GCSE MATHS
LEVEL C
(FOUNDATION)

Jean Holderness

Causeway Press Ltd

Published by Causeway Press Ltd
P.O. Box 13, Ormskirk, Lancashire L39 5HP

First published 1996

British Library Cataloguing-in-Publication Data.
A catalogue record for this book is available from the British Library.

ISBN 1-873929-17-X

The GCSE Maths Series
GCSE Maths: Level A (Higher) by Jean Holderness
GCSE Maths: Level B (Intermediate) by Jean Holderness
GCSE Maths: Level C (Foundation) by Jean Holderness

The Causeway Maths Series
Causeway Maths 1 by David Alcorn
Causeway Maths 2 by David Alcorn
Causeway Maths 3 by Jean Holderness
Causeway Maths 4 by Jean Holderness
Causeway Maths 5 by Jean Holderness
Causeway Maths 6 by Jean Holderness
Causeway Maths 7 by Jean Holderness

Other titles published by Causeway Press:
Mathematics: Levels 3 & 4 by David Alcorn
Mathematics: Level 5 by Jean Holderness
Mathematics: Level 6 by Jean Holderness
Mathematics: Level 7 by Jean Holderness
Mathematics: Level 8 by Jean Holderness
Mathematics: Levels 9 & 10 by Jean Holderness

GCSE Maths: Higher Level by Jean Holderness
GCSE Maths: Intermediate Level by Jean Holderness
GCSE Maths: Foundation Level by Jean Holderness
Pure Maths in Practice by Jean Holderness

Typeset and Printed in Great Britain by Alden, Oxford, Didcot and Northampton

Preface

This book is planned for use on a 2-year or a 1-year course leading to the Foundation level papers of the GCSE. It is based on the syllabuses published for examinations in 1998 onwards, which are all linked with the National Curriculum programme of study and attainment targets for Key Stage 4.

Students will have been learning Mathematics from an early age, so they will have already met many of the topics in this book. The earlier chapters will help to revise and consolidate the work of former years. A good understanding of the basic topics, leading to a sense of achievement, will form a firm foundation to build on when progressing through the syllabus.

The order of the book has been carefully planned, although, of course, it need not be followed rigidly. To some extent it follows the order of the topics in the National Curriculum. Chapters contain a mixture of straightforward questions for students who need to master the techniques, and more varied questions for others to do. Each chapter ends with a practice test.

After every 5 chapters there is a miscellaneous section which includes an aural exercise; revision exercises, which could also be used as practice tests; and suggestions for activities to link with AT1, 'using and applying mathematics'. There are puzzle questions throughout the book. Also there are suggestions to students for study, revision and preparation for the examination.

I should like to thank my brother Jim, and all my family and friends who have given me support and encouragement while I have been writing this book. I should also like to thank all those teachers, and others, who have provided helpful comments on the previous GCSE series.

Thanks also go to those who have helped with the production of the book, Andrew, Alan, Dave and the staff at Alden Bookset and Alden Press. From Causeway Press I have had great support from Mike and everyone else, and especially from David, who has given me a great amount of practical help and encouragement over several months.

I hope that you find this book useful and interesting.

Jean Holderness

To Winnie and Tom

Acknowledgements

Artwork created electronically by
David Alcorn
Mark Andrews
Alan Fraser
Lee Spencer

Cover design
Andrew Allen

Copyright photographs
Andrew Allen
Jim Holderness
Zefa Pictures (cover)

Contents

Topics for Activities (included in the miscellaneous sections)

To the teacher:

This book has been planned for a 2-year course or a 1-year course leading up to the GCSE examination at the Foundation level.

The first few chapters deal with elementary work to give a good start to the course. Students will gain a greater understanding of these topics which they may not have learnt fully at an earlier age, and thus they gain confidence. It is essential for them to have a good basic foundation of elementary work to build on later.

The main part of each chapter consists of bookwork and worked examples, followed by straightforward exercises. The bookwork has been kept to a minimum, leaving further explanations for the teacher to include, as these will depend on the ability and the previous knowledge of the students. The last exercise of each chapter is more varied, giving ideas for applications and activities. Some are purely mathematical and some relate the mathematics of the chapter to real-life applications. The teacher can decide how to use these questions with the class, whether using them for individual work, group work or as whole class activities.

There is a short test at the end of each chapter, covering the main topics of the chapter.

The book has 30 chapters, arranged in an order which interlinks arithmetic, geometry, algebra, statistics and probability, so that there is a variety of mathematics in each part of the book, but there is no need to keep to the exact order of topics.

After every 6 chapters, that is roughly one term's work if using the book over two years, there is a miscellaneous section. This includes the following:
Aural Practice. With many Examination Boards an aural test is no longer a separate part of the examination, but even so, these questions provide useful quick revision.
Revision Exercises. These are based on the work of the previous chapters, and they can be used as practice papers.
Activities. Time spent on these is invaluable for adding interest and understanding to the subject. A variety of suggestions have been included so that students can choose to work on a topic they enjoy. Some students may need help at the beginning, and you may have to modify some of the suggestions. Some of the ideas are more suitable for group work than individual work, and some students would be happier working in a group than alone.
For those students doing a coursework option in the examination, with a choice of coursework, some activities may be suitable to count as a component of this, but you must check with your own syllabus. For those doing a Paper 3, or coursework set by the Examination Board, many of these activities give useful practice in doing these types of questions.

There are puzzle questions fitted in at the ends of chapters. Some of these are traditional and some original. They are there to give interest, and perhaps to develop into further investigations. They are arranged in a miscellaneous order and are not necessarily matched to the work of preceding chapters.

Here are some other notes:

Arithmetic. Students who know the basic number work will take a more confident part in aural work and discussion, will do written work quickly and accurately, and will find Maths more enjoyable. These skills can be improved by doing the first 5 chapters without using a calculator, whenever possible.

Statistics. This work has been separated into small sections. Although it is an easy subject, if too many ideas are introduced too quickly they tend to get all muddled up. It is desirable to allow time for practical work to be carried out as this aids understanding so the suggestions for practical work in Statistics have been included in the relevant chapters.

Graphs. For graphical questions, graph paper with 2 mm squares is easier to use than that with 1mm squares, and for some questions, paper ruled in 1 cm squares is better still. In an examination the graph paper would be supplied and in many cases the axes will have already been drawn and labelled. To do the questions from this book, therefore, the students may need help in drawing and labelling the axes.

Calculators. The teacher should decide which type of calculator, a simple one or a scientific one, would be better for the students to use. Most simple calculators have a square root key, and they should be quite satisfactory for use at this level, and with fewer functions they will be easier to understand. On a scientific calculator many keys will not be needed, but the x-squared key, the fractions key and statistical functions (to find the mean) may be useful. Depending on which calculator is being used the relevant parts of Chapter 6 should be followed. Even so, not all calculators of one type work in the same way, so the teacher may have to sort out particular problems with the calculator being used.

Computers. References to using a computer are given in very general terms, as the development of computers is so rapid that detailed references would soon become outdated. Students should be encouraged to make good use of a computer for any topic where there is suitable software available.

Answers. The answers are given at the back of the book to the straightforward questions, but not usually to the activities questions where it is important that the students should make their own discoveries. The answers to the puzzles have not been included as the puzzles would not be so challenging if the answers were too readily available.

Syllabuses. The syllabuses of the different Examination Boards have a great deal in common as they are all based on the National Curriculum, but there are a few minor differences, so there may be some sections of the work which you may not need for your particular syllabus. Also, in some cases it is difficult to decide from the wording of the syllabus the depth of study needed for a particular topic. The specimen papers and, later on, the actual papers, will help to clarify these points. General advice would be to include everything in your course, unless you are sure that certain topics can be omitted.

I hope that you and your students find this book useful and interesting. **Enjoy your Maths.**

Jean Holderness

Tables

Time

60 seconds = 1 minute
60 minutes = 1 hour
24 hours = 1 day
7 days = 1 week
52 weeks = 1 year
365 days = 1 year
366 days = 1 leap year
12 months = 1 year

The Metric System   **British Units**

Weight

1000 mg = 1 g   16 ounces = 1 pound
100 cg = 1 g   14 pounds = 1 stone
1000 g = 1 kg   112 pounds = 1 hundredweight
1000 kg = 1 tonne   8 stones = 1 hundredweight
2240 pounds = 1 ton
20 hundredweights = 1 ton

Capacity

1000 ml = 1 ℓ   8 pints = 1 gallon
100 cl = 1 ℓ
1000 ℓ = 1 kl

1 litre = 1000 cm^3
1 litre of water weighs 1 kg   1 pint of water weighs $1\frac{1}{4}$ lb
1 cm^3 of water weighs 1 g   1 gallon of water weighs 10 lb

The Metric System
British Units

Length

1000 mm = 1 m	12 inches = 1 foot
100 cm = 1 m	3 feet = 1 yard
1000 m = 1 km	1760 yards = 1 mile

Approximate comparisons

1 inch ... $2\frac{1}{2}$ cm

1 foot ... 30 cm or 30.5 cm

1 yard ... 0.9 m

1 mile ... 1.6 km

5 miles ... 8 km

1 lb ... 450 g (nearly $\frac{1}{2}$ kg)

1 ton ... 1 tonne

1 pint ... just over $\frac{1}{2}$ litre

1 gallon ... $4\frac{1}{2}$ litres

1 cm ... 0.4 inches

1 m ... 40 inches = 4 ins longer than 1 yard

1 km ... $\frac{5}{8}$ mile

8 km ... 5 miles

1 kg ... 2.2 lb (just over 2 lb)

1 tonne ... 1 ton

1 litre ... $1\frac{3}{4}$ pints

1 litre ... 0.22 gallon

To change to the metric system

Length

1 inch = 2,54 cm

1 foot = 30.48 cm

1 yard = 91.44 cm = 0.9144 m

1 mile = 1.609 km

Weight

1 oz = 28.35 g

1 lb = 453.6 g

1 ton = 1016 kg = 1.016 tonne

Capacity

1 pint = 0.568 litre

1 gallon = 4.546 litre

To change from metric system

Length

1 cm = 0.394 in

1 m = 39.37 in = 1.094 yd

1 km = 1094 yd = 0.621 mile

Weight

1 kg = 2.205 lb

1 tonne = 0.984 ton

Capacity

1 litre = 1.76 pints = 0.220 gallons

Learning mathematics

Maths is not a new subject since you have been learning it all your life, but in this book are all the topics you need to learn for the Foundation level of the GCSE in Maths.

We hope that you will enjoy studying Maths. Just think of some of the ways in which Maths is linked with our lives, for example:
Shapes in the natural world involving symmetry, curves, spirals, etc.
Shapes in architecture and design.
Management of our money.
Understanding of diagrams, graphs and maps.
Ability to think logically, so as to plan ahead.
You can think of many more examples of how Maths is essential in today's world.

Learn to think for yourself. Do not rely on being told how to do everything. The more things you can work out for yourself the better you will do.

Try to discover things for yourself. Look for patterns in numbers and shapes. From a particular result, could you deduce a general formula ? As an example, suppose you have a spare moment waiting for a lesson to begin and you put your ruler down on your exercise book and draw lines on either side of it, then you move the ruler and cross the lines with two others, getting a shape in the middle. Now you can discover many things about that shape: What is it ?
Are there any equal lines or angles, or any axes or centre of symmetry ? What is the sum of its angles ? Join the diagonals of the figure and see what further discoveries you can make.

As you work through this book, try to learn the important facts and methods of each chapter. If you do not understand the main ideas, ask someone to help you, either your teacher, someone else in your class or anyone else who can explain them to you. But when you have to answer an unusual question, before you ask for help, try to use your own commonsense and reason it out.

If you work steadily your standard should improve and you should do well enough to obtain a satisfactory grade in GCSE Maths.

To do this course properly, you will need a calculator. You do not need a complicated one with all kinds of scientific functions on. A simple one which will do addition, subtraction, multiplication and division will be sufficient and will be easier to use, but make sure it has got a square root key $\boxed{\sqrt{}}$ on as well, as you will need that.

How this book is arranged

There are 30 main chapters. At the beginning of each chapter there is a list of topics included in that chapter. Then there are main facts or methods followed by worked examples, and an exercise to give you practice. The last exercise in each chapter has more varied questions. You may do them at this stage or you may leave them to return to later to give you more revision practice. Finally, there is a test on the ideas of the chapter.

There should be no need to do every part of every question in an exercise. More questions, rather than fewer, have been included for those students who need them. As soon as you have understood a topic you could go on to something else. Use your time wisely so that you complete the syllabus. Learn the important facts, methods and formulae as you go along.

After every 6 chapters there is a Miscellaneous Section. This can be used at any time. It includes an aural practice exercise, revision questions and suggestions for activities or independent work.

There are puzzle questions fitted in at the ends of some chapters. Try some of these, and remember that some may have a catch in them ! Many puzzles do not form part of the examination course but they may be useful for independent work, and may suggest ideas for further investigation.

Now, get started and **enjoy your Maths**.

1 **Numbers**

The topics in this chapter include:

- using number facts including multiplication up to 10×10,

- understanding and using common properties of numbers including multiples, factors, prime, even and odd numbers, the term square and the square root of a perfect square,

- understanding and using index notation for positive integral indices and knowing the words square and cube.

Numbers

A calculator is an invaluable tool for saving time and doing accurate calculations, but there are basic arithmetical operations which you should be able to do mentally, quickly and accurately, and for which you should not waste time pressing calculator keys.

You may be asked to multiply and divide mentally in questions such as 80×20 and $600 \div 20$, so you will need to know the basic tables.

There will be many situations in your life when you need to work something out quickly and you will not have your calculator available. So make sure you are mentally alert.

To learn your tables

On squared paper, or with columns drawn on lined paper, copy this chart.
Fill in the results of multiplication so that the first column is the 2 times table and the numbers in the first few squares are 4, 6, 8, ... from 2×2, 2×3, 2×4, ... (or 2×2, 3×2, 4×2, ... if you prefer to think of them that way).
When you have filled in all the squares and made sure they are correct, then you must learn all the results you do not already know.

You can look for some patterns in the table.
Which results are odd numbers ?
Which results have a unit figure of 5 ?
Which number appears most in the table ?
What do the digits add up to in the 9's column ?
What do the digits add up to in the 3's column ?

Learn the squares in the table. These are $2 \times 2 = 2^2 = 4$, $3 \times 3 = 3^2 = 9$, $4 \times 4 = 4^2 = 16$, and so on.

×	2	3	4	5	6	7	8	9	10	11	12
2	4										
3	6										
4	8										
5											
6											
7											
8											
9											
10											
11											
12											

If you wish, you can include columns for 0 and 1 in the table. The 1 times table has results such as $1 \times 3 = 3$, $8 \times 1 = 8$. The 0 times table has results such as $0 \times 3 = 0$, $8 \times 0 = 0$.

If you find it very hard to learn these tables, then you may find it easier if you leave out the columns and rows for 11 and 12 and concentrate on learning the tables up to 10×10.

To check your tables

This time you are going to rearrange the numbers in the headings of the rows and columns. Also leave out one number in each so that there are 10 rows and 10 columns, making 100 spaces to be filled in. Copy this chart.

×	2	8	6	9	4	11	3	7	5	12
6	12									
11	22									
5	10									
8	16									
12										
3										
10										
4										
9										
7										

Fill in the results of multiplication, so the numbers in the first few squares down the first empty column are 12, 22, 10, 16, etc. Work down each column in turn. Before you begin, note the time. Try to complete the chart within 5 minutes. If you take longer, then repeat the exercise, using numbers in a different random order, until you improve. Then check the accuracy of your work, which should be completely correct.

Make a similar chart for addition, so that the numbers down the first empty column are 8, 13, 7, . . .
See how quickly you can complete this.

The square of a number

This is the number multiplied by itself.
e.g. The square of 7 is 7×7 and equals 49.
7×7 can be written as 7^2 (read as 7 squared).

The sum and product of numbers

The **sum** of two or more numbers is the result of adding them together.
The **product** of two or more numbers is the result of multiplying them together.
e.g. If the numbers are 6 and 9, the sum is 15 and the product is 54.
If the numbers are 1, 4 and 7, the sum is 12 and the product is 28.

Exercise 1.1

These questions are intended to improve your speed and accuracy so concentrate and do them quickly.
Write down the answers only in questions 1 to 7.

1.   Work out, working downwards in columns.

8×7	$30 + 90$	$21 - 6$	6×12	$100 \div 5$
6×4	$8 + 7$	$30 \div 5$	6×0	$99 + 7$
20×1	11^2	30×8	$64 \div 8$	99×0
20×3	$56 \div 7$	$20 - 8$	13×1	12^2

2.   Work out

$32 \div 4$	$27 \div 9$	$55 \div 5$	$72 \div 12$	$15 \div 5$
$42 \div 7$	$132 \div 11$	$72 \div 9$	$30 \div 6$	$49 \div 7$
$96 \div 12$	$60 \div 6$	$36 \div 3$	$77 \div 11$	$45 \div 5$
$56 \div 8$	$144 \div 12$	$35 \div 7$	$60 \div 5$	$81 \div 9$

3.   What is the remainder when

   1   18 is divided by 5,   **4**   52 is divided by 4,
   2   39 is divided by 7,   **5**   100 is divided by 8 ?
   3   68 is divided by 11,

4.   What must be added to

   1 8×7 to make 60,   **4** 7×11 to make 80,
   2 4×3 to make 20,   **5** 9×9 to make 100 ?
   3 5×9 to make 50,

5.   Find the values of

   1 $5 \times 3 \times 1$ **5** $5000 \div 2$ **8** $(8 \times 12) - (7 \times 12)$
   2 $4 \times 2 \times 0$ **6** $89 + 99$ **9** $(6 \times 9) + (4 \times 9)$
   3 $8^2 - 2^2$ **7** $180 \div 5$ **10** $5 \times 2 \times 11$
   4 $8 \times 6 \times 2$

6.   **1**   How many more 4's than 5's are there in 40 ?
      2   How many more 8's than 12's are there in 96 ?
      3   How many more 4's than 6's are there in 36 ?
      4   How many more 5's than 6's are there in 60 ?
      5   How many more 7's than 9's are there in 63 ?

7.   **1**   Find two numbers whose sum is 13 and whose product is 36.
      2   Find two numbers whose sum is 11 and whose product is 30.
      3   Find two numbers whose sum is 16 and whose product is 48.
      4   Find two numbers whose product is 72 and which differ by 1.
      5   Find two numbers whose product is 24 and which differ by 5.

8.   **1**   Start from 100 and count down in 6's until you reach a number less than 10. What
              number is this ?

      2   Start from 1, then 2, then 4, and double the number every time until you reach a
              number greater than 1000. What number is this ?

      3   Start from 25 000 and keep dividing by 5 until you reach a number less than 10. What
              number is this ?

      4   Start with 1 and keep adding 7's until you reach a number greater than 100. What
              number is this ?

      5   Start from 0 and add 1, then 2, then 3, and so on until you reach a number greater
              than 100. What number is this ?

9.   **1**   Write down any number between 1 and 10, multiply this by 3, then to the result
              add 8. Double this answer. Now subtract 3, multiply by 5, add 7. Subtract 2 and
              divide by 10. Add 17, divide by 3 and take away the number you started with.
              What is your answer ?

9.   **2**   Write down any number between 1 and 10, add 3 and multiply the result by 6. Then subtract 12, divide by 3, multiply by 10. Add 5, divide by 5 and add 7. Subtract 12 then divide by the number you started with. What is your answer ?

     3   Write down any number less than 5, double it and add 3. Square the result, add 3 and divide by 4. Subtract 1 and multiply by 2. Subtract 4, divide by the number you started with, add 14 and halve the result. Take away the number you started with. What is your answer ?

10.   What is the missing number in each of these statements ?

    1 $\square + 11 = 30$ **4** $\square - 11 = 4$

    2 $\square \times 11 = 77$ **5** $(11 + 9) - \square = 4$

    3 $(\square \times 3) - 11 = 16$

11.   **1**   I think of a number, divide it by 3 and then add 5. The result is 12. What was the original number ?

     2   I think of a number, square it and add 3. The result is 39. What was the original number ?

     3   I think of a number, multiply it by 4 and take away 12. The result is 16. What was the original number ?

Even and odd numbers

An **even number** is a number which divides exactly by 2. The units figure is 2, 4, 6, 8 or 0.

An **odd number** is a number which does not divide exactly by 2. The units figure is 1, 3, 5, 7 or 9.

Multiples

e.g. The multiples of 7 are numbers which 7 divides exactly into, including 7 itself.
Some multiples of 7 are 7, 14, 21, 28, 140, 196, 700.

Factors

Example

1   Find all the factors of 24.

    Factors of 24 are numbers which divide exactly into 24.
    All numbers have a factor 1, and 24 has a factor 24.
    Also $24 = 2 \times 12 = 3 \times 8 = 4 \times 6$.
    So the factors of 24 are 1, 2, 3, 4, 6, 8, 12, 24.

Prime numbers

A prime number has no factors (except itself and 1). The first few prime numbers are 2, 3, 5, 7, 11, 13, 17, ...

Tests of divisibility

Divisibility by 2

If the units figure is even, i.e. 2, 4, 6, 8, 0, the number divides by 2.

Divisibility by 3

Add up the digits in the number, and if the answer is more than 9 you can add up the digits of that answer, and repeat until you get a 1-figure number. If this number divides by 3 then 3 is a factor of the original number.

For example, for 2841, $2 + 8 + 4 + 1 = 15$ (and $15 \rightarrow 1 + 5 = 6$). This divides by 3 so 3 is a factor of 2841.

(Also, if the 1-figure number is 9, the original number divides by 9.)

Divisibility by 5

If the units figure is 5 or 0 the number divides by 5.

To find whether a number is a prime number

Check that it does not divide exactly by any numbers (except itself and 1) by dividing by the first few prime numbers 2, 3, 5, 7, 11, ...

First, check that it does not divide exactly by 2.
Then check that it does not divide exactly by 3.
Then check that it does not divide exactly by 5. (Since $5 \times 5 = 25$, you do not need to do this or any further checks for numbers less than 25.)
Then check that it does not divide exactly by 7. (Since $7 \times 7 = 49$, you do not need to do this or any further checks for numbers less than 49.)
Then check that it does not divide exactly by 11. (Since $11 \times 11 = 121$, you do not need to do this or any further checks for numbers less than 121.)
You are unlikely to need to check for larger numbers but, if necessary, you would check whether the number divides exactly by 13, 17, 19, ...

Example

2   Find the prime numbers between 90 and 100.

The even numbers 90, 92, 94, 96, 98, 100 divide by 2 so they are not prime numbers.
This leaves the odd numbers 91, 93, 95, 97, 99 to be checked.
93 and 99 divide by 3 so they are not prime numbers.
This leaves 91, 95, 97 to be checked.
95 divides by 5 so this is not a prime number.
91 divides by 7 so this is not a prime number.
97 does not divide by 2, 3, 5 or 7. Since 97 is less than 121 there is no need to check that
it does not divide by 11 or any greater prime number.
97 is a prime number, and it is the only prime number between 90 and 100.

Index notation

5^2 (five squared) means 5×5 and equals 25.
4^3 (four cubed) means $4 \times 4 \times 4$ and equals 64.
10^6 (ten to the sixth) means $10 \times 10 \times 10 \times 10 \times 10 \times 10$ and equals $1\,000\,000$ (one million).

Square numbers are $1^2, 2^2, 3^2, 4^2, \ldots$ which worked out are 1, 4, 9, 16, $\ldots$

Cube numbers are $1^3, 2^3, 3^3, 4^3, \ldots$ which worked out are 1, 8, 27, 64, $\ldots$

Square roots

e.g. $5 \times 5 = 25$ so 25 is square number and its square root is 5.
     $12 \times 12 = 144$ so 144 is a square number and its square root is 12.

The symbol for square root is $\sqrt{}$.

e.g. $\sqrt{49} = 7$ since $7^2 = 49$.

Example

3   Find the value of $2^3 \times 5^2$.

$$2^3 \times 5^2 = 2 \times 2 \times 2 \quad \times \quad 5 \times 5$$
$$= 8 \times 25$$
$$= 200$$

Exercise 1.2

1.   Which of these numbers are prime numbers ?   21,   23,   25,   27,   29.

2.   What are the next two prime numbers after   **1**   30,   **2**   80 ?

3.   Find the values of

     1 2^4 **6** $2^3 \times 3^2$

     2 7^3 **7** $2^2 \times 5 \times 7$

     3 10^5 **8** $2^3 \times 11$

     4 $\sqrt{121}$ **9** $3^3 \times 10^2$

     5 $\sqrt{64}$ **10** $2 \times 5^2 \times 9$

4.   Which of these numbers are divisible by   **1**   2,   **2**   5,   **3**   3 ?

     132,   135,   156,   225,   400.

5.   Find a number which is a factor of both these numbers. If you can find more than one, give the highest one.

     1   88, 99   **5**   28, 16   **8**   48, 40

     2   18, 45   **6**   24, 8   **9**   14, 20

     3   45, 35   **7**   27, 6   **10**   77, 49

     4   18, 21

6.   Find a number which is less than 30 and is a multiple of both these numbers. If you can find more than one, give the lowest one.

     1   3, 5   **5**   10, 20   **8**   2, 3

     2   8, 12   **6**   11, 22   **9**   2, 10

     3   4, 5   **7**   6, 9   **10**   3, 7

     4   6, 8

7.   **1**   Find the squares of   11,   6,   2,   10,   1.

     2   Find the square roots of   64,   144,   49,   9,   25.

     3   Find two consecutive numbers whose squares differ by 11.

     4   Find two consecutive numbers whose squares add up to 181.

     5   Find three consecutive numbers whose squares add up to 50.

8.   Write the number 30

     1   as the product of three prime numbers,

     2   as the sum of three prime numbers.

9.   From the numbers   8,   12,   16,   19,   20:

     1   Which number is a prime number ?

     2   Which number is a square number ?

     3   Which number is a multiple of 5 ?

     4   Which number is a factor of 84 ?

     5   Which two numbers have a sum which is a square number ?

     6   Which two numbers have a sum which is a cube number ?

10.   From the numbers 18, 19, 20, 23, 25, 27, write down

    1   the prime numbers,
    2   a square number,
    3   the numbers which are multiples of 3,
    4   a cube number,
    5   two numbers whose sum is 44.

11.   From the numbers 60 to 70 inclusive,

    1   which numbers are odd numbers,
    2   which number is a square number,
    3   which numbers divide by 7,
    4   which numbers divide by 5,
    5   which number in index form is $2^2 \times 3 \times 5$,
    6   which number has factors 2, 3 and 11,
    7   which two numbers are prime numbers,
    8   which number is a cube number ?

12.   What number is this ?

It is less than 100, it is a prime number, it is one less than a multiple of 7 and its digits add up to 5.

13.   What number is this ?

It is less than 100, it is two more than a square number and it is a multiple of 11. When divided by 9 there is a remainder of 3.

Use of brackets

Operations inside brackets should be carried out first. If there are no brackets, multiplication and division should be carried out before addition and subtraction.

Examples

$4 \times 6 - 5 \times 3 = (4 \times 6) - (5 \times 3) = 24 - 15 = 9$
$4 \times (6 - 5) \times 3 = 4 \times 1 \times 3 = 12$
$4 + 6 \times 5 - 3 = 4 + (6 \times 5) - 3 = 4 + 30 - 3 = 31$
$(4 + 6) \times (5 - 3) = 10 \times 2 = 20$

A fraction line can take the place of a bracket.

$\dfrac{3 + 5}{6 - 2}$ means $(3 + 5) \div (6 - 2)$ which equals $\dfrac{8}{4} = 2$.

Exercise 1.3

1. Find the values of

1	$4 \times 7 + 5$	**5**	$\dfrac{5+4}{7-4}$	**8**	$7^2 - 4^2$
2	$4 \times (7 + 5)$	**6**	$4^2 + 7^2$	**9**	$(7 - 4)^2$
3	$4 + 7 \times 5$	**7**	$(4 + 7)^2$	**10**	$(7 + 4) \times (7 - 4)$
4	$(4 + 7) \times 5$				

2. Find the values of

1	$2 + 6 \times 8$	**6**	$6^2 + 8^2$
2	$(2 + 6) \times 8$	**7**	$8^2 - 6^2$
3	$2 \times 6 + 8$	**8**	$(8 - 6)^2$
4	$2 \times (6 + 8)$	**9**	$(8 + 6)(8 - 6)$
5	$\dfrac{8+6}{8-6}$	**10**	$\dfrac{8+6+2}{6-2}$

Exercise 1.4   Applications

1. **1** Write down the numbers from 80 to 90.
   2 List the even numbers.
   3 List the multiples of 3.
   4 List the multiples of 5.
   5 List the multiples of 7.
   6 From these numbers, numbers which do not divide by 2, 3, 5 or 7 are prime numbers. Which numbers are prime numbers ?

2. From the numbers   8,   37,   50,   73,   81,   91,   360:

   1 Which number is a square number ?
   2 Which number is a cube number ?
   3 Which two numbers are prime numbers ?
   4 Which number is a multiple of 13 ?
   5 Which number is a factor of 72 ?
   6 Which number can be written in index form as $2^3 \times 3^2 \times 5$?
   7 Which number is equal to the sum of two other numbers in the list ?
   8 Which number when divided by 9 leaves a remainder of 5 ?

3. Are the answers to the following questions even or odd numbers ?

   1 odd number + odd number
   2 odd number $\times$ even number
   3 even number − smaller odd number
   4 even number $\times$ (even number + even number)
   5 odd number $\times$ (odd number + even number)

4. Instead of writing down the question $(5 \times 3) + (4 \times 2)$, Andrea wrote down
    $(5 + 3) \times (4 + 2)$.

    1 What was the answer to the correct question ?

    2 What answer would Andrea get if she worked her question out correctly ?

5. **1** What number is this ?

    It is a factor of 180, it is 4 less than a square number, and when it is divided by 7
    there is a remainder of 3.

    2 What is this number ?

    It is less than 100. It is divisible by 11. It is 1 less than a square number.

6. Copy and complete this table.

    Is there any pattern in the unit figures
    1 in the squares column,
    2 in the cubes column ?

number	square	cube
1	1	1
2	4	8
3	9	
.		
.		
.		
10		

7. 6 is called a **perfect number** because its factors are 1, 2, 3 and when you add them up
    their sum equals 6.
    12 has factors 1, 2, 3, 4, 6 and their sum equals 16, not 12, so 12 is not a perfect number.
    However, there is one other number less than 50 which is a perfect number.
    Which is it ?

8. **1** In a knock-out competition there
    are 32 teams. How many matches
    must be played altogether to
    decide the winning team ?

    2 In a football competition there
    are 6 teams. Each team plays each
    other team twice, once at home
    and once away. How many
    matches are played altogether ?

Practice test 1

1. Find the values of

   1 $(9 \times 7) - (6 \times 10)$ **4** $(8 \times 6) - (9 \times 4)$
   2 $(9 + 12) \div 7$ **5** $(4 + 6) \times (8 + 2)$
   3 $40 \div (3 + 2)$

2. Give the squares of these numbers.

   7, 5, 12, 1, 6.

3. Give the square roots of these numbers.

   121, 100, 16, 81, 4.

4. Which of these numbers are cube numbers ?

   64, 6, 1000, 125, 81.

5. Find the values of

   1 $2^2 \times 3^2$
   2 2×5^2
   3 $(2^2 \times 3^2) + (2 \times 5^2)$

6. Write down all the numbers from 20 to 30 inclusive.

   1 Which numbers are even numbers ?

   2 Which numbers divide by 7 ?

   3 Which number is a square number ?

   4 Which number is a cube number ?

   5 Which number in index form is $2^3 \times 3$?

   6 Which number has factors 2, 3 and 5 ?

   7 Which number is a multiple of 11 ?

   8 Which two numbers are prime numbers ?

   9 Which number when divided by 8 gives a remainder of 7 ?

7. Write down an odd number between 10 and 20, add 12 and double the answer.
   Subtract 6 and divide by 4. Add 3 and double the answer, then take away the number
   you started with. Add 1 and take the square root.
   What is the final answer ?

2 Angles

The topics in this chapter include:

- measuring and drawing angles,
- drawing parallel lines,
- understanding and using properties associated with intersecting lines and parallel lines,
- understanding and using horizontal and vertical lines, clockwise and anticlockwise turns, and 8 points of the compass.

Angles

An angle is the amount of turning between two lines.

This is angle *ABC* (or ∠*ABC*) or angle *CBA*.
If there is no possibility of confusion it can be called ∠*B*.

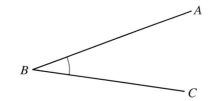

Angles can also be identified by small letters.
This angle is *b*.

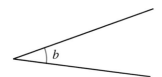

Measuring angles

1 complete turn or revolution is divided into 360 degrees (360°).

1 half-turn is 180°.

1 quarter-turn is 90°. This is also called a right angle.

The sign for a right angle is

Perpendicular lines are lines which meet each other at right angles.

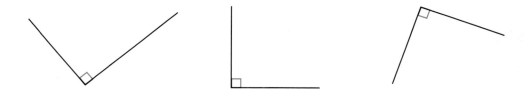

Types of angles

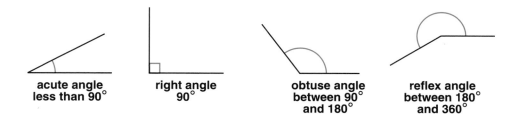

| acute angle | right angle | obtuse angle | reflex angle |
| less than 90° | 90° | between 90° and 180° | between 180° and 360° |

Using a protractor

1 To measure an angle

(1) Put the centre point of the protractor on the point of the angle.
(2) Put the 0° line of the protractor on one of the lines of the angle.
(3) Count round from 0° to read the size of the angle.
   If the 0° you are using is on the
   outside set of figures, use those
   figures, counting past 10°, 20°, 30°, etc.
   If the 0° you are using is on the
   inside set of figures, then you will use
   those figures.
   (Not all circular protractors are marked
   in the same way so yours may not be
   numbered like the one shown below.)

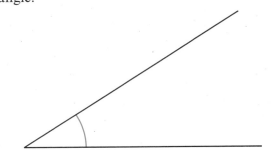

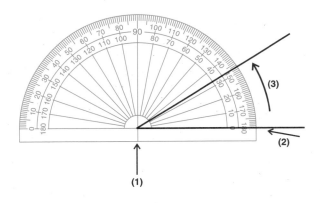

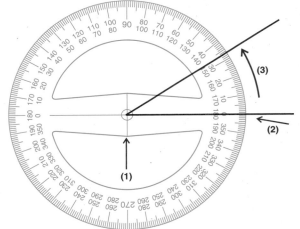

This is an angle of 33°.

Use the other 0° line if it is more convenient.

2 To draw an angle

Mark a point *P* on a line *PQ*, as shown.
At point *P*, using the line *PQ*, make an angle of 28°.

P   *Q*

(1) Put the centre point of the protractor on the point *P*.

(2) Put the 0° line of the protractor on the line *PQ*.

(3) Count round from 0° to 28°. Put a dot at 28°.

(Decide from where 0° is, whether you are using the inside or the outside set of figures.)

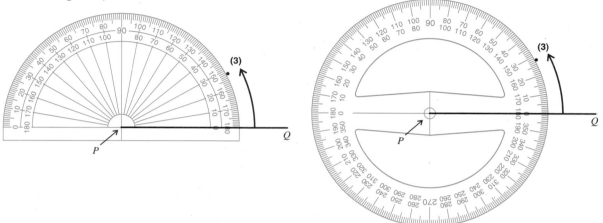

(4) When you have removed the protractor, join the dot to point *P*.

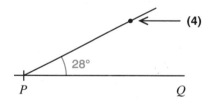

Exercise 2.1

1. State whether these angles are acute, obtuse or reflex angles.

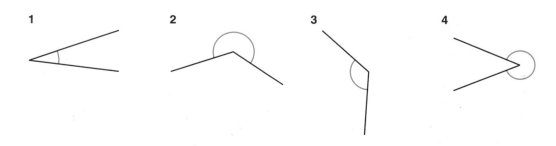

2.   Using your protractor, draw angles of

    1   20°   **2**   45°   **3**   90°   **4**   120°.

3.   Copy these figures, drawing the angles accurately.

1   **2**   **3** 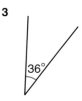   **4**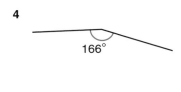

4.   Estimate the sizes of these angles, in degrees. Check your estimate by measuring with your protractor.

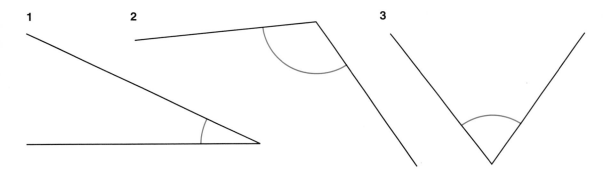

5.   Measure the angles *a*, *b*, *c* and *d*.

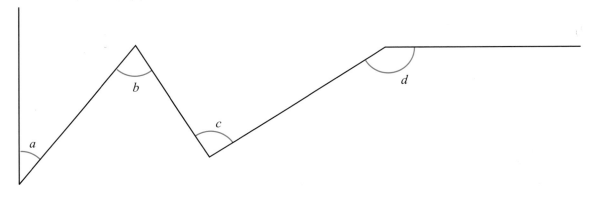

Calculations with angles

Angles at a point

These add up to 360°.

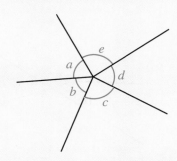

$$a + b + c + d + e = 360°$$

Adjacent angles (on a straight line)

These add up to 180°.

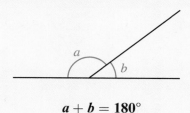

$$a + b = 180°$$

Vertically opposite angles

These are equal.

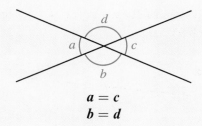

$$a = c$$
$$b = d$$

Example

Calculate the sizes of angles a, b, c, d.

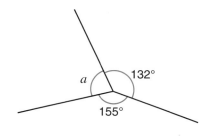

$a + 132° + 155° = 360°$ (angles at a point)
$a = 73°$

$b + 130° = 180°$ (angles on a straight line)
$b = 50°$
$c = 50°$ (opposite to b)
$d = 130°$ (opposite to $130°$)

Exercise 2.2

1. Estimate the sizes of the marked angles, in degrees. Check your estimates by measuring with your protractor. Verify that the angles at a point add up to 360°, adjacent angles on a straight line add up to 180°, and vertically opposite angles are equal.

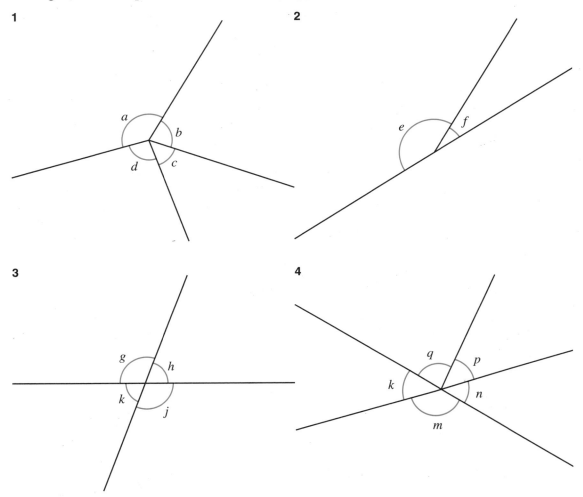

2. In the diagrams measure angle *a* with your protractor and use your answer to calculate the size of angle *b*.

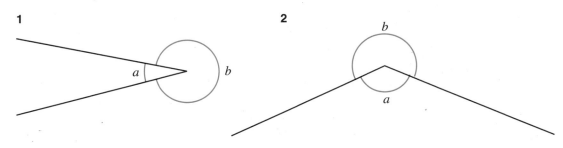

3.   Calculate the sizes of angles a, b, c, d, e.

1

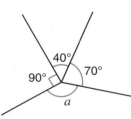

2

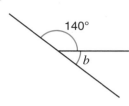

3

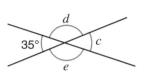

4.   Calculate the sizes of angles a, b, c, d, e.

1

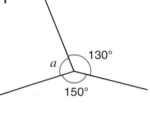

2

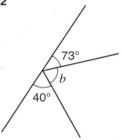

3

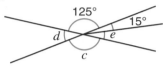

5.   **1**   If all the angles in the diagram are equal, find
          the size of angle a.

      2   If $a = 60°$ and the other angles are all equal,
          find their size.

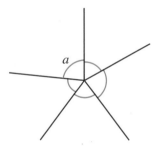

Parallel lines

Parallel lines are lines with the same direction. They remain the same distance apart, so never meet each other.
The sign for parallel lines is similar arrows on the lines.
The symbol // can be used for 'is parallel to'.

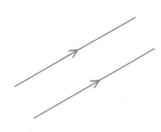

To draw parallel lines with a set-square

Example

Draw a line through C, parallel to AB.

Place the longest side of the set-square on AB so that, if possible, the set-square is placed over C. Place a ruler along one of the other sides of the set-square.

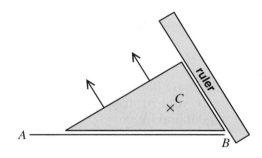

Keeping the ruler fixed, slide the set-square along the ruler until its longest side passes through C. Draw a line along this edge.

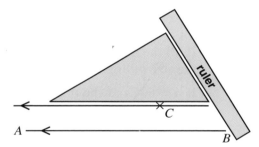

Practise drawing different parallel lines until you are sure that you can draw them correctly.

Calculations with angles and parallel lines

Corresponding angles

These are equal.

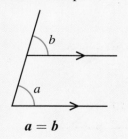

$a = b$

Alternate angles

These are equal.

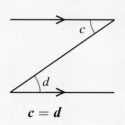

$c = d$

Interior angles

These add up to $180°$.

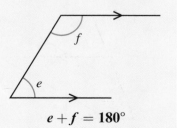

$e + f = 180°$

Example

Calculate the sizes of angles a, b, c and d.

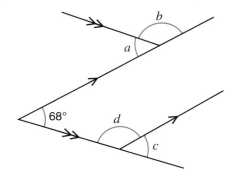

$a = 68°$ alternate angles
$b = 112°$ adjacent angle to a
$c = 68°$ corresponding angles
$d = 112°$ interior angles (or adjacent to c)

Exercise 2.3

1. Estimate the sizes of the marked angles, in degrees. Check your estimate by measuring with your protractor. Verify that corresponding angles are equal, alternate angles are equal and interior angles add up to $180°$.

1

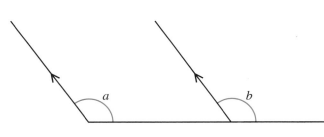

2

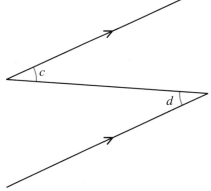

3

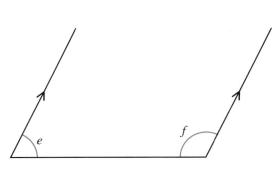

2. Calculate the sizes of angles f, g, h.

1

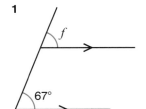

2

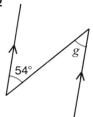

3

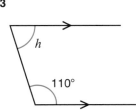

3.   Calculate the sizes of angles a, b, c, d, e, f.

1   **2**   **3**

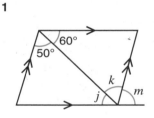

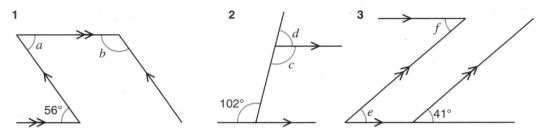

4.   Calculate the sizes of angles a, b, c, d, e.

1   **2**

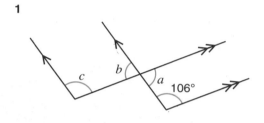

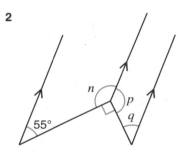

5.   Calculate the sizes of angles j, k, m, n, p, q.

1   **2**

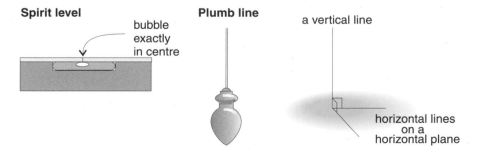

Horizontal and vertical lines

A spirit level shows whether lines are horizontal.
A plumb line (a heavy weight on a thin string) shows whether lines are vertical.

A horizontal line and a vertical line meet at right angles.

Spirit level

bubble
exactly
in centre

Plumb line

a vertical line

horizontal lines
on a
horizontal plane

Clockwise and anticlockwise turns

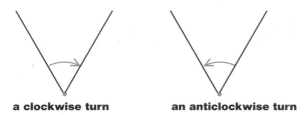

a clockwise turn   **an anticlockwise turn**

A clockwise turn is in the same direction as the hands of a clock turn.

Compass directions

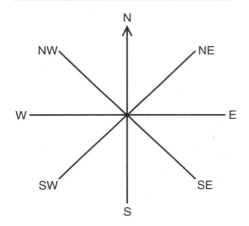

8-points compass directions

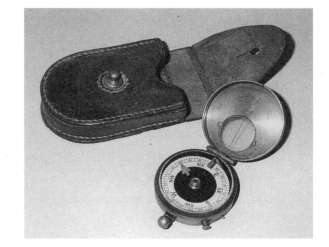

The angle between two adjacent directions, e.g. N and NE, is 45°.

Exercise 2.4

1. The diagram shows a sketch of a shed.
    On the shed, which of the lines shown will be
    1 horizontal lines,
    2 vertical lines,
    3 lines which are not horizontal nor vertical ?

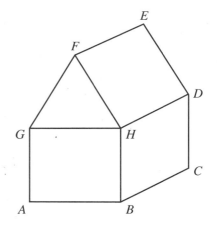

2. **1** On this weighing scale, when more weight is added, will the pointer move clockwise or anticlockwise ?

2 If the pointer on this speedometer moves anticlockwise, is the speed increasing or decreasing ?

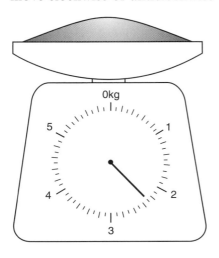

3. **1** Through how many degrees do you turn when facing South-East and turning clockwise to West ?

2 Through how many degrees do you turn when facing North-West and turning anticlockwise to South-West ?

3 In which direction are you facing if you start facing South and then turn through 135° anticlockwise ?

4 In which direction are you facing if you start facing North-East and then turn through 90° clockwise ?

5 If you are facing North-East after having turned 135° clockwise, in which direction were you facing originally ?

Exercise 2.5 Applications

1. **1** Through how many degrees does the hour hand of a clock turn in 1 hour ?

2 Through how many degrees does the hour hand of a clock turn between 1 pm and 3.30 pm ?

3 What is the size of the obtuse angle between the hands of a clock at half-past two ?

2.   On squared paper, trace out the path of a robot who follows these instructions. Mark the starting point as *A*.

Start facing the top of the page.
FORWARD 3 squares.
Turn clockwise through 90°.
FORWARD 6 squares.
Turn anticlockwise through 90°.
FORWARD 2 squares.
Turn anticlockwise through 90°.
FORWARD 1 square.
Turn clockwise through 270°.
FORWARD 5 squares.

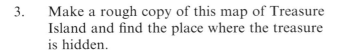

Where is the robot now ? Mark the point as *B*.
In which direction is the robot facing ?

Give instructions for the robot to return to *A*,
1   following its route in reverse,
2   going by a direct route.

3.   Make a rough copy of this map of Treasure Island and find the place where the treasure is hidden.

'Halve the distance in a straight line from *A* to *B*, and from this halfway point proceed in a straight line at right angles to the line *AB* until you reach the river.
Having crossed the river, march North to the coast.
Here you will find a cave where the treasure lies hidden.'

4.   Draw a line *AB* 10 cm long.
Measure an angle of 57° at *A* and measure off a length of 6 cm along this line to give the point *D*.
Through *D* draw a line parallel to *AB*.
Through *B* draw a line parallel to *AD*, and let this line meet the other line at *C*.
Measure *BC*, *DC* and angle *C*.

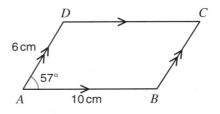

5.   The diagram shows the positions of some places in a village.

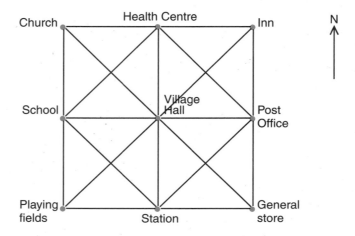

1   Which place is South-East of the Village Hall ?

2   In which direction is the Health Centre from the school ?

3   A boy who is at the Health Centre faces North and then turns clockwise through
     135°. Which place does he face then ?

4   A girl who is at the Village Hall faces East and then turns anticlockwise through 45°.
     Which place does she face then ?

5   A man who is at the Station is facing West. Through how many degrees must he
     turn, and in which direction, to face the Village Hall ?

6.   The diagram shows a triangle *ABC*.

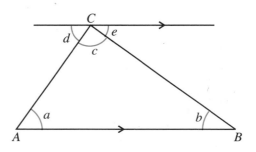

1   Name an angle equal to a, and say why
     they are equal.

2   Name an angle equal to b, and say why
     they are equal.

3   What is the sum of the 3 angles $c + d + e$,
     and why ?

4   What does this prove about the sum of
     the angles of the triangle, $a + b + c$?

Practice test 2

1.   Draw a line *PQ* of length 8 cm and at *P* make an angle *QPR* of 37°.

2. Draw accurately an angle *BAC* of 132°, making the lines *AB* and *AC* 6 cm long.
    Through *C* draw a line *CD* which is parallel to *AB*, making it 12 cm long.
    Measure ∠*ACD*.
    At *B* draw a line perpendicular to *AB* to meet the line *CD* at *E*.

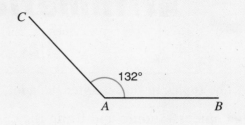

3. In the diagram, *AB* and *CD* are straight lines.

    1 Find the sizes of angles *a* and *b*.

    2 Angles *c* and *d* are equal. Find their size.

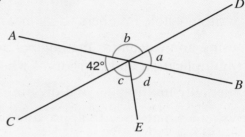

4. **1** Find the size of angle *a*.

    2 If ∠*DEF* = 150°, find the size of angle *b*.

    3 Find the size of angle *c*.

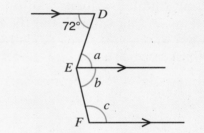

5. This box is lying on a horizontal table. On the box, which lines shown in the diagram are
    1 horizontal lines,
    2 vertical lines ?

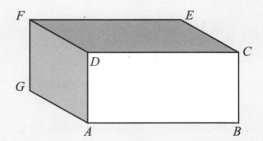

6. **1** Which compass direction is opposite to North-West ?

    2 In which direction will you be facing if you start facing East and then turn through 135° anticlockwise ?

    3 If you face North-West and then turn through 45° clockwise, in which direction will you then be facing ?

3 Arithmetic

The topics in this chapter include:

- understanding and using the concept of place value in whole numbers,

- reading, writing and ordering whole numbers of any magnitude,

- writing whole numbers to the nearest 10, 100, 1000, etc.

- using non-calculator methods of addition and subtraction of whole numbers and multiplication and division of whole numbers by whole numbers,

- mentally multiplying and dividing whole numbers by powers of 10,

- using estimation with approximations and using inverse operations to check solutions,

- selecting suitable sequences of operations and methods of computation to solve problems, giving solutions in the context of the problem.

Large numbers

100	one hundred
576	five hundred and seventy-six
1000	one thousand
3214	three thousand, two hundred and fourteen
10 000	ten thousand
82 100	eighty-two thousand, one hundred
100 000	one hundred thousand
504 030	five hundred and four thousand, and thirty
1 000 000	one million
9 876 543	nine million, eight hundred and seventy-six thousand, five hundred and forty-three

Place value

9 876 543   The figure 9 represents 9 millions,
             the figure 8 represents 8 hundred thousands (or 800 thousands),
             the figure 7 represents 7 ten thousands (or 70 thousands),
             the figure 6 represents 6 thousands,
             the figure 5 represents 5 hundreds,
             the figure 4 represents 4 tens,
             the figure 3 represents 3 units.

Approximations

Numbers to the nearest ten

e.g. For numbers between 50 and 60.
Any number less than 55 is given as 50, to the nearest ten.
Any number from 55 upwards is given as 60, to the nearest ten.
(Actually, 55 is exactly halfway between 50 and 60 but it is usual to round it **up** to 60.)

Numbers to the nearest hundred

e.g. For numbers between 200 and 300.
Any number less than 250 is given as 200, to the nearest hundred.
Any number from 250 upwards is given as 300, to the nearest hundred.

Numbers to the nearest thousand

e.g. For numbers between 7000 and 8000.
Any number less than 7500 is given as 7000, to the nearest thousand.
Any number from 7500 upwards is given as 8000, to the nearest thousand.

Examples

    64   = 60, to the nearest ten
   264 = 300, to the nearest hundred
9264 = 9000, to the nearest thousand
9764 = 10 000, to the nearest thousand

Exercise 3.1

1.   Write in words the numbers

    1   236   **4**   10 201
    2   1079   **5**   8 300 000
    3   441 358

2.   Write in figures these numbers.

    1   Two hundred and sixty-five thousand, three hundred and eighty-four.

    2   Twelve thousand and forty.

    3   One and a half thousand.

    4   Thirty thousand.

    5   Four million, four hundred and forty thousand, four hundred and four.

3.   **1**   What are the numbers which are one more than
      199, 9900, 219, 4009, 999 ?

    2   What are the numbers which are two less than
      300, 5000, 921, 7100, 9082 ?

4.   **1**   What are the numbers which are one hundred less than
      1800, 66 375, 2113, 10 297, 5013 ?

    2   What are the numbers which are one thousand more than
      386, 8219, 180 274, 9967, 369 000 ?

5.   **1**   In 100 567, what do the 1, the 5 and the 6 stand for ?

    2   In 2 908 134, what do the 2 and the 8 stand for ?

6.   **1**   Write these numbers correct to the nearest ten.
      46, 7693, 34, 1529, 96.

    2   Write these numbers correct to the nearest hundred.
      687, 9716, 323, 3751, 1970.

    3   Write these numbers correct to the nearest thousand.
      6501, 3127, 85 800, 12 499, 254 293.

Addition

Keep the numbers in columns.
Add up each column in turn, starting with the units column.
If the total of a column is more than 9, only write down the units figure, and carry the tens figure to the next column.

e.g.   364   Units column:
           859        $4 + 9 + 3 = 16$, write down 6 and carry 1.
      +1093   Tens column:
       2316 $6 + 5 + 9 + 1 = 21$, write down 1 and carry 2.
                      Hundreds column:
                      $3 + 8 + 0 + 2 = 13$, write down 3 and carry 1.
                      Thousands column:
                      $1 + 1 = 2$, write down 2.
                      The answer is 2316.

You may prefer to add smaller numbers in a different way.

e.g. $64 + 27 = 91.$ $64 + 20 = 84,$
                               $84 + 7\ = 91,$
                               or
                               $64 + 7\ = 71,$
                               $71 + 20 = 91.$

When adding a number ending in 9, you can do it like this:

e.g. $56 + 29 = 56 + 30 - 1 = 86 - 1 = 85.$

When adding a long list of small numbers, look for pairs of numbers making 10 and add these together.

e.g. $9 + 2 + 5 + 8 + 1 = (9 + 1) + (2 + 8) + 5 = 10 + 10 + 5 = 25.$

Subtraction

Keep the numbers in columns.
Work out each column in turn, starting with the units column.
Sometimes you may have to use 1 from the number in the next column as 10.

e.g.   3492   Units column:
         $-$ 854   You cannot take 4 from 2. Make 2 into 12. $12 - 4 = 8.$
           2638   Tens column:
                           You have used 1 from 9 so the tens column is now $8 - 5 = 3.$
                           Hundreds column:
                           $14 - 8 = 6.$
                           Thousands column:
                           There is now 2. $2 - 0 = 2.$
                           The answer is 2638.

(There is an alternative method, where you do not alter the numbers on the top line. Instead you add numbers to the bottom line. If this is the method you have learnt, continue to use it.)

Be very careful if there are no units and no tens to subtract from.

e.g.   400   You need to use 1 hundred to make 10 tens, then you can use
         $-$254   1 ten to make 10 units.
           146   Units column:
                           $10 - 4 = 6.$
                           Tens column:
                           The top number is now 9. $9 - 5 = 4.$
                           Hundreds column:
                           The top number is now 3. $3 - 2 = 1.$
                           The answer is 146.

You may prefer to subtract smaller numbers in a different way.

e.g. $63 - 26 = 37.$ $63 - 20 = 43,$
                                $43 - 6 = 37,$
                                or
                                $63 - 6 = 57,$
                                $57 - 20 = 37.$

Subtraction by the method of adding on. This is useful when subtracting from a number such as $100, 200, \ldots$

e.g. $100 - 63.$

To make 63 into 70 you need **7**, then to make 70 into 100 you need **30**.

The answer is 37.

e.g. $300 - 51.$

To make 51 into 60 you need **9**, to make 60 into 100 you need **40** and to make 100 into 300 you need **200**.

The answer is 249.

When subtracting a number ending in 9, you can do it like this:

e.g. $83 - 39 = 83 - 40 + 1 = 43 + 1 = 44.$

Exercise 3.2

You should do these questions without using a calculator.

1.   Work out the following.

	1		2		3		4		5
	7231		1745		931		2725		867
	7497		684		1602		1944		593
	+6280		+ 462		+ 387		+ 136		201
									+816

2.   Work out the following.

	1		2		3		4		5
	968		642		5234		560		2000
	−745		−197		−1192		−249		− 671

3.   Work out the following.

   1   $46 + 38$ 4 $86 + 19$
   2   $67 + 25$ 5 $51 + 29$
   3   $54 + 28$

4.   Work out the following.

   1   $98 - 16$ 4 $62 - 39$
   2   $87 - 28$ 5 $58 - 19$
   3   $53 - 37$

5. Add these numbers in the simplest way.

    $5 + 8 + 3 + 7 + 6 + 5 + 2$

6. Work out these subtractions by the method of adding on.

    1 $100 - 77$ **4** $500 - 362$
    2 $100 - 18$ **5** $800 - 14$
    3 $1000 - 523$

7. Tom's scores in 5 tries at a computer game were 1167, 5742, 1507, 6830 and 4891.

    1 What was his total score ?
    2 Peter's total score in his 5 tries was 15 297. How many points had Tom scored more
       than Peter ?

8. On 5 days training a cyclist travelled the following
    distances, 67 km, 53 km, 76 km, 49 km and 89 km.

    1 What was the total distance he cycled ?
    2 How many kilometres was this short of his
       target of 400 km ?

Multiplying whole numbers by 10

$$7 \times 10 = 70$$
$$87 \times 10 = 870$$
$$987 \times 10 = 9870$$
$$980 \times 10 = 9800$$
$$900 \times 10 = 9000$$

The figures 7 units, 8 tens and 9 hundreds have all become ten times bigger by moving up one
place to become 7 tens, 8 hundreds and 9 thousands. 0's are used to fill the empty spaces.

Multiplying whole numbers by 100 or 1000

To multiply by 100 is simply the same as multiplying by 10 and then by 10 again, so the
numbers move up two places.
To multiply by 1000 is the same as multiplying by 10, by 10 again and then by 10 again, so the
numbers move up three places.

$$8 \times 100 = 800 \qquad\qquad 23 \times 1000 = 23\,000$$
$$78 \times 100 = 7800 \qquad\qquad 123 \times 1000 = 123\,000$$
$$678 \times 100 = 67\,800 \qquad\qquad 4020 \times 1000 = 4\,020\,000$$
$$5670 \times 100 = 567\,000$$
$$5000 \times 100 = 500\,000$$

Multiplying whole numbers by 20, 30, 40, . . . , 200, 300, 400, . . . , 2000, 3000, 4000, . . .

$$70 \times 500 = 7 \times 10 \times 5 \times 100$$
$$= 7 \times 5 \times 10 \times 100$$
$$= 35 \times 1000$$
$$= 35\,000$$

$$800 \times 20 = 8 \times 2 \times 1000$$
$$= 16\,000$$

$$5000 \times 20 = 5 \times 2 \times 10\,000$$
$$= 100\,000$$

$$9000 \times 3000 = 9 \times 3 \times 1\,000\,000$$
$$= 27\,000\,000$$

Multiplying by numbers less than 10

Examples

1   Work out 728×6.

$$\begin{array}{r} 728 \\ \times \quad 6 \\ \hline 4368 \\ \hline \end{array}$$

$8 \times 6 = 48$. Write down 8 and carry 4 to the 10's column.
$2 \times 6 = 12$, and 4 makes 16. Write down 6 and carry 1 to the 100's column.
$7 \times 6 = 42$, and 1 makes 43. Write down 3, and write down 4 in the 1000's column.

2   Work out 5907×4.

$$\begin{array}{r} 5907 \\ \times \quad 4 \\ \hline 23628 \\ \hline \end{array}$$

$7 \times 4 = 28$. Write down 8 and carry 2.
$0 \times 4 = 0$, and 2 makes 2. Write down 2.
$9 \times 4 = 36$. Write down 6 and carry 3.
$5 \times 4 = 20$, and 3 makes 23. Write down 3, and write down 2 in the 10 000's column.

To multiply by a number between 10 and 100

Examples

3   Work out 328×46.

First multiply 328 by 6, then 328 by 40, and add the results together.

$$\begin{array}{r} 328 \\ \times \quad 46 \\ \hline 1968 \\ 13120 \\ \hline 15088 \\ \hline \end{array}$$
← Write down the 0 because this comes from multiplying by 10, then multiply 328 by 4.

or

$$\begin{array}{r} 328 \\ \times \quad 46 \\ \hline 13120 \\ 1968 \\ \hline 15088 \\ \hline \end{array}$$
} if you prefer to multiply by 40 before you multiply by 6.

Checking the size of the answer
328 is approximately 300.
46 is approximately 50.
$300 \times 50 = 15\,000$
The answer $15\,088$ seems to be about the right size.

4   173×91

$$\begin{array}{r} 173 \\ \times\quad 91 \\ \hline 173 \\ 15570 \\ \hline 15743 \end{array} \qquad \text{or} \qquad \begin{array}{r} 173 \\ \times\quad 91 \\ \hline 15570 \\ 173 \\ \hline 15743 \end{array}$$

Checking the size of the answer
173 is approximately 200.
91 is approximately 90.
$200 \times 90 = 18\,000$
We expect the answer to be less than $18\,000$ because 173 is quite a bit less than 200.
The answer $15\,743$ seems to be about the right size.

Normally you would use your calculator to do such questions but it is essential to know how to work out the answers yourself as you cannot always rely on having a calculator handy.

This method is called **long multiplication**. There are other methods of working and you can use any method you prefer as long as it gives the correct answer.

Exercise 3.3

You should do these questions without using a calculator.

1. 1 500×10 5 123×100 8 196×10
    2 92×1000 6 1060×10 9 10×100
    3 65×100 7 17×100 10 20×1000
    4 50×10

2. 1 30×20 5 400×2000 8 20×7000
    2 800×5 6 8000×30 9 6000×50
    3 500×30 7 300×600 10 70×400
    4 60×80

3. 1 46×3 5 529×7 8 805×7
    2 802×5 6 741×9 9 218×5
    3 53×8 7 180×4 10 370×6
    4 165×6

4. When you have answered each of these questions, check the size of the answer.

1	804×45	**5**	397×54	**8**	703×15
2	457×19	**6**	216×66	**9**	989×73
3	673×92	**7**	525×62	**10**	140×87
4	144×68				

5. **1** There are 1760 yards in a mile. How many yards are there in 10 miles ?

2 The distance round a playing-field is 653 m. Wayne goes round it 8 times on a sponsored run. How far has he run altogether ? How far is this to the nearest 100 m ?

3 On an excursion there were 16 coaches, each carrying 47 passengers. How many passengers were there altogether ?

Dividing whole numbers by 10, 100 or 1000

$9000 \div 10 = 900$
$6800 \div 10 = 680$
$6850 \div 10 = 685$

The figures have all become ten times smaller by moving down one place. 0's no longer needed disappear.

$9300 \div 100 = 93$ (Moving down 2 places)
$800 \div 100 = 8$
$30\,000 \div 1000 = 30$ (Moving down 3 places)
$34\,000 \div 1000 = 34$
$534\,000 \div 1000 = 534$

Dividing whole numbers by 20, 30, 40, . . . , 200, 300, 400, . . . , 2000, 3000, 4000, . . .

$6000 \div 30 = \dfrac{600\cancel{0}}{3\cancel{0}} = \dfrac{600}{3} = 200$

The 0's are crossed out because we are dividing both numbers by 10. (This can be called **cancelling**.)

What we are really doing is
$6000 \div 30 = (6000 \div 10) \div 3 = 600 \div 3 = 200$

$$800 \div 400 = \frac{8\cancel{0}\cancel{0}}{4\cancel{0}\cancel{0}} = \frac{8}{4} = 2$$

(We have divided both numbers by 10, and then by 10 again.)

$$30\,000 \div 5000 = \frac{30\,\cancel{0}\cancel{0}\cancel{0}}{5\cancel{0}\cancel{0}\cancel{0}} = \frac{30}{5} = 6$$

$$7200 \div 60 = \frac{720\cancel{0}}{6\cancel{0}} = \frac{720}{6} = 120$$

$$3500 \div 700 = \frac{35\cancel{0}\cancel{0}}{7\cancel{0}\cancel{0}} = \frac{35}{7} = 5$$

You can still use this method without writing anything down, if you have to do it in your head.
e.g. $40\,000 \div 800$ equals $400 \div 8$ which is 50, (mentally dividing by 100 first).

Dividing by numbers less than 10

Examples

1   Work out $148 \div 4$.

```
   37 Answer
4)148
```

The working is:
4's into 1 will not go.
4's into 14 go 3 times, remainder 2. Write 3 in the answer above the 4 of 14. Carry the 2 (tens) to the next figure, making it 28.
In the next place, 4's into 28 go 7 times exactly. Write 7 in the answer above the 8.
The answer is 37 and there is no remainder.

If you cannot do some of the working in your head you can set it down like this:

```
   37 Answer
4)148
   12
   28
   28
    0
```

2   Work out $966 \div 7$.

$$\begin{array}{r} 138 \text{ Answer} \\ 7\overline{)966} \end{array}$$ or $$\begin{array}{r} 138 \text{ Answer} \\ 7\overline{)966} \\ \underline{7} \\ 26 \\ \underline{21} \\ 56 \\ \underline{56} \\ 0 \end{array}$$

If the numbers do not divide exactly, it may be appropriate to leave a remainder, or alternatively you can continue the division using decimal places. (See Chapter 5.)

3   Work out $969 \div 7$, giving the answer and the remainder.

$$\begin{array}{r} 138 \text{ Answer, remainder 3.} \\ 7\overline{)969} \end{array}$$

To divide by a number between 10 and 100

Examples

4   Work out $988 \div 19$.

$19\overline{)988}$ First, think of 19 as nearly 20.
                        How many 20's in 98. Nearly 5.
                        Check whether 19×5 is less than 98. Yes, it is, so the first part of the
                        answer is a five.

$$\begin{array}{r} 5 \\ 19\overline{)988} \\ \underline{95} \\ 38 \end{array}$$ $19 \times 5 = 95$. Put the 5 above the 8 of 98, and 95 below 98.
                        Subtract 95 from 98 and put the 3 below. Bring down the next 8.

$$\begin{array}{r} 52 \text{ Answer} \\ 19\overline{)988} \\ \underline{95} \\ 38 \\ \underline{38} \\ 0 \end{array}$$ How many 19's in 38 ? (How many 20's ?)
                        There are nearly 2 20's, and there are exactly 2 19's.
                        $19 \times 2 = 38$. Write 2 in the answer above the 8 of 38.
                        Write 38 below 38 and subtract, leaving 0 so there is no remainder.
                        The answer is 52.

Checking the size of the answer

988 is approximately 1000.
19 is approximately 20.
$1000 \div 20 = 50$
The answer 52 seems to be about the right size.

You can also check by multiplication.

If $988 \div 19 = 52$,
then $52 \times 19 = 988$.

$$
\begin{array}{r}
52 \\
\times\ 19 \\
\hline
468 \\
520 \\
\hline
988 \\
\hline
\end{array}
$$

5   Work out $826 \div 14$.

First, 14 into 8 will not go.
14's into 82 go 5 times. Put 5 in the answer above the 2 of 82.
Multiply 14 by 5 (=70) and write this under the 82.
Subtract 70 from 82 leaving 12.
Bring down the next figure, 6, making 126.
14's into 126 go 9 times. Put 9 in the answer above the 6.
Multiply 14 by 9 (=126) and write this under the 126.
Subtracting leaves 0 so there is no remainder.
The answer is 59.

$$
\begin{array}{r}
59\ \text{Answer} \\
14\overline{)826} \\
70 \\
\hline
126 \\
126 \\
\hline
0 \\
\end{array}
$$

Checking the size of the answer

826 is approximately 800.
14 is approximately 10.
$800 \div 10 = 80$

We expect the answer to be less than 80 because 14 is quite a bit bigger than 10.
The answer 59 seems to be about the right size.

You can also check by multiplication.

If $826 \div 14 = 59$,
then $59 \times 14 = 826$.

$$
\begin{array}{r}
59 \\
\times\ 14 \\
\hline
236 \\
590 \\
\hline
826 \\
\hline
\end{array}
$$

The difficult part of such a question is deciding how many times 14 goes into 82 and into 126. You can do it the long way by working out the 14 times table until you get far enough:
$14 \times 1 = 14$, $14 \times 2 = 28$, $14 \times 3 = 42$, etc.
You could make a rough guess instead.
$14 \times 10 = 140$ so half of that, $14 \times 5 = \frac{1}{2}$ of $140 = 70$. Then $14 \times 6 = 70 + 14 = 84$, so 14 goes into 82 five times.

6   Divide 919 by 24, giving the answer and the remainder.

$$\begin{array}{r} 38 \\ 24\overline{)919} \\ \underline{72} \\ 199 \\ \underline{192} \\ 7 \end{array}$$ Answer 38, remainder 7.

Checking the size of the answer

919 is approximately 900.
24 is approximately halfway between 20 and 30.
$900 \div 20 = 45$
$900 \div 30 = 30$
The answer 38 is between 45 and 30 and seems to be about the right size.

Checking the answer by multiplication:

If $919 \div 24 = 38$ rem 7,
then $(38 \times 24) + 7 = 919$.

$$\begin{array}{r} 38 \\ \times\ 24 \\ \hline 152 \\ 760 \\ \hline 912 \end{array}$$

$912 + 7 = 919$

This method is called **long division**. There are other methods of working and you can use any method you prefer as long as it gives the correct answer.

Exercise 3.4

You should do these questions without using a calculator.

1. **1** $7000 \div 10$ **5** $570 \div 10$ **8** $1790 \div 10$
    2 $30\,000 \div 100$ **6** $16\,000 \div 100$ **9** $1000 \div 10$
    3 $6000 \div 1000$ **7** $10\,000 \div 1000$ **10** $18\,000 \div 1000$
    4 $4000 \div 100$

2. **1** $120 \div 40$ **5** $90\,000 \div 300$ **8** $20\,000 \div 50$
    2 $9000 \div 300$ **6** $800 \div 40$ **9** $600 \div 300$
    3 $4000 \div 40$ **7** $6000 \div 200$ **10** $5000 \div 20$
    4 $7200 \div 80$

3. **1** $57 \div 3$ **5** $525 \div 7$ **8** $708 \div 6$
    2 $805 \div 5$ **6** $196 \div 4$ **9** $938 \div 7$
    3 $488 \div 8$ **7** $747 \div 9$ **10** $390 \div 5$
    4 $162 \div 6$

4. Work out the answers to these questions and also give the remainders.

1	$605 \div 6$	5	$210 \div 8$	8	$503 \div 4$
2	$257 \div 7$	6	$146 \div 5$	9	$252 \div 5$
3	$124 \div 9$	7	$424 \div 7$	10	$732 \div 8$
4	$98 \div 3$				

Questions 5 and 6.

When you have answered each of these questions, check the size of the answer and check the answer by multiplication.

5.

1	$608 \div 16$	5	$423 \div 47$	8	$403 \div 31$
2	$438 \div 73$	6	$522 \div 18$	9	$374 \div 17$
3	$961 \div 31$	7	$221 \div 13$	10	$850 \div 25$
4	$378 \div 54$				

6. Work out the answers to these questions and also give the remainders.

1	$940 \div 18$	4	$475 \div 31$
2	$572 \div 47$	5	$358 \div 16$
3	$681 \div 54$		

7. 20 people together won £960, and shared the money equally. How much did they each get ?

8. A stove uses 15 kg of fuel each day. If there are 675 kg of fuel available, how long will it last ?

9. A farmer collects 1400 eggs. If he packs them in cartons each containing 12 eggs, how many cartons are used and how many eggs are left over ?

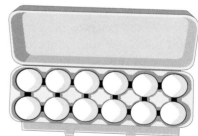

Exercise 3.5   Applications

You should do these questions without using a calculator.

1. The attendances at four cricket matches were 3242, 5671, 10 470 and 2835.

    1   Write 10 470 in words.
    2   What was the difference between the greatest and least attendances ?
    3   What was the total attendance for the four matches ?
    4   Write the answer to **3** correct to the nearest 1000.

2. Write down a 3-figure number whose digits are all different and do not include 0. Reverse it, i.e. write it down backwards. Take the smaller number of the two from the larger. Reverse this answer and add this number to the answer. What is your total ?

3. Ashton, Barton, Corton, Dayton and Elton are five villages. The distances between each are shown on the mileage chart, (for example, from Barton to Dayton is 15 miles).

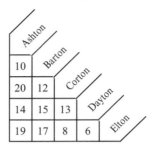

   1 What is the distance between Ashton and Dayton ?

   2 A cyclist travels from Elton directly to Ashton. On his return journey he takes the route via Corton. How much further does he travel on the return journey ?

   3 A motorist lives in Barton and works in Elton, and drives to and from work on 6 days each week. What is the total distance he has travelled in 3 weeks ?

4. Mr Sumner was paid £8 per hour for a week of 38 hours work. Overtime was paid as time-and-a-half, except on Sundays when it was paid as double time.
In one week Mr Sumner worked 8 hours each day from Monday to Friday, 4 hours on Saturday and 3 hours on Sunday. Find his total wages for that week.

5. In a theatre the price of tickets is £8 each. If there are 252 seats in the theatre, what are the total takings if all tickets are sold ?
If the price of tickets is increased to £9, how many tickets must be sold for a performance, for the total takings to match the previous total for a full theatre ?

6. 83 vases are bought for £19 each. What is the total cost ?
3 of the vases are broken, and the rest are sold to make an over-all profit of £423. For what price is each vase sold ?

7. How many square plots of length 17 metres can be made from a rectangular field which is 391 m long and 272 m wide ?

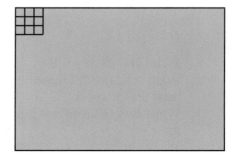

Practice test 3

You should do these questions without using a calculator.

1. Write the number thirteen thousand and ninety in figures.

2. What is the number which is 2 less than 600 ?

3. Write 3486
    1   to the nearest 10,
    2   to the nearest 100,
    3   to the nearest 1000.

4. In one sack of potatoes there are 29 kg and in another sack there are 17 kg. How many kilograms must be transferred to make equal amounts in the two sacks ?

5. Two candidates in an election received 36 865 and 25 917 votes.
    1   What was the total number of votes ?
    2   How many more votes did the winner get than the loser ?

6. Work out these calculations.

    1   100×100 4 $10\,000 \div 1000$
    2   700×50 5 $972 \div 6$
    3   38×4

7. A wheel makes 300 revolutions per minute. How long will it take to make 12 000 revolutions ?

8. Find the value of 271×41. Check your answer using approximate numbers.

9. A box holds 24 tins. How many boxes must be used to pack 360 tins ?
    Check your answer using multiplication.

10. How many books costing £14 each can be bought for £500, and how much money is left over ?

PUZZLE

1. A ship in the harbour has a ladder with 12 rungs, each 30 cm apart, hanging over the side. At low tide 4 rungs are covered by the sea. If the tide rises at 40 cm per hour, how many rungs will be covered 3 hours later ?

4 Introduction to algebra

The topics in this chapter include:

- using letters to represent variables,
- constructing, interpreting and evaluating formulae given in words and in symbols,
- substituting numbers into simple formulae,
- understanding and using basic algebraic conventions.

Algebra is a branch of Mathematics which uses letters to represent numbers.
e.g. $3x + 2y$ is an algebraic expression. It means three times number x plus twice number y.
The expression cannot be simplified but if we know particular values for x and y then we can find the value of the expression.
If $x = 4$ and $y = 7$, $3x + 2y = (3 \times 4) + (2 \times 7) = 12 + 14 = 26$.
If $x = 6$ and $y = \frac{1}{2}$, $3x + 2y = (3 \times 6) + \left(2 \times \frac{1}{2}\right) = 18 + 1 = 19$.

Small letters $a, b, c, \ldots$ are usually used to represent numbers although occasionally capital letters may be used instead. In any question, use the sort of letter which is given, do not change from small letters to capital letters or vice versa.
x and y are often used for numbers whose values have to be found. We also use them on graphs.

Write the letters carefully, otherwise your work will be difficult to read and understand.
Make b different from number 6. Make ℓ different from number 1. Make x different from $\times$ (a multiplication sign). Make z different from a 2 or a 3.
o and O are not normally used as letters in Algebra as it is too easy to confuse them with number 0.

Expressions

If apples cost 15 pence per lb, the cost of 10 lb of apples is 10×15 pence.
If apples cost a pence per lb, the cost of 10 lb of apples is $10 \times a$ pence $= 10a$ pence.
($10 \times a$ or $a \times 10$ are written as $10a$.)

If a girl is 10 years old and her younger brother is 3 years old, then the girl is $(10 - 3)$ years older than her brother.
If a girl is g years old and her younger brother is b years old, then the girl is $(g - b)$ years older than her brother.

The total weight of 8 parcels of 3 kg each and 6 parcels of 5 kg each is
$[(8 \times 3) + (6 \times 5)]$ kg.
The total weight of 8 parcels of b kg each and 6 parcels of c kg each is $(8b + 6c)$ kg.

If 20 people share £300 equally they each get £$\frac{300}{20}$.

If x people share £300 equally they each get £$\frac{300}{x}$.

Formulae

A rule for finding a suitable rise, in cm, on a
staircase, is to subtract the length of the tread, in cm,
from 60 and then divide by 2.

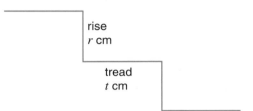

rise
r cm

tread
t cm

If the rise is r cm and the tread is t cm then the formula
is $r = \frac{1}{2}(60 - t)$.

Exercise 4.1

1. **1** What is the cost, in pence, of 5 kg of butter at 120p per kg ?
     What is the cost, in pence, of 5 kg of butter at a pence per kg ?

   2 How many minutes are there in 3 hours ?
     How many minutes are there in $2b$ hours ?

   3 If a man goes abroad with 200 francs and spends 180 francs, how many francs has he
     left ?
     If a man goes abroad with c francs and spends d francs, how many francs has he left ?

   4 What is the total cost, in pence, of 3 lb of apples at 20p per lb and 2 lb of pears at
     25p per lb ?
     What is the total cost, in pence, of 3 lb of apples at e pence per lb and 2 lb of pears at
     f pence per lb ?

   5 What is the change from 50p after buying 5 packets of sweets at 7p each ?
     What is the change from 50p after buying g packets of sweets at h pence each ?

2. **1** If a pencil costs k pence, what is the cost of 12 pencils ?

   2 What is the cost in pence of 4 eggs, if they cost m pence per dozen ?

   3 How many seconds are there in $3n$ minutes ?

   4 If x pence is shared equally among q children, how much do they each receive ?

   5 If a clock gains s seconds per hour, and it is set to the right time, how many seconds
     fast will it be t hours later ?

3. **1** The rule for finding the number of vertices (corners) on a certain type of solid figure is to subtract the number of faces from the number of edges and then add 2.
If the number of edges is E and the number of faces is F, find a formula for V, the number of vertices.

2 To find a bowler's average, divide the number of runs scored against his bowling by the number of wickets he has taken.
If a bowler takes w wickets for a cost of r runs, find a formula for his bowling average, B.

3 A ferry charges £40 for each car and £6 for each person.
If there were n people and c cars on a crossing, find a formula for T, where £T is the total cost.

4 The amount for the monthly payment on an interest-free credit sale is found by subtracting the deposit from the total price and dividing the result by the number of months of the loan.
If the total price is £T, the deposit is £D and the loan is to run for 12 months, find a formula for M, where £M is the monthly payment.

5 If a stone is dropped (e.g. from the edge of a cliff), the time in seconds it will take to fall a certain distance can be found by dividing the distance in metres by 5, and then taking the square root.
If the distance is d metres, find a formula for t, where t seconds is the time taken.

Simplifying expressions

Addition and subtraction

$a + a = 2a$
$5b - 4b = b$
$3c - 3c = 0$
$3d + 4e + d - e = 4d + 3e$

Multiplication and division

$5 \times a = 5a$

$1 \times b = b$

$c \times 3 = 3c$

$d \times 0 = 0$

$e \times f = ef$

$a \times a = a^2$

$2 \times b \times c = 2bc$

$d \times d \times d = d^3$

$e \div f = \dfrac{e}{f}$

$g \div g = 1$

Further expressions

$3a \times 4 = 12a$

$5b \times b = 5b^2$

$6c \times 2d = 12cd$

$3e \div f = \dfrac{3e}{f}$

$12g \div 4g = 3$

$h^2 + h^2 = 2h^2$

Removing brackets

$3(a + 4b) = 3a + 12b$

$2(3c - 5) = 6c - 10$

$3(2d + 1) + 2(d - 2) = 6d + 3 + 2d - 4 = 8d - 1$

$$5(f - 2g - h) + 3(f - g + 2h) = 5f - 10g - 5h + 3f - 3g + 6h$$
$$= 8f - 13g + h$$

Exercise 4.2

1.   Simplify these expressions.

   1 $3a + 5a$

   2 $b + b + 2b$

   3 $4c + 6c - 3c$

   4 $5d - d + 2d - d$

   5 $3c + 2c - 4c$

   6 $6d - 4d - 2d$

   7 $5e + f + 3e - f$

   8 $2g - 3h + g - h$

   9 $4j + k + 2j + 3k$

   10 $6m - 7m + 2m$

2.   Simplify these expressions.

   1 $a \times a \times 2$

   2 $b \times b \times b$

   3 $c \div c$

   4 $8d \div 2$

   5 $5e \times 4$

   6 $3f \times f$

   7 $2g \times 3h$

   8 $3j \div k$

   9 $20m \div 4m$

   10 $15pq \div 3$

3.   Remove the brackets in these expressions and, if possible, simplify the answers.

    1 $2(a + 3b)$ **6** $2(a + 2) + (a - 1)$

    2 $5(3c - d)$ **7** $4(b - 1) + 3(b + 2)$

    3 $10(2e - 3)$ **8** $(c - d) + 4(c + 2d)$

    4 $2(3f + 5)$ **9** $3(e + 8) - 2e$

    5 $3(6g - 5h)$ **10** $f(2f - 3) + 3f$

Substitution

If $a = 2$, $b = 5$ and $c = 0$,

$3a + b^2 = (3 \times 2) + 5^2 = 6 + 25 = 31,$

$4abc = 4 \times 2 \times 5 \times 0 = 0,$

$a^3 + 2b^2 = 2^3 + (2 \times 5^2) = 8 + 50 = 58.$

Note that $2b^2$ means $2 \times b^2 = 2 \times 5^2 = 2 \times 25 = 50$. It is not the same as $(2b)^2$ which means $2b \times 2b$ and equals 100.

Formulae

Examples

1   A formula used to find the area of a right-angled isosceles triangle is $A = \dfrac{x^2}{2}$.

    If $A = \dfrac{x^2}{2}$, find A when $x = 10$.

    $A = \dfrac{10^2}{2} = \dfrac{100}{2} = 50$

2   A formula used to find Simple Interest is $I = \dfrac{PRT}{100}$.

    If $I = \dfrac{PRT}{100}$, find I when $P = 800$, $R = 7$ and $T = 5$.

    $I = \dfrac{800 \times 7 \times 5}{100} = 280$

3   A formula used to convert temperatures from the Celsius to the Fahrenheit scale is $F = 1.8C + 32$.

    If $F = 1.8C + 32$, find F when $C = 40$.

    $F = (1.8 \times 40) + 32 = 72 + 32 = 104$

Exercise 4.3

1. If $p = 6$, $q = 2$, find the values of

   1 $2p + 3q$ **5** $p - 2q$ **9** $2(p + q)$

   2 $3p - 4q$ **6** p^2 **10** $\dfrac{p + 2q}{5}$

   3 pq **7** $3q^2$

   4 $\dfrac{4p}{q}$ **8** $\sqrt{8q}$

2. If $x = 4$ and $y = 3$, find the values of

   1 $2x^2$ **5** $\dfrac{x + 2}{y}$ **8** $4y - 3x$

   2 $x^2 + y^2$ **6** $2y^2$ **9** $\dfrac{y^2 + 1}{x}$

   3 $2x - y$ **7** y^3 **10** $\sqrt{x + 4y}$

   4 $2xy$

3. If $a = 5$, $b = 3$ and $c = 1$, find the values of x if

   1 $x = 4a + b$ **4** $x = 2a - 3b - c$

   2 $x = a^2 + b^2$ **5** $x = \dfrac{a}{c}$

   3 $x = 2a^2$

4. **1** If $distance = speed \times time$, what is $distance$ when $speed = 70$ and $time = 3$?

   2 If $paint = \dfrac{area}{18}$, what is $paint$ when $area = 45$?

   3 If $amount = principal + interest$, what is $amount$ when $principal = 800$ and $interest = 80$?

   4 If $weight = 6 \times (length)^2$, what is $weight$ when $length = 5$?

   5 If $radius = \sqrt{\dfrac{7 \times area}{22}}$, what is $radius$ when $area = 154$?

5. **1** If $a = 180n + 360$, find a when $n = 3$.

    2 If $s = a + ar$, find s when $a = 4$ and $r = \frac{1}{2}$.

    3 If $b = 2\sqrt{x}$, find b when $x = 25$.

    4 If $C = \frac{5}{9}(F - 32)$, find C when $F = 50$.

    5 If $s = \dfrac{n}{2}(a + l)$, find s when $n = 20$, $a = 6$ and $l = 24$.

6. A polygon with n sides has $\dfrac{n(n - 3)}{2}$ diagonals.

    How many diagonals has a polygon with 10 sides ?

Exercise 4.4 Applications

1. If £p is shared equally among q children, how much, in pence, do they each receive ?

2. A video recorder costs £60 deposit and then £25 per month for 12 months.

    How much has been paid after 1 month, 2 months, 3 months ?

    Find a formula for A, where £A is the amount paid, after n months, where n is less than or equal to 12.

    What is the total amount paid for the recorder ?

Deposit £60
£25 per month
for 12 months

3. Simplify

    1 $a + a$ | **2** $a - a$ | **3** $a \times a$ | **4** $a \div a$ | **5** $\sqrt{a^2}$

4. Simplify

    1 $5a - 2a$ **6** $3f - f$
    2 $b + 2b$ **7** $g - g$
    3 $9c - 4c$ **8** $2h + 5h - 6h$
    4 $2d - d$ **9** $5j - 2j + j$
    5 $7e + 2e$ **10** $9k - 7k - k$

5. Simplify

    1 $8x \times 2y$ **6** $3 \times 2xy$
    2 $4x \times x$ **7** $6 \times 4x^2$
    3 $2x \div x$ **8** $5x \div 5$
    4 $3x \times 9$ **9** $(3x)^2$
    5 $6x \div 6x$ **10** $0 \times 4xy$

6. Simplify

    1 $4(x-4)+3(x+5)$ **4** $8(1+x)+12(1-x)$

    2 $x+2(x+y)$ **5** $4(3x-1)+3(x+2)$

    3 $2(1+3x)+3(5-x)$

7. If $p=4$, $q=2$, $r=3$, find the values of

    1 $p+q$ **5** p^2+4r^2 **8** $4r^2-3q^2$

    2 $4p+3q$ **6** $\dfrac{p}{q}$ **9** $\dfrac{p+r}{7q}$

    3 $r-q$

    4 $8qr$ **7** $4r-3q$ **10** $q(2p+r)$

8.   **1**   If $A=P+PR$, find A when $P=700$ and $R=0.1$.

    2   If $t=180n-360$, find t when $n=4$.

    3   If $speed=\dfrac{distance}{time}$, find $speed$ when $distance=120$ and $time=4$.

    4   If $y=2x-4$, find y when $x=17$.

    5   If $P=\dfrac{V^2}{R}$, find P when $V=10$ and $R=20$.

9. The formula for the sum s of the numbers from 1 to n is $s=\frac{1}{2}n(n+1)$.
Put $n=12$ in this formula to find the value of $1+2+3+\cdots+11+12$.

10. Mr West's weekly wage is calculated according to the hours he has worked using this rule:
If the number of hours is less than 40, wage in £ = (4 × number of hours) + 70.
If the number of hours is 40 or more, wage in £ = (6 × number of hours) − 10.

    Find how much he will earn in a week when he works for

    1   30 hours,   **2**   50 hours.

Practice test 4

1.   **1**   If 20 lb of apples are bought for x pence per lb and sold for y pence per lb, what is the profit ?

    2   A man is paid £8 per hour for doing a job. What does he earn for x hours work ?

    3   How many grams are there in x kg ?

    4   There are x children in a Youth club. If 5 of them leave, how many remain ?

[Turn over]

2.   The time taken to cook a chicken is given as 40 minutes per kg plus 20 minutes extra.

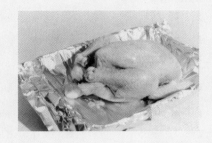

What are the cooking times for chickens weighing 1 kg, 2 kg, 3 kg ?

Find a formula for T, where T minutes is the time needed for a chicken weighing c kg.

3.   Simplify

1 $8a + 4a$ 4 $2e + 4f - 2e + f$
2 $8b - 7b$ 5 $8g - 4 + g + 5$
3 $c + 5d + c - 6d$

4.   Simplify

1 $2 \times 6a$ 4 $4e \div e$
2 $3b \times 4c$ 5 $5f \times f$
3 $6d \div 6$

5.   Remove the brackets in these expressions.

1 $2(3a - 5)$ 4 $e(e + 2)$
2 $3(6b + 5c)$ 5 $3(f - 4)$
3 $4d(d + 1)$

6.   If $a = 6$, $b = 5$ and $c = 1$, find the values of

1 $4a - b$ 4 $\dfrac{a - c}{b}$
2 $a^2 + c^2$ 5 $(3b - 5c)^2$
3 $b^2 + b$

7.   The cost of electricity, £E, is given by the formula $E = S + \frac{7}{100}n$, where £S is the quarterly charge and n is the number of units used in that quarter.

Find the cost when the quarterly charge is £9 and 500 units have been used in the quarter.

8. **1** If $ax - b = c$, find c when $a = 6$, $b = 10$ and $x = 4$.

    2 If $E = 3v^2$, find E when $v = 10$.

    3 If $v = u + at$, find v when $u = 30$, $a = 10$ and $t = 2$.

    4 If $s = t^2 - t$, find s when $t = 8$.

    5 If $area = length \times breadth$, find $area$ when $length = 12$ and $breadth = 7$.

PUZZLES

2. Five children were playing a game of cards.
    A set of cards numbered 1 to 10 are dealt so that they get two each. Paul has two cards which total 11, Mike has two cards which total 7, Laura has two cards which total 17, Kate has two cards which total 4 and Jane has two cards which total 16. In this game the winner is the person who has the card numbered 10.
    Who wins the game ?

3. How many triangles are there in this figure ?

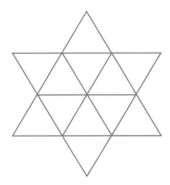

4. Copy the diagram and starting in the top left-hand square, draw a continuous line passing through each square once only, so that the sum of the numbers in each group of four squares is 24.

6	6	3	15	5	3
6	9	3	10	6	3
3	3	3	8	8	5
5	10	4	2	3	10
3	6	11	2	3	9
5	8	4	7	10	9

5 Decimals

The topics in this chapter include:

- ordering decimals and understanding place values,
- calculating with decimals using the four rules,
- calculating with money in £'s and pence,
- applying the four rules in the solution of problems,
- understanding decimal places and applying given degrees of accuracy.

Decimals

In the number 234.567 the figure 5 represents five-tenths because it is in the first decimal place, the 6 represents six-hundredths and the 7 represents seven-thousandths.
It is usual to write a nought before the decimal point if there is no other number there, e.g. 0.51, not just .51, and 0.02, not just .02.

Working without a calculator

Addition, subtraction; multiplication and division by whole numbers

When adding, subtracting, or when multiplying or dividing by whole numbers, keep the figures in their correct positions relative to the decimal point.

Examples

1 Work out $1.5 + 14.83$.

$$\begin{array}{r} 1.5 \\ +14.83 \\ \hline 16.33 \end{array}$$

2 Work out $12.1 - 3.02$.

$$\begin{array}{r} 12.10 \\ -\ 3.02 \\ \hline 9.08 \end{array}$$

3   Work out 12.6×4.

$$
\begin{array}{r}
12.6 \\
\times \quad 4 \\
\hline
50.4 \\
\hline
\end{array}
$$

4   Work out $27.6 \div 8$.

$$
\begin{array}{r}
3.45 \\
8{\overline{)27.60}}
\end{array}
$$

Powers of 10

When multiplying by 10, 100, 1000, ... the numbers grow larger, so the figures move upwards (to the left), 1, 2, 3, ... places, assuming that the decimal point is fixed. Add 0's to fill any empty places between the figures and the decimal point.

Examples

5 $2.56 \times 10 = 25.6$
$3.5 \times 100 = 350$
$0.0041 \times 1000 = 4.1$

When dividing by 10, 100, 1000, ... the numbers become smaller, so the figures move downwards (to the right), 1, 2, 3, ... places, assuming that the decimal point is fixed. Add 0's to fill any empty places between the decimal point and the figures.

Examples

6 $31.8 \div 10 = 3.18$
$23 \div 100 = 0.23$
$5.6 \div 1000 = 0.0056$

To multiply by 20, multiply by 10 and then multiply that answer by 2.
To divide by 20, divide by 10 and then divide that answer by 2.

Examples

7 $2.89 \times 20 = 28.9 \times 2 = 57.8$
$4.54 \div 20 = 0.454 \div 2 = 0.227$
$28.5 \times 30 = 285 \times 3 = 855$
$5.43 \times 40 = 54.3 \times 4 = 217.2$
$9.6 \div 80 = 0.96 \div 8 = 0.12$
$8.02 \times 200 = 802 \times 2 = 1604$
$648.6 \div 300 = 6.486 \div 3 = 2.162$
$3690 \div 900 = 36.9 \div 9 = 4.1$

For questions involving multiplying or dividing by decimal numbers, e.g. 3.8×1.25 or $300 \div 2.4$, use your calculator.

Exercise 5.1

In this exercise, do not use your calculator, except for checking your answers.

1. 1 $1.32 + 2.5 + 3.79$
    2 $5.87 + 1.03 + 0.1$
    3 $0.4 + 0.08 + 0.15$
    4 $9.99 + 0.03$
    5 $2.05 + 4.93 + 0.88$

2. 1 $21.03 - 0.07$
    2 $7.92 - 0.97$
    3 $0.5 - 0.13$
    4 $10 - 0.91$
    5 $5.82 + 2.19 - 3.13$

3. 1 3.87×4
    2 0.05×12
    3 0.8×7
    4 3.14×3
    5 1.92×5

4. 1 $3.88 \div 4$
    2 $0.056 \div 8$
    3 $0.8 \div 5$
    4 $19.8 \div 9$
    5 $35.4 \div 6$

5. 1 1.32×10
    2 2.5×100
    3 1.03×1000
    4 0.027×100
    5 3.1×100

6. 1 $3.79 \div 10$
    2 $0.15 \div 100$
    3 $21.3 \div 1000$
    4 $3.1 \div 1000$
    5 $3.4 \div 100$

7. 1 9.1×20
    2 0.6×300
    3 $8.2 \div 20$
    4 $930 \div 300$
    5 $56 \div 40$

8. Write down any even number between 1 and 11. Add 1.83 and multiply the total by 5. Now subtract 10.9 and then divide by 10. Add 0.675 and double the result. Subtract the number you started with. What is your answer ?

9. On a staircase there are 8 steps. The height of each rise is 18.5 cm. What is the total height from bottom to top of the staircase ?

10. A block of copper with volume $9 \, \text{cm}^3$ weighs 79.2 g. What is the weight of $1 \, \text{cm}^3$ of copper ?

Decimals in order of size

To compare 0.56 and 0.6, write 0.6 as 0.60 so that both numbers have the same number of decimal places.
Then 0.56 is 5 tenths and 6 hundredths, which is 56 hundredths, and 0.60 is 60 hundredths.
0.56 is smaller than 0.6.

To compare 0.24 and 0.231 write 0.24 as 0.240.
Then 0.240 is 240 thousandths, and 0.231 is 231 thousandths.
0.231 is smaller than 0.24.

To compare 0.77, 0.769 and 0.7, write all three numbers with 3 decimal places.
0.77 = 0.770 and this is 770 thousandths.
0.769 is 769 thousandths.
0.7 = 0.700 and this is 700 thousandths.
In order of size, smallest first, the numbers are 0.7, 0.769, 0.77.

Numbers to the nearest whole number

If you need an answer correct to the nearest whole number, continue the division to 1 decimal place.

e.g. For numbers between 14 and 15.
Any number less than 14.5 is given as 14 to the nearest whole number.
Any number from 14.5 upwards is given as 15 to the nearest whole number.
(Actually, 14.5 is exactly halfway between 14 and 15 but it is usual to correct it **up** to 15.)
So, if the figure in the 1st decimal place is 5 or more, correct up to the next whole number.

Examples

2.3   =   2, to the nearest whole number.
15.9 = 16, to the nearest whole number.
16.1 = 16, to the nearest whole number.
19.6 = 20, to the nearest whole number.
20.48 = 20, to the nearest whole number.

Decimal places

Sometimes when doing division the answer is not exact and it will be necessary to stop after a suitable number of decimal places. The method for this is similar to that used to correct numbers to the nearest whole number.

Look at the figure to the right of the last figure you need. If this extra figure is 5 or more, add 1 to the final figure of your answer.

Examples

1   Find the value of 29 ÷ 7, correct to 3 decimal places.

We want 3 decimal places, so find the figures in the first 4 decimal places, that is one more place than we need.

$$\begin{array}{r} 4.1428 \\ 7\overline{)29.0000} \end{array}$$

Since the figure in the 4th decimal place (8) is 5 or more, the figure in the 3rd decimal place must be corrected up from 2 to 3.

29 ÷ 7 = 4.143, correct to 3 decimal places.

2   Find the value of 36.86 ÷ 6, correct to 2 decimal places.

$$\begin{array}{r} 6.143 \\ 6\overline{)36.860} \end{array}$$

Since the figure in the 3rd decimal place (3) is less than 5, the figure in the 2nd decimal place is not changed.

36.86 ÷ 6 = 6.14, correct to 2 decimal places.

Here are some other examples:

3.2976 = 3.298 to 3 decimal places
0.8692 = 0.869 to 3 decimal places
0.0827 = 0.083 to 3 decimal places
0.00426 = 0.004 to 3 decimal places

0.849 = 0.85 to 2 decimal places
3.297 = 3.30 to 2 decimal places
1.0347 = 1.03 to 2 decimal places

0.849 = 0.8 to 1 decimal place
3.297 = 3.3 to 1 decimal place
1.0347 = 1.0 to 1 decimal place
1.0747 = 1.1 to 1 decimal place

Exercise 5.2

1.   Write these numbers in order of size, smallest first.

0.8, 0.75, 0.81, 0.7, 0.778.

2.   Write these numbers in order of size, smallest first.

62.5, 63.7, 60.9, 62.49, 63.72.

3.   Write these numbers correct to the nearest whole number.

    1 56.752   **2** 82.9804   **3** 253.312   **4** 206.789   **5** 1000.49

4.   Write these numbers correct to 2 decimal places.

    1 29.7122   **2** 1.62815   **3** 202.9157   **4** 4.6798   **5** 0.03527

5.   Find the answers to these questions, correct to 1 decimal place. Do not use your calculator, except for checking your answers.

1 $14.49 \div 5$	**5** $26.23 \div 4$	**8** $13.8 \div 5$
2 $3.85 \div 2$	**6** $47.76 \div 9$	**9** $24.1 \div 7$
3 $12.7 \div 8$	**7** $0.98 \div 6$	**10** $38.96 \div 3$
4 $108.4 \div 3$		

Money

Since there are 100 pence in £1, our money calculations use the decimal system.

£2 and 48 pence is £2.48
£3 and 5 pence is £3.05
£3 and 50 pence is £3.50

Examples

1   **Addition.** Work out £2.84 + £3.96.

    £
    2.84
    3.96
    ――――
    6.80   Answer £6.80

2   **Subtraction.** Work out £10 − £7.56.

    £
    10.00
     7.56
    ――――
     2.44   Answer £2.44

3   **Subtraction by the method of adding on.**

    This is the way a shopkeeper would count out the change.

    Work out £10 − £7.56.

    £7.56 and **4p** makes £7.60, and **40p** makes £8, and **£2** makes £10.
    You receive £2.44 in change.

4   **Multiplication**. Work out £3.75 × 8.

          £
          3.75
          ___8
          30.00   Answer £30 or £30.00 (whichever is more appropriate).

5   **Division**. Work out £75 ÷ 6.

          £
          12.5
          6)75.0   Answer £12.50

6   How many lollipops at 6p each can be bought for £5 ?

          Work in pence.   £5 is 500p.

            83, remainder 2
          6)500

          83 lollipops can be bought (and there is 2p change).

Amounts to the nearest penny

If you are working in pence,
29.3 pence = 29p, to the nearest penny.
12.62 pence = 13p, to the nearest penny.
(If the figure in the 1st decimal place is 5 or more, round up to the next penny.)

If you are working in £'s,
£3.776 = £3.78, to the nearest penny.
£2.494 = £2.49, to the nearest penny.
(The figures in the first two decimal places give the pence. If the figure in the 3rd decimal place
is 5 or more, round the pence up to the next penny.)

Approximations and estimations

When you go shopping, it is useful to make an approximate calculation of any bill so that
you can see if you have enough money, and you can check that you do not get the wrong
change.

For example, in a shop suppose you select 3 articles at £1.99 each, 2 at £2.95 each and 1 at
£4.90. Before you go to the cash desk you could do an approximate calculation to see if you
had enough money to pay for them. It is nearly 3 at £2, 2 at £3 and 1 at £5 so you would need
nearly £17. You also expect to get just over £3 in change if you pay with a £20 note.
(When the exact amount is shown on the till you can check your exact change.)

Exercise 5.3

In this exercise, do not use your calculator, except for checking your answers.

1. Mrs Martin spent £6.36 on meat and £3.84 on
    vegetables.

    1   How much was this altogether ?
    2   What change did she get from a £20 note ?

2. A shop's takings during the week were Monday £591.17, Tuesday £629.80, Wednesday
    £212.14, Thursday £859.75, Friday £905.22, Saturday £1028.60.

    1   What were the total takings for the week, to the nearest £1 ?
    2   The shopkeeper was hoping for total takings of £5000. How many £'s was he short of
    his target ?

3. From a mail-order catalogue Rachel orders 2 items at £6.99 each and 3 items at £11.99
    each. What is the approximate cost ?

4. Mr Seed bought toys at 5 for 45p and sold them at 4 for 52p. How much profit did he
    make on each one ?

5. 28 bars of chocolate cost £3.64. What would be the cost of 7 similar bars ?

6. Two books together cost £6.50, one being £1.20 more than the other. What did the
    cheaper one cost ?

7. The weekly wages paid by a firm to 5 workmen total £525. What will the weekly wages
    be if they employ two extra men, and pay them all at the same rate ?

8. 7 people won a competition and shared the prize money of £250 equally. How much did
    they each get, to the nearest penny ?

Exercise 5.4   Applications

In this exercise, do not use your calculator, except for checking your answers.

1. A glass weighs 278.2 g when empty and 543.1 g when it contains some
    water. What is the weight of the water ?

    If another 123.8 g of water are added, what is the new total weight ?

2. A wheel travels a distance of 2.7 m when making 1 revolution.

   1   How far does it travel when making 6 revolutions ?

   2   What is this distance to the nearest metre ?

3.   **1**   Divide $(27.3 - 12.7)$ by $(27.3 + 12.7)$.

   2   What is the answer correct to 1 decimal place ?

4. At a weather station in the South of England in a recent
year the rainfall in the first four weeks of January
(1st to 28th Jan) was, in mm,
12.2,   33.4,   3.5,   13.8.

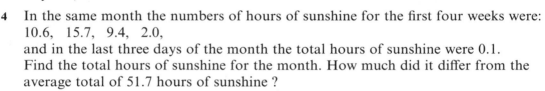

   1   Find the total rainfall for the four weeks.

   2   The total rainfall for the 29th, 30th and 31st January
was 0.2 mm. Find the total rainfall for the whole month.

   3   Find by how much the total rainfall for the whole month
differed from the average January total over a number
of years, which is 52.0 mm.

   4   In the same month the numbers of hours of sunshine for the first four weeks were:
10.6,   15.7,   9.4,   2.0,
and in the last three days of the month the total hours of sunshine were 0.1.
Find the total hours of sunshine for the month. How much did it differ from the
average total of 51.7 hours of sunshine ?

   5   Comment briefly on the weather in that month.

5. A rope 2.4 m long hangs over a nail. One end of the rope just
touches the floor and the other end is 0.6 m above the floor.
How high is the nail above the floor ?

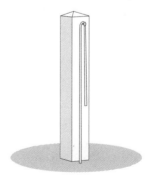

6. A book with 200 pages (100 sheets of paper) has a total thickness of 9.6 mm, including
the covers which are each 1.8 mm thick. Find the thickness of a single sheet of the paper
used for the book.

7. 300 ball-bearings weigh 1875 grams. What is the weight of 1 ball-bearing ? What is the
weight of 20 ball-bearings ?

8.   This is the fares table on the local bus. (Fares for Adults)

Town centre	**Fares in pence**			
25	Pollard Street			
35	30	Victoria Road		
40	37	25	Addison Road	
55	50	40	35	Long Lane

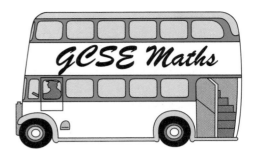

1   What is the total cost for Mr and Mrs Gray to travel from Addison Road to Pollard Street ?

2   Make a similar table for the children's fares. Children pay half-price (with $\frac{1}{2}$ penny counted as 1 penny, e.g. half-price for a 25p fare is 13p).

3   What is the total cost for 3 children to travel from the Town centre to Long Lane ?

4   What is the total cost for Mrs Gray and her 2 children to travel from Addison Road to Victoria Road ?

9.   Tomatoes at the market last week cost 56p per lb and lettuces were 30p each. The prices of both these items had risen by 5p when I went to buy them this week. But cucumbers had remained at 70p and cabbages had fallen in price by 2p to 28p.

1   Find the cost of last week's shopping when I bought 2 lb of tomatoes, 2 lettuces, 1 cucumber and 1 cabbage.

2   Find the cost of this week's shopping when I bought 1 lb of tomatoes, 1 lettuce, 1 cucumber and 2 cabbages.

Practice test 5

You should do these questions without using a calculator.

1. Find the values of

   1 $1.5 + 3.9 + 8.4$ **6** 0.91×1000
   2 $30.4 - 16.8$ **7** $3.1 \div 10$
   3 52.7×6 **8** $870 \div 100$
   4 $163.5 \div 5$ **9** 1.5×20
   5 20.3×100 **10** $36 \div 40$

2. Write these numbers in order of size, smallest first.

   1 0.6, 0.66, 0.06, 0.59, 0.059.

   2 25.19, 25.0, 25.9, 24.95, 24.59.

3. Write these numbers as stated:

   1 379.4 to the nearest whole number,
   2 19.85 to the nearest whole number,
   3 27.37 to 1 decimal place,
   4 105.926 to 2 decimal places,
   5 18.604 to 2 decimal places.

4. Find the value of $19.59 \div 7$, correct to 1 decimal place.

5. **1** How many 5p coins are worth £5 ?

   2 What is the change from £1 after buying 3 small loaves at 28p each ?

   3 If 4 apples cost as much as 5 pears and a pear costs 8p, how much does an apple cost ?

   4 Find the cost of 200 articles at 15p each ?

   5 What is the cost of 4 articles at 99p each ?

6. Find the missing item in this bill.   £11.29
                                                £ 6.09
                                                · · · ·
                                                £20.72

7. What is the price of a bar of chocolate if 9 of them cost £2.16 ?

PUZZLES

5. Mrs Richards left her umbrella on the bus so she went into the local gift shop to buy a new one at £6.75. She paid with a £20 note, but since it was early in the morning, Mr Jenkins who owned the gift shop had no change so he took the £20 note next door to Mrs Evans at the confectioner's, and got £20 in change. Then he gave Mrs Richards her £13.25 change and she went on her way.

    Later on, Mrs Evans came in, very worried, because she had just discovered that the £20 note was a forgery. Mr Jenkins had to give her a cheque for £20, and give the forged note to the police. Later on he told his wife the sad tale—that he had lost a good umbrella, £13.25 in change and a cheque for £20, total value £40.
    Was he correct ?

6. A group of six children have to send a team of four of them to take part in a quiz. But they all have their own views on whether they will take part or not.

    Laura won't be in the team unless Michelle is also in it.
    Michelle won't be in the team if Oliver is.
    Naomi won't be in the team if both Laura and Michelle are in it.
    Oliver won't be in the team if Patrick is.
    Patrick will be in the team with any of the others.
    Robert won't be in the team if Laura is, unless Oliver is in it too.

    Which 4 took part in the quiz ?

7. In the 'Tower of Hanoi' puzzle, there are 8 discs of different sizes on 1 peg, with two empty pegs.

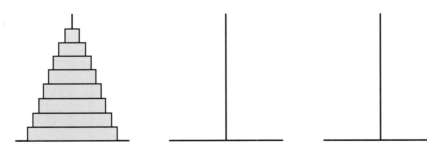

    The game is to transfer all the discs to one of the empty pegs.
    Only one disc can be moved at a time. A disc can only be placed on an empty peg or onto a larger disc, never onto a smaller one.
    Make your own version of this game using circles of cardboard, and see how many moves are needed. You may prefer to discover the pattern of moves by starting with less than 8 discs. Notice the moves of the smallest disc.
    The legend has it that there is such a peg with 64 discs on it. At the rate of 1 move per second, how long will it take to move all 64 discs ?

6 Using a calculator

The topics in this chapter include:

- using a calculator efficiently to plan a calculation and to evaluate expressions,

- reading a calculator display correct to a specified number of decimal places,

- applying appropriate checks of accuracy using inverse operations and estimates using approximations,

- calculating with money,

- selecting suitable sequences of operations and methods of computation including trial and improvement methods to solve problems,

- giving solutions in the context of the problem, interpreting the display on a calculator,

- understanding the meaning of $a \times 10^n$ (positive n) in the context of a calculator display.

Use of a calculator

A calculator will save you time in doing routine calculations but do not use it for simple arithmetic which you can do more quickly in your head. You can use it for addition, subtraction, multiplication and division, and there may be other function keys.

Practise using the **memory** keys. It is useful to know how to store a number in the memory, to add numbers to it or to take numbers from it, and then to recall the contents of the memory for further use.

It is advisable to start every new calculation by pressing the $\boxed{\text{C}}$ key (for CLEAR), but you may find that on your calculator this is unnecessary if you have just pressed the $\boxed{=}$ key. This also works after pressing some of the other keys.

Different makes of calculators work in slightly different ways. Read the instruction booklet of your own calculator and try the examples shown there. You may find there are quicker ways than you normally use to do some calculations. But you will not be allowed to use the instruction booklet in an examination so you must be really sure that any method you use is correct.

Further instructions

1. When doing multiplication and division, it is better to multiply first and divide last if the division is not exact.
    e.g. For $\frac{2}{3}$ of 20, find $2 \times 20 \div 3$ instead of $2 \div 3 \times 20$.
    The answer is 13.333 ...

2. If the answer is not exact, or has several figures, then round it up to a sensible degree of accuracy.

3. ### Checking calculator answers

    It is easy to get a wrong answer from a calculator by pressing the wrong keys, so look at the answer and see if it seems to be about right.
    You could also do the calculation twice, possibly entering the numbers in reverse order, to see if you get the same result.

    Check the size of the answer

    $5813 + 1967$
    The numbers are approximately 6000 and 2000.
    The answer should be approximately $6000 + 2000 = 8000$.
    (The exact answer is 7780.)

    5813×2
    The answer should be approximately $6000 \times 2 = 12\,000$.
    (The exact answer is 11 626.)

    $5813 - 1967$
    The answer should be approximately $6000 - 2000 = 4000$.
    (The exact answer is 3846.)

    $5813 \div 2$
    The answer should be approximately $6000 \div 2 = 3000$.
    (The exact answer is 2906.5.)

    Check by doing the inverse operation

    To check $5813 - 1967 = 3846$, do the calculation $3846 + 1967$ and you will get 5813.

    To check $5813 \div 2 = 2906.5$, do the calculation 2906.5×2 and you will get 5813.

    To check $\sqrt{121} = 11$, do the calculation 11×11 and you will get 121.

4.   **To find the remainder in a division sum**

Find the remainder when 79 is divided by 19.

Press 79 $\boxed{\div}$ 19 $\boxed{=}$ getting 4.157 ...
So 19 divided into 79 goes 4 times.
Now find out what 4×19 equals.
$4 \times 19 = 76$ and $79 - 76 = 3$, so the remainder is 3.

A simpler way to do this is:
79 $\boxed{\div}$ 19 $\boxed{=}$ 4.157...
Keeping this number on the calculator, subtract 4 to leave the decimals, then multiply by 19.
This should give the remainder, 3, but due to rounding errors it may not give 3 exactly.
So count a number such as 2.999 ... or 3.000 ... as 3.

5. $\boxed{\sqrt{}}$ is the square root key. It must be pressed after the number.

To find the square root of 169 press 169 $\boxed{\sqrt{}}$ and the answer is 13.
If you find the square root of a number on your calculator and the result is not an exact whole number then the original number is not a square number.

Exercise 6.1

1.   These numbers are approximations of the numbers used in question 2. Find the answers, if possible without using your calculator. Keep the answers to use in question 2.

1	$3 + 2 + 8$		**6**	4×300
2	0.1×2		**7**	$1 \div 2$
3	$7 \div 0.2$		**8**	$400 + 800 - 600$
4	$13 - 3$		**9**	$2 + 2 + 2$
5	$20 \times 20 + 10$		**10**	$1000 \div 5$

2.   Work out the following, using your calculator. Compare each answer with the corresponding answer from question 1. If they are very different, check your work again.

1	$3.17 + 2.4 + 7.73$		**6**	3.63×280
2	0.09×2.1		**7**	$1.32 \div 2.4$
3	$6.8 \div 0.17$		**8**	$379 + 821 - 560$
4	$13.3 - 2.84$		**9**	$2.35 + 2.4 + 1.85$
5	$22.1 \times 18.6 + 9.3$		**10**	$1008 \div 4.8$

3. Find approximate answers to the following, then use your calculator to work out the exact answers.

    1 1.4×2.32 **4** 5.8×6.1
    2 $203.7 - 114.9$ **5** $319.2 + 97.5$
    3 $8.74 \div 3.8$

4. Check the answers to question 3 by using the inverse operations.
    e.g. For part **1**, use your answer divided by 2.32 and you should get 1.4.

5. Work out the following using your calculator, and give the answers correct to 1 decimal place.

    1 $29.7 \times 18.6 \div 50.1$

    2 $\frac{4}{7} \times 29.3$

    3 $\dfrac{12 \times 1.03}{17.5}$

6. Find the whole number answers and the remainders when

    1 371 is divided by 12,   **4** 7 is divided into 2000,
    2 827 is divided by 23,   **5** 60 is divided into 400.
    3 1024 is divided by 13,

7. Use your calculator to find the square roots of these numbers.

    1 225   **5** 5625   **8** 1936
    2 1764   **6** 196   **9** 4225
    3 1089   **7** 441   **10** 10 201
    4 256

8. 329 marbles are shared equally among 32 children. How many did they each get, and how many were left over ?

9. When a certain number is divided by 28, the answer is 13 and the remainder is 19. What is the number ?

10. A box holds 50 oranges, which on average weigh 0.075 kg each. The box weighs 1.2 kg. What is the total weight of the oranges and the box ?

11. A model statue made of metal has to weigh 500 grams. If $1 \, cm^3$ of the metal weighs 7.7 grams, how many cm^3 of metal, to the nearest cm^3, will be used ?

Using a simple calculator

Instead of using the rule that multiplication or division should be carried out before addition and subtraction, a **simple calculator** will do all the operations in the order in which they are entered.

You must be careful if a question has an instruction $+$ or $-$ followed by an instruction $\times$ or $\div$.
e.g. $18 - 3 \times 5$
This means $18 - (3 \times 5) = 18 - 15$ and the correct answer is 3.
But the simple calculator will do $18 - 3 = 15$ and $15 \times 5 = 75$, and give the wrong answer 75.
Try this question on your calculator, and if you get the answer 75 then to do such questions you will have to use the memory.

Before you begin, make sure the memory is clear by pressing $\boxed{C}$, then when you press $\boxed{RM}$, 0 should be shown. $\boxed{RM}$ stands for 'recall memory'.

For $18 - (3 \times 5)$ press $3 \boxed{\times} 5 \boxed{M+} 18 \boxed{-} \boxed{RM} \boxed{=}$ and you will get the correct answer 3.

(You have worked out 3×5 first and put the answer in the memory, and then subtracted the memory contents from 18.)
Clear the memory again as soon as you have written down the answer.

If you are using a simple calculator, do these questions using the memory.

1. $29.2 - (3.5 \times 7.1)$

2. $100 - (225 \div 4)$

3. $(2 \times 11.3) + (27.3 \div 7)$

4. $(12 \times 36) - (15 \times 14)$

5. $(3 \times 15.9) + (0.3 \times 27.8)$

To find the square of a number if you do not have a key $\boxed{x^2}$, press number $\boxed{\times} \boxed{=}$.
e.g. For 52^2 press $52 \boxed{\times} \boxed{=}$ and you will get the answer 2704.

For a calculation such as $4000 - 52^2$, you will have to work out 52^2 first and store it in the memory, i.e. press $52 \boxed{\times} \boxed{M+} 4000 \boxed{-} \boxed{RM} \boxed{=}$ and you will get the answer 1296.

To find the cube of a number, press number $\boxed{\times} \boxed{=} \boxed{=}$.
e.g. For 7^3 press $7 \boxed{\times} \boxed{=} \boxed{=}$ and you will get the answer 343.

Using a scientific calculator

These instructions are for a scientific calculator.
With some calculators you may have to do some operations in a
different way.

Scientific calculator

1. If you have a question involving addition or subtraction together
    with multiplication, the calculator will read it as if there were
    brackets round the multiplication part, and do that part first.
    e.g. $25.1 + 76.2 \times 0.3$ is read as $25.1 + (76.2 \times 0.3)$ and the
    answer is 47.96.

    Similar rules work with addition or subtraction together with division.
    The calculator will do the division first.
    e.g. $5.93 - 0.86 \div 0.4$ is read as $5.93 - (0.86 \div 0.4)$ and the answer is 3.78.

2. If there are brackets then the part in brackets is worked out first.

    e.g. $(25.1 + 76.2) \times 0.3$
    Use the bracket keys on your calculator, or instead, you can press
    25.1 $\boxed{+}$ 76.2 $\boxed{=}$ $\boxed{\times}$ 0.3 $\boxed{=}$ so that the calculator works out the addition before
    multiplying by 0.3.
    The answer is 30.39.

    For $(5.93 - 0.86) \div 0.4$, use the bracket keys or press 5.93 $\boxed{-}$ 0.86 $\boxed{=}$ $\boxed{\div}$ 0.4 $\boxed{=}$.
    The answer is 12.675.

    $\dfrac{5.93 - 0.86}{0.4}$ is the same question, written in a different way.

3. ## Using the memory

    e.g. $\dfrac{23.5 + 12.9}{18.1 - 6.9}$

    First find $18.1 - 6.9$ and put the answer (11.2) in the memory.
    Then press 23.5 $\boxed{+}$ 12.9 $\boxed{=}$ $\boxed{\div}$ $\boxed{RM}$ $\boxed{=}$.
    The answer is 3.25.
    RM stands for 'recall memory'.

    Alternatively, you could find $(23.5 + 12.9) \div (18.1 - 6.9)$, using brackets.

4. $\boxed{x^2}$ is the squaring key.

    For 3.2^2 press 3.2 $\boxed{x^2}$ and you will get 10.24.

    To find the cube of a number press number $\boxed{\times}$ $\boxed{x^2}$ $\boxed{=}$.
    e.g. For 7^3 press 7 $\boxed{\times}$ $\boxed{x^2}$ $\boxed{=}$ and you will get 343.

Large numbers

An answer may be too big for the calculator to display it normally.

e.g. $50\,000^2 = 2\,500\,000\,000$

A **scientific calculator** will display this in the form

2.5 09, which means $2.5 \times 10^9 = 2.5 \times 1\,000\,000\,000$
$$= 2\,500\,000\,000$$

A **simple calculator** may display the result as 25.000000 E.
On this calculator E means that the number should be multiplied by 10^8.

So 25.000000 E $= 25.000000 \times 10^8 = 25 \times 100\,000\,000$
$$= 2\,500\,000\,000$$

You will have to clear E by pressing $\boxed{C}$ before you continue with further calculations.

Exercise 6.2

1. Write down the keys that you would use to do these questions using your calculator, and
    give the answers.
    Say whether you are using a simple calculator or a scientific calculator.

    e.g. $33 - (4 \times 5)$
    With a simple calculator, press 4 $\boxed{\times}$ 5 $\boxed{M+}$ 33 $\boxed{-}$ $\boxed{RM}$ $\boxed{=}$.
    With a scientific calculator, press 33 $\boxed{-}$ 4 $\boxed{\times}$ 5 $\boxed{=}$.
    Answer 13.

    1 $(3 + 4) \times 5$
    2 $6 \times (9 - 2)$
    3 $7^2 + (3 \times 8)$

2. Find the results of these calculations without using your calculator. Then repeat the
    questions using your calculator, making sure that you get the same results.

    1 $\dfrac{5 \times 3}{2}$ **6** $10^2 - 7^2$

    2 $(6 - 2) \times 3$ **7** $\dfrac{15 + 13}{4}$

    3 $7 + (5 \times 4)$ **8** $\dfrac{12}{4} + \dfrac{15}{3}$

    4 $60 - (4 + 2)$ **9** $(12 \times 4) - (10 \times 3)$

    5 $(5 \times 7) - 29$ **10** $\sqrt{64} - \sqrt{36}$

3. The numbers in these questions are approximations of the numbers used in question 4. Find the answers, if possible without using your calculator. Keep the answers to use in question 4.

    1 $\dfrac{200 \times 0.1}{10}$ **4** $20 \div (3 + 2)$

    2 $(35 - 30) \times 60$ **5** $(5 \times 3) - 5$

    3 $2 + \left(\frac{1}{4} \times 8\right)$

4. Work out the following, using your calculator. Compare each answer with the corresponding answer from question 3. If they are very different, check your work again.

    1 $\dfrac{216 \times 0.084}{9.6}$ **4** $23.75 \div (2.8 + 2.2)$

    2 $(35 - 29.7) \times 61.3$ **5** $(4.7 \times 3.1) - 5.07$

    3 $1.93 + (0.25 \times 7.64)$

5. Find
    1 the squares of 13, 29, 31.2,
    2 the cubes of 8, 21, 99.

6. Work out these questions on your calculator and write down the answers as 'ordinary' numbers.
    1 $110\,000 \times 1300$
    2 $51\,000^2$
    3 $251\,000 \times 51\,000$

Money

Our money calculations use the decimal system.
£2 and 48 pence is £2.48.
£3 and 5 pence is £3.05.
£3 and 50 pence is £3.50. On a calculator this may be displayed as 3.5. Remember that this means £3.50, not £3.05.

Examples

1 £1.32 + £5.28 = £6.60
On a calculator £6.60 will be shown as 6.6.

2 £10.00 − £7.56 = £2.44
On a calculator there is no need to enter 10.00 for £10.00.   10 will do.

3 £6.25 × 8 = £50 or £50.00, whichever is more appropriate.
A calculator will just show 50.

4   How many books at £5.60 can be bought for £50 ?

This is £50 ÷ £5.60.
On your calculator do 50 ÷ 5.6.
The answer is 8.92 . . . showing that 8 books can be bought and there is some money left over.
To find how much is left, multiply £5.60 by 8 and subtract the total from £50.
$50 - (8 \times 5.6) = 5.2$, so there is £5.20 left.

Exercise 6.3

1.   A shop was advertising some special offers. Mrs Parsons bought some dog food reduced from £9.99 to £7.49, 12 tins of cat food reduced from a total price of £4.69 to £3.50, and 3 packets of soap powder, each reduced from £5.45 to £4.09. How much did she save altogether ?

2.   What is the total cost of 24 notebooks at 28p each and 24 pens at 22p each ?

3.   Petrol costs 59.3p per litre. What is the cost of 30 litres ?

4.   Tessa works in a local shop from 1.30 pm to 5 pm on four afternoons each week. She is paid £3.70 per hour.
How much is her weekly wage ?

5.   Mrs Davies makes 200 soft toys. The material for each toy costs 48p. Other expenses amount to £50. She sells the toys for £1.95 each. What profit does she make ?

6.   Mr Rigby has a £20 voucher to spend at the garden centre. He decides to buy 4 bushes for £1.85 each and spend the rest on bulbs at 21p each. How many bulbs can he buy ?

7.   How many articles costing 75p each can be bought for £30 ?

8.   If £9.10 is made up of equal numbers of 5p, 10p and 20p coins, how many coins are there ?

9.   How many 26p stamps can be bought for £10, and how much change is there ?

10.   The first prize of £180 in a competition was shared equally among 32 winners.
      How much did they each get, in £'s and pence, and how much was left over ?

11.   A gas fire costs £479.99. Alternatively, the fire can be bought for a deposit of £24 and
      24 monthly payments of £24.59.
      How much extra does the fire cost if paid for monthly ?

Trial and improvement methods

Example

1   Two girls each write down a whole number. When they add the numbers together the
     sum is 80, and when they multiply the numbers the product is 1564. Find the numbers.

     First, think of pairs of numbers which add up to 80 and investigate their products.
     Begin with multiples of 10.

Smaller number	Larger number	Product
10	70	700
20	60	1200
30	50	1500
40	40	1600

This table of results suggests that the product grows larger as the numbers get nearer to
each other. We could test this if we were not sure by adding multiples of 5 to the table.

Smaller number	Larger number	Product
5	75	375
10	70	700
15	65	975
20	60	1200
25	55	1375
30	50	1500
35	45	1575
40	40	1600

This theory seems to work.

Since the product we want is 1564, it comes from somewhere between the pair 30 and 50
with product 1500, and the pair 35 and 45 with product 1575.

We can make a new table for these pairs of numbers and their products.

Smaller number	Larger number	Product
30	50	1500
31	49	1519
32	48	1536
33	47	1551
34	46	1564
35	45	1575

This table shows the solution.
The numbers were 34 and 46.

This is not the only way to do this question.
You may have decided to consider the unit figures of the two numbers.
Suppose you begin by investigating unit figures whose sum ends in 0, because 80 ends in 0.
They could be 0 and 0, 1 and 9, 2 and 8, 3 and 7, 4 and 6 or 5 and 5.
Their product has to end in 4, from 1564, so the only pair involved is 4 and 6.

So you might try

Smaller number	Larger number	Product
4	76	304
6	74	444
14	66	924
16	64	1024
24	56	1344
26	54	1404
34	46	1564
36	44	1584

and you have found the solution.

Square roots

Example

2   Find the square root of 784.

If your calculator is a simple one without a square root key, then you can find $\sqrt{784}$ using trial and improvement methods.
We know that $20^2 = 400$ and $30^2 = 900$, so $\sqrt{784}$ is a number between 20 and 30, and probably nearer to 30 than to 20.
The unit figure is 4 so it must come from 22^2 ($2 \times 2 = 4$) or 28^2 ($8 \times 8 = 64$).
So find 28^2.
$28^2 = 784$ so $\sqrt{784} = 28$.

Exercise 6.4

Use trial and improvement methods to solve these problems.
You may begin by copying and continuing the tables given, or you may prefer different ways.

1. Two positive whole numbers have a product of 918. One number is 7 larger than the other one. Find the numbers.

Smaller number	Larger number	Product
10	17	170
20	27	540
30	37	. . .
25	. . .	. . .
. . .		

2. Two positive whole numbers have a sum of 70 and a product of 1216. Find the numbers.

Smaller number	Larger number	Product
10	60	600
20	50	1000
. . .	. . .	

3. Kevin thinks of a number. He finds that the square of the number added to 8 times the original number is 468. What is the original number ?

Number	Square	8 × number	Sum
10	100	80	180
20	400	160	560
15	. . .	. . .	. . .
. . .			

4. The sum of the squares of 3 consecutive odd numbers is 1883. Find the numbers.

3 consecutive odd numbers	Squares	Sum of squares
11, 13, 15	121, 169, 225	515
21, 23, 25	441, 529, 625	1595
. . .	. . .	. . .

5. Ann is 4 years older than Bobby. The sum of the squares of their ages is 400. Find their ages.

Bobby	Ann	Squares	Sum
10	14	100, 196	296
. . .	. . .	. . .	. . .

6. Find the square root of 676 without using the square root key on your calculator.

Number	Square
10	100
20	400
30	. . .
. . .	

Exercise 6.5   Applications

1. Use your calculator to find the numbers represented by □ in these statements.

1   $\square + 22.5 = 103.1$

2   $\square \times 13 = 22.1$

3   $\square - 5.3 = 12.7$

4   $\square \div 2.4 = 1.5$

5   $1967 + \square = 1988$

6   $1760 - \square = 990$

7   $12.6 \times \square = 10.08$

8   $136.8 \div \square = 15.2$

9   $2 \times (\square + 5.3) = 17.8$

10   $(5.1 \times 7.3) - \square = 27.23$

2. In each of these calculations a mistake has been made. Find the correct answers. Can you also discover what mistake was made in each case ?

1   $1.32 + 2.5 + 3.79 = 7.09$

2   $10 - 0.918 = 0.82$

3   $(13.1 + 17.9) \times 1.2 = 34.58$

4   $5.32 \times 6.15 = 34.6332$

5   $1234 \div 0.032 = 3856.25$

3. 1   The Amazon river discharges 2×10^5 tonnes of water per second into the Atlantic Ocean, when it is in flood.
Write this number as an 'ordinary' number.

2   Write the calculator display 1.5   08   (or 1.5 E) as an ordinary number. This is the approximate distance, in km, of the Earth from the Sun.

4.   An insurance company quotes these rates for travel insurance. (Prices per person.)

	United Kingdom only	Europe	Worldwide
up to 8 days	£5.65	£13.10	£30.60
up to 12 days	£6.00	£13.90	£31.95
up to 17 days	£6.95	£15.25	£33.55
up to 24 days	£7.75	£16.40	£39.10

Winter sports in Europe insured at $1\frac{1}{2}$ times the Europe premium.
Double premium for persons aged over 65, Worldwide.

Find the cost of insurance for these people.

1   Next week Mr Stewart is going on a business trip to Scotland for 5 days.

2   For their honeymoon next January Alan and Jayne are going skiing in Switzerland, for 10 days.

3   Mrs Charnley is going to stay with her married daughter in America for 3 weeks. She is looking forward to the trip although at age 70 it will be the first time she has travelled by air.

5.   Mrs Sharples wants to buy 2 curtains size 108 by 66, and 4 curtains size 54 by 46. (The measurements are in inches.)

1   Show how she can find a quick estimate of the cost, and give the estimated total.

2   Use your calculator, or another method, to find the exact cost.

Very good value ! Price per pair			
54 × 46	£29.99	54 × 66	£49.99
72 × 46	£42.99	72 × 66	£59.99
90 × 46	£49.99	90 × 66	£74.99
108 × 46	£59.99	108 × 66	£89.99
54 × 90	£68.99	90 × 90	£99.99
72 × 90	£86.99	108 × 90	£124.99

Curtains *Special Offer*

6. This table gives the repayments due when goods are bought from a certain firm by a credit agreement. (Amounts are in £'s.)

Cash price	Credit agreement price		
	Repay over 1 year 12 monthly instalments	Repay over 2 years 24 monthly instalments	Repay over $2\frac{1}{2}$ years 30 monthly instalments
10	0.94	0.53	0.44
20	1.88	1.06	0.88
30	2.82	1.59	1.32
40	3.76	2.12	1.76
50	4.70	2.65	2.20
60	5.64	3.18	2.64
70	6.58	3.71	3.08
80	7.52	4.24	3.52
90	8.46	4.77	3.96
100	9.40	5.30	4.40
200	18.80	10.60	8.80

1   Mr Jones wants to buy a lawn mower with cash price £60, and decides to pay over 1 year. What is the monthly instalment ?

2   How much will the mower cost him altogether ?

3   Instead of this he then decides to take longer to repay so that he will be able to get a better mower. He finally settles for repayments of £3.96 per month for 30 months. What is the cash price of the mower he chooses ?

4   What will it cost him altogether ?

SALE

£3.96
per month
for
30 months

7. Copy and complete this electricity bill.

Meter reading		Units used	Pence per unit	Amount
Present	Previous			
41527	40342	—	6.6	—
			Quarterly charge	£9.50
			VAT	£7.01
			Total now due	‾‾‾‾

Practice test 6

1.   By using approximate values, estimate answers for these questions. Then find the correct answers, using your calculator.

     1 8.96×4.1 **2** $18.081 \div 2.87$

     2 $26.68 \div 9.2$ **5** 512×0.98

     3 6.3^2

2.   Use your calculator to work out the following.

     1 $\dfrac{98.4 + 103.2}{25.2}$ **4** $\sqrt{1521}$

     2 $24.48 \div (82.6 - 41.8)$ **5** $\sqrt{(1369 - 144)}$

     3 $11.6 - (1.4 \times 1.8)$

3.   A roll of ribbon is 90 m long. How many complete strips of length 2.7 m can be cut from it ?

4.   Mrs Rija buys 12 metres of dress material at £4.65 per metre. What is the total cost ?

5.   Mr Clark spends £10 on petrol for his car and this takes him 125 miles. What is the cost per mile ?

6.   How many pens at 35p each can be bought for £15, and how much change is there ?

7.   **1**   The speed of light is 1.86×10^5 miles per second.
        Write this number as an 'ordinary' number.

     2   Write the calculator display 5.1 08   (or 5.1 E) as an 'ordinary' number. This is the approximate area, in km^2, of the Earth's surface.

8.   Two numbers differ by 5 and their product is 1326.
    Copy and continue this table to find the numbers by trial.

Smaller number	Larger number	Product
10	15	150
20	25	500
30	. . .	. . .
. . .		

Miscellaneous Section A

Exercise A1   Aural Practice

If possible find someone to read these questions to you.
You should do the questions within 20 minutes.
Do not use your calculator.
Write down the answers only.

1.   Write in figures the number four million, fifty-three thousand.

2.   The numbers 14, 21, 28, 35, form a pattern. What are the next two numbers in the sequence ?

3.   Write down an expression for the change in pence if an article costing x pence is paid for with a £1 coin.

4.   What is the smallest number into which both 6 and 10 divide exactly ?

5.   There were 7524 spectators at a football match. What is this number to the nearest 100 ?

6.   If £15 was equally divided among 6 children, how much would they each receive ?

7.   Denise thought of two numbers. When she added the numbers together she got 14, and when she multiplied the numbers together she got 24. What were the two numbers she thought of ?

8.   What is the total cost of 5 articles at 99 pence each ?

9.   There are two adjacent angles on a straight line. If one of them is 70°, how big is the other ?

10.   Simplify the expression $3x \times 4x$.

11.   What is the next prime number after 23 ?

12.   Give an approximate answer to 29×41.

13.   What is left when 0.8 is subtracted from 1 ?

14.   How many packets of sweets costing 8 pence each can be bought for £1, and how much change is there ?

15.   A formula for area is $A = lb$. What is the value of A when $l = 11$ and $b = 7$?

Additional aural questions using data from pages 444 to 447.

16. Use table **1**.
     In the distance chart, which of the places listed is furthest away from London, and how many kilometres away is it ?

17. Use diagram **2**.
     Estimate the size of the acute angle between *AB* and *CD*.

18. Use table **3**.
     What is the cost of insurance for a 14-day summer holiday in France ?

19. Use table **5**.
     Jayne has £200 invested in Savings Certificates. What will they be worth at the end of 4 years ?

20. Use table **17**.
     What are the weekly payments on a loan of £5500 taken out for 10 years ?

Exercise A2   Revision

1. **1** The distance by sea from Marseilles to Port Said is one thousand, five hundred and six miles. Write this distance in figures.

    2 The distance by sea from Southampton to New York is 3091 miles. Write this distance in words.

2. 702,   800,   891,   900,   1161.

    1 Which of these numbers are odd numbers ?
    2 Which of these numbers divide exactly by 5 ?
    3 Which of these numbers does not divide exactly by 9 ?

3. **1** Through how many degrees do you turn when facing North and turning clockwise to face South-East ?

    2 In which direction are you facing if you start facing North-West and turn through 45° anticlockwise ?

    3 If you are facing South-West after having turned through 90° clockwise, in which direction were you facing originally ?

4. Write these numbers correct to the nearest whole number.

    1 562.8   **2** 322.96   **3** 3728.3   **4** 9.76   **5** 6.512

5. **1** Write down the square roots of
        25, 64, 81, 100, 4.

    2 Write down the cube roots of
        64, 27, 1, 125, 8.

6. If $a = 3$, $b = 4$ and $c = 0$, find the values of these expressions.

    1 $ab + 2bc$ **4** $\dfrac{2a + 3b + 4c}{2a - b}$

    2 $2b^2 + a^3$ **5** $\sqrt{a^2 + b^2}$

    3 $3c(a + b)$

7. The table shows the dinners ordered for the year 7 forms at a school, for a week in September.

	7P	7Q	7R	7S	Total
Mon	35	28	22	25	110
Tues	34	28	18	26	
Wed	33		21	26	104
Thur	33	21			
Fri		26	22		106
Total for week	166		105	131	

    Copy the table and fill in the missing figures, including the total number of dinners ordered for the week by all the year 7 forms.

    1 On which day were the fewest dinners ordered ?
    2 If the dinners cost 90p each, what was the total cost of the dinners ordered for the week by form 7Q ?

8. Write these numbers in order of size, smallest first.

    10.91   11.19   10.99   10.09   10.9

9. A man worked 48 hours in a week. For the first 40 hours he was paid £3.60 an hour. For the rest he was paid at the overtime rate of £5.40 an hour.

    1 What were the man's wages that week ?
    2 How many hours altogether had he worked in a week when he earned £198 ?

10.   Draw an angle ABC of 127°.
        Through a point A draw a line AD,
        parallel to BC.
        Measure $\angle DAB$.

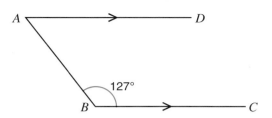

Exercise A3   Revision

1.   Write these numbers correct to the nearest ten.
        1   687   **2**   528   **3**   274.9

        Write these numbers correct to the nearest thousand.
        4   63 912   **5**   26 357   **6**   9501

2.   Find the values of the following.

        1 $2^2 \times 7$ **4** $2 \times 5 \times 7$
        2 3^3 **5** $2^3 \times 3$
        3 2×5^2

3.   Simplify the following.

        1 $4a + 7a$ **4** $8d \div 2$
        2 $2b - b$ **5** $5e \div e$
        3 $4c \times 3c$

4.   In the diagram, AC and BD are straight lines.

        1   If $a = 35°$ and $b = 51°$, find the sizes
                of c, d, e.

        2   If $a = b$ and c is a right angle, find the sizes
                of a, d, e.

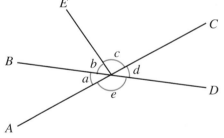

5.   A National Savings Certificate bought in March 1996 for £100 gains in value according
        to this table.

Years after purchase	Value at end of year
1	£103.75
2	£108.06
3	£113.46
4	£120.44
5	£129.77

(The rates are for the 43rd issue.
The rates will vary for other issues.)

        Margaret invested £500 in these savings certificates.
        She planned to keep the certificates for 5 years. How much would they be worth then
        altogether ?

6. **1** If 1 franc is worth p pence, how many pence will f francs be worth ?

   2 If x kg of potatoes are bought for y pence, what is the price per kg ?

   3 The sum of two numbers is 12. One of them is x. What is the other ?

   4 Elaine is 3 years younger than Eric. If Eric is x years old, how old will Elaine be next year ?

   5 A man earned £x per month and his wife earned £y per week. What were their total earnings in a year ?

7. Find the values of

   1 $8 \times 7 - 4 \times 6$ **4** $12 + 8 \div 4$
   2 $(8 + 7) \times (4 + 6)$ **5** $(12 + 8) \div 4$
   3 $(8 - 7) \times (6 - 4)$

8. Equal numbers of 20p and 26p stamps were bought for £19.78. How many of each kind were there ?

9. This prism is standing on a horizontal table.

   1 Which lines are horizontal ?
   2 Which lines are vertical ?

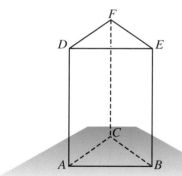

10. Use your calculator to find the numbers represented by □ in these statements.

   1 $122 + \square = 975$

   2 $\square \times 17 = 442$

   3 $\square - 169 = 2978$

   4 $\square \div 36 = 1944$

   5 $893 - \square = 578$

   6 $125 \times (\square + 89) = 52\,875$

   7 $\dfrac{187 + 99}{\square} = 13$

   8 $(47 \times 63) + \square = 3852$

   9 $\dfrac{127 + \square}{3} = 49$

   10 $(80 \times \square) - 1939 = 2221$

To the student : 2

Activities

As part of your Mathematics course, you should choose and make use of knowledge, skills and understanding of Mathematics in practical tasks, in real-life problems and to investigate within Mathematics itself.

You may be tested on this section by doing practical work during your course, or you may be tested by taking an extra examination paper which includes suitable practical tasks.

Some suggestions are given here for activities. If you are being tested by coursework, you should discuss with your teacher the sort of activities which will be acceptable. As well as the activities suggested here, you may gain ideas from other sources. There may be cross-curricular activities, school or locally-based projects, national or international current affairs which may suggest suitable investigations. You can also get ideas from other textbooks, library books, worksheets, etc.

If you are being tested in an extra examination paper you should use some of the activities here for practice in doing the investigational type of questions.

The organisation of an activity

First of all, decide what is to be the **aim** of the activity or investigation, and write this down. Decide how much time you have available for it, and then make a detailed plan of what you are actually going to do.
Decide where you are going to find any further information you need. Sources can include library books, newspapers, magazines, or asking other people.
Carry out the activity. Work methodically and check information and results. Write a logical account of your work. Give reasons for any choices made. Examine and comment on any results and justify any solutions.

You may choose to present your work in a booklet, on a poster or by another form of display, including drawings or photographs.

After doing an activity you may be able to extend your investigations and make further discoveries.

Exercise A4   Activities

1.   ### The Sieve of Eratosthenes and prime numbers

Write down the numbers from 1 to 200 in 6 columns.

```
 1    2    3    4    5    6
 7    8    9   10   11   12
13   14    .    .    .
```

Draw a circle round 2 and then cross out all other numbers
which divide by 2. The next number not circled or crossed out
is 3. Draw a circle round 3 and then cross out all other numbers
which divide by 3. The next number not crossed out or circled is
5. Draw a circle round 5 and then cross out all other numbers
which divide by 5. The next number not crossed out is 7.
Draw a circle round 7 and then cross out all other numbers
which divide by 7.
Continue similarly with the numbers 11 and 13.
Now draw a circle round all the remaining numbers which are
not crossed out, except 1.
The circled numbers are the prime numbers.
Why was it sufficient to stop at 13 ? If we had made a list up to 300 what other number
would need to be crossed out ?

This method can be used to find the prime numbers up to any large number.

1 is a special number, so mark it in a different way. It is not counted as a prime number
although it has no factors other than itself.

This method is known as 'The Sieve of Eratosthenes'. See if you can find out anything
about Eratosthenes who lived a long time ago.

Carry out further investigations with prime numbers.
First, get a list of more prime numbers, up to 500 or 1000.
Does the number of prime numbers in a range of 100 numbers decrease as the numbers
get larger ? E.g. Are there fewer prime numbers between 400 and 500 than between 300
and 400 ?
Prime numbers with a difference of 2 are called **prime pairs**. Examples are 29, 31; 41, 43.
Make a list of these for numbers less than 200. It is thought that the number of prime
pairs is infinite.
However, there is sometimes a sequence of consecutive numbers which are not prime, for
example, between the prime numbers 113 and 127 there are 13 numbers which are not
prime. Can you find a longer run of numbers which are not prime ?

With modern computers, searches can be made for larger prime numbers. The largest one
found (in 1994) was $2^{859433} - 1$. By now, a larger one may have been discovered. But it
can be proved that the number of prime numbers is infinite, so there is no such thing as
the largest prime number, only the largest one **known**.

2. Coins

1 Make a table showing the coins needed to pay amounts from 1p to 19p using the least number of coins.

		Coin				Total
		10p	5p	2p	1p	
Amount	1				1	1
(p)	2			1		1
	3			1	1	2
	4			2		2
	.					
	.					

Look for patterns in the table and comment about them.
What would happen for amounts 20p and above, up to £1 ?

2 Make a table showing the different number of ways you can pay an amount from 1p to 10p.

e.g. $6p = 5p + 1p$
$= 2p + 2p + 2p$
$= 2p + 2p + 1p + 1p$
$= 2p + 1p + 1p + 1p + 1p$
$= 1p + 1p + 1p + 1p + 1p + 1p$ (5 ways)

Comment about any patterns that you notice.

What would happen for amounts from 11p to 19p ?

3. Sevenths

Work out the recurring sequences of decimals for $\frac{1}{7}, \frac{2}{7}, \frac{3}{7}, \frac{4}{7}, \frac{5}{7}, \frac{6}{7}$.
Investigate the patterns formed.
Also try adding the 1st and 4th figures, the 2nd and 5th, the 3rd and 6th.
Add the 1st 2 figures as a 2-figure number, with the 3rd and 4th, and 5th and 6th.
Add the 1st 3 figures as a 3-figure number with the last 3 figures as a 3-figure number.

Investigate the decimals for the thirteenths, $\frac{1}{13}, \frac{2}{13}$, etc.

4. History of numbers and calculation

Counting can be traced back to very ancient times, and yet it is only a few years ago that modern calculators and computers were invented. You could make a topic booklet about this, including early methods of writing numbers in different parts of the world, and methods of calculation such as the abacus, Napier's bones and logarithms, and ending with a section on the development of the computer.

5. **A holiday abroad**

Plan a holiday abroad for your family. (It is an imaginary holiday so you can decide for yourself the type of holiday you want and how much you want to spend on it.)

Get details of costs from travel agents' brochures. (The old ones for last year that they no longer need will do.) Do not forget costs of things such as passports, travel to the airport, excursions, extras like postcards and presents, money for snacks and drinks. Make a list of all the costs.

Plan a timetable for the holiday, starting from the time you must leave home.

Find your destination in an atlas. How far from home is it, and in roughly what direction ? What sort of weather do you expect ? What is the usual temperature at the time of year when you will going ?

Plan the list of things to take. Find out the weight of luggage you are allowed, and whether you are limited to 1 suitcase. Give some idea of things you plan to do while on holiday. Is it to be a lazy fortnight on the beach or a more energetic holiday ? Are you going sightseeing, and if so, where ?

Find out the rate of exchange and make a conversion table for use while you are away, e.g. 10 pesetas = 5p, 20 pesetas = 10p, and so on.

There are other details you can add to make your booklet more interesting.
Illustrate it with pictures and a map.

6. ## Banking

Many people have a bank account nowadays. Many firms pay wages directly into the employees' bank accounts as this is safer and quicker than paying by cash.

Find out:

1   the names of the biggest banks in the country, and which of them have branches in your district.

2   the types of bank account they offer, and the advantages and disadvantages of each, e.g. which accounts include a cheque book, and which pay interest. Do the banks charge you for having an account?

3   how to write a cheque, and what a cheque stub is.

4   the procedure for paying money into your account.

5   what a bank statement is.

6   what a cheque card is, and how it is used. What should you do if you lose it?

7   what a credit card is, and how it is used.

8   how to use a cashpoint machine.

9   the usual banking hours in your district.

10 what other services the banks offer.

11 whether there are any special terms for students and what they are.

12 the procedure for opening an account.

7. **NIM**

This is a very old mathematical game for 2 players.
It is played with a number of counters (or match sticks) which are placed in 3 groups.

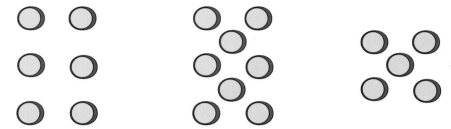

When it is your turn you can remove one or more counters, but they must all be taken from one group only.
You win the game if your opponent takes the last counter.

Play several games, beginning with a number of counters between 12 and 30. It need not be the same number in each game, and the 3 groups can contain unequal numbers of counters at the start of a game.

After playing several games, you may have noticed that if you leave one counter in each of 3 piles then you are bound to win.

You can also win if one pile is empty and there are 2 counters in each of the other two piles.

If you leave 3 counters in one pile, 2 in another and 1 in the third pile, show that whatever your opponent takes away, you can win.

In some cases, this is because you can reduce the position to 1, 1, 1 or 2, 2, 0 and then win, as above.

Find other positions which are such that whatever your opponent moves, you can reduce the counters to 3, 2, 1; 1, 1, 1; 2, 2, 0 or another winning position already discovered.

Make a list of all positions which guarantee you a win if you play carefully.

When you have worked out a winning strategy you can challenge all your friends to try to beat you. You can only lose when it is your first turn and the groups already form a winning combination.

8. ## A mystic rose pattern

Use a sharp pencil.
Draw a circle and divide the circumference into 24 equal parts. (If you choose a radius just larger than that of your protractor you can mark off points every 15° along the protractor edge.)
Join every point to every other one.

A mystic rose extended pattern

Draw another circle with the same centre and a radius 2 cm or 3 cm larger than the main circle. When you join two points extend the line in both directions until it meets the outer circle.

A coloured mystic rose pattern

Number the points from 1 to 24.
Draw the diameters first, i.e. 1 to 13, 2 to 14, etc. all in the same colour.
Then in another colour draw the lines 1 to 12, 12 to 23, 23 to 10, etc. counting on 11 points each time.
Use another colour for the lines 1 to 11, 11 to 21, etc. counting on 10 points each time.
Repeat similarly until you finish by joining 1 to 2, 2 to 3, etc.

You can also make the mystic rose using curve stitching (cardboard and embroidery thread). Start the stitching with the diameters.

The mystic rose also makes a good pattern for string art, using nails on a board and coloured thread, but it would be better to use a number of points which is a prime number, such as 23.

PUZZLES

8. What is the next letter in this sequence ?

N N N E N E E N E E E — — —

9. Using the figures 1 to 7 and the multiplication sign, as in these examples, 6 × 325 714, 341 × 5276, 21 × 56 × 473, which arrangement gives the largest product ?

10. The rail journey from Ashfield to Beechgrove takes exactly 4 hours and trains leave each way on the hour and on the half-hour. If you were on a train going from Ashfield to Beechgrove, how many trains going from Beechgrove to Ashfield would you pass during the journey ?

7 Sequences and patterns

The topics in this chapter include:

- recognising, describing, continuing and explaining patterns in number,

- interpreting, generalising and using simple relationships,

- describing rules for generating number patterns and sequences,

- describing a rule for the next term in a sequence,

- finding the nth term of a sequence where the rule is linear.

Sequences of numbers

Whole numbers   1, 2, 3, 4, ...

Odd numbers   1, 3, 5, 7, ...

Even numbers   2, 4, 6, 8, ...

Multiples of 5   5, 10, 15, 20, ...

Prime numbers   2, 3, 5, 7, 11, ... (These do not follow a regular pattern, but apart from 2 and 5 they all have unit figures of 1, 3, 7 or 9.)

Square numbers   1, 4, 9, 16, ... from 1^2, 2^2, 3^2, 4^2, ...

Cube numbers   1, 8, 27, 64, ... from 1^3, 2^3, 3^3, 4^3, ...

Triangular numbers   1, 3, 6, 10, 15, ... from 1, $1 + 2$, $1 + 2 + 3$, ...

Fibonacci sequence   1, 1, 2, 3, 5, 8, 13, ... (Each number after the first two is found by adding the two preceding numbers.)

There are many other sequences of numbers.
If you have to identify a sequence and continue it, see if you can recognise anything special about it. Also look at the differences between successive terms.

e.g. 8, 17, 26, 35, ...
You might notice that the difference between successive numbers is always 9. You get the next term by adding on 9.
You might notice that the unit's figures go down in 1's and the ten's figures go up in 1's, so the next term is 44. This will give you terms up to 80, although the sequence continues beyond that. You might notice that the digits add up to 8 each time.

e.g. 6, 12, 24, 48, 96, ...
The differences between successive terms are 6, 12, 24, 48. These are the same numbers as in the sequence, so the sequence is a doubling one. The next term is $96 \times 2 = 192$.

e.g. $\frac{1}{2}, \frac{1}{4}, \frac{1}{6}, \frac{1}{8}, \dots$
These are fractions which are getting smaller. The numerators are all 1. The denominators in turn go 2, 4, 6, 8 so they increase by 2 each time and the next one is 10. So the next number in the sequence is $\frac{1}{10}$.

e.g. 2, 3, 5, 9, 17, 33, ...
The sequence is growing more and more rapidly and after 2 the numbers are all odd. Investigate the differences between successive terms. They are 1, 2, 4, 8, 16. These are always doubled, the next difference is 32 and the next number in the sequence is $33 + 32 = 65$.

The sequence beginning 1, 2, 4, ...

These three terms are not enough to give us sufficient information to identify which sequence it is.
It could be 1, 2, 4, 8, 16 ... or 1, 2, 4, 7, 11.
What are the rules for these sequences ?

Unless you know the rule, you need enough terms to identify the sequence.
Sometimes there is more than one possible sequence, but if one sequence is obvious, do not try to find a more unlikely one.

Exercise 7.1

1. Copy and continue these sequences for 3 more terms. Describe the rule for continuing the sequence in each case.

   1   4, 10, 16, 22, 28, ...   6   3, 4, 6, 9, 13, ...

   2   3, 6, 9, 12, 15, ...   7 $3, 1, \frac{1}{3}, \frac{1}{9}, \frac{1}{27}, \dots$

   3   5, 10, 20, 40, 80, ...   8   3, 7, 15, 31, 63, ...

   4   3, 9, 27, 81, 243, ...   9   3, 8, 18, 38, 78, ...

   5   32, 29, 26, 23, 20, ...   10   1, 2, 6, 24, 120, ...

2. Write down the first 5 terms of these sequences. In each one, the first term is 12.

   1   Add 4 each time.
   2   Subtract 2 each time.
   3   Multiply by 5 each time.
   4   Divide by 2 each time.
   5   Add 1, then add 2, 3, 4, ...

3. Every term of these sequences is obtained from the sum of the previous two terms. Write down the next 3 terms of each one.

    1 1, 4, 5, . . .   **4** 3, 1, 4, . . .
    2 2, 8, 10, . . .   **5** 3, 4, 7, . . .
    3 0, 1, 1, . . .

4. Copy and complete the table, of the number of lines needed to join 2, 3, 4, . . . points. (The diagrams may help you to discover the pattern.)

Number of points	2	3	4	5	6	7	8	9	10
Number of lines needed	1	3	6						

2 points
1 line

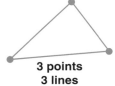

3 points
3 lines

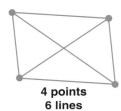

4 points
6 lines

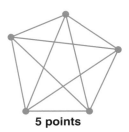

5 points

5. ## Geometrical representation of sequences

    Draw the next picture in each of these sequences.

    1 Square numbers

    1   4   9   16

    2 Triangular numbers

    1   3   6   10   15

3   Rectangular numbers

Here the rectangle is 2 units longer than wide.

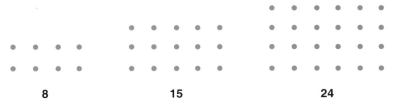

8   15   24

4   Trapezium numbers

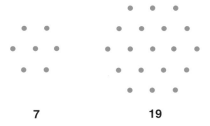

9   12   15

5   Hexagonal numbers

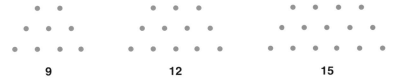

7   19

6.   What do you notice about the sum of any two consecutive triangular numbers ?
Can you show why this is so, using a dots pattern ?

Number patterns

Exercise 7.2

1.   Copy and continue this pattern to 9×999.

$$1 \times 999 =\ \ 999$$
$$2 \times 999 = 1998$$
$$3 \times 999 = 2997$$
$$\ldots$$

2.   Copy and continue this number pattern to 65^2.

   $5^2 = 0 \times 10 + 25 = 25$
   $15^2 = 10 \times 20 + 25 = 225$
   $25^2 = 20 \times 30 + 25 = 625$

   Use the pattern to find the value of 85^2.

3.   Copy and complete this number pattern.

   $142857 \times 1 = 142857$
   $142857 \times 5 =$
   $142857 \times 4 =$
   $142857 \times 6 =$
   $142857 \times 2 =$
   $142857 \times 3 =$

   What do you notice about the answers ?

4.   Copy and complete this number pattern to the eighth line.

   $8 \times 9 = 72$
   $88 \times 99 = 8712$
   $888 \times 999 = 887112$
   $\ldots$

5.   There is one mistake in this pattern. Copy the pattern, replacing the wrong number by the correct one.

   $1 = 1$
   $1 + 3 = 4$
   $1 + 3 + 5 = 8$
   $1 + 3 + 5 + 7 = 16$

   Fill in the next 3 rows of the pattern.
   What do you notice about the totals ?
   If this pattern was continued, what would be the total of numbers in the 20th row ?

Finding other terms of a sequence

We can find other terms of a sequence if the terms increase or decrease by a constant number.

In the sequence 4, 7, 10, 13, ... the rule is 'add 3'.
To get the 10th term you must add 3, 9 times.
The 10th term is $4 + 3 \times 9 = 31$.

In the sequence 87, 83, 79, 75, ... the rule is 'subtract 4'.
To get the 10th term you must subtract 4, 9 times.
The 10th term is $87 - 4 \times 9 = 51$.

By looking at the pattern of the numbers in a sequence we can find an expression for the nth term.

e.g. 3, 8, 13, 18, ... goes up by 5 each time.
The nth term will include a term $5n$.
In fact, it is $5n - 2$.

If the sequence decreases by a constant number:

e.g. 28, 25, 22, 19, ... goes down by 3 each time.
The nth term will include a term $-3n$.
In fact, it is $31 - 3n$.

You can use the expression for the nth term to find any term of the sequence.

Example

The nth term of a sequence is $70 - 5n$.

The 1st term is $70 - 5 \times 1 = 65$,
the 2nd term is $70 - 5 \times 2 = 60$,
the 3rd term is $70 - 5 \times 3 = 55$,
the 9th term is $70 - 5 \times 9 = 25$,
and so on, for any term.

Exercise 7.3

1.   Find the 10th terms in these sequences.

    1   1, 3, 5, 7, ...
    2   2, 8, 14, 20, ...
    3   100, 95, 90, 85, ...
    4   1, $1\frac{1}{2}$, 2, $2\frac{1}{2}$, ...
    5   69, 66, 63, 60, ...

2.   Find the terms stated, in these sequences.

   1   14, 17, 20, 23, ...   (11th term)
   2   25, 21, 17, 13, ...   (7th term)
   3   12, 18, 24, 30, ...   (16th term)
   4   3, 8, 13, 18, ...   (12th term)
   5   49, 46, 43, 40, ...   (15th term)

3.   Write down the next 2 terms in these sequences, and find an expression for the nth term.

   1   3, 7, 11, 15, ...   **4**   86, 81, 76, 71, ...
   2   16, 15, 14, 13, ...   **5**   14, 20, 26, 32, ...
   3   10, 13, 16, 19, ...

4.   These expressions are the nth terms of sequences. By putting $n = 1, 2, 3$ and 4 in turn, write down the 1st 4 terms of each sequence.

   1 $3n - 1$ **4** $15 - n$
   2 $100 - 10n$ **5** $\frac{1}{2}n + 3$
   3 $8n + 5$

Exercise 7.4   Applications

1.   These matchstick patterns form sequences. For each one, draw the next pattern, write down the next 3 terms of the sequence, and find an expression for the nth term.

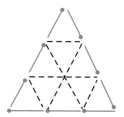

   1   Number of small triangles, 1, 4, 9, ...
   2   Number of matches used on the perimeters, 3, 6, 9, ...

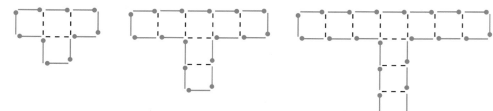

   3   Squares enclosed, 4, 7, 10, ...
   4   Number of matches used on the perimeters, 10, 16, 22, ...

2.   **Making number patterns with your calculator**

Press 2 $\boxed{\times}$ $\boxed{=}$ $\boxed{=}$ $\boxed{=}$ ... and see what you get.
(On some calculators you may have to press 2 $\boxed{\times}$ $\boxed{\times}$ $\boxed{=}$ $\boxed{=}$ $\boxed{=}$ ...)

Try 7 $\boxed{+}$ $\boxed{=}$ $\boxed{=}$ $\boxed{=}$ ... (or 7 $\boxed{+}$ $\boxed{+}$ $\boxed{=}$ $\boxed{=}$ $\boxed{=}$ ...)

Try 1 $\boxed{+}$ 7 $\boxed{=}$ $\boxed{=}$ $\boxed{=}$ ... (or 7 $\boxed{+}$ $\boxed{+}$ 1 $\boxed{=}$ $\boxed{=}$ $\boxed{=}$ ...)

Try 100 $\boxed{-}$ 6 $\boxed{=}$ $\boxed{=}$ $\boxed{=}$ ... (or 6 $\boxed{-}$ $\boxed{-}$ 100 $\boxed{=}$ $\boxed{=}$ $\boxed{=}$ ...)

Use your calculator to invent or discover other number patterns.
You can also explore number patterns using a computer.

3.   The numbers in this sequence go in pairs:

14, 10, 20, 16, 32, 28, 56, ...

The rule is: First time subtract 4, next time multiply by 2, and repeat these two
operations in order.

1   Find the 1st 8 terms of a sequence using this rule and beginning with 10.

2   What is the rule for this sequence ?

3, 9, 4, 12, 7, 21, 16, 48, ...

3   What are the next 2 terms of the sequence in part **2** ?

4   Find the 20th term of the sequence beginning with 1 and using the rule: First time
multiply by 2, next time subtract 1, and repeat the two operations in order.

4.   **Number chains**

These change a number into another number by a certain rule.
Then the new number is changed and the process is repeated.

Example
Rule:
For 2-figure numbers, multiply the 10's digit by 4 and add to the units digit.
Stop the chain when you get a single figure.

e.g. $29 \rightarrow (2 \times 4) + 9 = 17 \rightarrow (1 \times 4) + 7 = 11 \rightarrow (1 \times 4) + 1 = 5.$
$94 \rightarrow (9 \times 4) + 4 = 40 \rightarrow (4 \times 4) + 0 = 16 \rightarrow (1 \times 4) + 6 = 10 \rightarrow (1 \times 4) + 0 = 4.$

Carry out this rule for some 2-figure multiples of 6. What do you notice ?
Try it out for other 2-figure numbers.
Make other number chains using different rules.

5. This is a multiplication table pattern using the numbers 1, 3, 5, 7 only.
Make a similar table but instead of writing the answer down, for numbers greater than 7, divide them by 8 and just write the remainder down.
e.g. $5 \times 7 = 35$ and $35 \div 8 = 4$ remainder 3, so write down 3.
Do you notice any patterns ?

×	1	3	5	7
1	1	3	5	7
3	3	9	15	21
5	5	15	25	35
7	7	21	35	49

Make a similar table for the numbers 1, 3, 7, 9 just writing the units figures down, and another one for the numbers 2, 4, 6, 8 just writing the units figures down.

Make a similar table for the numbers 1, 2, 3, 4, dividing the answers by 5 and just writing the remainders down.

Do you notice any similarities ?

6. **Difference methods**

Look at the sequence on the right.
Find the differences between consecutive terms.
Find the differences between those numbers.

$$2 \quad 5 \quad 10 \quad 17 \quad 26$$
$$3 \quad 5 \quad 7 \quad 9$$
$$2 \quad 2 \quad 2$$

Assuming that the 3rd row is a row of 2's, you can continue the middle row and use it to write more terms in the sequence on the top row.

$$2 \quad 5 \quad 10 \quad 17 \quad 26 \longrightarrow 37 \longrightarrow 50 \longrightarrow 65 \longrightarrow 82$$
$$3 \quad 5 \quad 7 \quad 9 \longrightarrow 11 \longrightarrow 13 \longrightarrow 15 \longrightarrow 17$$
$$2 \quad 2 \quad 2 \quad 2 \quad 2 \quad 2 \quad 2$$

Here is another example.

$$2 \quad 3 \quad 7 \quad 14 \longrightarrow 24 \longrightarrow 37 \longrightarrow 53$$
$$1 \quad 4 \quad 7 \longrightarrow 10 \longrightarrow 13 \longrightarrow 16$$
$$3 \quad 3 \quad 3 \quad 3 \quad 3$$

Continue these sequences for the next 3 terms, using the difference method.

1 1, 5, 11, 19, 29, ...
2 2, 7, 13, 20, 28, ...
3 3, 5, 10, 18, 29, ...
4 4, 8, 14, 22, 32, ...
5 5, 10, 20, 35, 55, ...

Practice test 7

1.   Find the next 2 numbers in these sequences.

   1 1, 2, 5, 10, 17, ...
   2 288, 144, 72, 36, ...
   3 0, 4, 8, 12, ...
   4 81, 27, 9, 3, ...
   5 3, 7, 11, 15, ...

   6 $\frac{1}{3}, \frac{1}{6}, \frac{1}{9}, \frac{1}{12}, \ldots$
   7 45, 36, 27, 18, ...
   8 2, 5, 8, 11, ...
   9 1, 10, 100, 1000, ...
   10 100, 91, 82, 73, ...

2.   Copy and complete this number pattern to the row which begins 123456789.

   $$1 \times 8 + 1 \quad = \quad 9$$
   $$12 \times 8 + 2 \quad = \quad 98$$
   $$123 \times 8 + 3 \quad =$$
   $$1234 \times 8 + 4 \quad =$$

   ...

3.   Write down the next 5 terms of the Fibonacci sequence 1, 1, 2, 3, 5, 8, 13, ...
   Copy and complete this number pattern to the line beginning '10th term'.

   1st term $\times$ 3rd term $- 1 = 1 \times 2 - 1 = 1 = 1^2$
   2nd term $\times$ 4th term $+ 1 = 1 \times 3 + 1 = 4 = 2^2$
   3rd term $\times$ 5th term $- 1 = \ldots$
   4th term $\times$ 6th term $+ 1 = \ldots$

   ...

   Comment on the pattern.

4.   Write down the next 3 terms in these sequences, and find an expression for the
   nth term.

   1 11, 19, 27, 35, ...
   2 4, 8, 12, 16, ...
   3 25, 21, 17, 13, ...

   4 0, 6, 12, 18, ...
   5 46, 41, 36, 31, ...

PUZZLE

11.   A man has a wad of £5 notes numbered consecutively from 232426 to 232440.
   What is their total value ?

8 *Measures*

The topics in this chapter include:

- using standard units of length, mass, capacity and time,

- interpreting numbers on a range of measuring instruments,

- developing an understanding of the relationship between units, converting one metric unit to another,

- making sensible estimates in everyday situations,

- knowing British units in daily use and their approximate metric equivalents.

The metric system

Length

The main unit of length is called the **metre** (m).
One-thousandth part of a metre is a millimetre (mm).
One-hundredth part of a metre is a centimetre (cm).
One thousand metres is a kilometre (km).

$$1000\,mm = 1\,m$$
$$100\,cm = 1\,m \qquad (so\ 10\,mm = 1\,cm)$$
$$1000\,m = 1\,km$$

Weight

The main unit of weight is the **gram** (g).
One-thousandth part of a gram is a milligram (mg).
One-hundredth part of a gram is a centigram (cg).
One thousand grams is a kilogram (kg).
Since a kilogram is rather a small weight, a larger unit is often needed.
One thousand kilograms is a tonne, sometimes called a metric ton.

$$1000\,\text{mg} = 1\,\text{g}$$
$$100\,\text{cg} = 1\,\text{g}$$
$$1000\,\text{g} = 1\,\text{kg}$$
$$1000\,\text{kg} = 1\,\text{tonne}$$

Capacity

The main unit of capacity is the **litre** (ℓ).
One-thousandth part of a litre is called a millilitre (ml).
One-hundredth part of a litre is called a centilitre (cl).
One thousand litres is a kilolitre (kl).

$$1000\,\text{ml} = 1\,\ell$$
$$100\,\text{cl} = 1\,\ell$$
$$1000\,\ell = 1\,\text{kl}$$

$$1\,\text{litre} = 1000\,\text{cm}^3$$

It is useful to know that:

1 millilitre of water weighs 1 gram.

1 litre of water weighs 1 kilogram.

To change from one unit to another

centimetres into millimetres

To change centimetres into millimetres multiply by 10, because $1\,\text{cm} = 10\,\text{mm}$.
$5\,\text{cm} = 50\,\text{mm}$
$6.2\,\text{cm} = 62\,\text{mm}$

millimetres into centimetres

To change millimetres into centimetres divide by 10, because 10 mm = 1 cm.
30 mm = 3 cm
24 mm = 2.4 cm

metres into centimetres

1 m = 100 cm, so to change metres into centimetres multiply by 100.
3.2 m = 320 cm
5.61 m = 561 cm

centimetres into metres

100 cm = 1 m, so to change centimetres into metres divide by 100.
62 cm = 0.62 m
560 cm = 5.6 m

metres into millimetres

1 m = 1000 mm, so to change metres into millimetres multiply by 1000.
2 m = 2000 mm
1.5 m = 1500 mm
0.07 m = 70 mm

millimetres into metres

1000 mm = 1 m, so to change millimetres into metres divide by 1000.
2500 mm = 2.5 m
6 mm = 0.006 m

The methods are similar for changing units of weight and capacity.

e.g.   To change grams into kilograms, divide by 1000.
       To change litres into millilitres, multiply by 1000.

Exercise 8.1

1.   **1**   Write 2380 g in kg.
     2   Write 20 cm in m.
     3   Write 5 litres in ml.
     4   Write 12 cm in mm.
     5   Write 2.6 m in cm.
     6   Write 3.1 kg in g.
     7   Write 28 mm in cm.
     8   Write 512 cm in m.
     9   Write 3200 cl in litres.
     10 Write 0.25 kg in g.

2. Equal pieces of ribbon 28 cm long are cut from a strip 5 m long.
   1 How many pieces are there ?
   2 How many centimetres are left over ?

3. If 40 equal packets weigh 100 kg, what does one weigh ?

4. How many lengths of wood 0.4 m long can be cut from a piece 2.8 m long ?

5. 1 500 sheets of paper weigh 3 kg. What is the weight, in g, of 1 sheet ?
   2 The pile of sheets is 7 cm thick. What is the thickness, in mm, of 1 sheet ?

6. How many mm is 80 mm short of 1 metre ?

7. A caterer uses 300 g of potatoes per day for each person. Find the cost of providing potatoes for 40 people for 5 days at 25p per kg.

8. Which size of packet of this tea is the better value for money ?

9. How many packets of sweets, each containing 110 g, can be made up from $5\frac{1}{2}$ kg of sweets ?

10. If a car travels 12 km on a litre of petrol, how much will petrol cost for a journey of 270 km, if the price is 60p per litre ?

Accuracy of measurements

There is a difference between counting, which is usually in whole numbers, but in any case goes up in jumps, and measurement, which goes up continuously.

We can never measure **exactly**, but by using appropriate instruments we can get measurements as accurately as they are needed for a particular purpose.

When measuring a line in Geometry, it is usual to give the length to the nearest mm.
In measuring the width of a desk, it is probably sufficient to measure to the nearest cm. In measuring larger distances the measurement would be taken to the nearest 10 cm, the nearest metre, the nearest 10 m or 100 m, or the nearest km.

With weighing, 1 gram is such a small weight that it would only be used for scientific or medical purposes or when an expensive substance was being bought. In cookery it is sufficient to weigh to the nearest 25 g. Heavier items can be weighed to the nearest kg, and very heavy objects are weighed in tonnes.

For capacity, medicines are often given using a 5 ml spoonful, and in the kitchen liquids are measured in a litre jug, with markings for every 50 ml. Larger quantities can be measured to the nearest 10 ℓ, 100 ℓ, etc.

Time can be measured to the nearest hour, to the nearest minute or to the nearest second. Athletes will want to measure their times to tenths or hundredths of a second.

Reading numbers on scales

Example

What reading is shown by the arrow on this scale ?

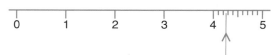

Decide between which two whole numbers the reading lies. This one lies between 4 and 5, so starts 4.

Here is an enlargement of the part of the scale between 4 and 5.
Decide between which two tenths the reading lies. This one lies between 2 and 3 so it is 4.2.
If you have to answer correct to 1 decimal place decide whether it is nearer to 2 or to 3. This one is nearer to 3 so give the answer as 4.3.

If you have to estimate the answer to 2 decimal places, imagine an enlargement of the part of the scale between 4.2 and 4.3. The reading is nearer to 4.3 than to 4.2, so it is bigger than 4.25. It is approximately 4.27.

Drawing and measuring lines

This is line *AB*.

A and *B* are the points at the ends of the line.

If a line *AB* has to be **drawn to an accurate length** it is useful to draw the line slightly longer than needed and then mark points *A* and *B* by small marks crossing the line.

e.g. Draw a line *AB*, 7 cm long.

The part of the line between the cross-marks for *A* and *B* should be 7 cm long.

Lines are usually **measured** in centimetres and millimetres, to the nearest millimetre.

e.g.

CD is 6 cm 4 mm, which is written as 6.4 cm. It could also be written as 64 mm.

Exercise 8.2

1.   Name a sensible metric unit for measuring or weighing

    1   the height of a tall tree,

    2   the amount of sugar in a bowl,

    3   the amount of water in a pond,

    4   the perimeter of a field,

    5   the height of a child,

    6   the weight of a loaded lorry,

    7   the capacity of a car's fuel tank,

    8   the weight of a letter, to be sent by air-mail,

    9   the distance between two towns,

    10   the width of a piece of paper.

2. **1** Rob says that he is 1.62 m tall.
         How accurately do you think he has measured his height ?

    2 Rob says that his weight is 38 kg.
         To what accuracy do you think he has weighed himself ?

3. Write these measurements as stated.

    1   8.732 m, to the nearest 0.1 m,
    2   279.3 g, to the nearest 10 g,
    3   4160 ℓ, to the nearest 100 ℓ,
    4   5.51 m, to the nearest metre,
    5   156.92 cm, to the nearest mm,
    6   4.087 ℓ, to the nearest 0.1 ℓ,
    7   4.96 m, to the nearest 0.1 m,
    8   5.438 kg, to the nearest 10 g,
    9   2504 ℓ, to the nearest 10 ℓ,
    10 47.03 s, to the nearest 0.1 s.

4. Give the readings shown on these instruments.

    1 Weight in kg.

    2 Weighing scale in kg and g.   **3** Measuring glass.

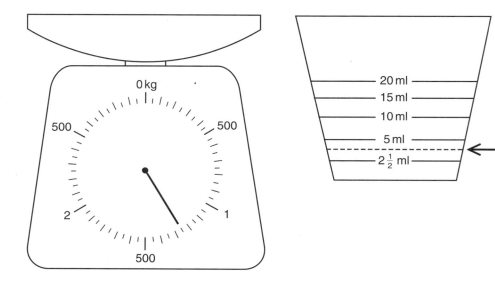

5. **1** Draw a line of length 1 cm, a line of 5 cm and a line of 10 cm. Estimate the lengths of other lines by comparing them with these lengths.

   2 Estimate the lengths of the lines AB, CD, EF, GH and check your estimates by measuring them to the nearest mm.

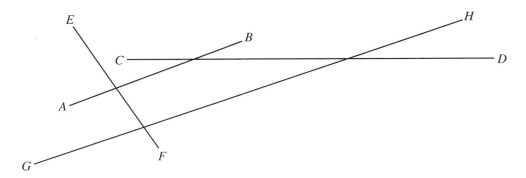

6. Draw accurately a line JK of length 11.4 cm.
   By measurement, find points M and N which divide the line into three equal parts JM, MN and NK.

Time

The units for time are unlikely to be changed in the near future although since they are not based on ten they are not easy to use on a calculator. Perhaps, eventually, things will be changed so that there could be 10 new hours in a day, 10 new minutes in an hour, and even 10 days in a new week. But we cannot change the length of a year because that is the length of time that the Earth takes to go round the Sun, and that is approximately $365\frac{1}{4}$ days.

Here is the present table for time:

60 seconds = 1 minute	52 weeks = 1 year
60 minutes = 1 hour	365 days = 1 year
24 hours = 1 day	366 days = 1 leap year
7 days = 1 week	12 months = 1 year

Recording the time of day can either be by the 12-hour clock, when morning times are denoted by a.m. and afternoon times by p.m., or by the 24-hour clock. To avoid confusion, timetables are often printed with times using the 24-hour clock.

Examples

	12-hour clock	*24-hour clock*
1 o'clock early morning	1.00 am	1.00 or 01.00
5 past 1 early morning	1.05 am	1.05 or 01.05
Noon	12.00 pm	12.00
Quarter-to-1 early afternoon	12.45 pm	12.45
1 o'clock early afternoon	1.00 pm	13.00
Half-past 8 in the evening	8.30 pm	20.30
One minute to midnight	11.59 pm	23.59
Midnight	12.00 am	0.00 or 00.00
One minute past midnight	12.01 am	0.01 or 00.01

(The day changes at the instant of midnight so when the time is shown as 12.00 am or 0.00 the date has changed.)

On a timetable the 24-hour times would be printed as 4-figure numbers. The full stop separating the hours and minutes could be left out.
e.g.   1.23 am would be printed as 0123,
1.23 pm would be printed as 1323.

1323 would be pronounced as thirteen twenty-three or thirteen twenty-three hours. But 1300 would be pronounced as thirteen hundred hours.

Use of a calculator

You cannot use your calculator directly for mixed calculations involving hours and minutes, minutes and seconds, days and weeks, etc. since these are not based on a scale of ten. You will have to do the calculations for the different units separately. Here are some examples:

1   A plumber does two jobs. The first one takes 1 hour 37 minutes and the second takes 2 hours 46 minutes. What is the total time taken ?

$$\begin{array}{r} 1\,\text{hr}\ 37\,\text{min} \\ \underline{2\,\text{hr}\ 46\,\text{min}} \\ \underline{4\,\text{hr}\ 23\,\text{min}} \end{array}$$

Use your calculator to add 37 and 46. This makes 83. 83 min = 1 hr 23 min so write down 23 min and carry 1 hour forward, making 4 hours altogether.

2   Of a school day of 5 hours, 2 hours 25 minutes was spent on rehearsals for a display. How much time was left for lessons ?

$$\begin{array}{r} 5\,\text{hr}\ \ 0\,\text{min} \\ 2\,\text{hr}\ 25\,\text{min} \\ \hline 2\,\text{hr}\ 35\,\text{min} \end{array}$$

Use your calculator to take 25 from 60, since you cannot take 25 from 0. This gives 35 min. Then adjust for the 1 hour you changed into 60 minutes, so, depending on the way you normally do subtraction, you will have either 5 hr − 3 hr or 4 hr − 2 hr. This gives 2 hours.

3   Work out 12 hr 22 min ÷ 7.

$$\begin{array}{r} 1\ \text{hr}\ 46\,\text{min} \\ 7\overline{)12\ \text{hr}\ 22\,\text{min}} \end{array}$$

Do the hours part first. 7 into 12 goes 1 remainder 5. Write down 1 hr.
Change the remainder, 5 hr, into 5 × 60 min = 300 min, so altogether there are 322 min.
322 ÷ 7 = 46,
so the answer is 1 hr 46 min.

4   A train left London at 12.25 pm and arrived in Penzance at 6.04 pm. How long did the journey take ?

One way to do this is by adding on.
From 12.25 pm to 1 pm is 35 minutes,
from 1 pm to 6 pm is 5 hours,
from 6 pm to 6.04 pm is 4 minutes,
Total time, 5 hours 39 minutes.

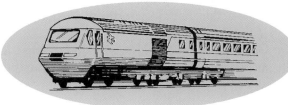

Exercise 8.3

1.   Change these times to the 24-hour clock.

     4.05 am   2.00 pm   3.15 pm   6.05 pm   11.55 pm

     Change these times to the 12-hour clock.

     01.10   5.18   10.30   17.05   21.50

2.   Work out the following. (If you use your calculator, take care with the mixed units.)

     1   2 hr 50 min + 1 hr 20 min
     2   12 hr 20 min − 5 hr 40 min
     3   7 hr 30 min ÷ 6

3.   Mike set off on a training ride at 11.50 am and cycled for $4\frac{1}{4}$ hours. At what time did he stop ?

4. Write down the time shown on this clock
    when it is in the afternoon,
    1 in the 12-hour system,
    2 in the 24-hour system.

5. A school's lessons begin at 9.20 am and end at 3.20 pm with an hour's break at lunchtime
    and 20 minutes break mid-morning. If there are 7 lessons of equal length, how long is a
    lesson ?

6. Tessa works in a local shop from 1.30 pm to 5 pm on four afternoons each week. She is
    paid £2.70 per hour. How much is her weekly wage ?

7. Tara says that it takes her 20 minutes to cycle to school.
    How accurately do you think she has stated this time ?

8. On a timetable, a plane was due to leave an
    airport at 20.55 and arrive at its destination
    at 02.05 the next day.

    1 How long should the journey take ?
    2 The plane actually arrived 45 minutes early. At what time did it arrive ?

British units

The metric system originated in France at the time of the French Revolution. Since it is based
on 10 and powers of 10 it is a very useful system for scientific work.
The British system of units for weights and measures is much older. It is still partly in use
although it is not so convenient for use with calculators, not being based on 10.

Length

We use inch, foot, yard, mile.

> 12 inches = 1 foot
>
> 3 feet = 1 yard
>
> 1760 yards = 1 mile

The **approximate comparisons** with the metric system which are useful are:

1 inch ... $2\frac{1}{2}$ cm	1 cm ... 0.4 inches
1 foot ... 30 cm	1 m ... 40 inches = 4 ins longer than 1 yard
1 yard ... 0.9 m	1 km ... $\frac{5}{8}$ mile
1 mile ... 1.6 km	8 km ... 5 miles
5 miles ... 8 km	

More accurate comparisons are:
  1 foot ... 30.5 cm   1 m ... 39.37 inches

Weight

We use ounces, pounds, stones, hundredweights and tons.

16 ounces	= 1 pound
14 pounds	= 1 stone
112 pounds	= 1 hundredweight
8 stones	= 1 hundredweight
2240 pounds	= 1 ton
20 hundredweights	= 1 ton

The symbol for ounces is oz, for pounds is lb (from Latin, libra for pound), for stones st, for hundredweight cwt (from the Roman C for a hundred).

The **approximate comparisons** with the metric system which are useful are:

1 lb ... 450 g (nearly $\frac{1}{2}$ kg)	1 kg ... 2.2 lb (just over 2 lb)
1 ton ... 1 tonne	1 tonne ... 1 ton

Capacity

We use pint, gallon.

8 pints = 1 gallon

The **approximate comparisons** with the metric system which are useful are:

1 pint ... just over $\frac{1}{2}$ litre   1 litre ... $1\frac{3}{4}$ pints
1 gallon ... $4\frac{1}{2}$ litres   1 litre ... 0.22 gallon

It is useful to know that:

1 pint of water weighs $1\frac{1}{4}$ lb.
1 gallon of water weighs 10 lb.

More exact comparisons with the metric system

You may need more accurate figures, and these are given at the front of the book on page xv. You can also find them in many diaries and reference books. There is no need to learn them.

Use of a calculator

As with calculations with time, be careful if using your calculator when dealing with mixed units not based on 10, such as lb and oz, gallons and pints, feet and inches. You will have to deal with the different units separately.

Example

One parcel weighs 14 lb 9 oz and another weighs 10 lb 12 oz. What is the total weight ?

14 lb 9 oz	First, do the ounces part. $9 + 12 = 21$.
10 lb 12 oz	Since 16 oz = 1 lb, this is 1 lb 5 oz.
25 lb 5 oz	Write down 5 oz and carry forward 1 lb, making 25 lb altogether.

(It is usual to have only 2 units in our measurements, which is why stones are not used in this question, where there are already lbs and oz.)

Exercise 8.4

1.   John is 6 feet 6 inches tall and his son Keith is 5 feet 8 inches tall. How many inches is John taller than Keith ?

2.   A farmer has 108 gallons of milk to sell. How many pint bottles can he fill with this milk ?

3.   Give approximate metric equivalents for these measures.

       1   6 inches   **4**   2 tons
       2   4 lb   **5**   10 miles
       3   10 gallons

4.   Give approximate British equivalents for these measures.

       1   3 m   **4**   12 km
       2   5 kg   **5**   6 tonnes
       3   4 litres

5.

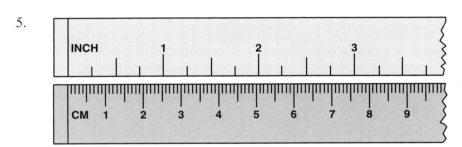

       The two rulers show measurements in inches and in centimetres. The top ruler is marked in inches and is divided into quarter inches. The other ruler is marked in centimetres and is divided into millimetres.

       1   What measurement in centimetres is equivalent to $2\frac{3}{4}$ inches ?

       2   What measurement in inches is equivalent to 3.8 cm ?

6.   The distance all round the equator is approximately 24 900 miles. Taking 1 mile as equivalent to 1.6 km, find this distance in kilometres, to the nearest 1000 km.

7.   An old knitting pattern for a child's jumper requires 8 oz of wool. How many 50 g balls of wool should Mrs Walsh buy to have enough to knit the jumper ?
       (16 oz = 1 lb, 1 lb = 450 g.)

Exercise 8.5   Applications

1.   How many

       1   mm in 5 cm   **6**   mm in 2 m
       2   g in 3 kg   **7**   minutes in $2\frac{1}{2}$ hours
       3   cm in $\frac{1}{2}$ m   **8**   weeks in a year
       4   days in a year   **9**   seconds in $\frac{1}{2}$ minute
       5   m in 4 km   **10** ml in 1 litre ?

2.   **1**   If 1 nail weighs 3 g, what do 1000 weigh ?

     2   If $1 \, cm^3$ of liquid weighs 1.1 g, what will $1000 \, cm^3$ of the liquid weigh ?

3.   Add together the number of grams in 3 kg, the number of seconds in 4 minutes and the number of mm in 8 cm, then divide the total by the number of pence in £8.30. What is the answer ?

4.   For these statements 4 alternatives are given in brackets. Which one makes the most sensible statement ?

     1   Jim's 20-year old brother is (1.2) (1.8) (2.4) (6) metres tall.

     2   Mary's baby sister weighs (35 g) ($3\frac{1}{2}$ kg) (35 kg) (350 lb). Her other young sister weighs (35 g) ($3\frac{1}{2}$ kg) (35 kg) (350 lb).

     3   Sam's car does 40 miles to the gallon. On his holiday he expects to drive about 500 miles, and he estimates that he will need about (£3) (£20) (£30) (£300) for petrol, which costs £2.50 per gallon.

5.   Here is a list of postage rates.

Weight not over	First Class	Second Class	Weight not over	First Class	Second Class
60 g	26p	20p	500 g	£1.30	£1.05
100 g	39p	31p	600 g	£1.60	£1.25
150 g	49p	38p	700 g	£2.00	£1.45
200 g	60p	45p	750 g	£2.15	£1.55
250 g	70p	55p	800 g	£2.30	Not
300 g	80p	64p	900 g	£2.55	admissible
350 g	92p	73p	1000 g	£2.75	over 750 g
400 g	£1.04	83p	Each extra 250 g		
450 g	£1.17	93p	or part thereof 70p		

     1   A letter weighs 180 g. How much does it cost to send it second class ?

     2   How much extra would it cost to send it first class ?

     3   Two packages each weighing 240 g are to be sent to the same address by 2nd class post. How much would be saved by tying them together to go as one package ?

     4   How much does it cost to send a package weighing just under 1.5 kg ?

  (Note that these rates may not be up-to-date.)

6.   The diagram shows a thermometer marked in degrees Celsius
     and degrees Fahrenheit.

     1   What temperature does the thermometer show
             in °F, and in °C ?

     2   What would be the temperature in °F if it was 35°C ?

     3   In cold weather, elderly people are advised to heat their
             living rooms to 68°F.
             What is this temperature in °C ?

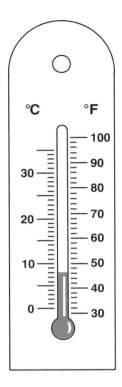

7.   If 4 pints of fuel are needed to keep a heater burning for 14 hours, how many gallons are
     needed to keep it burning continuously, day and night, for a week ?

8.   This distance chart gives distances in km.

Bristol	Dover	Exeter	LONDON	Oxford	Penzance	Southampton
299						
122	400					
185	114	277				
119	206	208	92			
298	568	179	452	402		
122	230	169	124	105	349	

     1   Which two places on the chart are 400 km apart ?

     2   How far is it from London to Southampton, in km ?

     3   How far is it in miles from London to Southampton ?
             (1 km = 0.62 miles. Give the answer to the nearest mile.)

9. This is an evening's programmes on a local TV station.

6.25	Weather
6.30	News
6.50	Entertainment 88
7.20	Sports Today
9.30	The Golden Age (play)
11.05	Local lives
11.45	Closedown

1 How long was the programme 'The Golden Age'?

2 If someone switched on at the end of the News and watched TV until closedown, for how long had they been viewing?

10.   Here is part of a bus timetable:

Ashmead School	1554	1602	1608	1616	1622	1629
Brook Lane	1604	1612	1618	1626	1632	1639
Carlton Village	1619	1627	—	1641	—	1654
Denham Station	—	—	1640	—	1654	—

1 Helen finishes school at 4.00 pm but it takes her 3 minutes to reach the bus stop. What is the time of the next bus she can catch to get to her home in Carlton Village? How long does the journey take?

2 Ismail usually catches a train from Denham station at 4.45 pm. On which bus must he travel from school? One day he stays late at school and catches the 1622 bus. The next train leaves at 5.30 pm. How long will Ismail have to wait at the station, for that train?

Practice test 8

1. 1 Write 0.75 kg in g.
    2 Write 126 mm in cm.
    3 Write 2.6 m in cm.
    4 Write 400 ml in ℓ.
    5 Write 160 cm in m.
    6 Write 1520 g in kg.
    7 Write 0.7 ℓ in cl.
    8 Write 7.8 cm in mm.
    9 Write 1.2 m in cm.
    10 Write 3040 kg in tonnes.

2. Write down the number and the unit which together make the most sensible statement.

    1 A packet of 4 video tapes will weigh about (1, 10, 100)   (g, kg).

    2 A good runner can run a mile in about (4, 20, 60)   (seconds, minutes, hours).

    3 If 200 new pencils were placed end-to-end to make a long straight line, the line would stretch for about (2, 10, 30)   (cm, m, km).

3. The line PQ is $4\frac{1}{2}$ inches long. Measure its length in cm, to the nearest mm.

4. Give the readings shown on these diagrams.

    1   2

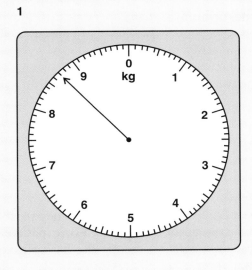

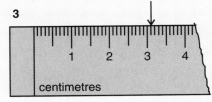

    3

5. 1 A joint of meat weighs 2.5 kg. What is this weight, approximately, in lbs ?

    2 A length of curtain material is 10 feet long. What is this length, approximately, in metres ?

    3 A bucket holds 2 gallons of water. What is this amount, approximately, in litres ?

    4 The distances between two villages is 24 km. What is this distance, approximately, in miles ?

6. A train left a station at 9.30 am and arrived at its destination at 2.13 pm. How long did the journey take ?

9 Collecting data

> **The topics in this chapter include:**
>
> - designing and using data collection sheets,
> - understanding and using tallying methods,
> - sorting, classifying and tabulating data,
> - extracting information from tables and lists,
> - designing and criticising questions for a questionnaire.

Statistics

Statistics involves numerical data.

Firstly, the data must be collected. Sometimes you carry out an investigation or experiment and collect data for yourself. Sometimes you can use data which someone else has collected. This includes data in government publications, newspapers, scientific textbooks, etc.

Secondly, the data is displayed in the form of a list, a table or a diagram.

Thirdly, it is studied, in order to make conclusions from it, often involving decisions for the future.

Data collection sheets

Example

1   The vehicles passing along a road were as follows:
    lorry, bus, car, lorry, lorry, lorry, car, lorry, bus, bus, lorry, car, car, van, car, car, bus, car, car, lorry, car, lorry, car, car, lorry, car, van, lorry, lorry, car, van, car, bus, van, lorry, car, bus, car.

The items are entered in a tally chart as they occur.

Vehicle	Tally	Total
Car	IIII IIII IIII I	16
Van	IIII	4
Bus	IIII I	6
Lorry	IIII IIII II	12
		38

Notice that the numbers are grouped in fives, the fifth number going diagonally through the first four. IIII
The groups of 5 are kept in neat columns.
Grouping in 5's makes the totals easier to count.

Presenting data in a table

Example

2   **Method of transport to and from school**
Copy the table and fill in the figures to show this information.
Of the 50 boys, 10 walk to school, 5 cycle, 3 come on their motorbikes, 8 come by car and 4 come by train. The rest come by bus.
All go home by the same method except that 2 who walk to school go home by car and 3 who come by car go home by bus.

	Morning			Afternoon		
	Boys	Girls	Total	Boys	Girls	Total
Walk						
Cycle						
Motorbike						
Car						
Bus						
Train						
Total						

Of the girls, 12 walk to school, 8 cycle, 1 comes on her motorbike, 3 come by car and 16 come by bus. No-one comes by train. 4 of the girls who come by bus walk home and 2 others go home by car instead of by bus.

How many pupils come to school by public transport (bus or train)?
How many go home by public transport?

Exercise 9.1

1. The numbers of matches in 60 boxes were counted. Tally the information and show the totals in a separate column.

48	49	47	45	48	49	48	49	49	49	49	48
48	44	48	47	49	45	49	50	48	49	47	48
49	46	50	48	46	46	47	48	47	49	45	47
45	46	47	47	48	45	50	49	46	47	49	48
46	49	46	49	47	46	49	49	49	45	49	49

2. A firm made a table to show the sales of a product.

	Standard model	De-luxe model	Total
Red			
Green			
Blue			
Total			

Copy the table and fill in the details.
In the standard model there were 60 sold altogether of which $\frac{1}{2}$ were red and $\frac{1}{5}$ were green.
For sales in the de-luxe range, 5 more red ones were sold than of the standard model and 4 fewer blue ones than of the standard model.
Altogether 31 green items were sold.
What fraction of the total items sold were blue ones ?

3. 24 teenagers going on an Activity Day each have to choose from these five activities: abseiling, orienteering, canoeing, archery, mystery event. They have to give their choice of activity (1) for the morning session, (2) for the afternoon session, (3) as a reserve, in case they cannot do one of their choices for (1) or (2).

   Design a sheet which the organiser could use to record the choices from each person and the totals for each category.

Questionnaires

To conduct a survey amongst a group of people one way is to ask them to answer a questionnaire. You can either give them the questionnaire to fill in themselves or you can ask the questions and write down their answers.
Decide exactly what information you want and how you are planning to use the answers.
Keep the questionnaire as short as possible, and keep the questions short, clear and precise.
Avoid questions which people may not be willing to answer because they are embarrassing or offensive.

The best questions can be answered by categories, such as the ones below, where you can put a tick in one of the boxes.

Age

Under 20	
20–under 40	
40–under 60	
60 or over	

No	
Yes	
Don't know	

Strongly agree	
Agree	
Don't know/ no opinion	
Disagree	
Strongly disagree	

'How long do you spend watching TV ?' This is a very vague question, and will produce equally vague answers, so you will find it difficult to analyse the data.

'How long did you spend watching TV yesterday ? Tick one of the following:'

Not at all	
Up to 1 hour	
Between 1 and 3 hours	
Between 3 and 5 hours	
Over 5 hours	

This is much more precise, and you have only to count the ticks in each category to have some useful data about viewing habits.

It is a good idea to try out your questionnaire on a few people first to see if it is clear enough and likely to give you the data you need, or whether it needs improving. This is called a **pilot survey**.

If you are asking members of the public for their views, you have not the resources, time or authority to make a proper sample. You will probably have to question people in the street or shopping area, and your sample will have to consist of people in that area at that time. (But a survey on where people shop could be biased if you select your sample from outside the largest supermarket in the area.)
Try to make your sample representative by including people of different ages, and equal numbers of men and women. Be very polite when you approach people, and thank them afterwards for their help. Remember that some people will be in too much of a hurry to stop to talk to you. Before you do such a survey, discuss your plans with your teacher and with your parents.

Analysing a questionnaire

After you have collected all the answers to a questionnaire you should list the results and study them.

For example, you may have been testing people's opinion on a particular matter, and you would have included a question about this in your questionnaire.

Now if you asked 100 people and 90 of them had answered giving a particular opinion, then you would consider that the majority of people would agree with this.

If only 30 agreed with this opinion, then you would consider that the majority of people did not agree with the opinion.

The difficulty is knowing what conclusions to draw if only about 55 people out of 100 agreed with the opinion. With a slightly different group of people you could have got different results, so if the result is near 50% you cannot be so sure what the majority of people would think. A statistician would have further tests to use in making a decision, but as a rough rule, out of 100 people, only accept that you have a majority decision when you get at least 60 people agreeing with it.

Exercise 9.2

1. Here are some questions which might be used in surveys.
    In each case, re-write the question, or the answer categories, so that the answers will be more useful for the survey.

    1   How much water do you think your household uses ?

More than average	
About average	
Less than average	

    (A survey about water meters.)

    2   How often do you drink our product ?

Daily	
Weekly	
Monthly	
Other (please specify)	

    (A health-food drink.)

3 Which figure best describes your annual household income ?

Less than £25 000	
£25 001–£30 000	
£30 001–£40 000	
£40 001–£50 000	
More than £50 000	

(A holiday survey given to a group of friends.)

4 How many times do you eat out at restaurants ?

Seldom/never	
Once a month	
2–4 times a month	
More than 4 times a month	

(Market research survey.)

2. Imagine that you are the cook at an adventure holiday centre for teenagers.
Design a questionnaire which you could give to a group of teenagers at the end of their
stay, to see whether the meals you are providing are satisfactory, or whether any
improvements should be made.
(Include about 4 to 8 questions.)

3. Certain community leaders thought that there ought to be a swimming pool and other
community amenities in the local area. They sent questionnaires to 500 households. One
question was: Do you think a local swimming pool is needed ?

Highly desirable	
Desirable	
Not needed	

Replies were received from 170 households and of these:
        72 ticked 'Highly desirable',
        20 ticked 'Desirable',
        63 ticked 'Not needed',
        15 did not answer that question.

On the basis of these replies, do you think that the community leaders should approach
the Council saying that there is a good local demand for a swimming pool ?

Exercise 9.3   Applications

1. Imagine that you are the manager of a seaside caravan park.
    Design a questionnaire which you could ask your customers to fill in, to give you some
    idea of whether the amenities on the site are satisfactory, and whether certain extra ones
    would be welcomed.

2. The owners of a local radio station wish to obtain information
    on any improvements that could be made to increase the listening
    figures. They decide to send out a questionnaire, asking the
    following questions:

    1   What is your name ?

    2   Do you enjoy listening to our station ?

    3   What type of programme do you enjoy most ?

    4   Do you listen in the mornings ?

    5   Do you like quizzes and competitions ?

    6   What kind of work do you do ?

    7   How much do you earn ?

    Are the questions suitable ? Where necessary, replace them by more useful ones,
    including categories of answers.

3. You are trying to test whether people prefer a certain brand of a product rather than any
    other brand.
    You ask a sample of people whether they prefer this brand.

    'Do you like this brand in preference to other brands ?'

	Number of replies
Strongly prefer	52
Prefer	81
Don't know	21
Prefer some other brand	67

    On the basis of these results, assuming that the sample was correctly chosen, would you
    say that this brand is preferred ?

4. The scores in 42 matches on a particular Saturday were as follows:

0–2	0–2	2–2	0–3	1–4	1–0	1–0	2–1	4–1	5–1	5–0
3–2	2–1	1–4	2–0	3–0	1–1	2–1	0–1	1–2	2–1	2–0
1–1	1–2	0–0	2–2	1–2	0–3	2–0	1–0	0–0	1–0	1–2
1–0	2–2	3–0	2–0	3–1	1–2	1–2	2–2	1–3		

Copy and fill in this table showing the **number of matches** in each category.

Number of matches		Goals by home team						
		0	1	2	3	4	5	Total
Goals by away team	0							
	1							
	2							
	3							
	4							
	Total							

What was the total number of goals scored by the home teams?
What was the total number of goals scored by the away teams?

Comment briefly on the results.

5. **A statistical investigation**

Choose a topic that interests you, or has some practical purpose, and carry out an investigation.
First of all, decide what is the **aim** of the investigation. It is no use spending time collecting data without knowing whether it will be of any use.
If you are collecting data for yourself, you will probably need to make a data collection sheet on which to record it.

You need not collect the data for yourself. You may use data that someone has already collected, or you may use data from books, magazines, etc. or from a computer database.

When you have carried out the investigation, you should then display your information in an interesting way, so that other people can read about it. Make neat lists or tables, and include statistical diagrams.

Nowadays there are many types of computer programs which you can use to present and analyse your data. After you have entered your data, many programs produce a variety of diagrams to illustrate the data, and will work out averages. This is very useful, especially if you have a large amount of data.

On the next page are some brief notes which may give you ideas for choosing what to do.

(Read the notes on the previous page.)

These investigations have been listed here, but for some of them you will need to complete them by using the methods of Chapters 12 (Averages and range), 17 (Statistical diagrams), 24 (Frequency distributions) or 29 (Scatter diagrams).

1   Investigations into heights of people, shoe sizes, heights of teenagers compared with parents' heights, etc.

2   Financial matters, e.g. children's spending money, family budgets, money spent on leisure, transport, etc.

3   Television, e.g. amount of time devoted to different kinds of programmes, comparing different channels. Time taken by advertising, kinds of advertising. Time people spend watching TV or videos. Favourite types of programme. Percentage of people who have satellite or cable television.

4   Sports, e.g. football results, goals scored, differences between home and away matches, comparisons with other years. Similar analysis of other sports. Popularity of various sports by people taking part, by spectators or by watching them on television.

5   Leisure interests, e.g. costs of a hobby, time needed for it.

6   Holidays, e.g. destinations, type, cost, length of time, method of travel.

7   Traffic, e.g. surveys, number of people in each car. Ages of cars. Traffic flow at different times. Distances travelled. Use of public transport or taxis. Travel costs.

8   School or college issues, e.g. any plans to alter existing arrangements for uniform, meals, homework. Survey of attendance and punctuality. Distances from homes to school. Examination results.

9   Local issues, e.g. whether people want a new by-pass built and their views for and against. Council spending. Ages of local population.

10   Employment, e.g. types of work and numbers of jobs available locally. Pay and prospects.

11   National issues, e.g. whether people support Government proposals on some matter and their views for or against.

12   Health issues, e.g. healthy eating, types of exercise.

13   International problems such as third world famine. Ecological issues.

14   Work linked with other school or college subjects such as experiments in Biology and other Sciences, links with Geography fieldwork, plans in technology.

Practice test 9

1. A group of children gave information about the number of children in their families, including themselves.
   Here are the results:

3	4	1	2	2	5	2	3	2	3	3	1	4	3	4
1	2	1	2	3	2	4	2	3	2	2	3	6	2	2
2	2	3	2	2	3	3	6	3	3	2	2	1		

   1 Make a tally table of the information.
   2 Comment briefly on the results of the survey.

2 You want to carry out a survey about the pets kept by local children, including the kinds of pets and the number of each kind.
   Design a data collection sheet on which to record the data.

3. These questions were suggested for use in a questionnaire for an investigation involving schoolchildren.
   Say why the questions are not very suitable, and give a better form for each one.

   1 Do you get a lot of pocket money ?
   2 Do you get too much homework ?
   3 Do you like sports ?

4. Attendances at an exhibition.

	Wed	Thur	Fri	Sat	Sun	Total
Adults	83	120	176	216	313	
Children	104	185	287	384	529	
Total						

   Copy the table and complete it.

   1 How many children altogether attended the exhibition ?
   2 On which day was there the greatest attendance ?
   3 The organisers had been hoping for a total attendance of 200 on the first day.
       How many visitors were they short of that target ?
   4 How many people altogether attended the exhibition ?

5. Design a table which could be used by a doctor to record the number of patients visiting the surgery on any one day. The table could include separate categories for men, women and children, and also the numbers for the morning surgery and the evening surgery, and all totals.

 **Fractions**

The topics in this chapter include:

- understanding and using fractions, and the equivalences between fractions and decimals,
- calculating fractions of quantities and fractional changes,
- expressing one number as a fraction of another,
- adding and subtracting simple fractions.

Fractions

Fractions are numbers such as $\frac{1}{4}, \frac{1}{3}, \frac{2}{5}, \frac{5}{9}$.

The number on top is called the **numerator** and the number underneath is called the **denominator**.

The shaded part represents $\frac{1}{4}$ (one-quarter) of the circle.
(The whole circle is divided into 4 equal parts and 1 part is shaded.)

The unshaded part represents $\frac{3}{4}$ (three-quarters) of the circle.

The shaded part represents $\frac{2}{5}$ (two-fifths) of the rectangle.
(The whole rectangle is divided into 5 equal parts and 2 parts are shaded.)

The unshaded part represents $\frac{3}{5}$ of the rectangle.

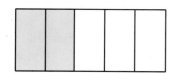

Equivalent fractions

This diagram shows that $\frac{2}{5}$ is equivalent to $\frac{4}{10}$.

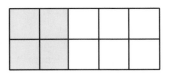

This diagram shows that $\frac{2}{5} + \frac{1}{10} = \frac{4}{10} + \frac{1}{10} = \frac{5}{10} = \frac{1}{2}$.

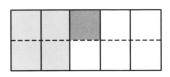

Improper fractions are numbers with a greater numerator than denominator, such as $\frac{6}{5}$ and $\frac{5}{2}$.

Mixed numbers are numbers with a whole number part and a fraction part, such as $1\frac{1}{5}$ and $2\frac{1}{2}$.

This diagram shows that $\frac{6}{5} = 1\frac{1}{5}$.

This diagram shows that $\frac{5}{2} = 2\frac{1}{2}$.

Examples

1   Reduce $\frac{60}{75}$ to its lowest terms.

60 and 75 both divide by 5 so reduce the fraction by dividing the numerator and the denominator both by 5. This process can be called **cancelling**.

$\overset{12}{\underset{15}{\cancel{\dfrac{60}{75}}}}$ This gives the fraction $\frac{12}{15}$ but this is still not in its lowest terms because 12 and 15 both divide by 3. So divide the numerator and the denominator both by 3.

$\overset{4}{\underset{5}{\cancel{\cancel{\dfrac{60}{75}}}}} = \frac{4}{5}$ This is the fraction in its lowest terms.

2   Change $\frac{5}{6}$ into a fraction with denominator 24.

6 becomes 24 when multiplied by 4, so multiply the numerator and the denominator by 4.

$$\frac{5}{6} = \frac{5 \times 4}{6 \times 4} = \frac{20}{24}$$

3   Change $3\frac{7}{8}$ into an improper fraction.

Multiply the whole number 3 by 8 to change it into eighths. This is 24 eighths and another 7 eighths makes 31 eighths.

$$3\frac{7}{8} = \frac{24}{8} + \frac{7}{8} = \frac{31}{8}$$

4   Change $\frac{45}{7}$ to a mixed number.

Divide 7 into 45. It goes 6 times so there are 6 whole ones. $6 \times 7 = 42$ and the remainder is 3 so there is also $\frac{3}{7}$.

$$\frac{45}{7} = \frac{42+3}{7} = 6\frac{3}{7}$$

Exercise 10.1

1.   What fraction of the shape is shaded ?

1
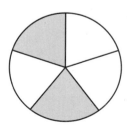

2
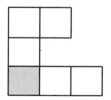

3
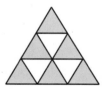

4
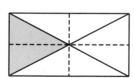

5
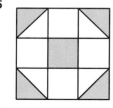

Copy these figures and shade the fraction stated.

6 $\frac{3}{8}$ 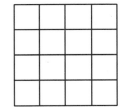   7 $\frac{5}{12}$ 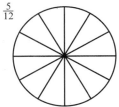   8 $\frac{1}{2}$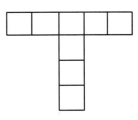

9 $\frac{2}{3}$ 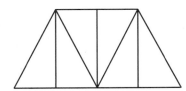   10 $\frac{1}{4}$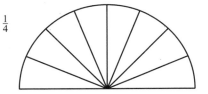

2. **1** Find one-half of each of these numbers.
    88   18   8   14   60   24   42   52   90   96

    2 Find one-third of each of these numbers.
    18   99   60   24   45   27   3   21   39   75

    3 Find one-quarter of each of these numbers.
    8   28   80   100   52   44   4   24   160   36

    4 Find one-fifth of each of these numbers.
    60   20   45   10   100   15   35   75   55   200

    5 Find two-thirds of each of these numbers.
    6   15   24   9   30   60   33   90   75   18

3. Reduce these fractions to their lowest terms.

    1 $\frac{6}{9}$ **5** $\frac{24}{80}$ **8** $\frac{21}{56}$

    2 $\frac{10}{12}$ **6** $\frac{18}{45}$ **9** $\frac{24}{54}$

    3 $\frac{5}{30}$ **7** $\frac{35}{56}$ **10** $\frac{15}{20}$

    4 $\frac{30}{100}$

4. **1** Change $\frac{7}{9}$ into a fraction with denominator 18.

    2 Change $\frac{3}{5}$ into a fraction with denominator 20.

    3 Change $\frac{5}{6}$ into a fraction with denominator 18.

    4 Change $\frac{7}{8}$ into a fraction with denominator 24.

    5 Change $\frac{3}{10}$ into a fraction with denominator 20.

5. Change these mixed numbers to improper fractions.

  1 $1\frac{3}{4}$ **5** $2\frac{7}{8}$ **8** $7\frac{1}{2}$

  2 $2\frac{1}{3}$ **6** $4\frac{2}{5}$ **9** $3\frac{1}{3}$

  3 $3\frac{7}{10}$ **7** $1\frac{1}{8}$ **10** $2\frac{3}{10}$

  4 $1\frac{5}{6}$

6. Change these improper fractions to mixed numbers.

  1 $\frac{23}{5}$ **5** $\frac{11}{4}$ **8** $\frac{17}{4}$

  2 $\frac{17}{6}$ **6** $\frac{20}{3}$ **9** $\frac{25}{3}$

  3 $\frac{31}{10}$ **7** $\frac{13}{5}$ **10** $\frac{13}{4}$

  4 $\frac{21}{8}$

To find one quantity as a fraction of another

Examples

1   Express 24 pence as a fraction of £3.

$$\frac{24\text{p}}{£3} = \frac{24\text{p}}{300\text{p}} = \frac{\overset{2}{\cancel{24}}}{\underset{25}{\cancel{300}}} = \frac{2}{25}$$

Both quantities must be in the same units before cancelling.

2   Express 56 min as a fraction of 1 h 10 min.

$$\frac{56\,\text{min}}{1\,\text{h}\,10\,\text{min}} = \frac{56\,\text{min}}{70\,\text{min}} = \frac{\overset{8}{\cancel{56}}}{\underset{10}{\cancel{70}}} = \frac{4}{5}$$

Cancelling by 7 and then by 2.

To find a fraction of a quantity

Examples

3   Find $\frac{2}{3}$ of £2.40.

     $\frac{1}{3}$ of £2.40 = 80 pence   Dividing £2.40 by 3.

     So $\frac{2}{3}$ of £2.40 = £1.60   Multiplying 80p by 2.

     Alternative method

     $\frac{2}{3}$ of £2.40 = £$\frac{2}{3}$ × 2.40   On your calculator, press 2 $\boxed{\times}$ 2.4 $\boxed{\div}$ 3 $\boxed{=}$.
                = £1.60

4   Find $\frac{7}{8}$ of 480 m.

$\frac{1}{8}$ of 480 m = 60 m   Dividing 480 m by 8.

So $\frac{7}{8}$ of 480 m = 420 m   Multiplying 60 m by 7.

Alternative method

$\frac{7}{8}$ of 480 m = $\frac{7}{8} \times$ 480 m   On your calculator, press 7 $\boxed{\times}$ 480 $\boxed{\div}$ 8 $\boxed{=}$.

            = 420 m

Converting fractions to decimals

1.   **Simple fractions, with denominators which are factors of 10 or 100**

e.g. $\frac{1}{2} = \frac{5}{10} = 0.5$

$\frac{1}{4} = \frac{25}{100} = 0.25$

$\frac{2}{5} = \frac{4}{10} = 0.4$

$\frac{3}{20} = \frac{15}{100} = 0.15$

$\frac{1}{25} = \frac{4}{100} = 0.04$

2.   **Using your calculator**

If the denominators are powers of 2, i.e. 2, 4, 8, 16, ..., or powers of 5, i.e. 5, 25, 125, ..., or combinations of these such as 20, 40, 50, ..., then there will be an exact decimal.

e.g. $\frac{3}{8} = 3 \div 8 = 0.375$

$\frac{7}{16} = 7 \div 16 = 0.4375$

$\frac{9}{125} = 9 \div 125 = 0.072$

3.   **Fractions with other denominators**

These will not give exact decimals so, since you are unlikely to need several decimal places, you should give the decimal correct to 2 or 3 decimal places, as needed.

e.g. $\frac{1}{3} = 1 \div 3 \quad = 0.3333\ldots$ =0.33 to 2 decimal places,
                                =0.333 to 3 decimal places.

$\frac{1}{6} = 1 \div 6 \quad = 0.1666\ldots$ =0.17 to 2 decimal places,
                                =0.167 to 3 decimal places.

$\frac{5}{7} = 5 \div 7 \quad = 0.7142\ldots$ =0.71 to 2 decimal places,
                                =0.714 to 3 decimal places.

$\frac{27}{31} = 27 \div 31 = 0.8709\ldots$ =0.87 to 2 decimal places,
                                =0.871 to 3 decimal places.

Converting decimals to fractions

e.g. $0.6 = \dfrac{6}{10} = \frac{3}{5}$ Cancelling by 2.

$0.35 = \dfrac{35}{100} = \frac{7}{20}$ Cancelling by 5.

$0.625 = \dfrac{625}{1000} = \dfrac{125}{200} = \dfrac{25}{40} = \frac{5}{8}$ Cancelling by 5, 3 times.

Exercise 10.2

1.   **1**   Express 8 hours as a fraction of 1 day.
     2   Express 20° as a fraction of 1 right angle.
     3   Express 10 cm as a fraction of 1 metre.
     4   Express 45 seconds as a fraction of 1 minute.
     5   Express 60p as a fraction of £1.
     6   Express £1.60 as a fraction of £2.40.
     7   Express 250 g as a fraction of 1 kg.
     8   Express 50p as a fraction of £4.50.
     9   Express 24 minutes as a fraction of 1 hour.
     10   Express 120° as a fraction of 1 complete turn.

2.   **1**   Find $\frac{3}{4}$ of £3.60.   **6**   Find $\frac{1}{6}$ of 1 right angle.
     2   Find $\frac{2}{3}$ of 1 foot.   **7**   Find $\frac{3}{8}$ of 16 litres.
     3   Find $\frac{3}{10}$ of £2.   **8**   Find $\frac{1}{9}$ of 360 g.
     4   Find $\frac{3}{5}$ of 1 hour 40 minutes.   **9**   Find $\frac{1}{4}$ of 2 m.
     5   Find $\frac{5}{8}$ of 24 cm.   **10**   Find $\frac{7}{10}$ of 1 kg.

3.   Write as decimals

     1 $\frac{3}{4}$ **2** $\frac{2}{5}$ **3** $\frac{7}{10}$ **4** $\frac{37}{100}$ **5** $\frac{7}{8}$

4.   Write as fractions in their simplest terms

     1   0.6   **2**   0.25   **3**   0.15   **4**   0.125   **5**   0.08

5.   2 pints of milk are poured into an urn containing 10 pints of coffee. What fraction of the mixture is milk ?

6.   In a club, two-fifths of the members are Junior members. The remaining 90 members are Senior members. How many members are there altogether ?

Adding and subtracting fractions

Examples

1   Addition

$\frac{5}{8} + \frac{3}{4}$

Change $\frac{5}{8}$ and $\frac{3}{4}$ into fractions with denominator 8, because 8 is the smallest number into which the denominators 8 and 4 both divide.

$\frac{3}{4} = \frac{6}{8}$

$\frac{5}{8} + \frac{3}{4} = \frac{5}{8} + \frac{6}{8} = \frac{11}{8} = 1\frac{3}{8}$

$\left(\text{The stage } \frac{5}{8} + \frac{6}{8} \text{ can be written as } \frac{5+6}{8}\right)$

2   Subtraction

$\frac{7}{8} - \frac{1}{16} = \frac{14-1}{16} = \frac{13}{16}$

$1 - \frac{2}{5} = \frac{5-2}{5} = \frac{3}{5}$

3   In addition and subtraction questions with **mixed numbers** do the whole number part and the fraction part separately.

$3\frac{5}{8} + 2\frac{3}{4} = 5\frac{5+6}{8} = 5\frac{11}{8} = 5 + 1 + \frac{3}{8} = 6\frac{3}{8}$

$3\frac{7}{8} - 1\frac{1}{16} = 2\frac{14-1}{16} = 2\frac{13}{16}$

$3\frac{5}{8} - 1\frac{3}{4} = 2\frac{5-6}{8} = 1\frac{8+5-6}{8} = 1\frac{7}{8}$ Since we cannot take 6 from 5, one of the whole numbers was changed into 8 eighths.

Exercise 10.3

1.   Find the values of the following.

   1 $\frac{1}{2} + \frac{1}{8}$
   2 $\frac{5}{8} + \frac{1}{16}$
   3 $5\frac{1}{4} + 1\frac{1}{2}$

   4 $2\frac{1}{2} + 2\frac{3}{4}$
   5 $4\frac{3}{4} + 1\frac{7}{16}$

2.   Find the values of the following.

   1 $\frac{5}{8} - \frac{1}{4}$
   2 $\frac{15}{16} - \frac{1}{2}$
   3 $2 - \frac{3}{8}$

   4 $2\frac{3}{4} - \frac{5}{8}$
   5 $3\frac{1}{4} - \frac{7}{8}$

3.   Eleanor had a box of chocolates. She put aside $\frac{1}{4}$ of them for her sister and $\frac{1}{8}$ of them for her brother. What fraction had she left ?

4. Mr Brown decided to dig
    his garden. On the first fine
    day he dug $\frac{1}{2}$ of it. On the
    next day he dug $\frac{3}{8}$ of it, then
    he stopped because it was
    raining.

    1   What fraction had he
        dug altogether ?

    2   What fraction remained
        to be dug ?

5. A plank of wood is $10\frac{1}{2}$ feet long. A piece $1\frac{3}{4}$ feet long is cut off. What length remains ?

Exercise 10.4 Applications

1. There were two candidates, Mr A and Mr B, in an election.
    Mr A got $\frac{7}{12}$ of the votes.
    What fraction did Mr B get ? Who won the election ?
    If 2400 people altogether voted, how many extra votes did
    the winner get more than the loser ?

2. How many half-pint glasses of fruit juice can be filled from a container which holds
    2 gallons ?

3. An engine turns at 1200 revolutions per minute. Find, as a fraction of a second, how
    long it takes to turn through one revolution ?

4. I think of a number. Two-thirds of this number is 18. What is the number ?

5. Maureen was trying to save £7. For 6 weeks she saved 70p a week. What fraction of the
    £7 had she still to save ?

6. A tank containing liquid is two-thirds full. When 60 more litres of liquid are put in the tank is full. How many litres does the tank hold altogether ?

7. Mrs Khan earns £4.20 per hour for a basic week of 40 hours. Overtime is paid at time-and-a-half. If she works 42 hours one week, what will she earn ?
If one week she earns £199.50, how many hours altogether did she work ?

8.

Pauline's ruler measures in inches and twelfths. From A to B is $3\frac{5}{12}$ inches and from B to C is $2\frac{1}{12}$ inches. What is the distance from A to C ?

9. Two rods, AB of length $4\frac{1}{2}$ inches and CD of length $5\frac{5}{8}$ inches, overlap by $\frac{3}{4}$ inch. What is the total length AD ?

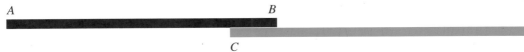

10. The outside measurements of a picture frame are $14\frac{7}{8}$ inches and $10\frac{3}{4}$ inches. The frame is $\frac{5}{8}$ inch wide.
What are the inside measurements ?

11. On a canal holiday, the family planned to make a round trip of 72 miles in 4 days.
On the first 3 days the distances they covered were $12\frac{3}{4}$ miles, $20\frac{1}{2}$ miles, $23\frac{3}{4}$ miles.

   1 How far would they have to travel on the 4th day ?

   2 What fraction of the total distance is this ?

12.   **Using a calculator with a fractions key**

This key is labelled $\boxed{a^b/_c}$.
The second function on the key is labelled $\boxed{d/_c}$.

To enter a fraction

e.g. To enter $\frac{5}{8}$, press 5 $\boxed{a^b/_c}$ 8. The display will show 5 ⌐ 8.
To enter $\frac{13}{8}$, press 13 $\boxed{a^b/_c}$ 8.

To enter a mixed number

e.g. To enter $2\frac{5}{8}$, press 2 $\boxed{a^b/_c}$ 5 $\boxed{a^b/_c}$ 8. The display will show 2 ⌐ 5 ⌐ 8.

To change a fraction to a decimal

Enter the fraction then press $\boxed{=}$ $\boxed{a^b/_c}$.
e.g. enter $2\frac{5}{8}$ then press $\boxed{=}$ $\boxed{a^b/_c}$ and the display will show 2.625.
Press $\boxed{a^b/_c}$ again to change the number back to a mixed number.

To reduce a fraction to its lowest terms

Enter the fraction and then press $\boxed{=}$ or $\boxed{+}$, $\boxed{-}$, $\boxed{\times}$ or $\boxed{\div}$.

To change a mixed number to an improper fraction

Enter the mixed number then press the second function key then $\boxed{d/_c}$.
To change it back, press $\boxed{=}$.
To change it to a decimal, press $\boxed{a^b/_c}$.

To change an improper fraction to a mixed number

Enter the improper fraction and then press $\boxed{=}$.

To find a fraction of a number

Press fraction $\boxed{\times}$ number $\boxed{=}$.
e.g. To find $\frac{2}{3}$ of $4\frac{1}{2}$ kg press 2 $\boxed{a^b/_c}$ 3 $\boxed{\times}$ 4 $\boxed{a^b/_c}$ 1 $\boxed{a^b/_c}$ 2 $\boxed{=}$ and you will get the answer 3 (kg).

Use the fractions key on your calculator to do some of the questions of Exercises 10.1 and 10.2, checking that you get the same answers as before.

Do not rely on your calculator entirely. You still need to know the methods for working out fractions.

Practice test 10

1. **1** Reduce $\frac{45}{72}$ to its lowest terms.

    2 Write $\frac{3}{4}$ as a fraction with denominator 24.

    3 Change the mixed number $3\frac{4}{5}$ into an improper fraction.

    4 Change $\frac{26}{5}$ into a mixed number.

2. Write these fractions as decimals.

    1 $\frac{4}{5}$ **2** $\frac{3}{4}$ **3** $\frac{7}{10}$ **4** $\frac{6}{100}$ **5** $\frac{3}{20}$

3. Change these decimals into fractions in their simplest terms.

    1 0.6   **4** 0.25
    2 0.03   **5** 0.16
    3 0.001

4. **1** Express 75 cm as a fraction of 2 metres.
    2 Find $\frac{2}{3}$ of £2.25.

5. There are 60 eggs in a crate. One-fifth of them are cracked. How many are whole ?

6. A farmer had 240 animals on his farm. $\frac{5}{8}$ of them were sheep, $\frac{1}{10}$ of them were pigs, he had 2 horses, 4 dogs and the rest were cows. How many cows had he ? What fraction of the total were cows ?

7. Mr Taylor's weekly wage is £280. He reckons that $\frac{1}{4}$ of his wages go in tax and insurance. Of the amount remaining, $\frac{1}{5}$ of it pays the rent and $\frac{1}{10}$ of it is put aside to pay the household fuel bills. How much has he left to spend ?

PUZZLES

12. Robert has to saw a 10-metre pole into 1-metre lengths. How long will it take him if he cuts one length every 3 minutes ?

13. What is the next prime number after 113 ?

14. In a dress shop there were six dresses in the window, marked for sale at £15, £22, £30, £26, £16 and £31. Five of the dresses were sold to two customers, the second customer spending twice as much as the first one. Which dress was unsold ?

Triangles

> **The topics in this chapter include:**
>
> - knowing the properties of and classifying triangles,
> - using the angle properties of triangles,
> - constructing triangles.

Kinds of triangle

Angles in a triangle

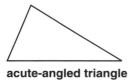      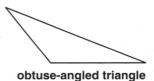

acute-angled triangle **right-angled triangle** **obtuse-angled triangle**

Sides in a triangle

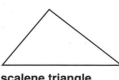

scalene triangle
(3 sides of different lengths) **isosceles triangle**
(two sides equal) **equilateral triangle**
(all 3 sides equal)

(The sign for lines of equal length is similar small marks crossing the lines.)

Angle properties of a triangle

Angle sum of a triangle

The sum of the angles of a triangle is 180°.

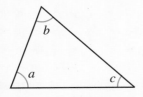

$$a + b + c = 180°$$

Exterior angle of a triangle

If a side is extended, the exterior angle is equal to the sum of the two opposite interior angles.

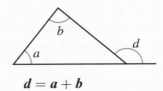

$$d = a + b$$

Isosceles triangle

The angles opposite the equal sides are equal.

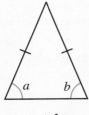

$$a = b$$

Equilateral triangle

All angles are 60°.

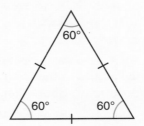

Example

Find the sizes of angles d and e.

$d = 73°$ (isosceles triangle, equal angles)

$e = d + 73°$ (exterior angle of triangle)

$e = 146°$

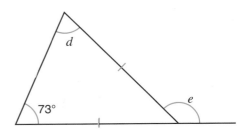

Naming of triangles

A triangle with vertices at points A, B and C is called triangle ABC.
This can be written as $\triangle ABC$.

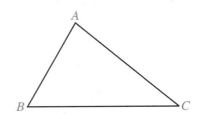

Exercise 11.1

1. Estimate the sizes of the angles in these triangles. Check your estimates by measuring with your protractor. Show that the sum of the angles is 180°.
   (The sum may not be exactly 180°, because you have to measure the angles to the nearest degree.)

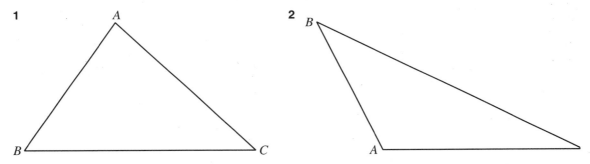

2. Estimate the sizes of the angles in these isosceles triangles. Check your estimates by measuring with your protractor. Show that the angles opposite the equal sides are equal.

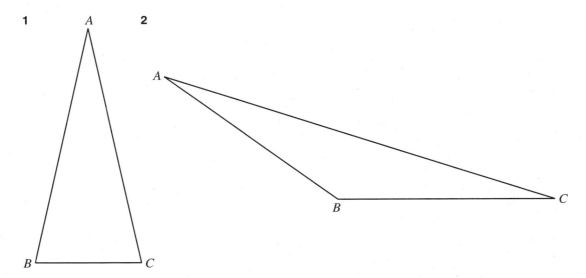

3. Calculate the sizes of the third angles in these triangles.

1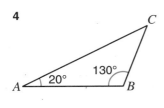

2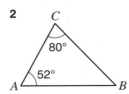

3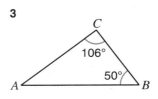

4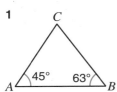

5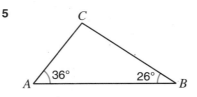

4. Calculate the third angle in each triangle.
    Say whether the triangle is acute-angled, right-angled or obtuse-angled, and say if it is
    isosceles or equilateral.

    1 Two angles are 130°, 36°.   **4** Two angles are 60°, 60°.
    2 Two angles are 72°, 36°.   **5** Two angles are 24°, 36°.
    3 Two angles are 54°, 36°.

5. Calculate the sizes of the marked angles in these figures.

1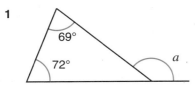

2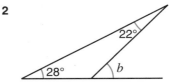

3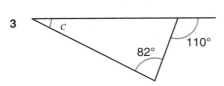

4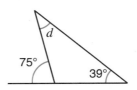

6. Calculate the sizes of angles a, b, c, d.

1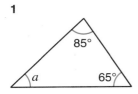

2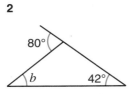

3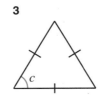

4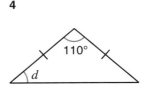

7. Find the sizes of ∠ACB and ∠DCB.

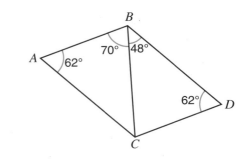

8. Find the sizes of a and b.
    What sort of triangle is it ?

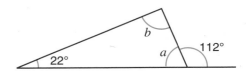

Constructing triangles

Follow the instructions and draw these triangles accurately.

1 To draw a triangle, given 1 side and 2 angles

Example

Draw a triangle *ABC* with *AB* = 9 cm,
∠*A* = 48° and ∠*B* = 77°.

Draw *AB*, 9 cm long.
Measure an angle of 48° at *A* and an angle
of 77° at *B*. Continue these lines until
they meet at *C*.

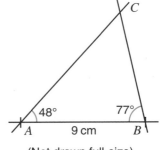

(Not drawn full-size)

(If a line *AB* has to be drawn to an accurate length it is useful to draw the line slightly
longer than needed and then mark *A* and *B* by small marks crossing the line.)

(If instead of being given the size of ∠*B* you have been told that ∠*C* = 55°, you could
have calculated the size of ∠*B*, since the 3 angles of a triangle have a sum of 180°, and
then you could continue as above.)

6. Calculate the sizes of the angles marked with small letters.

1

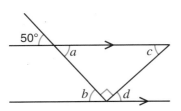

2

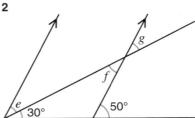

3

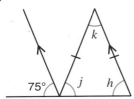

4

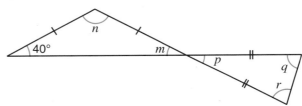

7. In $\triangle ABC$, $AB = AC$, and the bisectors of $\angle B$ and $\angle C$
    meet at I. (Bisectors of angles are lines which
    cut the angles in half.)

    Find the sizes of
    1 $\angle ABC$,
    2 $\angle IBC$,
    3 $\angle BIC$,

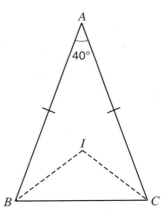

8. Construct $\triangle ABC$ full-size.
    Measure AC, BC and $\angle C$.

    D is the mid-point of AC. Mark D on
    your diagram.
    Through D draw a line parallel to AB.
    Let this line cut BC at E.
    Measure BE and CE.
    What do you notice ?

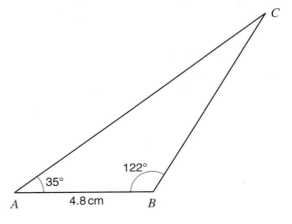

9. Construct △ *DEF* full-size.
    Measure *EF*, ∠*E* and ∠*F*.

    The mid-points of *DE*, *EF* and *DF* are *P*, *Q*
    and *R*. Mark *P*, *Q* and *R* on your diagram.
    Join *FP*, *DQ* and *ER*.
    What do you notice ?

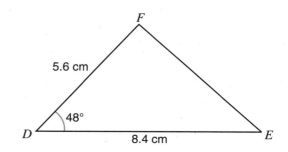

Practice test 11

1. Find the sizes of angles *a*, *b*, *c*.

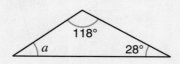

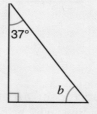

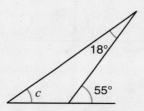

2. Find the sizes of angles *j* and *k*
    What sort of triangle is △ *HJK* ?

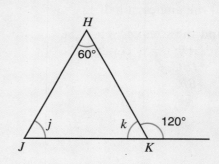

3. Find the sizes of angles *p*, *q*, *r*.

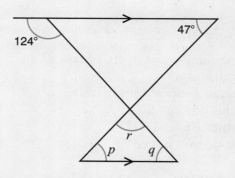

4.   Calculate the sizes of
      1   ∠ACD,
      2   ∠CDB,
      3   ∠DBC,
      4   ∠BCD.

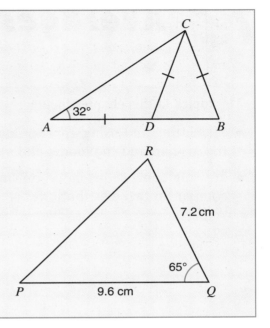

5.   Construct △ PQR full-size.
      Measure PR, ∠P and ∠R.

      Mark S, the mid-point of PQ and
      T, the mid-point of PR.
      Join ST and measure it.

PUZZLES

15.   How many squares are there in this figure,
      and how many contain the dot ?

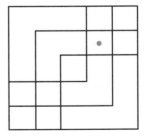

16.   Whilst Mr Mercer's car was being repaired, he travelled to and from work either by
      train or by bus. When he went to work on the train, he came home on the bus. If he
      came home on the train, he had taken the bus to work. During this time he travelled
      on the train 9 times and travelled on the bus 10 times going to work and 15 times
      coming home from work. For how many days was his car off the road ?

17.   Copy this long division sum and fill in the missing figures.

```
              2 *
      * 3 )1 2 4 *
          * 6
          3 * *
          3 * *
```

12 Averages and range

The topics in this chapter include:

- calculating and using appropriate measures of central tendency, i.e. the mean, the median and the mode; and also the range,
- drawing conclusions based on simple statistics for a single distribution, and comparing two distributions.

Averages

When statistical data has been collected, we often need to find an average measurement. There are several kinds of average. Here we will use the mean, the median and the mode.

1   **The mean** $= \dfrac{\text{the total of the items}}{\text{the number of items}}$.

The formula is written as

$$\bar{x} = \frac{\Sigma x}{n}$$

where $\bar{x}$ (read as x bar) is the symbol for the mean;

Σ, the Greek capital letter sigma, means 'the sum of', so Σx means the sum of the x values;

n is the number of items.

2   **The median**. When the items are arranged in order of size, the median is the value of the middle item, or the value halfway between the middle two if there is an even number of items.

3   **The mode** is the value which occurs most often. (Sometimes a set of values will not have a mode, as there may not be any value which occurs more often than any of the others.)

Example

1   **Numbers of members of a club attending the meetings**

Week number	1	2	3	4	5	6	7	8	9	10	Total
Attendance	20	19	24	22	20	23	20	28	24	20	220

Find the mean, median and mode attendances.

The mean

$$\bar{x} = \frac{\Sigma x}{n} = \frac{220}{10} = 22$$

The median

(Arrange the items in order of size.)

19	20	20	20	20	22	23	24	24	28

↑
middle

The median is halfway between 20 and 22, i.e. 21.
(Half the values are less than 21 and half are greater than 21.)

The mode

The value which occurs most often is 20 (as there were 4 weeks when 20 members were present), so the mode is 20.

Summary:– Mean = 22, median = 21, mode = 20.

All these averages can be used in different circumstances, although the most usual one is the mean, as this is the one which involves all the values. If one of the values is very high or low compared to the others, this will affect the mean and in this case the median might be a better average to use. The mode is the simplest average to find, but generally it is not as useful as the other two.

Example

2   In a class test, the marks were
     5   10   25   25   25   30   30   30   30   35

     The mean mark is 24.5, the median mark is 27.5 and the mode mark is 30.

     Comment about the averages.

     The fairest average to quote here is the median. Half the students have less than 27.5 and
     half have more.
     The mean has been distorted by the two low values, and only two students have marks
     less than the mean.
     The mode is not a representative average, as only 1 student has a better mark.

If the word 'average' is used without specifying which one in an arithmetical question, it refers
to the mean.

In your answers, remember to give the unit of measurement, e.g. cm, kg.
Check that your answers seem to be reasonable.
Do not give too many decimal places. If the data is accurate to the nearest whole number then
it is reasonable to give the averages to 1 decimal place.

Using a statistical calculator to find the mean

e.g. To find the mean of 23, 24, 28, 29, 31.

Set the calculator to work in statistical mode, then press

23 $\boxed{\text{DATA}}$ 24 $\boxed{\text{DATA}}$ 28 $\boxed{\text{DATA}}$ 29 $\boxed{\text{DATA}}$ 31 $\boxed{\text{DATA}}$

When you have entered all the data, pressing
$\boxed{n}$ will tell you the number of items entered, 5,
$\boxed{\Sigma x}$ will tell you the sum of the items entered, 135,
$\boxed{\bar{x}}$ will tell you the mean of the items entered, 27.

The range

The average (mean, median or mode) gives us a general idea of the data, but two sets of
numbers can have the same mean but be very different in other ways. The other main statistic
we find is a measure of dispersion (or spread).

The range is the simplest measure of dispersion to find.

    Range = highest value − lowest value

The range only uses the extreme values so it is not always very representative.

In example 1 on page 159, the range = 28 − 19 = 9 members.
In example 2 above, the range = 35 − 5 = 30 marks.

Exercise 12.1

1. Find the mean (average) of these sets of numbers.

    1 4 5 5 7 7 8 9 10 12 15 17

    2 12 20 31 35 39 48 55 71 85

    3 2 14 5 12 7

    4 25 53 37 17 62 93 41 27 33 19

    5 1.5 1.7 1.8 1.9 2.0 2.0 2.1 2.2

2. Find the median (halfway value) of the sets of numbers in question 1.

3. Find the median (halfway value) of these sets of numbers.

    1 4 5 5 7 7 7 8 9 9 10 12 12 12 12 13

    2 26 27 29 25 31 33 27 32 28 27 33

    3 3 5 1 6 2 5 4 8 1 5 2 5

4. Find the mode (most frequent value) of the sets of numbers in question 3.

5. Find the mean (average) of

    1 59.2, 90.0, 75.8, 32.6.

    2 £985, £863, £904, £967, £868.

    3 80 min, 150 min, 105 min, 190 min, 128 min, 73 min.

    4 1.2 cm, 2.6 cm, 3.7 cm.

    5 2.5 kg, 3.4 kg, 2.7 kg, 1.9 kg, 4.0 kg.

6. **1** The weights in kg of 10 children are
        54, 52, 62, 49, 61, 56, 51, 64, 54, 67.
        Find the mean (average) and the median
        (halfway value) of the weights.

    2 The ages of 5 boys are
        12 y 1 m, 12 y 5 m, 13 y 7 m, 11 y 2 m, 11 y 7 m.
        Find the median (halfway value) age.

    3 The weights of 10 helpings of potatoes (to the nearest 10 g) are
        150 g, 170 g, 190 g, 160 g, 180 g, 140 g, 170 g, 170 g, 150 g, 160 g.
        Find the mean (average) weight.

7. The temperature in a city each day of a summer week was (in °C)
    22 22 23 24 23 20 20
    Find the mean (average) temperature.

8. Find the range for the sets of numbers in question 1.

9. Find the range of the data in question 5.

Exercise 12.2 Applications

1. 20 men and 20 women were asked what size of shoes they wore.
    Here are the replies:

Men	7	10	8	9	8	6	7	10	9	8
	9	8	8	8	10	9	8	10	9	7
Women	5	5	6	4	6	7	5	5	6	5
	7	6	5	7	6	5	4	6	5	3

    1 What is the mode size for the men ?
    2 What is the mode size for the women ?

2. The weights of a team of oarsmen are, in kg, 84, 79, 72, 83, 65, 66, 73 and 89. The cox
    weighs 52 kg.

    1 Find the mean weight of the team, including the cox.
    2 Find the mean weight of the team, excluding the cox.

3. 12 men and 10 women who normally travel to work by car were asked how far they lived
    from their place of work.
    Their replies, in miles, were:

    Men   3, 2, 10, 30, 1, 2, 26, 1, 5, 4, 4, 12.

    Women 4, 2, 7, 5, 12, 1, 17, 3, 3, 4.

    1 Find the mean and median distances for the men.
    2 Which of these two averages do you think is the fairer one to use, and why ?

    3 Find the mean and median distances for the women.
    4 Which of these two averages do you think is the fairer one to use, and why ?

    5 Find the range of distances for the men.
    6 Find the range of distances for the women.

    7 Comment briefly on the differences between the data for the men and the women.

4. The number of hours of sunshine recorded during the first 7 days of June in a particular
    year at a weather observatory were:

    6.3, 4.5, 3.2, 6.5, 2.7, 0.3, 6.5.

    1 Find the mean and median of the number of daily hours of sunshine.
    2 Find the range of the number of hours of sunshine.
    3 In the previous year the figures were:
       mean 4.8 hours, median 5.2 hours, range 5.6 hours.
       Comment on how the weather differed in the two years.

5.   The weights of 9 apples of a particular variety were, in grams:

121,   100,   99,   96,   125,   108,   123,   102,   116.

    1   Find the mean and median weights of the apples.
    2   Find the range of the weights.

A sample of 10 apples of a different variety were also weighed. The weights, given in grams, were:

136,   128,   128,   120,   115,   119,   118,   108,   114,   124.

    3   Find the mean and median weights of this sample.
    4   Find the range of the weights of this sample.
    5   Comment on how the weights of the two varieties differed.

6.   **Collect other data** suitable for finding averages.

Some suggestions are:
The shoe sizes of boys or girls in your class.
The number of pets kept by a sample of children.
The number of children in a sample of families.
The number of goals scored in football matches by home teams, compared with the number of goals scored by away teams.
The number of passengers in cars.
The number of customers entering a shop in 1-minute intervals, compared at different times of the day.
The heights of students in your year-group.
The times students spend on their homework.
The ages of cars in a car park. (Estimates based on the registration letter.)
The weekly amounts spent by students on snacks, sweets, drinks, etc.
The distances people travel to work.
The length of time of phone calls.
Guesses from people of the length of a line, the weight of an object or the number of sweets in a jar.

Practice test 12

1.   Find the mean, median, mode and range of these sets of data.

    1   15 9 10 14 9 15 14 7 11 9 8

    2   £16, £18, £19, £20, £21, £21, £21, £24.

[Turn over]

2.   6 cassette tapes have the following playing-times (in minutes):

80   64   60   76   78   74.

Find
1   the mean playing-time,
2   the median playing-time,
3   the range of the playing-times.

3.   The daily attendances at an exhibition open for 6 days were:

235, 330, 350, 549, 318, 684.

1   Find the mean daily attendance.
2   Find the median daily attendance.
3   Find the range of the daily attendances.

4.   In one week a motorist travelled these distances, in miles,

38, 37, 18, 164, 51, 62, 8.

1   Find the mean daily distance.
2   Find the median distance.
3   Find the range of the distances.
4   Which of the two averages do you think is the more useful one to use, and why ?

5.   In one group of children (group A) the marks in a test were:
2, 3, 4, 4, 5, 5, 5, 6, 7, 8.

In a second group (group B) the marks in the same test were:
3, 5, 5, 5, 6, 6, 6, 6, 7, 7.

1   Find the mean, median and mode of the marks of group A.
2   Find the mean, median and mode of the marks of group B.
3   Find the range of marks for each of the two groups.
4   Which group had the higher mean mark ?
5   Which group had the greater range of marks ?
6   Comment briefly on the differences between the marks in the two groups.

PUZZLES

18.   A shop sells one brand of chocolate bars which are priced at, small, 16p; medium, 23p and large 39p; and a second brand where the prices are, small, 17p; medium, 24p and large 40p. A customer buys some of these bars of chocolate and they cost him exactly £1. What does he buy ?

19. A Cross-figure

Across

1   Number of miles I can travel in 24 minutes at 60 mph.

3   Number of diagonals of a parallelogram.

4   Number of mm in 1 cm.

5   Three angles of a quadrilateral are 16°, 27° and 150°. What is the 4th angle ?

7   $\sqrt{\text{LXIV}}$

8   75% of (11 across) − 40% of (4 across)

9   $\left(1\frac{3}{4} - 1\frac{1}{3}\right) \times 7.2$

10 The base of a triangle, in cm, if its height is 8 cm and its area is 20 cm^2.

11 A is south-west of C, B is on a bearing of 273° from C. What is the size of angle ACB, in degrees ?

12 $1.8 \div 0.3$

13 Number of days in a leap year + number of degrees in the angles of a triangle − number of sides of a triangle.

15 $3^2 + 4^2 + 5^2$

16 If the numbers 4 to 12 are placed in a magic square so that each row, column and diagonal add up to 24, what is the number in the centre square ?

17 An article cost £1.80 less a discount of 15%. What was the discount, in pence ?

Copy this diagram and fill in the answers on your copy.

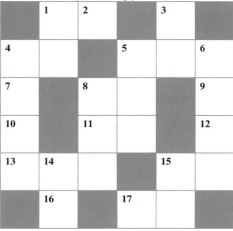

Down

1   If 5 pumps all working together can empty the water out of a tank in 36 minutes, how long would it take if there were 9 pumps working ?

2   A circular running-track has diameter 70 yards. How many times must an athlete run round it to run $\frac{1}{2}$ mile, to the nearest whole number ?

3   In a cuboid, number of faces + number of edges + number of vertices.

4   If 'THE LOVELY FIRE' is coded as 'pug cksgcz bang', decode 'puanpz-basg' and 'babpz-pungg' and write down their product.

5   The next number in the sequence 8, 16, 32, 64.

6   The number of metres in 8 km − the number of cm in 8 metres + the number of articles in 8 score.

8   One number in this sequence is incorrect. What should it be ?
1, 8, 27, 64, 125, 216, 333, 512, 729, 1000.

14 A lawn is 12 m long and 8 m wide. There is a path 1 m wide all the way round. How many metres of fencing would be needed to go all round the outer edge of the path ?

15 125 equal cubes are placed on the table to form a solid cube. The top and the four side faces of this large cube are then painted red. How many of the original cubes have just one face painted red ?

17 Write down any number less than 6. Double it and to the result add 2. Then square the total, subtract 4 and then divide by 4. Divide then by the number you started with, and finally subtract the number you started with. What is your answer ?

Miscellaneous Section B

Exercise B1 Aural Practice

If possible find someone to read these questions to you.
You should do the questions within 20 minutes.
Do not use your calculator.
Write down the answers only.

1. Pauline arrived at school at 12 minutes to 9. School begins at 5 minutes past 9. How many minutes early was she ?

2. Which is the larger fraction, one-third or one-fifth ?

3. Derek jogs $5\frac{1}{2}$ km every evening. How far does he jog altogether in 4 evenings ?

4. How many pieces of ribbon of length 50 cm can be cut from a piece 3 metres long ?

5. Approximately how many pounds are equivalent to 5 kg ?

6. What is the median of the numbers 6, 7, 9, 10, 10 ?

7. If 1 kg of a mixture costs 16 pence, what will 100 kg cost ?

8. Simplify the expression $4x + x$.

9. Three parcels weigh 6 kg, 7 kg and 11 kg. What is their average (mean) weight ?

10. If I face South and turn clockwise through 90°, in which direction am I then facing ?

11. Write down an expression for the number of grams in k kilograms.

12. If my digital clock shows the time as eighteen twelve, what time is it in the am/pm system ?

13. A water tank holding 36 litres of water lost one-quarter of it through a hole. How much was left ?

14. 4 cups of tea and a cake cost £1.80. If the cake cost 40 pence, what was the cost of a cup of tea ?

15. If 20 equal packages weigh 120 kg, what is the weight of 1 package ?

Additional aural questions using data from pages 444 to 447.

16.   Use diagram **2**.
       AB is 6 cm long. Estimate the length of *CD*.

17.   Use table **7**.
       How long is the 'Sports Today' programme ?

18.   Use the thermometer of diagram **8**.
       What is the approximate Celsius temperature equivalent to a temperature of
       80° Fahrenheit ?

19.   Use diagram **10**.
       Estimate the size of the largest angle in triangle *ABC*.

20.   Use table **14**.
       What is the total cost for 3 people to travel from Long Lane to Victoria Road ?

Exercise B2   Revision

1.   How many

      1   cm in 1 metre,   **5**   cm^3 in 1 litre,
      2   m in 1 km,   **6**   pence in £1,
      3   seconds in 1 minute,   **7**   mm in 1 metre,
      4   g in 1 kg,   **8**   minutes in 1 hour ?

2.   Change these mixed numbers to improper fractions.

      1 $4\frac{5}{6}$ **2** $7\frac{7}{10}$ **3** $9\frac{1}{11}$

      Change these improper fractions to mixed numbers.

      4 $\frac{37}{10}$ **5** $\frac{25}{8}$ **6** $\frac{55}{9}$

3.   This shows the reading when Bert had filled his car
      with some petrol.

      1   How many litres had he bought ?

      2   He paid for the petrol with a £20 note.
             How much change did he get ?

      3   What is the price per gallon, to the nearest
             penny, if 1 gallon = 4.546 litres ?

THIS SALE
£ 0 1 0 . 5 6
LITRES
0 2 0 . 0 0
PENCE PER LITRE
0 5 2 . 8

4. Calculate the sizes of the angles marked
    with small letters.

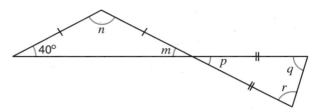

5. From this list of numbers:

    15 21 24 27 31 34 44 47 51 57

    1 Find the largest prime number.
    2 Find two numbers whose product is 765.
    3 Find two numbers whose sum is 104.
    4 Find two numbers which as numerator and denominator of a fraction reduce to $\frac{2}{3}$.
    5 Find two numbers which as numerator and denominator of a fraction simplify to 1.8.

6. $C = \dfrac{1000P}{V}$, where P is power in kilowatts, V is voltage in volts, C is current in amps.

    If the local voltage is 230 volts, what is the current for a 2 kW fire, to the nearest amp ?

7. Fence posts are 3 metres apart. If there are 3 strands of barbed wire nailed to each post,
    how much wire is needed to stretch between the first and the twentieth posts ?

8. The weights of 8 eggs were, in grams,

    47, 53, 53, 57, 48, 57, 55, 46.

    Find the mean and the range of the weights.

9. Copy and complete this number pattern to the line which begins 123456789.

    $0 \times 9 + 1 = \quad 1$
    $1 \times 9 + 2 = \quad 11$
    $12 \times 9 + 3 =$
    $123 \times 9 + 4 =$

10.   This is a timetable of the bus service on market days.

Picton Village	dep.	10.50
Renton Green	dep.	11.30
Suntown	arr.	12.15
Suntown	dep.	3.30
Renton Green	arr.	4.25
Picton Village	arr.	5.05

1   What is the time taken for the
     journey from Picton Village to Suntown ?

2   How much longer does the return journey take ?

3   Mrs Lloyd uses this service from Picton Village to visit her mother in Renton Green.
     How long can she spend with her mother, if her mother lives 10 minutes walk from
     the bus stop in Renton Green ?

Exercise B3   Revision

1.   Reduce these fractions to their simplest forms.

   1 $\frac{24}{88}$ **2** $\frac{60}{84}$ **3** $\frac{33}{132}$ **4** $\frac{26}{39}$ **5** $\frac{75}{200}$ **6** $\frac{11}{110}$

2.   Find the size of angle c.

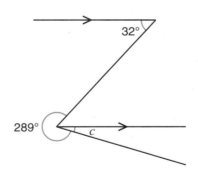

3.   A stallholder had 200 kg of potatoes to sell but $\frac{1}{4}$ were bad and $\frac{2}{5}$ of the remainder were
      too small for sale. What quantity were fit for sale ?

4.   Find the mean, the median and the mode of this set of numbers.

      1   2   2   2   5   7   8   10   14   17   20

5. Find the total cost of 4 kg of sugar at 67p per kg, $\frac{1}{4}$ kg of cheese at £4.68 per kg, $\frac{1}{2}$ kg of apples at 74p per kg and 2 dozen eggs at 42p for 6.
    How much change would there be from a £20 note ?

6. Find the next 2 numbers in these sequences.

    1 6, 13, 20, 27, 34, ...   **4** 4, 5, 8, 13, 20, ...
    2 21, 25, 29, 33, 37, ...   **5** 64, 32, 16, 8, 4, ...
    3 4, 20, 100, 500, 2500, ...

7. The arrows show the weights of two parcels, A and B.

    1 What are the weights of the two parcels ?

    2 How much heavier is parcel A than parcel B ?

    3 What is the total weight of the two parcels together ?

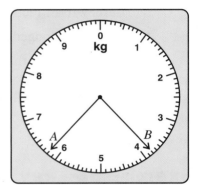

8. △ABC is an equilateral triangle.
    Find the sizes of angles a, b and d.

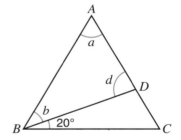

9. A newspaper advertisement to sell a car is charged at £1.80 per line, with a minimum charge of £5.40.

    1 What is the cost of an advert which takes 5 lines ?
    2 Mrs Barker decided to sell her car. The advert cost her £14.40. How many lines long was it ?

10. Imagine that you decide to do a statistical investigation about pocket money of young children. For example, you might like to find out how much pocket money they get, what it is spent on, and whether any is regularly saved in a savings account.
    Write a brief questionnaire (about 4 to 8 questions) which you could use to give you suitable information.

Exercise B4   Activities

1.   **Planning for a wedding**

This is a most important occasion in a couple's life and it deserves proper planning.
You can imagine it is your own wedding in a few years' time or the wedding of
imaginary friends.

Decide what type of wedding. Church, other place of worship, Registry Office ? It can be
a very simple wedding with just two witnesses or a very grand one. Plan all the details of
the wedding, and make a list of costs involved, with a separate note of who pays for
each. Traditionally the bride's father paid for most things but that is not always the case
nowadays. There are many small details to include, for instance, transport to the
wedding, legal costs, wedding ring or rings.

Plan the timetable for the day, so that the ceremony begins on time, and the couple leave
for their honeymoon on time, especially if they have a train or plane to catch.

Illustrate your booklet with pictures, e.g. of the bride's dress.

2.   **History of measurement**

It is interesting to find out about the measures which were used long ago in Britain. Land
is still measured in acres. An acre is the area of land that could be ploughed in a day, in
the days when oxen were used for ploughing.

If you have an interest in another country, maybe you could find out about how its
system of measurement developed.
In France at the time of the Revolution, the old measures were abolished and the Metric
System adopted. This is now used worldwide for scientific work and is being introduced
gradually into Britain.

You could make a topic booklet about measurement. You could include weights as well.
You could also find out about the measurement of time, and about coinage, or these
could be separate topics.

3. **'Casting out nines'**

This is an extra check for a multiplication or addition sum. It is not a foolproof check but it will often indicate an error, and it is an interesting method to learn.

First, we must learn how to reduce a number to a 1-figure number by adding its digits, and if necessary adding again.

e.g.   for $5813 \rightarrow 5 + 8 + 1 + 3 = 17 \rightarrow 1 + 7 = 8$
          $492567 \rightarrow 4 + 9 + 2 + 5 + 6 + 7 = 33 \rightarrow 3 + 3 = 6$

To save time, any 9 or figures which add up to 9 can be crossed out first without affecting the result, as long as we leave the last 9 if there is no other number, so as not to be left with nothing.

e.g. for 5813, cross out 8 and 1 which make 9.
$5813 \rightarrow 5 + 3 = 8$, (or we could have crossed out 5 and 3 and 1 instead, leaving 8).

492567. Cross out 9, 4 and 5, 2 and 7, leaving 6.

918. Cross out 9, **or** 1 and 8, but not both, leaving 9, because we do not want to be left with 0.

Now, to check multiplication,   e.g. $5813 \times 1967 = 11634171$
                                                    $\downarrow$ $\downarrow$ $\downarrow$
Reduce the numbers to single figures.   8   5   6
Make a cross.

Put the two figures of the question in a and b.
Put the answer figure in c.
Multiply the figures in a and b, reduce this answer and put it in d.

$8 \times 5 = 40 \rightarrow 4 + 0 = 4$

If the numbers in c and d are not the same, as here, the answer is wrong.
It should have been 11434171, so $c = 4$.
This gives

and here $c = d$, so the answer satisfies the check. (However this does not definitely prove that the answer is correct, as other answers could also satisfy the check.)

Practise using this method by checking the answers to these multiplication questions. If the check shows that an answer is incorrect, find the correct answer and check that also.

1 $568 \times 24 = 13\,642$ **4** $509 \times 17 = 8553$
2 $1734 \times 72 = 124\,848$ **5** $187 \times 56 = 10\,472$
3 $331 \times 85 = 28\,035$

How can this method be used to check addition?

4. **Triangular numbers**

1, 3, 6, 10, 15, ...

1   3   6   10   15

1 Copy down the sequence and continue it up to the 25th triangular number.

2 What can you discover about the triangular numbers 3, 10 and 15?

$3 + 10 + 15 =$
$3 \times 10 + 15 =$
$3 \times 15 + 10 =$
$10 \times 15 + 3 =$
$3 \times 10 + 3 \times 15 + 10 \times 15 =$

3 What can you discover about the sum of two consecutive triangular numbers?

$1 + 3 =$
$3 + 6 =$
$6 + 10 =$
...

4 What can you discover about the squares of consecutive triangular numbers?

$1^2 + 3^2 \;=$ and $3^2 - 1^2 =$
$3^2 + 6^2 \;=$ $6^2 - 3^2 =$
$6^2 + 10^2 =$ $10^2 - 6^2 =$
...   ...

5. **Make your own Maths Magazine**

Or at least, issue No. 1. for a beginning.

Do not be too ambitious. Use a plain sheet of A4 paper and fold it down the middle to make a leaflet.
On the first page you need a title in the top half, and then an article or a puzzle.
On the next three pages you need further articles, puzzles, cartoons or jokes.
You could make up a Maths cross-figure, similar to a crossword but with numbers instead of words for the answers. Articles could be about something you have learnt recently, or you could use library books to find out about great Mathematicians and their discoveries. You could describe how to do paper folding or how to make Maths models.

Try to keep some variety in your magazine. Keep your writing neat and perhaps use plenty of colour, unless you intend to make photocopies, when you should use dark colours only.

You could have a display in your class if you all made magazines.

6. **Estimation**

It is useful to be able to make good estimates of weights and measurements. Here are some suggestions to improve your skill. You should think of others.

Lengths. Find out the measurements of your thumb as far as the knuckle, the width of your hand across four fingers, the length of your hand-span, the length of your foot with a shoe on, your height, the distance you can reach with arms stretched out, the height you can reach on tiptoe, and so on. Use a measured distance of 100 m to find the length of your pace when you walk normally, and how long your stride is. Practise estimating distances by comparing them with these lengths.

Time. See how many times you take a breath normally, in 1 minute, and then practise estimating 1 minute by counting your breathing.

Weight. Get used to the weight of 1 kg (a bag of sugar) and 2.5 kg (a bag of potatoes). Find your own weight in kg and the weight of a small child. Estimate other weights by comparing them with these known weights.

Capacity. Estimate how much water various containers hold and check by using a measuring jug, a litre bottle (or a pint bottle for British measures). A bucket or a watering can may have measuring lines marked on it. It is useful to remember that 1 litre of water weighs 1 kg. In British measures 1 gallon of water weighs 10 lb.

Area. Find the area of a local football pitch and compare other large areas with that. For smaller areas, compare with $1 \, m^2$ or $1 \, cm^2$.

Angles. Practise drawing an angle of 45° by eye by imagining a right angle cut in half. Then practise making angles of 30° and 60° by splitting a right angle into 3 equal parts. Practise guessing the sizes of angles, then check with your protractor.

7. **Curves of pursuit**

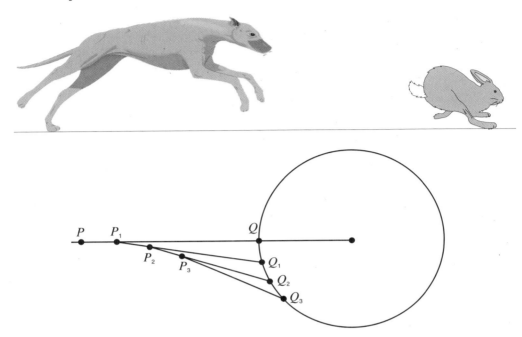

Example

A dog at P chases a rabbit at Q, which is running along a circular track.

Mark PQ to represent the dog's intended path.
The rabbit runs to Q_1 whilst the dog reaches P_1.
Mark P_1Q_1 which is the dog's new direction.
In the next interval the rabbit reaches Q_2 and the dog reaches P_2, and so on.

Decide on their speeds, e.g. represent the dog's speed by 1 cm so that
$PP_1 = P_1P_2 = P_2P_3 = \cdots = 1$ cm.
If you want the rabbit to be slower choose a length such as 0.7 cm. Mark
$QQ_1 = Q_1Q_2 = Q_2Q_3 = \cdots = 0.7$ cm, using compasses to mark off the distances along
the circle.

When the rabbit is caught, or the dog gives up the chase, go over $PP_1, P_1P_2, P_2P_3, \ldots$ in
colour as this is the curve of pursuit.

What happens if
(1)   the dog goes faster, or slower,
(2)   the rabbit starts from a different part of the circle,
(3)   the dog starts nearer to the circle,
(4)   the rabbit runs along a line instead of a circle ?

Try the curve of pursuit for 3 dogs A, B, C starting from the 3 corners of an equilateral
triangle with equal speeds, if A is chasing B, B is chasing C and C is chasing A.

Make up some other investigations for yourself.

8. **The cost of keeping a pet**

Make a survey of your friends and relatives to find out the sort of pets people have. You could also work out the average number of pets per family. Then ask these people about the costs of keeping their various pets. Here are some of the costs to consider:

Somewhere for the pet to live—hutch, cage, fish tank, stable.
Weekly food bill, including different sorts of food for a healthy diet.
Costs of cleaning out—cat litter, sawdust for cage, straw for stable.
Necessary Vet's bills, for inoculations, etc.
Unexpected Vet's bills, an average cost of treatment for illnesses.
Insurance, and any other costs.

You could also make a survey asking people what sort of pet they would like to own.

You could also ask about the amount of time people spend each week on looking after their pets, from the goldfish which needs very little attention to the dog or pony which needs regular exercise.

PUZZLES

20. If $1000 + 1 + 50 + 500$ spells **MILD**, what does $100 + 1 + 5 + 1 + 50$ spell ?

21. What is the next symbol in this sequence ?

22. Alan, Bob and Charles are allowed to pick apples in an orchard. Alan picks 7 sackfuls containing 16 kg each, Bob picks 7 sackfuls containing 14 kg each, Charles has smaller sacks and he picks 10 sackfuls holding 9 kg each. They had agreed beforehand that they would share the fruit equally. How can they do this without opening any of the sacks ?

To the student : 3

Improving your work

Check your handwriting and if necessary, improve it. It must be legible even when you are working quickly. Badly written work means that you confuse 6 with 0 or *b*, 2 with *z*, 5 with *s*, and so on. Show minus signs clearly. Do not alter figures, e.g. a 2 into a 3, by overwriting. Cross the 2 out and write the 3 nearby. Do not change + into − except by crossing it out and re-writing clearly. + which might mean either + or − cannot be marked as correct because you have not made it clear which it is. Altered figures which are not clear cannot be marked as correct. So always make clear alterations.

Try to work at a reasonable speed. If you tend to work slowly, try to speed up, because in an examination you must give yourself a reasonable chance of completing the paper to gain good marks. When you are doing a question, concentrate completely on it so that you immediately think about the method, start it quickly, and continue working it out without a pause until you finish it. Work out any simple arithmetic in your head so that you do not break your concentration, and waste time, by pressing calculator keys. (You could do a check later, using the calculator, if you want to.)

Make sure that you use brackets correctly. $180 - 30 + 40$ is not the same as $180 - (30 + 40)$. The first expression equals 190, the second one equals 110. Be careful when you work out algebraic expressions or equations, especially those involving brackets.

Sketch diagrams, or rough plans of what you are going to do, are very useful even if they are not required as part of the answer.

When you have found an answer, consider if it is reasonable, especially if you have pressed calculator keys to get it. Look at the relative sizes of lengths or angles on the diagram, which should give a general idea even if the diagram is not drawn to an exact scale. A man earning £12 000 per year would not pay £30 000 per year in tax ! If a triangle has an angle of over 90°, then a second angle cannot also be over 90°. (Why ?) If the answer to a simple question is an awkward number such as $3\frac{10}{71}$, this **could** be correct, but it is more likely that you have made a mistake.
When you have found an answer, give it correct to a suitable degree of accuracy, e.g. to the nearest whole number, and do not forget the units, e.g. £, cm, m^2, kg, where necessary.

13 Percentages

The topics in this chapter include:

- understanding and using percentages,
- understanding and using the equivalences between decimals or fractions and percentages,
- calculating percentages of quantities,
- finding one number as a percentage of another,
- working out percentage changes and related calculations.

Percentages

'Per cent' means 'per hundred', so 17% means $\dfrac{17}{100}$ or 0.17.

Examples

1   Express 45% as a fraction.

$$45\% = \frac{45}{100} = \tfrac{9}{20}$$

2   Express 63% as a decimal.

$$63\% = \frac{63}{100} = 0.63$$

To change a fraction or decimal to a percentage

Multiply the fraction or decimal by 100 and write the % sign.

Examples

3    $\dfrac{2}{5} = \dfrac{2}{5} \times 100\% = \dfrac{200}{5}\% = 40\%$

4    $0.57 = 0.57 \times 100\% = 57\%$

It is useful to learn the percentages corresponding to simple fractions or decimals.

Fraction	Decimal	Percentage
$\frac{3}{4}$	0.75	75%
$\frac{1}{2}$	0.5	50%
$\frac{1}{4}$	0.25	25%
$\frac{1}{5}$	0.2	20%
$\frac{1}{10}$	0.1	10%
$\frac{1}{100}$	0.01	1%

Also, $33\frac{1}{3}\%$ is equivalent to the fraction $\frac{1}{3}$, and $66\frac{2}{3}\%$ is equivalent to the fraction $\frac{2}{3}$.

To find a percentage of a sum of money

Change the percentage into a fraction, if it is a simple fraction such as $\frac{1}{2}$, $\frac{1}{4}$, $\frac{1}{5}$, $\frac{1}{10}$, $\frac{1}{20}$, or change it into a decimal and use your calculator.

Examples

5   Find 20% of £360.

$20\% = \dfrac{20}{100} = \frac{1}{5}$, so find $\frac{1}{5}$ of £360.

$\frac{1}{5}$ of £360 = £72.

6   Find 27% of £250.

27% is 0.27 so find $0.27 \times £250$.
$0.27 \times £250 = £0.27 \times 250 = £67.50$

Use a similar method to find a percentage of a quantity.

Example

7   Find 24% of 60 cm.

24% is 0.24 so find 0.24×60 cm, which is 14.4 cm.

To find one quantity as a percentage of another

Example

8   What percentage is 34 g of 2 kg ?

(First find what fraction 34 g is of 2 kg, then change this fraction to a percentage.)

$\dfrac{34\,\text{g}}{2\,\text{kg}} = \dfrac{34\,\text{g}}{2000\,\text{g}} = \dfrac{34}{2000} \times 100\% = 1.7\%$

Exercise 13.1

1. Express these percentages as fractions in their simplest forms.

   1 30%   **2** 35%   **3** 15%   **4** 40%   **5** 60%

2. Express as decimals.

   1 47%   **2** 95%   **3** 22%   **4** 6%   **5** 99%

3. Change these fractions or decimals to percentages.

   1 $\frac{3}{4}$ **2** $\frac{4}{5}$ **3** 0.15   **4** $\frac{7}{10}$ **5** 0.87

4. **1** Find 72% of £5.   **4** Find 75% of £3.20.

   2 Find 80% of 75p.   **5** Find 20% of 65p.

   3 Find 15% of £4.20.

5. **1** Find 48% of 200.   **4** Find 10% of 50 cm.

   2 Find 30% of 400 g.   **5** Find 62% of 50 litres.

   3 Find 5% of 40 minutes.

6. Find what percentage the 1st quantity is of the 2nd.

   1 £3.60, £5.00.   **4** 750 g, 2 kg.
   2 16 cm, 2 m.   **5** 50p, 75p.
   3 36 minutes, 1 hour.

7. In a school, pupils can learn either French or German or Spanish. In a year group of 150 pupils, 50% of the pupils learn French and 40% learn German.

   1 What percentage learn Spanish ?
   2 How many pupils learn each language ?
   3 If there are 25 pupils in each French class, 20 pupils in each German class and just 1 class for Spanish, how many classes are there altogether ?

Increase or decrease by a percentage

Examples

1 Increase £50 by 15%.

Find 15% of £50, which is £0.15 × 50 = £7.50.
Add this to the original £50, making £57.50.

Alternative method

The new amount will be $(100 + 15)$%, i.e. 115% of £50.
115% of £50 = £1.15 × 50 = £57.50

2   Decrease £900 by 12%.

Find 12% of £900, which is £0.12 × 900 = £108.
Subtract this from the original £900, leaving £792.

Alternative method

The new amount will be (100 − 12)%, i.e. 88% of £900.
88% of £900 = £0.88 × 900 = £792

Profit and Loss

Examples

3   A dealer buys an article for £60 and wants to make a profit of 25% on it. What price must he sell it for ?

$25\% = \dfrac{25}{100} = \frac{1}{4}$, so he wants to make $\frac{1}{4}$ of £60 profit.

$\frac{1}{4}$ of £60 is £15 so he adds £15 onto the cost price of £60.
He sells it for £75.

4   A car salesman buys a car for £480 and has to sell it making a loss of 5%. How much does he sell it for ?

$5\% = \dfrac{5}{100} = \frac{1}{20}$ so he loses $\frac{1}{20}$ of £480.

$\frac{1}{20}$ of £480 (or 0.05 × £480) = £24 so he loses £24.
He sells it for £(480 − 24) = £456.

5   A shopkeeper buys a vase for £75 and sells it for £90. What is his percentage profit ?

Percentage profit is always based on the cost price, unless otherwise stated.
Here the profit is £15 on a cost price of £75.

$\% \text{ profit} = \dfrac{15}{75} \times 100\% = 20\%$

6   A trader bought a clock for £150 and sold it for £129.
What was his percentage loss ?

Percentage loss is always based on the cost price, unless otherwise stated.
Here the loss is £21 on a cost price of £150.

$\% \text{ loss} = \dfrac{21}{150} \times 100\% = 14\%$

Exercise 13.2

1. **1** Increase £6 by 4%.

    2 Increase £2.60 by 15%.

    3 Decrease £120 by 10%.

    4 Decrease £75 by 20%.

    5 Increase £300 by 12%.

2. **1** Find the selling price of a toy which cost £4.50 to make, and is sold making a profit of 20%.

    2 Find the selling price of a book which was bought for £4 and sold making a loss of 25%.

    3 Find the selling price of a car which was bought for £800 and sold making a profit of 12%.

    4 Find the selling price of some furniture which a dealer bought for £600 and had to sell making a loss of 12%.

    5 William bought a bike for £40. Later on he sold it, making a gain of 5%. How much money did he gain on the sale ?

3. **1** Find the percentage profit if an article costing £2.50 to make is sold for £3.

    2 Find the percentage loss if an article costing £3 is sold for £2.50.

    3 Find the percentage profit if a picture is bought for £800 and sold for £980.

    4 Find the percentage loss if a computer which cost £600 is sold for £480.

    5 A restaurant bill for £15 became £16.80 after a service charge was added. What was the percentage rate of the service charge ?

4. **1** A dealer bought a table for £1200 and made 40% profit when he sold it. What price did he sell it for ?

    2 To clear goods during a sale a shopkeeper reduced the prices by 10%. What would you pay for a vase previously priced at £3.60 ?

    3 A bottle of shampoo normally holds 300 ml of liquid. A special bottle marked '10% extra' is put on sale. What quantity should it hold ?

    4 Miss Scott earned £9000, then she was given an 8% pay-rise. What was her new salary ?

    5 A meal in a restaurant cost £15. To this a service charge of 10% was added. What was the total cost ?

Value Added Tax (VAT)

This tax is added to the cost of many things you buy. In most shops the price marked includes the tax so you do not have to calculate it.

Occasionally, however, the prices are given without VAT and it has to be added to the bill.

The present rate of this tax is $17\frac{1}{2}\%$ so to find the amount added on for VAT, multiply the original price by 0.175.

The final price is $117\frac{1}{2}\%$ of the original price. To find the final price, multiply the original price by 1.175.

Example

1   A builder says he will charge £80 for doing a small job. To this, VAT at $17\frac{1}{2}\%$ is added. What is the total cost ?

The VAT is $17\frac{1}{2}\%$ of £80.
This is £0.175 × 80 = £14.
The total cost is £80 + £14 = £94.

Alternatively, you can find the total cost by multiplying the original price by 1.175.
The original price is £80.
The total cost is £1.175 × 80 = £94.

The rate of tax might be changed. If it has, work out this example using the up-to-date rate.

Interest

If you invest money, this money earns money which is called **interest**. e.g. If you invested money in a Building Society which was paying interest at 8% (per year), then for every £100 invested you would get £8 every year your money was invested.

With **Simple Interest**, the interest is paid out each year, not added to the investment.

Example

2   If £600 is invested at 8% per annum for 4 years, what is the Simple Interest ?
     ('per annum' means 'for a year'. It is sometimes abbreviated to 'p.a.')

Every £100 invested gains £8 interest per year.
So £600 invested gains £48 interest per year.
£600 invested for 4 years gains £48 × 4 = £192.
The Simple Interest is £192.

This can also be worked out using the formula

$$I = \frac{PRT}{100}$$ where I is the Simple Interest
                         P is the Principal, (the money invested)
                         R is the rate per cent (per annum)
                         T is the time (in years)

In this example, $P = £600$, $R = 8$, $T = 4$.

$$I = \frac{PRT}{100} = £\frac{600 \times 8 \times 4}{100} = £192.$$

Loans

If you borrow money then you probably have to pay interest on the loan. Usually you agree
to make repayments at so much per month or per week and these amounts include the interest,
so that you pay back more than you borrowed. The sooner you repay a loan the less the
interest will be. The bank, finance company or other lender must tell you the true rate of
interest. In advertisements look for the letters APR (Annual Percentage Rate), for instance
APR 24.6% means that you will pay at that rate of interest over the period of the loan. It
might be possible to find another source from which you could borrow money at a cheaper
rate of interest.

Using a calculator

There may be a % key on your calculator, but unless you use it a great deal for the different
kinds of percentage calculations so that you know exactly what you are doing, it may be safer
to stick to the methods shown here, rather than use this key.
If you do want to use the % key, find out from your instruction booklet how to use it in the
different types of calculations. Always make a rough estimate to see if the answer seems
correct.

Exercise 13.3

1. Find the VAT, at $17\frac{1}{2}$%, which must be added to these costs, and then find the total cost of each item.

   1 A self-catering holiday cottage costs £360 + VAT.
   2 A plumber charges £32 + VAT.
   3 Goods at a wholesale warehouse cost £124 + VAT.
   4 The phone bill is £78 + VAT.
   5 A builder charges £890 + VAT.

2. Mr Parmar buys some DIY materials marked £24. VAT at $17\frac{1}{2}$% is added to this price. What is the total cost, including the tax?

3. Mrs Evans wants to borrow some money to finance a special project. Four firms are willing to lend her the money.

   1 Which firm charges the cheapest rate of interest?

   2 Which firm charges the dearest rate of interest?

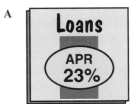

4. How much interest must be paid each year on the following loans?

   1 Loan £1500, interest 12% p.a.
   2 Loan £600, interest 10% p.a.
   3 Loan £240, interest 7% p.a.

5. Find the Simple Interest if

   1 £250 is invested for 3 years at 8% per annum,
   2 £600 is invested for 4 years at 11% p.a.,
   3 £840 is invested for 2 years at 10% p.a.

Exercise 13.4   Applications

1. A car insurance premium is £450 but there is a deduction of 60% of this for 'no claims discount'. How much is deducted, and how much remains to be paid?

2. A grocer bought 10 cases of tinned fruit at £7.50 per case, each case containing 24 tins. He sold 200 tins at 42p each but the remainder were damaged and unfit for sale. Find his percentage profit.

3. If £1000 is invested at 9% per annum, find the interest paid at the end of the first year. If the interest is added to the money invested, find the interest which will be paid at the end of the second year.
   What is the total interest paid for the 2 years ?

4. Machinery which cost £5600 when new was reduced in value by 20% in its first year and by 10% in the second year.

   1 How much did it lose in value in the first year ?
   2 What was its value after 1 year ?
   3 How much did it lose in value in the second year ?
   4 What was its value after 2 years ?

5. A house was valued at £42 000. During the next year, due to a rise in house prices, its value increased by 10%. In the second year its value increased over the year by 8%. What was the house worth at the end of the 2 years ?

6. Here is an advertisement for a loan.

   | Secured Loans Weekly Equivalent Payments | | | | e.g. £8250 over 5 yrs = £227.98 per month. |
LOAN	10 yrs	$7\frac{1}{2}$ yrs	5 yrs	Total cost of repayment = £13 678.80.
£2250	£10.52	£11.69	£14.34	APR 22.4% variable.
£3200	£14.96	£16.63	£20.40	Total cost greatly reduced on early
£5500	£25.71	£28.58	£34.89	settlement.

   1 What does the advertisement quote for the annual percentage rate of interest ?

   Mr Parker wishes to borrow £3200 to buy a car and he decides he can afford to repay about £15 per week.

   2 For how long will he take out the loan ?
   3 What will the total payment be ?
   4 Instead of this, he thinks he ought to pay more weekly, so as to repay the loan in 5 years. How much extra per week will this cost him, and what will the total payment be in this case ?

7. Copy and complete this phone bill.

Call charges	£52.16
Line rental	£20.24
Subtotal excluding VAT	
VAT at 17.5%	
Total amount now due	

Practice test 13

1. **1** Write down the percentages equivalent to these fractions.

    $\frac{1}{2}$, $\frac{1}{4}$, $\frac{1}{5}$, $\frac{1}{10}$, $\frac{1}{20}$, $\frac{1}{100}$.

    2 Write down the fractions equivalent to these percentages.

    30%, $33\frac{1}{3}$%, 40%, $66\frac{2}{3}$%, 75%.

2. What is 450 g as a percentage of 1.25 kg ?

3. In an election 40 000 people voted. Of the 3 candidates A, B, C; A got 25% of the votes, B got 35% and C got the rest.

    1 What percentage of votes did C get ?
    2 Who won the election ?
    3 How many votes did the winner get ?

4. Mr Turner buys this car and is allowed a discount of 5%.

    1 What discount does he get ?

    2 What does he actually pay for the car ?

5. Debbie knits a jumper from 12 balls of wool costing 60p per ball. In addition the pattern costs 30p. She sells the jumper for £12. What is the percentage profit on her outlay ?

6. One firm will lend £800 at 10% per annum Simple Interest while another will lend it at 9% per annum Simple Interest. If the money is needed for 2 years, how much cheaper would it be to borrow from the second firm ?

PUZZLES

23. Mine cost 52p, my neighbour's cost 26p and I got some for my friend who lives at the far end of the road, and they cost 78p. What was I buying in the hardware shop ?

24. If it takes a clock 6 seconds to strike 6, how long does it take to strike 12 ?

25. A farmer has 70 m of fencing available and he wants to enclose a rectangular area of 300 m^2. What measurements will his rectangle have ?

14 Probability (1)

> **The topics in this chapter include:**
>
> - understanding and using simple vocabulary of probability,
> - using a probability line and ordering the likelihood of events,
> - giving and justifying an estimate of probability,
> - recognising situations where estimates must be based on experimental evidence, and making these estimates,
> - understanding and using relative frequency as an estimate of probability.

Probability

Probability or chance is the likelihood of an event happening.

A probability line

We can mark the probability on a probability line.
At one end there is the probability that the event cannot possibly happen, at the other end there is the probability that the event is certain to happen.
Other events can be unlikely to happen, or likely to happen.

If there is an even chance of an event happening this means that it is just as likely to happen as not to happen, e.g. if you toss a coin fairly it is equally likely to show heads or tails, so there is an even chance of it showing heads. This is sometimes called a fifty-fifty chance.

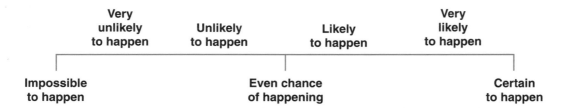

There are many times in life when we have to estimate the probability or chance of something happening.

Exercise 14.1

1.   Here are some statements. For each one, decide how likely it is to happen and give the probability as impossible, very unlikely, unlikely, an even chance, likely, very likely or certain to happen.

   1   You will travel to Australia this year.
   2   On tossing a coin 3 times you will get at least one head.
   3   You will get an odd number when you throw a fair die.
   4   There will be a thunderstorm locally, during the next week.
   5   On choosing a card from a pack of playing cards, it will be a picture card (Jack, Queen or King) or an Ace.
   6   You will eat some crisps tomorrow.
   7   Soon you will meet a man who has been to the planet Mars.
   8   It will go dark tonight.
   9   On choosing a card from a pack of cards, it will be a heart or a diamond.
   10   You will watch television tonight.

2.   Name an event, not mentioned in question 1, which is
   1   impossible or very unlikely to happen,
   2   certain or very likely to happen,
   3   more likely than unlikely to happen,
   4   more unlikely than likely to happen,
   5   just as likely to happen as not to happen.

A numerical scale

We can measure probability on a numerical scale from 0 to 1, and it can be given as a fraction, a decimal or a percentage.

A probability of 0 means that there is no chance of the event happening.
A probability of 1 means that it is certain that the event will happen.
A probability of $\frac{1}{2}$ means that there is a 50–50 chance of the event happening. In the long run, $\frac{1}{2}$ of the trials will give successful results.
A probability of $\frac{2}{3}$ means that in the long run $\frac{2}{3}$ of the trials will give successful results.
The nearer the value of the probability is to 1, the more chance there is of a successful outcome.
The nearer the value of the probability is to 0, the less chance there is of a successful outcome.

Example

What is the probability that this year there will be a
White Christmas ?
(This means that there will be snow on Christmas Day.)

Now if you live in Northern Canada, you might estimate the
probability as 1 (certain to happen), and if you live in the
Sahara Desert you might estimate the probability as 0 (certain
not to happen).
If you live in Southern England, and there has never been
snow on Christmas Day for many years, you may think that
there is a very slight chance, and estimate the probability as
0.1, or 0.05.
If you live in the Scottish Highlands, and most years there
has been snow, you might estimate the probability as 0.8, 0.9
or 0.95.
For other parts of Britain you might make estimates at some
other point on the probability scale. If you think there is an even
chance, the probability will be 0.5. If it is more likely to snow
than not, the probability will be over 0.5. And so on ...

Some people may have a bet on an outcome such as this. For other people, the result is more
serious. Shepherds have to make sure the sheep are safe. Transport authorities have to keep
their vehicles running, and people planning journeys may have to change their plans.

Exercise 14.2

1.   Here are some statements. Some of them may not apply to you, or they may be
       certainties. Choose 5 statements from the rest and put them in order of likelihood. Then
       decide which probabilities are less than 0.5 and which are greater than 0.5. Finally, give
       estimated probabilities for them.

       (a)   Tomorrow will be wet.
       (b)   You will give some useful help at home this evening.
       (c)   You will be late for school/college one day next week.
       (d)   You will go to the cinema next weekend.
       (e)   During the next fortnight, you will get some new clothes.
       (f)   During the next month, you will win a prize in a competition.
       (g)   For your next holiday you will go to the USA.
       (h)   When you take GCSE Maths you will achieve a satisfactory result.
       (i)   Next year, you will continue your education (at school or college).
       (j)   When you take your driving test, you will pass at the first attempt.
       (k)   Make up your own statement.

2.   Draw a probability line from 0 to 1. Mark on it points labelled *A*, *B*, *C*, *D*, *E*, to show the estimated probabilities of these events happening during the next week.

   A   You will travel somewhere on a bus or a train.
   B   You will watch a sports match or take part in one.
   C   You will be absent from school/college because of illness.
   D   There will be a foggy morning.
   E   The car registration number on the next car you see passing your house will be an odd number.

When we know the probability of an event happening we can use its value to predict the likelihood of a future result. That is why Probability is linked to Statistics. Government departments, business firms, industrialists, scientists, medical researchers and many other people and organisations use the figures from past events to predict what is likely to happen in the future, and thus they can plan ahead. For example, insurance companies use their knowledge of past claims to predict future ones, and they can then decide what premiums they must charge. If you want to gamble on a sporting event it is useful to estimate the probability of winning. You might then realise that you are unlikely to win in the long run and decide not to waste your money on the bet.

You learn about probability by doing simple experiments with coins, dice, cards, etc. but probability is an important subject, and affects all our lives.

Relative frequency

If we have trials with different outcomes, some of which are successful, then

the relative frequency of a successful outcome $= \dfrac{\text{number of successful outcomes}}{\text{total number of trials}}$.

The relative frequency gives an estimate of the probability of a successful outcome.

Example

There are a number of beads in a bag, some red and some blue. To find the probability of picking a red bead out if picking a bead at random, a large number of trials are made. A bead is picked out, its colour noted, and the bead is replaced. This experiment is repeated 1000 times altogether, and the number of red beads noted was 596.

So, the probability of a red bead $= \dfrac{\text{number of trials giving a red bead}}{\text{total number of trials}}$

$= \dfrac{596}{1000} = 0.60$, to 2 dec. pl.

We can only use this method for **estimating probability** if we do enough trials to show that the fraction is settling down to a steady value. Some events are completely unpredictable and in those cases the fraction would not settle down and we could not find a value for the probability.

Exercise 14.3 includes suggestions for experiments.

All the trials should be done randomly and fairly. Toss a coin properly. Give a die (dice) a good shake before rolling it out onto a flat surface. Shuffle a pack of cards properly and for most experiments you should take out the jokers first so that the pack contains the 52 cards of the 4 suits. If you have not got proper equipment it is often possible to think of a substitute. If you can combine other people's results with yours to give more trials, do so. Keep a record of your results to use again later.

If you compare your results with another person's, you will probably find that the outcomes are different, but for a large number of trials the final estimates for probability should be similar.

Using random numbers to simulate results

Instead of actually doing the experiments, you may prefer to use a graphics calculator or a computer to produce random numbers.
To simulate the throwing of a die, on the graphics calculator, press

$$\boxed{\text{Int}}\ \boxed{(}\ \boxed{\text{Ran\#}}\ \boxed{\times}\ \boxed{6}\ \boxed{+}\ 1\ \boxed{)}\ \boxed{\text{EXE}}\ \boxed{\text{EXE}}\ \boxed{\text{EXE}}\ \dots$$

and you will get a sequence of random numbers between 1 and 6. By changing 6 into 2 in the instructions, you will get a sequence of 1's or 2's which you can use as the results of tossing coins, with 1 for heads and 2 for tails.

You can produce similar results on a computer using a simple program.
However, you may have commercial computer programs available which will do these and other simulated experiments.

Exercise 14.3

1.   Toss a coin 200 times. Record your results in order, in a grid of 10 columns by 20 rows.
     Put H for head and T for tail.
     The grid starts like this:

H	H	T	H	T	T	H			

Before you begin, estimate how many heads you are likely
to get.

Make a table similar to this one and fill it in.

Number of tosses (n)	Number of heads (h)	Fraction $\dfrac{h}{n}$	$\dfrac{h}{n}$ to 2 decimal places
1			
2			
3			
4			
5			
10			
20			
50			
100			
150			
200			

Is $\dfrac{h}{n}$ settling down to a steady value ? If so, this gives the estimated probability of a toss
of a coin showing a head.
The value from 200 tosses gives the most reliable estimate, as it involves most trials.
From your results, what is the estimated probability of a toss showing a head ?

Keep a record of your results for the estimated probability in questions 1, 2, 3, 6 and 7, to
compare them with the theoretical probabilities, explained in Chapter 22.

2.   Instead of tossing coins again, use the results of question 1 in pairs, as if you had tossed two coins together, so that the possible results are HH, HT, TH, TT. If you had 200 single results you will have 100 results for pairs. Count the number of heads in each pair and put your results on a tally chart. Before you begin estimate how many of each you will get.

Heads	Tally marks	Frequency (f)
0		
1		
2		
		100

What is the most likely result ?
What are your estimates for the probabilities of 0 heads, 1 head, 2 heads ?

3.   Throw a die 400 times. Record the number which lands face upwards, in a grid of 20 columns by 20 rows.
If the total number of throws is n and the number of sixes is s,
find the fraction $\dfrac{s}{n}$, to 2 decimal places.
This gives the estimated probability of a throw showing a six.
Work out the probabilities of getting the other numbers, 1 to 5.
Is the die a fair one ?

4.   Put 10 similar drawing-pins into a cup and holding it approximately 20 cm above a table, gently tip the drawing-pins out so they land on the table. They come to rest point upwards, like this ⊥, or on their side, like this ⋋. Count and record how many land point upwards. Repeat the experiment 50 times.

If the total number of drawing-pins tipped out is n, and the number which rest point upwards is s, find the fraction $\dfrac{s}{n}$, to 2 decimal places, after 5, 10, 20, 30, 40 and 50 repetitions.
If the results are settling down to a certain value this gives the value of the probability that a drawing-pin in this type of experiment will land point upwards. (There is no theoretical way of checking this result.)

The height through which the drawing-pins fall may affect the result. You could investigate this by repeating the experiment from different heights. Different makes of drawing-pins may also give different results.

5.   Shuffle a pack of cards and pick out 3 cards.
      Record as P if they contain at least one
      picture-card (i.e. Jack, Queen or King).
      Record as N if there is no picture card.
      Replace the cards, shuffle and repeat
      100 times altogether.
      Before you begin, estimate how many times
      P will occur.

      Find the fraction $\dfrac{\text{number of times P occurs}}{\text{total number of trials}}$

      as a decimal to 2 decimal places.
      From your results, what value would you give
      for the probability that of three cards drawn at
      random, at least one card is a picture-card ?

6.   Collect 200 single-figure random numbers by taking the last figure of a list of phone
      numbers out of a random page of a directory. (If a firm has consecutive numbers listed,
      only use the first one.) Record these numbers in a grid, as in question 1.
      Before you begin, estimate how many of each number 0 to 9 you expect to get.

      Count up your results and show them in a table.

      Now add up the frequencies of the odd numbers.

      Find the fraction $\dfrac{\text{number of odd numbers}}{\text{total number of numbers}}$ as a decimal

      to 2 decimal places.

      From your results, what value would you give for the
      probability that a number picked at random from the
      numbers 0 to 9 is odd ?

Number	Frequency
0	
1	
2	
3	
4	
5	
6	
7	
8	
9	

7.   Use the results for throwing a die, from question 3, taking them in pairs. You will have
      200 pairs.
      Record as H is the 2nd number is higher than the 1st number and as N if it is not.
      Before you begin, estimate how many times H will occur.
      Use your results to estimate the probability that if a die is thrown twice, the 2nd throw
      will show a higher number than the 1st throw.

Exercise 14.4   Applications

1.   Imagine a young couple, Mr and Mrs Kaye, who are going to spend 10 days holiday in Greece.
     Give estimated probabilities for these statements.

   1   The plane's departure will be delayed.
   2   There will be fine, sunny weather every day during the holiday.
   3   The hotel accommodation will be satisfactory.
   4   The couple will spend more money than they expected to.
   5   They will make new friends.
   6   Mrs Kaye will buy some new clothes.
   7   Mr Kaye will go water-skiing.
   8   One of them will need medical treatment during the holiday.
   9   They will buy some duty-free goods on the plane coming home.
   10   They will go again to the same place next year.

2.   Use a set of dominoes going up to double six.
     (If you have no dominoes, label cards 0–0, 0–1, up to 0–6; then 1–1, 1–2, up to 1–6; then 2–2, etc., ending 6–6. There are 28 cards altogether.)
     Pick out a domino at random and record the total score. Replace and repeat 200 times.
     The scores range from 0 to 12. Make a tally chart of the results.

     What is the estimated probability of getting a score of 6 if a domino is picked at random ?

3.   Ask as many people as you can on what day of the week their birthday falls this year. Tally the results. What is the estimated probability that if a person is chosen at random, his/her birthday is on a Saturday ?

Practice test 14

1.

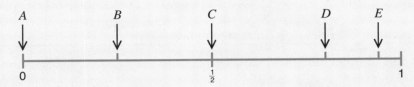

The events listed below have probabilities shown by the arrows *A, B, C, D* or *E* on the probability line.

Say whether each event is represented by *A, B, C, D* or *E*.

1   The probability of getting a number greater than 2, if cards labelled from 1 to 10 are placed in a bag and one is drawn out at random.

2   The probability of getting a domino which is a double, when a domino is picked at random from the 28 dominoes of a set going from double blank (0–0) to double six (6–6).

3   The probability that a woman will be picked, if there are 30 workers in a workshop of which 2 are men and the rest are women, and a worker is picked at random.

4   The probability of getting one head and one tail when two coins are tossed.

5   The probability that you meet someone whose birthday is on 31st February.

2.   In an experiment with a biased (unfair) die, the following results were obtained for the number facing uppermost when the die was thrown 400 times.

Number	1	2	3	4	5	6
Number of times	39	72	57	111	25	96

Using these results, find the probability of throwing
1   number 6,
2   an odd number,
3   a number greater than 3.

PUZZLES

26.   Write in figures; eleven thousand, eleven hundred and eleven.

27.   If it takes 5 men 5 days to plough 5 fields, how long does it take 1 man to plough 1 field, working at the same rate ?

15 Quadrilaterals

The topics in this chapter include:

- knowing and classifying types of quadrilaterals,
- constructing quadrilaterals,
- knowing and using the properties of quadrilaterals.

Quadrilaterals

A **quadrilateral** is a figure with 4 sides.

The sum of the angles of a quadrilateral is 360°.

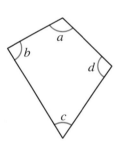

$$a + b + c + d = 360°$$

Special sorts of quadrilaterals

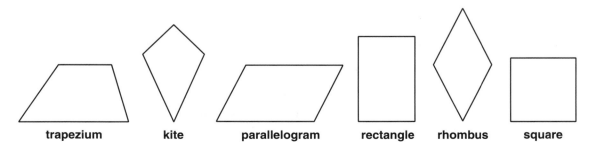

| trapezium | kite | parallelogram | rectangle | rhombus | square |

Here is a summary of the special quadrilaterals with their definitions and properties.

Trapezium

One pair of parallel sides.

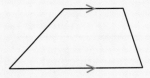

If the other 2 sides are equal it is an
isosceles trapezium.

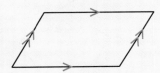

Kite

Two adjacent sides are equal and the
other two adjacent sides are equal.

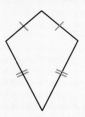

Parallelogram

Opposite sides are parallel.

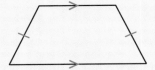

Opposite sides are equal.
Opposite angles are equal.

Rectangle

It is a parallelogram with one angle a
right angle.

Opposite sides are parallel and equal.
All angles are right angles.

Rhombus

It is a parallelogram with one pair of
adjacent sides equal.

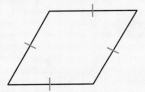

Opposite sides are parallel.
All sides are equal.
Opposite angles are equal.

Square

It is a rectangle and a rhombus.

Opposite sides are parallel.
All sides are equal.
All angles are right angles.

Example

ABCD is a parallelogram.
What is the size of $\angle A$?
Find the size of $\angle AYX$.
What sort of triangle is $\triangle AYX$?

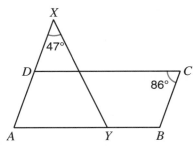

$\angle A = 86°$ opposite angles of a parallelogram are equal
$\angle AYX = 180° - (86° + 47°)$ sum of angles in $\triangle AYX = 180°$
          $= 47°$

In $\triangle AYX$, $\angle AYX = \angle AXY$, so it is an isosceles triangle, with $AY = AX$.

Exercise 15.1

1.   Estimate the sizes of the angles in these figures, in degrees. Check your estimates by
      measuring with your protractor.
      For each figure, find the sum of the 4 angles.
      Notice which angles are equal.

1

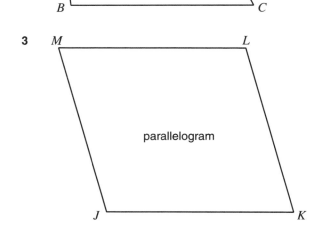

quadrilateral

2

kite

3

parallelogram

4

isosceles trapezium

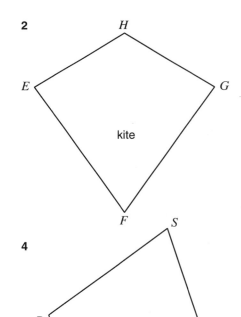

2.   Three angles of a quadrilateral are 50°, 75° and 123°. Find the size of the fourth angle.

3.   Two angles of a quadrilateral are 72° and 118° and the other two angles are equal. What size are they ?

4.   In the diagrams, find the sizes of angles a, b, c, d, e, f.

1
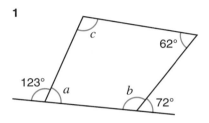

2
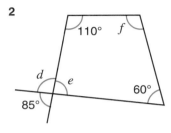

5.   Two angles of a trapezium are 106° and 93°. Find the size of each of the other two angles.

6.   Find the sizes of the marked angles in this parallelogram.

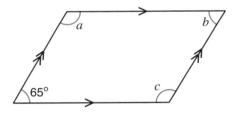

7. $ABCD$ is a rectangle and ABX is an equilateral triangle.
Find the sizes of angles a and b.

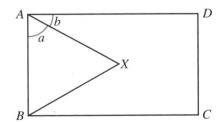

8. $ABCD$ is a kite with $AB = BC$ and $AD = DC =$ diagonal AC. $\angle ABC = 80°$.
Find the size of $\angle BAD$.

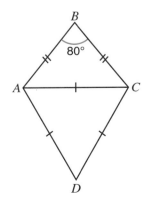

9. In the parallelogram *ABCD*, ∠*B* = 76°.
    E is a point on *BC* such that *BA* = *BE*,
    and ∠*EDC* = 27°.
    Find the sizes of the marked angles.

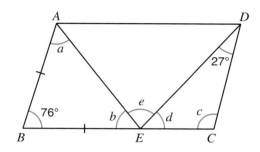

10. Four rods are placed together to make the outline of a plane shape.

    1 If the rods are, in order, 4 cm, 6 cm, 4 cm and 6 cm, what two possible shapes can be
        made ?

    2 If the rods are, in order, 4 cm, 4 cm, 6 cm and 6 cm, what shape can be made ?

    3 If all the rods are 8 cm long, what two possible shapes can be made ?

Drawing parallelograms

You can use the facts that:
    opposite sides are parallel,
    opposite sides are equal,
    opposite angles are equal,
    the interior angles between parallel lines add up to 180°.

In addition:
    for a rhombus, all sides are equal,
    for a rectangle, all angles are right angles,
    for a square, all sides are equal and all angles are right angles.

Exercise 15.2

1. Construct the parallelogram *ABCD*, as follows:
    Draw *BC* = 9 cm.
    Make an angle of 62° at *B*.
    Measure off 6 cm to get point *A*.
    Draw *CD* parallel to *BA*, using your set-square or by
    making ∠*C* = 118° (since ∠*B* + ∠*C* = 180°).
    Measure off 6 cm to get point *D*.
    Join *AD*.

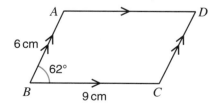

    You can check the accuracy of your drawing by
    measuring ∠*A* (=118°), ∠*D* (=62°) and *AD* (=9 cm).

2.   Construct the rhombus *ABCD*, using a similar method
      to that of question 1.

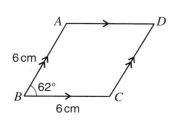

3.   Construct the rectangle *ABCD*, as follows:
      Draw $BC = 9$ cm.
      Make a right angle at *B*.
      Measure off 6 cm to get point *A*.
      Make a right angle at *C*.
      Measure off 6 cm to get point *D*.
      Join *AD*.

      Check that $\angle A$ and $\angle D$ are right angles and $AD = 9$ cm.

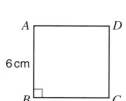

4.   Construct the square *ABCD*, using a similar
      method to that of question 3.

5.   Draw a triangle *ABC* with $BC = 6$ cm, $\angle B = 70°$, $\angle C = 55°$.
      Find, using compasses, a point *D* to complete the quadrilateral *ABCD* such that
      $AD = CD = 8$ cm.
      Measure the length of *AC* and the size of the angle *ADC*.
      What sort of quadrilateral is *ABCD* ?

Diagonals

A diagonal of a quadrilateral is a line which joins opposite
points.

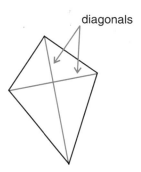

diagonals

Here is a summary of the properties of diagonals.

Isosceles trapezium

Diagonals are equal (but do not bisect each other).

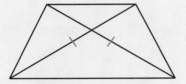

Kite

One diagonal is a line of symmetry. It bisects the other diagonal at right angles.

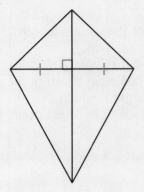

Parallelogram

Diagonals bisect each other.

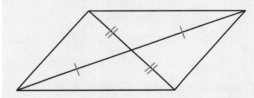

Rectangle

Diagonals bisect each other.
Diagonals are equal.

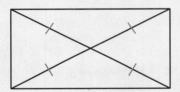

Rhombus

Diagonals bisect each other at right angles.
They also bisect the angles of the rhombus.

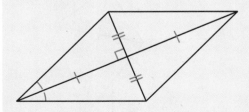

Square

Diagonals bisect each other at right angles.
Diagonals are equal.
Diagonals make angles of 45° with the sides of the square.

Exercise 15.3

1. Of the figures parallelogram, rhombus, rectangle and square,

    1 which have diagonals which bisect each other,
    2 which have diagonals which cut each other at right angles,
    3 which have diagonals which are equal ?

    Write your results in a table, putting 'yes' or 'no' in the columns.

	Diagonals bisect each other	Diagonals cut each other at right angles	Diagonals are equal
Parallelogram			
Rectangle			
Rhombus			
Square			

2. What sort of triangles are these ?

    1 $\triangle ABC$, where $ABCD$ is a rectangle.
    2 $\triangle PQR$, where $PQRS$ is a square.
    3 $\triangle XYZ$, where $WXYZ$ is a rhombus.

3. Draw accurately a parallelogram $ABCD$ with $AB = 8.5\,\text{cm}$, $BC = 5\,\text{cm}$ and $\angle ABC = 42°$. Draw its diagonals and measure the acute angle between them.

4. Construct a square $ABCD$ with side $AB = 5\,\text{cm}$.
    Join its diagonals and let them meet at X.
    Measure AC and BD, and also measure the sizes of the angles at X.

5. In this rectangle, find the sizes of a and b.

    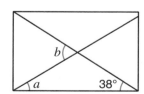

6. In this square, find the sizes of d, e, f.

    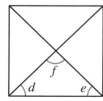

Exercise 15.4 Applications

1. **1** Draw 2 right-angled triangles of the same size and
         shape, on paper, and cut them out.
         Put the 2 triangles together so that they meet exactly
         along one edge. (The triangles can be turned over.)
         Sketch the different shapes which can be made and give
         their names.

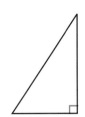

    2 Repeat this with 2 equilateral triangles of the same size.

2. *ABCD* is a square and *CDEF* is a rhombus.
    Explain why *AD* = *DE*.
    Find the sizes of the angles *a*, *b*, *c*, *d*, *e*.

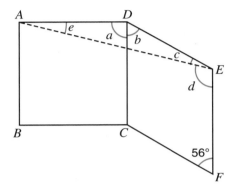

3. **1** Draw a line *AC* = 10 cm.
         Let *O* be the mid-point of *AC*.
         Draw a line through *O* making an
         angle of 56° with *OC*.
         Find points *B* and *D* on this line such
         that *BO* = *OD* = 3.4 cm.
         Join *AB*, *BC*, *CD*, *DA*.
         Measure these lines.

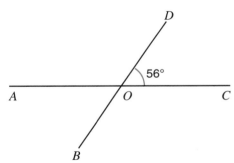

       What sort of quadrilateral is *ABCD* ?

    2 Repeat the question, but making *BO* = *OD* = 5 cm.

    3 Repeat part **1**, but making the line *BOD* at right angles to the line *AOC*.

Practice test 15

1.   In the rectangle, find the size of angle *a*.

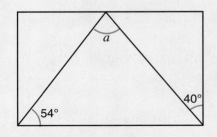

2.   In the diagram, ADE is a straight line and $CD = CE$. Find the sizes of angles a, d, e, c.

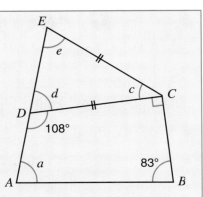

3.   Which of the quadrilaterals, kite, trapezium, parallelogram, rectangle, rhombus or square, is described here ?

    1   Both pairs of opposite sides are parallel, but there are no right angles.

    2   Two adjacent sides are equal and the other two adjacent sides are equal.

    3   All sides are equal and all angles are right angles.

    4   Two opposite sides are parallel, but not equal.

    5   Two opposite sides are equal and the other two opposite sides are equal, and all angles are right angles.

4. $ABCD$ is a trapezium with AD parallel to BC and diagonals cutting at X.

    1   If $BX = XC$, which angles are equal to $\angle XBC$?

    2   Explain why $AX = XD$.

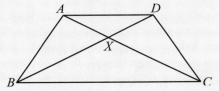

5.   Construct a rhombus $ABCD$ with sides 8.5 cm long and $\angle A = 48°$. Draw the diagonals.

    If the diagonals cross at E, measure AE, EC and $\angle AEB$.

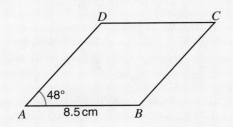

PUZZLES

28.   How many squares are there on a chessboard ?

29.   A weighty problem. Which would you rather have, half a tonne of 10 pence coins or a tonne of 5 pence coins ?

30.   Is it correct to say 'Half of 13 **is** $7\frac{1}{2}$' or 'Half of 13 **are** $7\frac{1}{2}$' ?

16 Directed numbers

The topics in this chapter include:

- understanding and using directed numbers in practical situations,
- ordering directed numbers,
- adding and subtracting with negative numbers,
- using and interpreting coordinates in all 4 quadrants.

Directed numbers

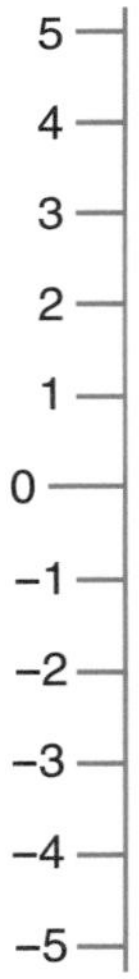

The diagram shows a number scale where the numbers go below 0.
This can happen, for example, on a temperature scale where 0° is the temperature at which water freezes, and the temperature can drop below this. Temperatures below zero are given as $-1°$, $-2°$, $-3°$, etc.
Temperatures above zero are given as ordinary numbers, $1°$, $2°$, $3°$, etc, or they can be given as plus numbers, $+1°$, $+2°$, $+3°$, etc. $+3°$ is the same as $3°$.

Draw your own number scale diagram, extending it further in both directions than this one.
Follow these examples on your number scale, counting up or down.

Start at 2 and go up 4. You get to 6.
Start at -5 and go up 4. You get to -1.
Start at -5 and go up 7. You get to 2.
Start at 5 and go down 2. You get to 3.
Start at 5 and go down 8. You get to -3.
Start at -3 and go down 1. You get to -4.

These questions can be written as follows:

$2 + 4 = 6$
$(-5) + 4 = -1$
$(-5) + 7 = 2$
$5 - 2 = 3$
$5 - 8 = -3$
$(-3) - 1 = -4$

```
5 ─
4 ─
3 ─
2 ─
1 ─
0 ─
-1 ─
-2 ─
-3 ─
-4 ─
-5 ─
```

To get from 3 to 2, go down 1.
To get from 3 to −5, go down 8. (You go down 3 to 0 then down another 5 to −5.)
To get from −2 to 5, go up 7.
To get from −1 to −5, go down 4.
To get from −2 to 0, go up 2.

Ordering numbers

The **order** of two numbers depends on their position on the number scale.

Example

> −2 is less than 1 because −2 is lower on the scale.
> −5 is less than −3 because −5 is lower on the scale.

Exercise 16.1

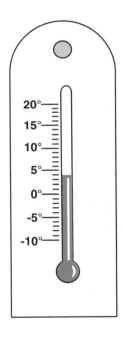

1.   Find the new temperature in the following cases.

  1   The temperature is +4° and it falls 3°.
  2   The temperature is −5° and it falls 2°.
  3   The temperature is +3° and it rises 6°.
  4   The temperature is −1° and it rises 1°.
  5   The temperature is −4° and it rises 2°.
  6   The temperature is 0° and it falls 5°.
  7   The temperature is −3° and it falls 4°.
  8   The temperature is +2° and it falls 5°.
  9   The temperature is +6° and it falls 7°.
  10 The temperature is −2° and it rises 8°.

2.   Say how many degrees the temperature has risen or fallen in the following cases.

  1   It was +8° and is now +11°.   **6**   It was +10° and is now −17°.
  2   It was +6° and is now −3°.   **7**   It was −8° and is now +2°.
  3   It was −4° and is now +2°.   **8**   It was −3° and is now 0°.
  4   It was −9° and is now −7°.   **9**   It was +5° and is now +1°.
  5   It was 0° and is now −6°.   **10** It was −1° and is now −4°.

3.   (Give the answer in the form '10 minutes to 1' or '10 minutes past 1'.)

  1   If the time is 13 minutes to 1 o'clock, what will be the time in 20 minutes ?
  2   If the time is 7 minutes to 2 o'clock, what was the time 5 minutes ago ?
  3   If the time is 4 minutes past 3 o'clock, what was the time 10 minutes ago ?

4. 1 If the time is 12 minutes past 4 o'clock, how many minutes have passed since it was 5 minutes to 4 o'clock ?
   2 If the time is 5 minutes to 5 o'clock, in how many minutes will it be 5.15 ?
   3 If the time is 20 minutes to 6, in how many minutes will it be 5 minutes to 6 ?

5. Write these numbers in order, smallest first.
   e.g. -2, 5, -6 in order are -6, -2, 5.

   1 $-2, 4, -1$ 4 $-3, 1\frac{1}{2}, 1\frac{3}{4}$
   2 $3, 0, -4$ 5 $4, -4\frac{1}{2}, -3\frac{1}{2}$
   3 $-1, 4, -5$

Addition and subtraction

Use your number line for counting up, when the sign is $+$, or down, when the sign is $-$.

Examples

$4 + 2 = 6$
Start at 4 and go up 2, getting to 6.

$4 - 7 = -3$
Start at 4 and go down 7, getting to -3.

$(-3) + 5 = 2$
Start at -3 and go up 5, getting to 2.

$(-3) + 1 = -2$
Start at -3 and go up 1, getting to -2.

$(-3) - 6 = -9$
Start at -3 and go down 6, getting to -9.

```
5 —
4 —
3 —
2 —
1 —
0 —
-1 —
-2 —
-3 —
-4 —
-5 —
```

Sometimes you may have to work out expressions such as $(-4) - (+3)$ or $5 - (-6)$. These are best done by changing the middle two signs into one according to rules.

$+ +$ should be replaced by $+$
$+ -$ or $- +$ should be replaced by $-$
$- -$ should be replaced by $+$

So there are two stages to working out such questions.
If two signs follow each other, replace them by one sign.
Then use the number line to work out the answer.

Here are some examples:

$(-5) + (+1)$ Replace $++$ by $+$, which means 'go up'.
$= (-5) + 1$ Start at -5 and go up 1, getting to -4.
$= -4$

$(-5) - (+3)$ Replace $-+$ by $-$, which means 'go down'.
$= (-5) - 3$ Start at -5 and go down 3, getting to -8.
$= -8$

$5 + (-7)$ Replace $+-$ by $-$, which means 'go down'.
$= 5 - 7$ Start at 5 and go down 7, getting to -2.
$= -2$

$5 - (-1)$ Replace $--$ by $+$, which means 'go up'.
$= 5 + 1$ Start at 5 and go up 1, getting to 6.
$= 6$

If your calculator has a $\boxed{+/_-}$ key, then you can enter negative numbers, and you can do calculations with the calculator, although it is better just to use the rules and manage without the calculator.

e.g.   For $(-4) + (-3)$ press 4 $\boxed{+/_-}$ $\boxed{+}$ 3 $\boxed{+/_-}$ $\boxed{=}$ and you will get the answer -7.
       For $(-4) - (-3)$ press 4 $\boxed{+/_-}$ $\boxed{-}$ 3 $\boxed{+/_-}$ $\boxed{=}$ and you will get the answer -1.

Exercise 16.2

Work out the answers to these calculations.

1.   **1** $4 + 3$ **8** $(-1) + 11$ **15** $(-8) + 0 + 4$
     2 $4 - 1$ **9** $(-8) - 1$ **16** $(-12) + 6 - 2$
     3 $(-2) + 1$ **10** $(-5) + 8$ **17** $3 - 1 - 5$
     4 $2 - 8$ **11** $(-7) + 6 + 1$ **18** $(-2) - 5 + 3$
     5 $(-3) + 3$ **12** $2 - 5 + 4$ **19** $6 - 1 - 5$
     6 $(-4) - 4$ **13** $10 - 5 + 6$ **20** $(-5) + 4 + 2$
     7 $9 - 12$ **14** $(-1) + 6 - 3$

2.   **1** $3 - (+4)$ **7** $0 - (+5)$
     2 $(-2) + (-5)$ **8** $(+4) - (-3)$
     3 $(-6) - 0$ **9** $(-5) + (+2)$
     4 $(+1) + (-1)$ **10** $(+7) - (+6)$
     5 $(-2) - (-4)$ **11** $(-4) - (-4)$
     6 $(-6) + (+3)$ **12** $(-6) - (-3) - (+6)$

Graphs

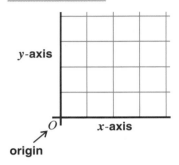

Coordinates

A point on a graph can be specified by giving its coordinates, i.e. its x-value and y-value.

Example

1   Point A has x-value 1 and y-value 2.
This can be written as the point (1, 2).
(The x-value is always written first.)

A is (1, 2),
B is (0, 4),
C is (4, 6).

Copy this diagram and plot the point D (5, 4).

Join AB, BC, CD, DA.

What sort of figure is $ABCD$?

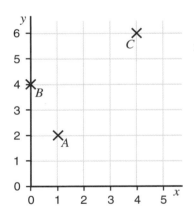

Graphs extended to negative numbers

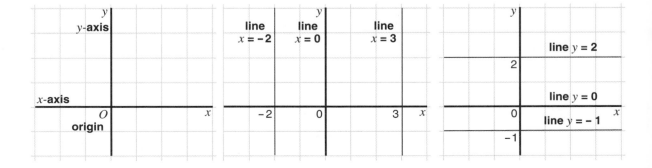

Example

2   Point *A* has *x*-value 1 and *y*-value 2.
     This can be written as the point (1, 2).
     A is (1, 2),
     B is (−2, 1),
     C is (0, −3).

     Copy this diagram and plot the
     point *D* (3, −2).

     Join *AB*, *BC*, *CD* and *DA*.

     What sort of figure is *ABCD* ?

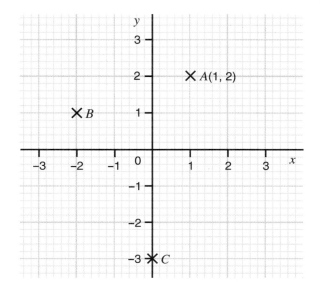

Exercise 16.3

1.   Draw the *x*-axis from 0 to 4 and the *y*-axis from 0 to 3. Plot the points *A*, *B*, *C*, *D* where
     A is (3, 0), *B* is (4, 1), *C* is (1, 3) and *D* is (0, 2).
     Join *AB*, *BC*, *CD* and *DA*.
     What sort of quadrilateral is *ABCD* ?

2.   Draw the *x*-axis from 0 to 8 and the *y*-axis from 0 to 10 using equal scales on both axes.
     On this graph:

     1   Plot the points *A* (1, 7), *B* (4, 8), *C* (5, 10), *D* (2, 9).
          Join *AB*, *BC*, *CD*, *DA*.
          What sort of quadrilateral is *ABCD* ?

     2   Plot the points *P* (4, 3), *Q* (5, 6), *R* (8, 5). Join *PQ* and *QR*.
          Mark a point *S* and join *PS* and *RS*, such that *PQRS* is a square.
          What are the coordinates of *S* ?

     3   Plot the points *J* (0, 2), *K* (2, 4), *L* (3, 6), *M* (8, 10).
          Three of these points lie on a straight line. Draw this line.
          Write down the coordinates of 4 more points which lie on the line.
          What is the connection between the *x* and *y* values for all points on the line ?

     4   Complete this pattern.

          (0, 6), (1, 5), (2, 4), (3, _), (4, _), (5, _), (6, _).

          Plot these points and join them with a line.
          What are the coordinates of the point where this line crosses the line drawn in **3** ?

3.   Draw axes for x and y from -8 to 8 using equal scales on both axes.

   1   Plot points A $(0, 2)$, B $(8, 6)$, C $(6, 8)$, D $(2, 6)$.
         Join AB, BC, CD, DA.
         What sort of quadrilateral is $ABCD$?

   2   Plot points F $(-8, 5)$, G $(-6, 2)$, H $(-3, 4)$.
         Join FG and GH.
         Find a point J such that $FGHJ$ is a square. Complete the square.
         What are the coordinates of J ?

   3   Plot points K $(-7, -6)$, L $(-4, -8)$, M $(-1, -6)$, N $(-4, -4)$.
         Join KL, LM, MN, NK.
         What sort of quadrilateral is $KLMN$?

Exercise 16.4   Applications

1.

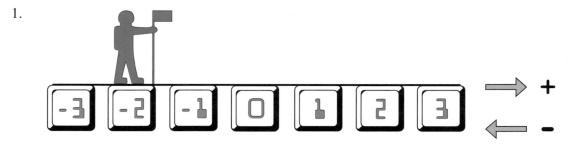

   Steve is playing a computer game. To make the robot go to the right he presses the
   $+$ key. To make the robot go to the left he presses the $-$ key.

   e.g.   To get from $\boxed{-2}$ to $\boxed{0}$ he would press $+2$,
           to get from $\boxed{-1}$ to $\boxed{-3}$ he would press -2.

   What must he press to move the robot

   1   from $\boxed{-3}$ to $\boxed{3}$,   **4** from $\boxed{2}$ to $\boxed{-2}$,

   2   from $\boxed{0}$ to $\boxed{3}$,   **5** from $\boxed{-2}$ to $\boxed{1}$?

   3   from $\boxed{1}$ to $\boxed{-1}$,

   Where does the robot end up if

   6   it was at $\boxed{-1}$ and Steve pressed -2,   **9**   it was at $\boxed{-2}$ and Steve pressed $+4$,

   7   it was at $\boxed{0}$ and Steve pressed $+2$,   **10** it was at $\boxed{-1}$ and Steve pressed $+1$?

   8   it was at $\boxed{3}$ and Steve pressed -6,

2. Mr Bramwell has an agreement with his bank to overdraw money, that is, to spend more money than is in his account.

    1   If he has £300 in his account and writes a cheque for £450, by how much will his account be overdrawn ?
    2   If his account is overdrawn by £200 and he takes out another £60, by how much is he overdrawn now ?
    3   If his account is overdrawn by £150 and he puts £80 into the account, by how much is he overdrawn now ?
    4   If his account is overdrawn by £100 and he puts £130 into the account, by how much is his account in credit ?

3. Trixie and Marian are playing a game with cards marked with + numbers or − numbers. At the end of the game they score according to the numbers on their cards.
    e.g. For $\boxed{+8}$ $\boxed{-6}$ $\boxed{-3}$ Trixie scores $8 - 6 - 3 = -1$.

    What do they score with these cards ?

    1   $\boxed{-1}$ $\boxed{-3}$ $\boxed{+4}$
    2   $\boxed{+2}$ $\boxed{-7}$ $\boxed{+9}$
    3   $\boxed{-3}$ $\boxed{-5}$ $\boxed{-4}$
    4   $\boxed{+5}$ $\boxed{-3}$ $\boxed{-3}$
    5   $\boxed{-3}$ $\boxed{-1}$ $\boxed{+7}$

4. Draw the x-axis from −5 to 9 and the y-axis from −3 to 10 using equal scales on both axes. Draw triangles labelled A to F by plotting and joining the 3 points given in each case.

    Triangle A   (2, 6), (2, 9), (3, 10)
    Triangle B   (5, 3), (6, 6), (7, 6)
    Triangle C   (9, 0), (6, −2), (6, −3)
    Triangle D   (−5, 7), (−3, 10), (−2, 10)
    Triangle E   (−5, 4), (−2, 4), (−1, 5)
    Triangle F   (−4, −2), (−4, −3), (−1, −1)

    Which pairs of triangles are exactly the same shape and size ? (They may need to be turned over to fit.)

5. On a graph, draw the x-axis from −3 to 5 and the y-axis from −1 to 6, using equal scales on both axes.
    Plot the points A (3, 2), B (5, 6) and C (0, 4). Join AB and BC.
    Plot point D such that AD is parallel and equal in length to BC.
    What are the coordinates of D ?
    Join AD and DC. What kind of quadrilateral is ABCD ?

6.   ## Multiplication and division

$(+4) \times (+3)$ is the same as 4×3 and equals 12.

$(+4) \times (-3)$ is the same as $4 \times (-3)$ and equals -12.

$(-4) \times (-3)$ is the tricky one. It equals 12 (not -12).

$$+ \times + = +$$
$$+ \times - = -$$
$$- \times - = +$$

The rules for division follow those for multiplication, and are

$(+12) \div (+3) = 4$

$(+12) \div (-3) = -4$

$(-12) \div (+3) = -4$

$(-12) \div (-3) = 4$

$$+ \div + = +$$
$$+ \div - = -$$
$$- \div + = -$$
$$- \div - = +$$

Work out the answers to these calculations.

(1) 1 $(-2) \times 8$ 7 $0 \times (-10)$
     2   $(-6) \times (-4)$ 8 $(-2) \times (-1)$
     3   $(+7) \times (-5)$ 9 $(-3) \times 3$
     4   $5 \times (-2)$ 10 $(-8) \times (-8)$
     5   $(-1) \times (-3)$ 11 $(-1) \times (+2)$
     6   $(-7) \times 0$ 12 $(-1) \times 1$

(2) 1 $6 \div (-3)$ 7 $49 \div (-7)$
     2   $(-15) \div (+5)$ 8 $(-1) \div (+1)$
     3   $18 \div (-6)$ 9 $(-24) \div (-3)$
     4   $(-36) \div (-4)$ 10 $(+30) \div (+5)$
     5   $(-4) \div 4$ 11 $8 \div (-4)$
     6   $36 \div (-6)$ 12 $0 \div (-2)$

(3) 1 $2 \times \left(-2\frac{1}{2}\right)$ 6 $0 \times (-6)$
     2   $(-5)^2$ 7 $(-1) \times (-2) \times (-3)$
     3   $0 \div 8$ 8 $(-12) \div (+12)$
     4   $(-1) \div (-1)$ 9 $3 \div (-6)$
     5   $(-1) \times (+1)$ 10 $(-3)^2$

7.   ## Negative numbers in expressions or formulae

(1)   If $p = 1$, $q = -1$ and $r = 0$, find the values of

      1   $q - p$ 4 $p^2 + q^2 + r^2$
      2   pqr 5 $6q - 4p$
      3   $4(p + q)$

(2)   1   In the formula $v = u + at$, find the value of v when $u = 70$, $a = -10$ and $t = -2$.
      2   In the formula $K = \frac{1}{2}mv^2$, find the value of K when $m = 8$ and $v = -4$.
      3   In the formula $F = 1.8C + 32$, find the value of F when $C = -40$.

Practice test 16

1. **1** If the temperature is $+3°$ and it falls by $10°$, what is the new temperature ?

    2 If the temperature is $-6°$, by how many degrees must it rise to become $+7°$?

    3 If the temperature is $+10°$ and it falls to $-5°$ overnight, through how many degrees has it fallen ?

    4 After rising 9 degrees the temperature is $+1°$. What was it originally ?

    5 After falling 4 degrees the temperature is $-9°$. What was it originally ?

2. Find the values of

    1 $4 - 6$ **5** $(-2) + 2$ **8** $0 - 8$
    2 $(-5) - 3$ **6** $(-10) - 10$ **9** $2 - 3$
    3 $(-5) + 7$ **7** $7 - 12$ **10** $(-3) + 1$
    4 $6 - 4$

3. Find the values of

    1 $8 + (-5)$ **4** $4 - (-1)$
    2 $(-3) - (+3)$ **5** $(-5) - (-5)$
    3 $(-2) + (+7)$

4. Draw the x-axis from 0 to 7 and the y-axis from 0 to 5 using equal scales on both axes.
    Plot points A (3, 1) and B (7, 3), and join AB.
    Plot the point C (6, 5) and join BC.
    Find the point D such that $ABCD$ is a rectangle.
    Join AD and DC.
    What are the coordinates of D ?

5. On a graph draw the x-axis from -3 to 4 and the y-axis from -3 to 4, using scales of 1 cm to 1 unit on both axes.
    Plot points A (4, 0), B (1, 4), C (−3, 1) and D (0, −3).
    Join AB, BC, CD, DA.
    What kind of quadrilateral is $ABCD$?

17 Statistical diagrams

The topics in this chapter include:

- constructing appropriate diagrams and graphs to represent data, including pictograms, bar charts, pie charts and line graphs,
- interpreting a wide range of graphs,
- drawing conclusions based on the shapes of graphs,
- recognising that graphs can be misleading.

Statistical diagrams

Here are shown some types of diagrams which can be used to display data.

Pictogram

Example

1

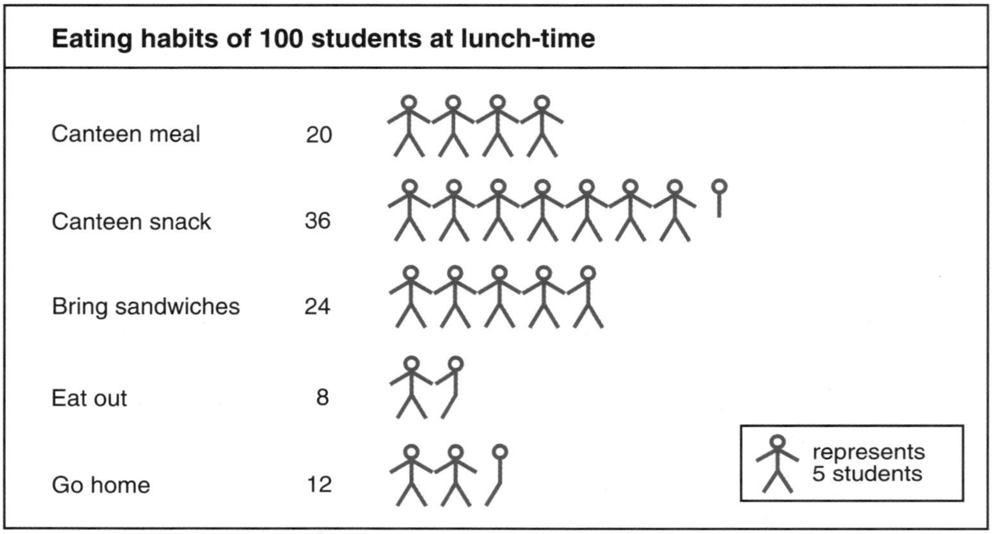

Eating habits of 100 students at lunch-time		
Canteen meal	20	
Canteen snack	36	
Bring sandwiches	24	
Eat out	8	
Go home	12	

represents 5 students

Unless you are spending time on a special project, do not draw elaborate symbols. Use simple ones that are quick and easy to draw.

If you make pictures of different kinds, for example, cars, vans and buses, make them of equal length or you will not be able to compare the frequencies by looking at the diagram.

For example,
use

not

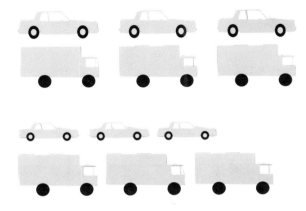

Bar chart

Example

2   **Favourite sports of 20 children**

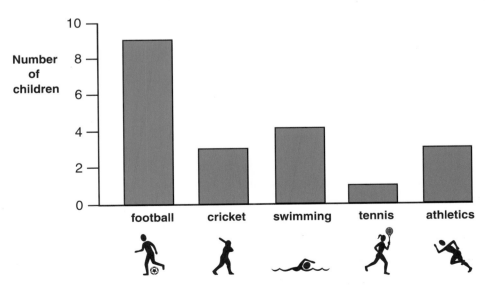

(The rectangles should all have the same width.)

Bar charts could be horizontal instead of vertical.

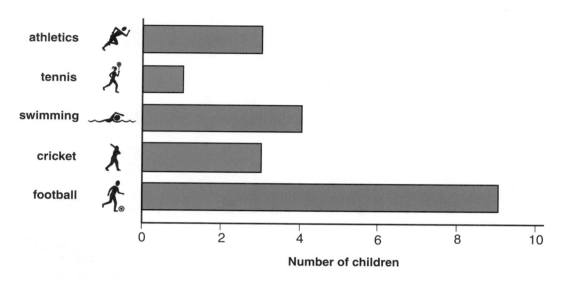

Favourite sports of 20 children

Number of children

Statistical diagrams and graphs should have headings to describe them.
Scales should be clearly marked. Axes should be labelled.

The modal category

The category with most items in is called the modal category.
Here, the modal sport is football, as more children (9) choose football than any other sport.

Exercise 17.1

1.   The numbers of livestock in Britain in a certain year included the following:

Sheep	44 million
Cattle	14 million
Pigs	8 million

(Figures are given to the nearest million.)
Represent the data on a pictogram or bar chart.

2. In a particular year, the destinations of British
    holidaymakers travelling to other European countries
    were as follows:
    Spain 30%, France 14%, Italy 8%, Greece 7%, Eire 5%,
    Other countries 36%.

    Represent the data on a pictogram or bar chart.

3. Each £1 collected in Council Tax was used by a Council as follows:

Education	53p
Social services	17p
Police	12p
Highways and transport	8p
Fire Services	3p
Other expenses	2p

    The rest was kept in reserve. How much
    per £1 was this ?
    Represent this information on a pictogram.

4. A family's income of £200 in a particular week was spent as follows:

Food	£60
Rent	£35
Car expenses	£30
Clothes	£15
Fuel	£20
Miscellaneous	£40

    Represent the data on a bar chart.
    What is the modal category ?
    What fraction of the total income is spent on this item ?

5. The bar chart shows how a family spent its weekly income of £220.

    The rest of the income was saved for the
    holiday fund.
    1   How much was saved that week ?
    2   The following week the income was increased
        by a bonus to £260, so £24 extra was spent
        on food, £6 extra on other expenses and the
        rest of the increase went into the holiday fund.
        Draw a bar chart showing the spending and
        saving for this second week.

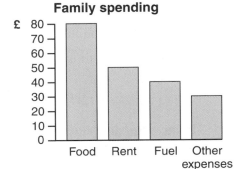

Family spending

Line graph (Time-series graph)

Example

These figures show the numbers attending a youth club over the past ten weeks.

20, 35, 28, 25, 33, 41, 37, 46, 48, 42.

We can plot these figures on a graph, putting time on the horizontal axis and attendance on the vertical axis.

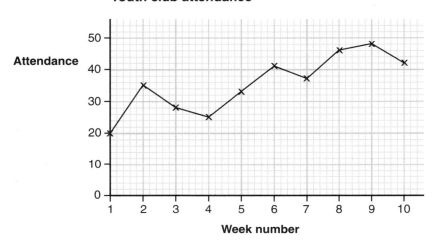

The points are joined from one to the next by straight lines, because this shows increases and decreases more easily, but in this graph the lines have no other meaning. We cannot use the graph to find the attendance at in-between times, because that would be meaningless. The graph does show an upward trend in attendance and we might use this to make a very cautious prediction for future attendances.

From the graph find
1   in which week the attendance was greatest,
2   between which two weeks there was the greatest increase in attendance.

Exercise 17.2

1.   The assets of a building society for 7 consecutive years (to the nearest million £'s) were

Year number	1	2	3	4	5	6	7
Assets (in £1 000 000)	19	21	25	29	34	39	47

Draw a line graph to represent the data.
(Label the vertical axis from 0 to 50.)

2. The graph shows the number of passengers carried by a bus company on 14 consecutive days.

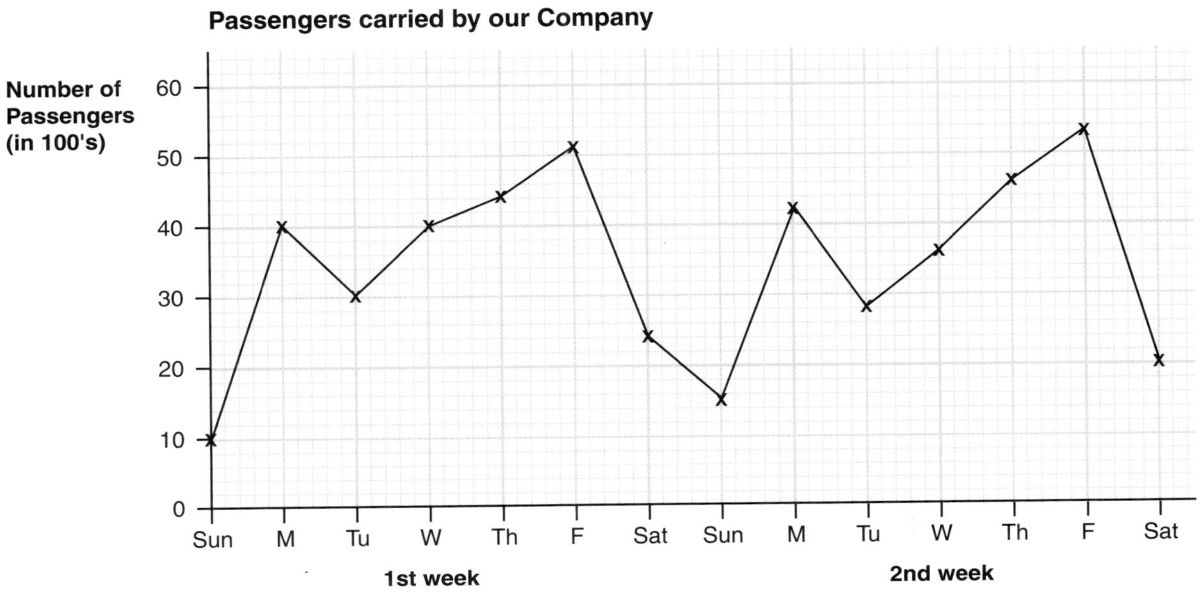

Passengers carried by our Company

Number of Passengers (in 100's)

1st week   2nd week

1 On which day were fewest passengers carried, and how many were there ?

2 On which day were most passengers carried, and how many were there ?

3 On one weekday there are usually fewer passengers because many of the shops close in the afternoons. Which day do you think this is ?

3. The figures show the profits of a firm for 6 years.

Year	1990	1991	1992	1993	1994	1995
Profit (million £'s)	26	28	34	45	60	80

Draw a line graph to represent these figures.
Comment briefly about the profits.

4. The UK population figures are given in this list. (Figures to the nearest million.)

Year	1901	1911	1921	1931	1941	1951	1961	1971	1981	1991
Population (in millions)	38	42	44	46	48	51	53	56	56	58

Draw a line graph to represent the data.
(Label the vertical axis from 0 to 60.)

Pie chart

Example

A family with a weekly income of £240 spend it as follows:

	£
Rent	54
Fuel	40
Food	80
Clothing	30
Household goods	16
Other expenses	20
	240

Spending by a family

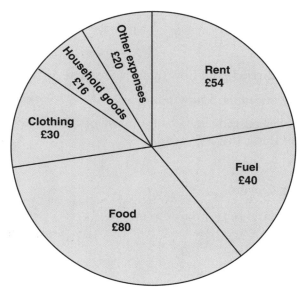

(Working for the pie chart.)
Since £240 is represented by 360°,

£1 is represented by $\frac{360°}{240} = 1.5°$.

Rent	$54 \times 1.5° =$	$81°$
Fuel	$40 \times 1.5° =$	$60°$
Food	$80 \times 1.5° =$	$120°$
Clothing	$30 \times 1.5° =$	$45°$
Household goods	$16 \times 1.5° =$	$24°$
Other expenses	$20 \times 1.5° =$	$30°$

Total $= 360°$

this is a useful check

(It is not necessary to mark the sizes of angles on the diagram but show your working clearly as above. The diagram shows the statistical figures and is clearer without the angle markings.)

Which diagram to draw

A **pictogram** shows information in a similar way to a bar chart, but by making attractive drawings it makes it look more interesting than a bar chart, so people are more likely to look at it.

A **bar chart** shows clearly the different frequencies. It is easy to compare them. You can see at a glance which of two similar bars is longer.

A **pie chart** shows more easily the fraction of the total which each item takes. A sector using more than half of the circle represents more than half of the total, a sector with a small angle represents a small part of the total, and so on. It is not so easy to compare sectors with each other if they are nearly the same size.

Exercise 17.3

1.   Of 24 school leavers, 9 went to the Further Education College, 8 found employment in a local factory, 5 found other employment and the others joined a training scheme.

   1   How many joined the training scheme ?
   2   What angle on a pie chart will represent 1 school leaver ?
   3   Represent the data on a pie chart.

2.   18 children are asked about their pets.
   3 have a dog.
   5 have a cat.
   2 have a budgie.
   1 has a guinea-pig.
   The others have no pets.

   1   How many children do not have a pet ?
   2   Represent the data on a pie chart.

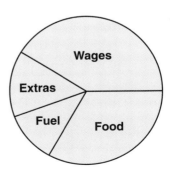

3.   Mrs Harris puts aside £30 a week from her wages as personal spending money.
   In one particular week she spent £12 on a restaurant meal, £4 on magazines and £7 on a birthday present. She gave £2 to a charity collection, and saved the rest for her holidays.

   1   How much did she save ?
   2   What fraction of the £30 did she save ?
   3   Represent the data on a pie chart.

4.   This pie chart shows the expenses of a catering firm.
   The total expenses were £54 000.

   1   What amount is represented by 1° ?

   2   If the angles at the centre of each sector were:
      Wages, 150°; Food, 120°; Fuel, 40°; Extras, 50°;
      find the cost of each item.

Misleading pictograms

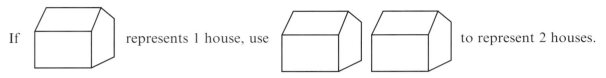

If [house] represents 1 house, use [two houses] to represent 2 houses.

If you double the measurements of the house instead, the proportion is all wrong. (In fact the new house has eight times the volume of the other one and should represent 8 houses.)

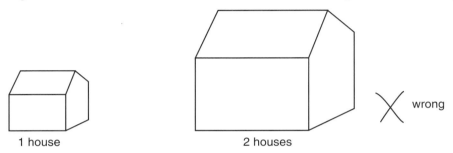

1 house   2 houses   ✕ wrong

People might use this method when they want to give a misleading impression.
The method is acceptable if the measurements are calculated properly so that the volumes, or areas in a two-dimensional picture, are in the correct proportion.

In advertisements, notice the effect of colour or shading. On a diagram the parts with brighter colours seem to be more important than the others.

Look out for examples of misleading statistical diagrams.

Misleading bar charts

Because the scale does not start at 0, there seems to be a rapid increase. Sometimes, also, the scale is distorted.

This gives the true picture.

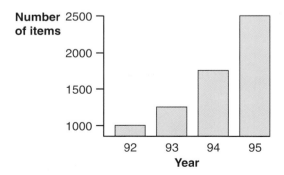

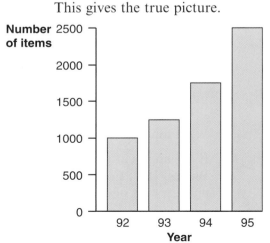

Misleading line graphs

1. When the scale does not start at 0, there seems to be a rapid increase. Sometimes, also, the scale is distorted.

This gives the true picture.

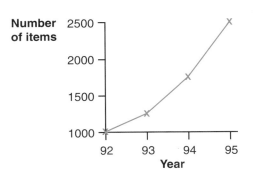

2. Although the profits have increased, the dotted line suggests a greater increase to follow in the future.

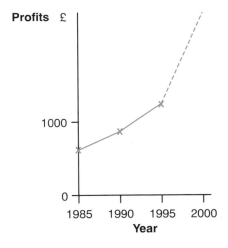

3. This is meaningless as there are no scales or units given. It gives the impression that 'ours is best'.

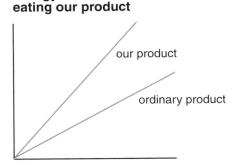

Exercise 17.4

1. This line graph shows the profits of a company. Give two reasons why the diagram is misleading.

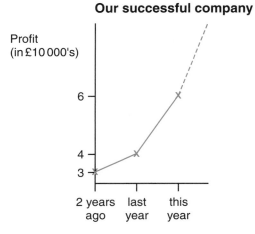

Our successful company

Profit (in £10 000's)

2. The diagram represents the milk sold by a dairy in 1994 and 1995.

   1 Why is the diagram misleading ?
   2 Draw a more suitable diagram.

1994
1000 gallons

1995
2000 gallons

3. This bar chart shows the takings at the local fete for 3 years.

   1 Why is the diagram misleading ?
   2 Draw a more suitable bar chart.

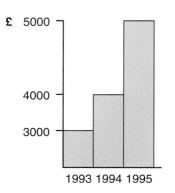

£ 5000

4000

3000

1993 1994 1995

Exercise 17.5 Applications

1. A camping holiday cost £36. This pie chart shows how the money was used.

    Measure the angles with your protractor to the nearest 5° in each case.

    Find how much was spent on each of the four items.

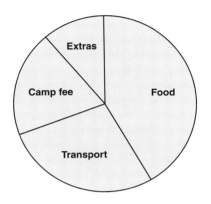

2. The graphs show the sales of two products for the years 1991 to 1995.

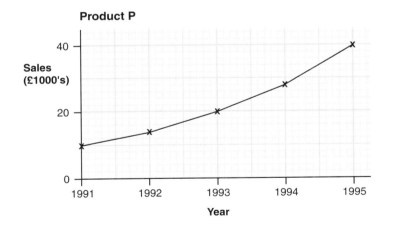

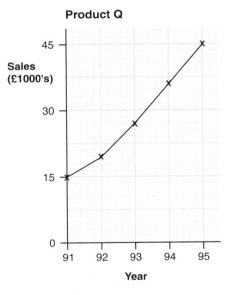

1 What is the increase in sales for each product over the 5 years ?

2 What misleading impression about the increase in sales do the graphs give ?

3 Draw the graph for product Q so that it gives a better comparison with the graph for product P.

3.   In a shopping survey, 4 different brands of butter, which we will call brands A, B, C and
      D, were on sale. The first 60 customers' choices were as follows:

      C   C   A   D   D   D   C   C   D   C   B   A
      C   A   D   D   C   C   A   D   C   A   A   C
      C   A   B   C   C   A   A   A   A   C   D   C
      C   C   A   A   A   A   A   C   C   C   A   C
      B   B   D   C   D   C   C   C   B   D   B   D

      1   Show in a list the total number of choices for each brand.
      2   Draw a pie chart to illustrate the choices.

4.   In Chapter 9, Exercise 9.3, several suggestions were given for data which could be
      collected for statistical investigations.
      If you have carried out any investigations, you could illustrate your data with suitable
      diagrams.

Practice test 17

1.   The types of dwellings in a district of a town are as follows:
      (Figures to the nearest 10.)

      | Owner occupied | 1470 |
      | Local authority | 610 |
      | Housing association | 130 |
      | Private rented | 490 |
      | Unoccupied | 400 |

      Draw a pictogram or bar chart to illustrate these figures.
      What is the modal type of dwelling ?

2.   An arable farm of 90 hectares grows four main crops.

      | Barley | 56 hectares |
      | Potatoes | 11 hectares |
      | Carrots | 9 hectares |
      | Green vegetables | 14 hectares |

      (1 hectare $= 10\,000\,\text{m}^2$)

      1   What angle on a pie chart will represent 1 hectare ?
      2   Represent the data on a pie chart.

3.   The temperature in a classroom was recorded at the same time each day for 3 weeks. The results are shown on this graph.

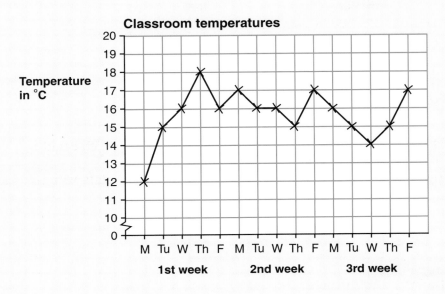

1   On which day was it very cold in the classroom ? Give a possible reason for this.
2   How many degrees warmer was it on the next day ?
3   On which day was it warmest ?
4   On how many days was the temperature below 16°C ?

4.   A firm selling cars advertise the fact that its sales have doubled.

Why is the diagram rather misleading ?
Draw a sketch of a more suitable diagram.

$\mathit{18}$ Simple equations

The topics in this chapter include:

- using letters to represent unknowns,
- solving linear equations,
- forming and manipulating simple equations in order to solve problems, selecting the most appropriate method for the problem concerned.

Solving equations

You can add equal numbers to both sides.
You can subtract equal numbers from both sides.
You can multiply both sides by the same number.
You can divide both sides by the same number, (not 0).

Examples

1     $x + 10 = 17$
     Subtract 10 from both sides.
       $x = 7$

2     $x - 8 = 5$
     Add 8 to both sides.
       $x = 13$

3     $5x = 15$
     Divide both sides by 5.
       $x = 3$

4     $\frac{1}{4}x = 5$
     Multiply both sides by 4.
       $x = 20$

Exercise 18.1

Solve these equations.

1. $5x = 20$
2. $x - 6 = 9$
3. $\frac{1}{3}x = 7$
4. $x + 8 = 19$
5. $4x = 24$
6. $\frac{1}{4}x = 9$
7. $x - 1 = 10$

8. $x + 2 = 14$
9. $5x = 45$
10. $x + 7 = 22$
11. $x + 11 = 11$
12. $x - 3 = 12$
13. $5x = 0$
14. $x - 8 = 1$

15. $x + 6 = 25$
16. $\frac{1}{2}x = 6$
17. $x - 14 = 4$
18. $x + 3 = 13$
19. $x - 9 = 0$
20. $12x = 72$

21. In the formula $P = 4l$, find the value of l when $P = 32$.

22. In the formula $y = x + c$, find the value of x when $y = 12$ and $c = 1$.

23. In the formula $a = 3b + d$, find the value of d when $a = 23$ and $b = 6$.

24. When 10 is subtracted from a certain number the answer is 17. What is the number ?
(Let the number be x. Write down an equation and solve it to find the number.)

Example

$13x - 20 = 6x + 8$

Subtract $6x$ from both sides.
  $7x - 20 = 8$
Add 20 to both sides.
    $7x = 28$
Divide both sides by 7.
      $x = 4$

To check the equation, substitute $x = 4$ into both sides of the equation separately.
The two sides should be equal.
Left-hand side (LHS) $= 13x - 20 = (13 \times 4) - 20 = 52 - 20 = 32$.
RHS $= 6x + 8 = (6 \times 4) + 8 = 24 + 8 = 32$.
The two sides are equal, both 32, so the solution $x = 4$ is correct.

If you are not required to do a check as part of the answer, do it at the side of your
work, as rough working, or even mentally.

Exercise 18.2

1. Solve these equations and check the answers.

1	$3x + 1 = 13$		**11**	$7 + 2x = 32 - 3x$
2	$16 + 4x = 24$		**12**	$15x - 4 = 3x + 8$
3	$12x - 5 = 19$		**13**	$3 - x = 12 - 4x$
4	$2x + 7 = 31 + x$		**14**	$72 - 2x = 12 + 3x$
5	$3 + 5x = 31 + x$		**15**	$9 - 5x = x + 9$
6	$3x = x + 6$		**16**	$4x + 2 = 17 - x$
7	$5x = 18 - x$		**17**	$12x - 6 = 14 + 8x$
8	$4x = 5 - x$		**18**	$2x + 5 = 29 - 4x$
9	$7x + 3 = 33 + x$		**19**	$4 + 6x = 12 + 2x$
10	$16 - 4x = 0$		**20**	$8x - 13 = 3x + 2$

2. I think of a number, multiply it by 3 and add 8. The result is the same as if I multiply the original number by 7 and subtract 8.
    Let the original number be x. Write down an equation and solve it to find the number.

3. Use angle properties to write down an equation involving x and hence find the value of x in the following figures.

    1

    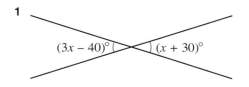

    $(3x - 40)°$ $(x + 30)°$

    2

    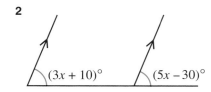

    $(3x + 10)°$ $(5x - 30)°$

Example

$5(x - 3) + 2x = 20$

Remove the bracket.
$5x - 15 + 2x = 20$
$7x - 15 = 20$
Add 15 to both sides.
$7x = 35$
Divide both sides by 7.
$x = 5$

To check the equation, substitute $x = 5$ into the left-hand side of the equation.

$$\text{LHS} = 5(x - 3) + 2x = 5 \times (5 - 3) + 2 \times 5$$

$$= 5 \times 2 + 10$$

$$= 20$$

RHS $= 20$
The two sides are equal, both 20, so the solution $x = 5$ is correct.

Exercise 18.3

1. Solve these equations.

    1 $3(x + 2) - x = 26$ **4** $2(x - 9) = x - 2$
    2 $3(1 + 2x) = 45$ **5** $8x = 4(3x - 6)$
    3 $6(x + 1) - 6 = 0$

2. Solve these equations and check the answers.

    1 $5(x + 3) = 40$ **4** $3(8 - x) = 15$
    2 $(x + 1) + 2(x + 2) = 29$ **5** $5(x - 2) = 0$
    3 $4(3x - 1) + 10 = 18$

3. A certain number has 7 added to it and the result is multiplied by 3. The answer is 36.
    Let the number be x. Write down an equation and solve it to find the original number.

4. Jane has saved a sum of money and Ruth has saved £20 more than Jane.
    Let the amount Jane has be £x. How much has Ruth ?

    If together they have £44, write down an equation and solve it to find how much each girl has.

Exercise 18.4   Applications

1. I think of a number, multiply it by 5 and add 28. The result is 5 less than eight times the original number.
    Write down an equation, letting x be the original number, and solve it. What number did I start with ?

2. A woman is 3 times as old as her daughter. In 9 years time she will only be twice as old as her daughter.
    If the daughter's age now is x years, find the woman's age now, and both their ages in 9 years time.
    Write down an equation to find the value of x.
    What are the ages of the woman and her daughter now ?

3. There are 4 consecutive odd numbers. If the smallest one is n, what are the others in terms of n ?

    The sum of the 4 numbers is 48.
    Write down an equation and solve it to find the 4 numbers.

4. £5 is divided among Ann, Barbara and Chris so that Barbara has 40p more than Ann and Chris has 60p more than Barbara.
    If Ann has a pence, find expressions for the amounts Barbara and Chris have.

    Write down an equation and solve it to find the value of a. (£5 = 500 pence.)
    What are the amounts that the 3 girls received ?

5.   (In each part of this question write down an equation involving x, and solve it.)

1   The three angles of a triangle are $(x + 25)°$, $(x + 35)°$ and $2x°$. Find x. What is the size of the largest angle ?

2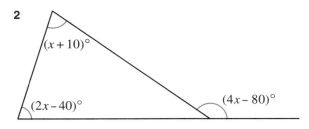

Find x. What sort of triangle is it ?

3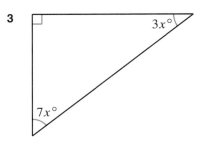

Find x.

6.   **1**   Write down an equation involving x and solve it to find the value of x.

2   Write down an equation involving y and solve it to find the value of y.

3   Write down an equation involving z and solve it to find the value of z.

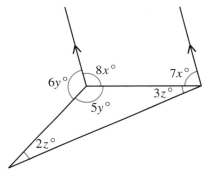

7.   Equations can have solutions which are not necessarily whole numbers. Use fractions rather than decimals in cases where the fraction would not be an exact decimal.
e.g. If $x = 1\frac{1}{2}$, you could give the answer as $x = 1.5$, but if $x = 1\frac{2}{3}$, you should leave the answer as a fraction as you cannot express $\frac{2}{3}$ as an exact decimal. However, if the answer was wanted correct to 2 decimal places it would be 1.67.

Sometimes equations have solutions which are negative numbers.

Examples

1   Solve $5x - 3 = 0$.

Add 3 to both sides.
$$5x = 3$$
Divide both sides by 5.
$$x = \tfrac{3}{5} \text{ (or } 0.6\text{)}$$

2   Solve $5x + 20 = 3x + 14$.

Subtract $3x$ from both sides.
$$2x + 20 = 14$$
Subtract 20 from both sides.
$$2x = -6$$
Divide both sides by 2.
$$x = -3$$

Solve these equations.

1	$6x = 3$	**6**	$2x + 17 = 3$
2	$5x - x = 1$	**7**	$1 - 3x = 10$
3	$5x + 3 = x + 5$	**8**	$5(x + 3) = 0$
4	$10x = 5x + 2$	**9**	$3x + 16 = x$
5	$6 + 3x = 7x - 4$	**10**	$2(3x - 4) = 14x$

Practice test 18

1. Solve these equations.

    1 $a - 7 = 14$ **4** $\dfrac{d}{7} = 20$

    2 $b + 17 = 36$ **5** $11e - 6 = 71$

    3 $7c = 56$

2. Solve these equations and check the answers.

    1 $3(2x - 5) = 21$ **4** $x + 1 = 4(x - 5)$

    2 $5x = x + 32$ **5** $8x - 5 = 2x + 4$

    3 $6x - 1 = 2x + 15$

3. (In these questions let the number be x. Write down an equation and solve it to find the number.)

    1 A certain number when multiplied by 3 and the result added to 7 makes 25. What is the number ?

    2 When 15 is subtracted from 4 times a certain number the answer is 17. What is the number ?

4. There are 3 consecutive numbers. If the smallest one is n, what are the others, in terms of n ?

    The sum of the 3 numbers is 63.
    Write down an equation and solve it to find the 3 numbers.

5. Write down two equations, one involving x, the other involving y, and solve them.

    Hence find the numerical values of the lengths of the sides of this parallelogram.

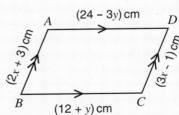

Miscellaneous Section C

Exercise C1   Aural Practice

If possible find someone to read these questions to you.
You should do the questions within 20 minutes.
Do not use your calculator.
Write down the answers only.

1.   What fraction of an hour is 40 minutes ?

2.   If a car costing £5000 is sold at a profit of 20%, what is the selling price ?

3.   What is 6 less than one-quarter of 44 ?

4.   If 9 cm was cut from 1 metre of ribbon, how much was left ?

5.   Three angles of a quadrilateral are each 100°. What is the size of the 4th angle ?

6.   What is the value of x if $6x - 1 = 29$?

7.   A train which was due at 4.55 pm arrived 25 minutes late. At what time did it arrive ?

8.   There are two parcels with total weight 10 kg. One is 3 kg heavier than the other. What does the heavier one weigh ?

9.   If the total amount of time represented on a pie chart is 24 hours, what angle is needed for a sector representing 8 hours ?

10.   What is the square root of 100 ?

11.   What will 200 lollipops cost at 6 pence each ?

12.   What is the mean of the numbers 2, 3, 5, 10 ?

13.   In dropping a drawing-pin onto a table, it came to rest point upwards 70 times out of 100. What is an estimate of the probability that the next time it is dropped it will land point upwards ?

14.   I think of a number, multiply it by 8 and subtract 5. The answer is 67. What was the number I thought of ?

15. Trees are to be planted 10 metres apart along one side of a driveway of length 350 m. If there are to be trees at both ends of the driveway, how many are needed altogether ?

Additional aural questions using data from pages 444 to 447.

16. Use table **9**.
     Mrs Smith needs a pair of curtains either 90 by 90 inches or 108 by 90 inches. What is the difference in price ?

17. Use diagram **10**.
     Estimate the size of angle *A*.

18. Use diagram **10**.
     AB is 6 cm long. Estimate the length of *BC*.

19. Use the graph **11**.
     How many more passengers were carried on Friday than on Monday ?

20. Use diagram **12**.
     What is the mathematical name for the shape of the diamond symbol ?

Exercise C2   Revision

1. The number of insects in a colony doubles each week. If there were 100 insects initially, how many would there be after 5 weeks ?

2. Do not use your calculator in this question.

    Write down any number less than 10, add 3 to it and square the result. Then add 1 and multiply by 10. Subtract 100 and divide by the number you started with. Add 5 and then divide by 5. Subtract 9 and halve the result. Subtract the number you started with. What is your answer ?

3. Find the size of angle *b*.

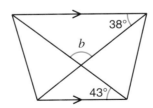

4. Find the values of

    1 $\frac{1}{8}$ of £5.20,   **4** $\frac{2}{3}$ of 45 min,

    2 $\frac{3}{4}$ of 68 kg,   **5** $\frac{7}{10}$ of 500 ml.

    3 $\frac{3}{5}$ of 80 cm,

5. The rainfall records for a town in England for one year were as given in this bar diagram.

    1   Which was the wettest month and how much rain fell then ?
    2   Which was the driest month and how much rain fell then ?
    3   In which month was the rainfall double that of the preceding month ?

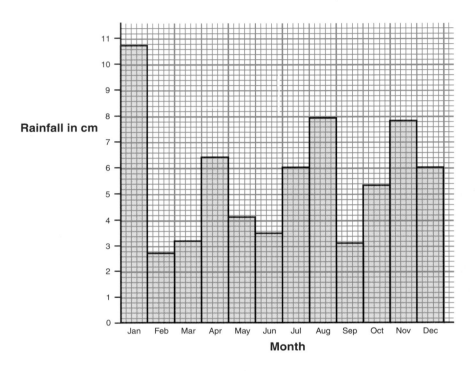

6. Find the approximate value (to the nearest whole number) of 3.92×9.08.
    Use your calculator to find a value correct to 1 decimal place.

7. 100 discs with letters A, E, I, O or U printed on them are placed in a bag.
    Here are the numbers of discs with each letter.

Letter	A	E	I	O	U
Number of discs	10	38	20	30	2

    Describe the probabilities as very unlikely, unlikely, an even chance, likely or very likely, that a disc drawn out at random will have these letters.
    1   O,
    2   E, I, O or U,
    3   A, E or U.
    4   U,
    5   A, E, I or U.

8. *ABCD* is a rhombus with $\angle ABC = 60°$.

    What sort of triangles are
    1   $\triangle ABC$,
    2   $\triangle ABD$,
    3   $\triangle ABX$?

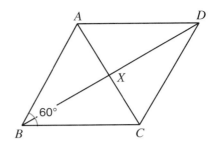

9. A plumber does three repair jobs as follows: the first from 9.35 am to 11.15 am, the second from 11.45 am to 12.50 pm and the third from 2.05 pm to 3.50 pm.
    Find the average (mean) time taken for a job.

10. In a certain firm there were 4 workshops, A, B, C, D, with men and women workers in each.
    Design a table to show the categories of (1) men, (2) women, (3) total workers, in each workshop, and the totals in the firm.

    Fill in the table using this information. There were 175 workers in workshop A of whom 40% were men and the rest were women. There were 200 men and 50 women in workshop B. There were 45 women in workshop C and twice as many men, and in workshop D there were 80 workers of whom 15% were men.

    How many workers were there altogether ?

Exercise C3   Revision

1. Change these fractions to decimals.

    1   $\frac{3}{4}$ 2 $\frac{3}{20}$ 3 $\frac{3}{8}$

    Change these decimals to fractions in their simplest forms.

    4   0.25   5   0.2   6   0.24

2. Five people measured the length of a field and their measurements were 53 m, 55 m, 56 m, 52 m, 55 m.
    Find the mean, median and range of the measurements.

3. Which one of the following statements referring to a parallelogram is **not** correct ?

    A   opposite angles equal   B   sum of angles $= 360°$
    C   opposite sides equal   D   opposite sides parallel
    E   diagonals equal

4.   Solve the equations.

   1 $2a + 3 = 17$ **4** $d - 5 = 0$
   2 $b + 3b = 24$ **5** $15 - e = 12$
   3 $3c = 90 - c$

5.   **1** The marks on a harbour wall
           show the water level at -2 (feet).
           Where will it be when the water
           has risen 6 feet ?

      2 At its highest point the water level was at
           6 (feet), and several hours later it was
           at -6 (feet).
           What was the fall in the tide ?

6.   Find the total cost of the ingredients used in making a cake from 150 g of butter, 150 g of
      sugar, 3 eggs and 200 g of flour, when flour costs 45p for a 1.5 kg bag, butter 65p for
      250 g, sugar 60p for a kg bag and eggs £1 per dozen.

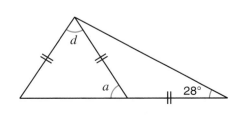

7.   **1** If $s = ut + \frac{1}{2} ft^2$, what is the value of s when $u = 9$, $f = 10$, $t = 4$?

      2 If $I = \dfrac{PRT}{100}$, what is the value of I when $P = 750$, $R = 8$, $T = 4$?

      3 If $g = \dfrac{v - u}{t}$, find g when $v = 90$, $u = 20$ and $t = 10$.

      4 If $S = 90(2n - 4)$, find S when $n = 6$.

      5 If $a = \dfrac{b(100 + c)}{100 - c}$, find a when $b = 6$ and $c = 20$.

8.   Find the sizes of angles a and d.

9.   A man bought 600 eggs for £48 and planned to sell them at £1.20 per dozen.
      What percentage profit would he have made on his cost price ?

      However, 60 of the eggs were broken and he could not sell them.
      What was his percentage profit after he had sold the rest ?

10.   A baby was weighed at the Health Clinic every month. The weights recorded for the
      first year were as follows:

Age in months	1	2	3	4	5	6	7	8	9	10	11	12
Weight in kg	4.5	5.0	6.0	6.5	7.0	7.5	8.0	8.5	9.0	9.2	9.4	9.5

Show this information on a graph, joining the points
with a series of straight lines.

In which month was there the greatest gain in weight ?

Exercise C4 Revision

1.   Write these numbers correct to 2 decimal places.

      1   5.628   4   0.0976
      2   3.2296   5   0.0628
      3   37.283

2.   The marks of 12 students in a test are 5, 5, 6, 6, 6, 7, 8, 8, 10, 10, 14, 17.

      Find
      1   the mode,
      2   the median,
      3   the mean,
      4   the range, of the marks.

3.   Philip buys a computer game for £25. Later he sells it to a friend for £22. What is the
      percentage loss he makes on the sale ?

4.   What is the total weight of 34 boxes, each weighing 25 kg ?

5.   In the diagram, ∠*DBC* is cut in half by *BE*.
      ABC is a straight line.
      Find the size of angle *b*.

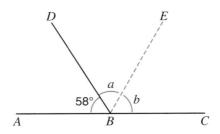

6.   **1** A shop allows a discount of 10% on all purchases during a sale.
           What was the sale price of an article which was originally marked at £39 ?

      2 A shopkeeper buys an article for £2.70. His marked selling price is 10% more than
           the cost price. What is the marked selling price ?

7.   Write down the next 2 terms in these sequences and find an expression for the *n*th term.

      1   1, 11, 21, 31, ...   **4**   20, 23, 26, 29, ...
      2   60, 56, 52, 48, ...   **5**   71, 80, 89, 98, ...
      3   39, 37, 35, 33, ...

8.   20 paperback books are bought, some costing £1.80 each and the others costing £3.20
      each. The total cost was £54.20. How many of the cheaper kind were there ?
      (Let there be *x* at 180p and (20 − *x*) at 320p.)

9.   A householder paid £360 in council
      tax last year. This compound bar
      chart shows how this money is used
      by the County.

      1 How much goes into the Reserve
           Fund ?

      2 What percentage of the tax is spent
           on Education, to the nearest whole
           number ?

      3 Show the data on a pie chart.

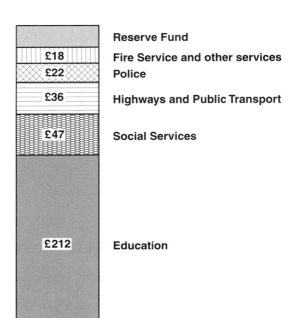

10. Draw an accurate, full-size drawing of this figure.

Join *AD* and measure it to the nearest mm.

What sort of figure is *ABCD* ?

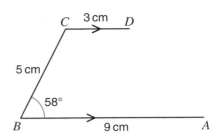

Exercise C5   Activities

1. **Adding a column of numbers**

Write down any two numbers, one underneath the other, then continue
making a column of numbers by adding the two numbers together and
writing the sum down underneath. Repeat this, always adding the last
two numbers together, until there are six numbers altogether.
Then, finally, find the total of all six numbers.

Repeat this a few more times, beginning with two different numbers.

Can you find a connection between the total and the 5th number in
the column, which is true for all your examples ?

You may like to extend this idea by continuing the columns until you have ten numbers
and then adding them up.
See if you can find a connection between the total and one of the other numbers in the
column.

22
52
74
126
200
326
800

2. **The number of throws of a die needed to get a six**

In many children's dice games, you need to get a six to begin, and sometimes it seems a
long time before you get one. What is the average number of throws needed ?

Before you begin the experiment, estimate
(1)   what is the most likely number (mode number) of throws
        until you get a six,
(2)   what is the average number (mean number) of throws
        until you get a six.

Throw the die and count the number of throws until you get a six. e.g. 5, 3, 3, 6 counts
as 4.
Repeat about 200 times. (You can use the results of a previous experiment if you have
kept them. You can also use simulated numbers from a computer or calculator.)

Put the results in a tally chart.
Draw a bar-line graph of the results and describe its shape.
Find the mode number and the mean number of throws.

How close were your estimates ?

3. **Motoring**

How much does it cost to run a car?

Imagine that you are planning to buy a car and want to see how much it will cost you.

Decide what make of car you want, and whether you will buy a new one or a secondhand one.

Find the cost of the car, or of a bank loan to buy the car, or the credit sale payments.

Find other costs, such as road tax, insurance. For the cost of petrol, find out how many miles per gallon your car should do on average, decide how many miles you will travel in a year, (ask other drivers how many miles they do), and work out the cost of the petrol.

There are other costs such as oil, car cleaning, repairs and replacements, garage rent, parking fees, membership of a motoring association, MOT if the car is over 3 years old, and so on. Make an estimate of these.

Find the estimated total cost for a year, and see from this how much you will need per week.

Illustrate your booklet with a picture of the car.

If you prefer you can imagine you are buying a motor bike instead of a car.

Here is a list of costs of running a car, from 1935.
You may like to compare your costs with these and comment about the differences.
(Amounts less than £1 have been converted to decimal currency.)

Cost for 20 000 miles	
	£
Petrol, 20 mpg at $7\frac{1}{2}$p per gallon	75.00
Oil at 25p per gallon (1000 mpg)	5.00
Tyres	15.00
Insurance	15.75
Tax	11.25
Garage, 50p per week	26.00
Cleaning, at 25p per week	13.00
Depreciation, first year	125.00
Repairs	5.00
Total	291.00

4. **Using a computer to investigate shapes**

If you have a computer which will **draw**, you can investigate
quadrilaterals.

If you have had no previous experience, begin by finding out
how to draw rectangles and squares. Then by altering the
angles you can produce parallelograms or rhombuses, and by
altering lengths you can make trapeziums and kites. You can
investigate the diagonals of such figures. For instance, by
making a sequence of small changes to the angles of a
parallelogram until it becomes a rectangle, you can notice
how the diagonals which are unequal in length finally become equal. Similarly you can
watch what happens to the diagonals when you turn a parallelogram into a rhombus.

You can also draw polygons, especially regular polygons, on the screen, and use these to
make patterns such as tessellations. You can also include curves such as circles, or arcs of
circles, into your designs. You can reflect shapes in a line, or lines, or rotate them about
a point. You can move shapes around the screen by translation, or enlarge or reduce
them.

5. **Hexominoes**

Hexominoes are arrangements of 6 equal squares which join together with edges of
adjacent squares fitting exactly together, such as

Pieces which would be identical if turned round or turned over are counted as the same.

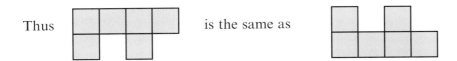

There are 37 different pieces. Try to find all of them.
Some of them will form the net of a cube. Which ones ?
Which pieces can be used to make tessellations ?

6. ## Savings

Investigate the different places or ways in which money can be saved or invested, such as banks, building societies, shares, savings certificates, life insurance policies, or hidden in the house.

Consider the advantages and disadvantages of each, such as
1   safety of your money,
2   interest gained (a) if you are a taxpayer or (b) if you are not,
3   easy access to your money.

Does it make any difference if you have
(a)   only a small amount of money,
(b)   quite a large sum of money ?

If someone saves regularly out of his or her wages, e.g. saving £10 per week for several years, make a table or graph to show how this money would grow if invested in a regular savings scheme.

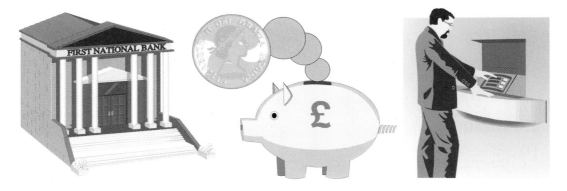

7. ## An ABC book

You know many Mathematical facts now. You could make a 'Maths ABC' book. Put one letter on each page and choose a mathematical word beginning with that letter, e.g. A is for Angle. Then illustrate that page with an angle, if you want a simple, attractive book, or with facts about angles, such as types of angles, with illustrations, if you want to do more research.
Even letters like Q, X, Y and Z give no difficulty. The most difficult letter to find a suitable word for seems to be J. There is 'join', as in 'Join the points', or 'Joule', whose name is used for a unit of work.

PUZZLE

31.   How many times in 12 hours do the hands of a clock point in the same direction ?

To the student : 4

Making plans for revision

As the time of the examination draws nearer you should look back over your progress and see if you are satisfied with it, and make a plan of action for the future. If you have been working steadily from the beginning of the course, you may not need to make any extra effort. If you enjoy the challenge of Maths you are probably working well and learning everything as you go along. But if you find some of the work difficult and are feeling discouraged, perhaps a little extra effort at this stage, and perhaps a change in the way you approach your work, will help to improve your standard, and you will feel more confident.

In addition to lessons and set homework you should spend some time each week on individual study. Make a plan for this depending on how much time you have available and what you need to learn or practise. In addition to Maths, you will have work to do in all your other subjects, so take these into consideration. If you have to do a 'Project' in any subject, then start it in good time or you will find yourself at the last minute spending all your time on it, and your other work is neglected.

You must plan how you are going to revise the work. You could work through this book again in order, spending so much time on each chapter. Choose a suitable selection of questions to do, either straightforward ones if you need practice in these, or the more challenging questions if you are more confident with the topic. Alternatively, you could use the revision exercises in the miscellaneous sections A to E of the book. You might prefer to revise all the arithmetic, then the algebra, then the geometry, and so on. The important thing is that **you** should decide for yourself what **you** need to do, and then plan how you are going to do it.

Sort out your difficulties as you go along. Try to think things out for yourself as far as possible, rather than having to be shown how to do everything. But if you need extra help, then **ask** someone to help you, either your teacher, someone in your class or a higher class, a parent or a friend.

Keep a list of what you are doing. At first there will be a lot to do and not much done, but you will find it encouraging when after a few weeks you can see that you are making real progress.

Symmetry and polygons

The topics in this chapter include:

- understanding the symmetry properties of 2-D shapes and using these to solve problems,
- knowing and using the properties of polygons,
- constructing polygons.

Axes of symmetry

The diagrams show axes of symmetry, marked by dotted lines.

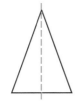

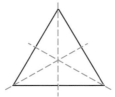

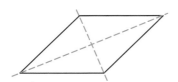

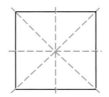

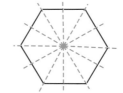

Exercise 19.1

1. Copy these figures onto tracing paper and fold them so that one half fits on top of the other half.
    The fold line is the axis of symmetry.

    1   **2**    **3**

2. Sketch these figures and mark in the axes of symmetry.

    1    **2** 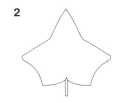   **3**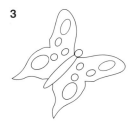

3. Sketch these figures roughly and complete them, so that the dotted line is an axis of symmetry.

    1 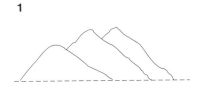   **2** 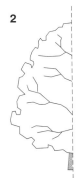   **3**

4. For each of these diagrams, state how many axes of symmetry there are.

    1 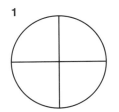   **2** 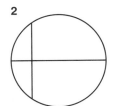   **3** 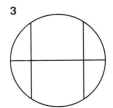   **4**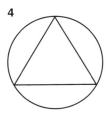

5. This square tile has two axes of symmetry shown
    by the dotted lines. Copy the figure and complete
    the rest of the pattern.

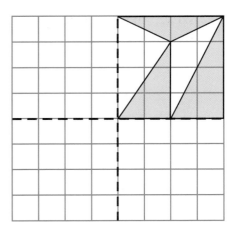

Rotational symmetry

order 2

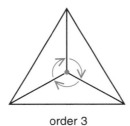

order 3

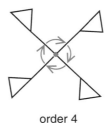

order 4

order 5

The dot shows the centre of rotational symmetry.

Exercise 19.2

1. Do these figures look the same upside-down ? If so, they have rotational symmetry of
    order 2. Copy the figures and mark the centres of symmetry.

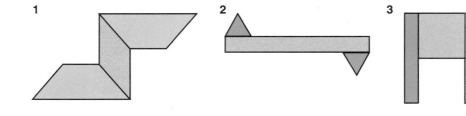

2. Sketch and complete these drawings so that they have rotational symmetry of order 2, about the point marked ●.

3. Copy these figures and complete them so that they have rotational symmetry of order 3 about the point marked ●.

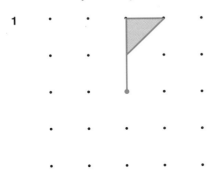

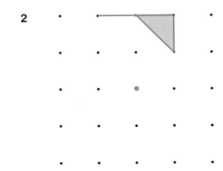

4. Copy the figures onto dotted or squared paper and complete them so that they have rotational symmetry of order 4 about the point marked ●.

5. What is the order of rotational symmetry of these figures ?

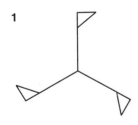

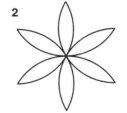

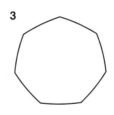

The outline of a
20 pence coin.

Triangles and quadrilaterals

Triangles

An isosceles triangle has one axis of symmetry.

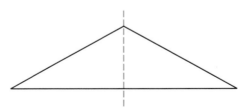

An equilateral triangle has 3 axes of symmetry.

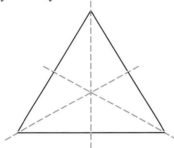

An equilateral triangle has rotational symmetry of order 3.

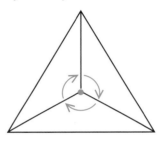

Quadrilaterals

An isosceles trapezium has one axis of symmetry.
A kite has one axis of symmetry.
A parallelogram has no axes of symmetry.
A rectangle has 2 axes of symmetry.
A rhombus has 2 axes of symmetry.
A square has 4 axes of symmetry.

The parallelogram, rectangle, rhombus and square have a centre of rotational symmetry at the point where the diagonals cross each other. They have rotational symmetry of order 2, except for the square, which has rotational symmetry of order 4.

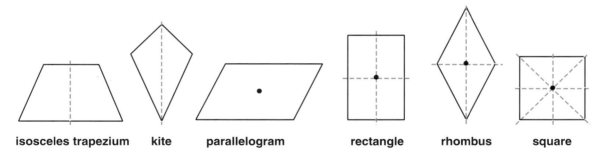

isosceles trapezium   kite   parallelogram   rectangle   rhombus   square

Exercise 19.3

1. **1** Draw accurately an equilateral triangle ABC with all sides 7.4 cm long.
    2 Draw on the diagram all the axes of symmetry.
    3 Mark point O, the centre of rotational symmetry. What is the order of rotational symmetry ?

2. In this figure, AC is an axis of symmetry.

    1 Name an angle equal to $\angle ABC$.

    2 Name a line equal to BX.

    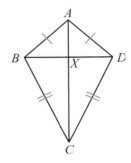

3. $ABCD$ is a rhombus.

    1 Name the axes of symmetry.

    2 If $\angle BAD = 64°$, what is the size of $\angle BAC$?

    3 Name a line equal to AE.

    4 Name 3 angles equal to $\angle AEB$.

    5 What is the size of $\angle AEB$?

    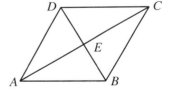

4. **1** In this parallelogram, name the centre of rotational symmetry.

    2 Name an angle equal to $\angle DAB$.

    3 Name lengths equal to AX, and BX.

    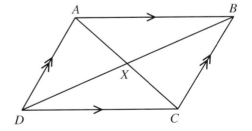

5. What is the order of rotational symmetry of

    1 a parallelogram,
    2 a rectangle,
    3 a rhombus,
    4 a square ?

Polygons

A **polygon** is a figure with straight sides.

Number of sides	Name
3	triangle
4	quadrilateral
5	pentagon
6	hexagon
7	heptagon
8	octagon

pentagon

hexagon

octagon

Regular polygons

A regular polygon has all sides equal and all angles equal.

Number of sides	Name
3	equilateral triangle
4	square
5	regular pentagon
6	regular hexagon
7	regular heptagon
8	regular octagon

Regular polygons

pentagon

hexagon

heptagon

octagon

Sum of the angles in a polygon

Split the polygon into triangles as shown. The sum of the angles in each triangle is 180°. The number of triangles is 2 less than the number of sides of the polygon.

Pentagon

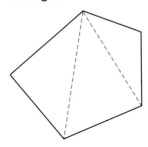

Hexagon

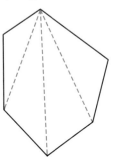

Octagon

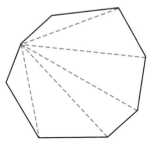

3 triangles
Sum of angles in a pentagon
= 3 × 180°
= 540°

4 triangles
Sum of angles in a hexagon
= 4 × 180°
= 720°

6 triangles
Sum of angles in an octagon
= 6 × 180°
= 1080°

Size of each angle in a regular polygon

To find the size of an angle in a **regular** polygon, divide the sum of the angles by the number of sides.

Example

1   Find the size of the angles in a regular pentagon.

The sum of the angles is 540°.
There are 5 sides, and so there are 5 angles.
Each angle = 540° ÷ 5 = 108°.

Angles of regular polygons

Number of sides	Name	Sum of angles	Each angle
3	equilateral triangle	180°	60°
4	square	360°	90°
5	regular pentagon	540°	108°
6	regular hexagon	720°	120°
8	regular octagon	1080°	135°

Exterior angles of a convex polygon are the angles formed when each side is extended in order.

The sum of the exterior angles is 360°.

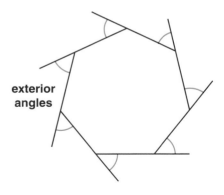

exterior
angles

An alternative way to find the size of each angle in a regular polygon

At each vertex,
  interior angle + exterior angle = 180°,
so interior angle = 180° − exterior angle.

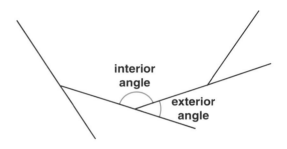

interior
angle

exterior
angle

Example

2   Find the angles of a regular octagon.

Sum of the exterior angles = 360°.
Each exterior angle = 360° ÷ 8 = 45°.
Each interior angle = 180° − 45° = 135°.

Symmetry of regular polygons

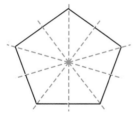

A regular pentagon has 5 axes of symmetry.   It has rotational symmetry of order 5.

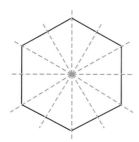

A regular hexagon has 6 axes of symmetry.

It has rotational symmetry of order 6.

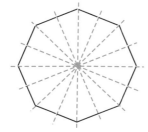

A regular octagon has 8 axes of symmetry.

It has rotational symmetry of order 8.

Diagonals of a polygon

A diagonal is a line which joins two non-adjacent points.

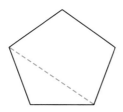

A diagonal of a pentagon.

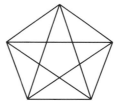

A pentagon with all diagonals drawn.

Exercise 19.4

1. What is the sum of the angles of a pentagon ?
    Four of the angles of a pentagon are 75°, 110°, 124° and 146°. Find the size of the fifth angle.

2. What is the sum of the angles of a hexagon ?
    Five of the angles of a hexagon are 108°, 106°, 115°, 120° and 124°. Find the sixth angle.

3.   What is the sum of the angles of an octagon ?
     Five of the angles of an octagon are each 130°, two other angles are 140° and 155°. Find
     the size of the remaining angle.

4.   Five of the exterior angles of a hexagon are 45°, 55°, 60°, 65° and 85°. Find the sixth
     exterior angle.

5.   *ABCD* is part of a regular pentagon. *PCBQ* is
     part of a regular octagon.
     State or find the sizes of ∠*BCD* and ∠*BCP* and
     hence find the size of angle *a*.

     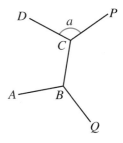

6.   Sketch these figures and mark any axes of symmetry or centres of rotational symmetry:
     equilateral triangle, square, regular pentagon, regular hexagon, regular octagon.

     Copy and complete this table.

Name of figure	Number of axes of symmetry	Order of rotational symmetry
equilateral triangle		
square		
...		

     Is there a pattern in your answers ?

7.   *ABCDEF* is a regular hexagon. *O* is the centre of rotational
     symmetry, and *AD*, *BE*, *CF* are axes of symmetry.

     1   State or find the size of an interior angle of the hexagon.
     2   Find the sizes of the angles *a*, *b*, *c*.
     3   What sort of triangle is △*OAB* ?
     4   What sort of quadrilateral is *ABCO* ?

     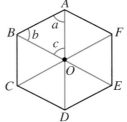

8.   The diagram shows part of a regular polygon
     with 8 sides.

     1   What is the size of an exterior angle
         of the polygon ?
     2   What is the size of an interior angle
         of the polygon ?
     3   Find the size of angle *a*.

     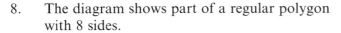
     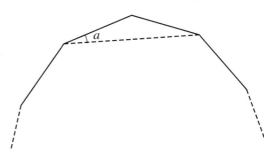

Exercise 19.5 Applications

1. From these capital letters:

   A B C F H I M N S T U X Y Z

   1 Which have one axis of symmetry which is a vertical line ?

   2 Which have one axis of symmetry which is a horizontal line ?

   3 Which have two axes of symmetry ?

   4 Which have rotational symmetry but no axes of symmetry ?

   5 Which have rotational symmetry as well as axes of symmetry ?

2. Copy and complete the figure *PQRSTU* so that *PS* is a line of symmetry. State the coordinates of *T* and *U*.

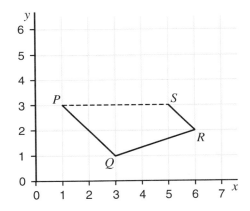

3. In the diagrams the dotted line is an axis of symmetry. Calculate the marked angles.

   1 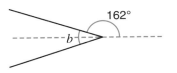 **2** 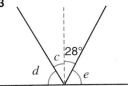 **3**

4. Copy the diagram on squared paper and complete the figure so that it has rotational symmetry of order 2 about the centre *O*.

   On a separate diagram, complete the figure so that it has rotational symmetry of order 4.

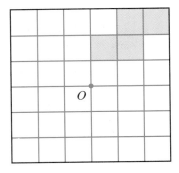

5.   Here are 2 flow charts for finding the size of each interior angle of a regular polygon.

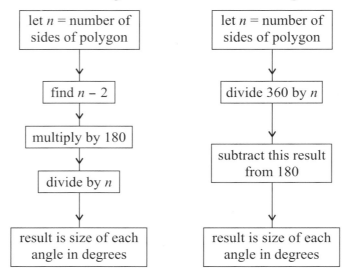

Use each flow chart to find the size of an interior angle in

1   a hexagon,   2   an octagon.

Which flow chart do you prefer to use ?

6.   Three regular polygons fit exactly together at a point P.

1   If they all have the same number of sides,
     what are the sizes of the angles at P ?
     What sort of polygons are they ?

2   If one polygon is a square and the other two have
     an equal number of sides, what are the sizes of the
     angles of P ?
     What sort of polygons are they ?

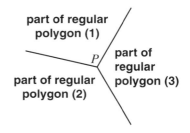

7.   Sketch the regular pentagon $ABCDE$ and join points as
      necessary to answer the following.

1   What is the size of $\angle A$?
2   What sort of triangle is $\triangle BCD$?
3   What is the size of $\angle CBD$?
4   What is the size of $\angle ABD$?
5   What sort of figure is $ABDE$?
6   If CE cuts BD at K, what sort of figures is $ABKE$?

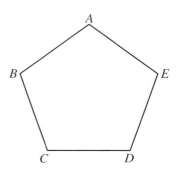

8.   **To construct a regular pentagon *ABCDE***

Method 1

Draw $AB = 6$ cm, make angles of $108°$ for $\angle BAE$ and $\angle ABC$.
Mark off 6 cm on these lines for points E and C.
To find D, with compasses centre C, draw an arc of radius
6 cm, with centre E draw an arc of radius 6 cm, to meet
the first arc at D.
Join CD and ED.

Check the accuracy of your drawing by measuring angles
C, D and E, which should all be $108°$.
Measure the distance from A to D. (You can also measure
the other 4 diagonal lengths of the pentagon, which should
all be equal.)

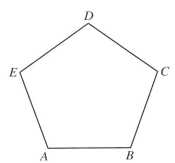

Method 2

Starting at a point O, draw 5 lines OA, OB, OC, OD and
OE, each 5 cm long, with an angle of $72°$ between each
one and the next.
Join AB, BC, CD, DE, EA and measure these lines
(which should be equal in length).

Similar methods can be used to construct other regular
polygons.

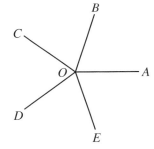

9.   **To construct a regular hexagon *ABCDEF* of side 6 cm**

With compasses mark a centre O and draw a circle,
radius 6 cm.
Take 1 point on the circumference to be A.
With compasses, radius 6 cm, centre A, mark off an
arc to cut the circumference at B.
Repeat with centre B to get point C.
Continue this method to get points D, E and F.
As a check, $FA = 6$ cm.
Join the sides AB, BC, CD, DE, EF and FA.

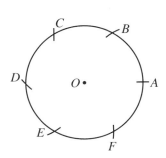

10. **To construct a regular octagon**

Draw 2 lines *AOE* and *COG*, cutting
at right angles, and making
AO = *OE* = *OC* = *OG* = 6 cm.

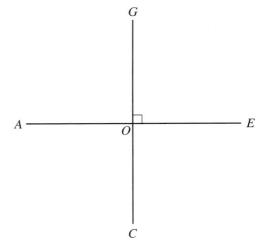

Draw 2 other lines *BOF* and *DOH* making
angles of 45° with the other lines at *O*, and
making *BO* = *OF* = *OD* = *OH* = 6 cm.
Join *AB*, *BC*, *CD*, *DE*, *EF*, *FG*, *GH*, *HA*.

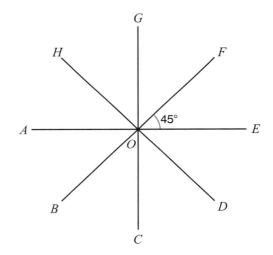

Practice test 19

1. From the letters **S H A P E**, which has

    1 only one axis of symmetry, which is horizontal,
    2 2 axes of symmetry,
    3 rotational symmetry but no axes of symmetry ?

2. In this figure, C is the centre of
rotational symmetry.

    1 Name a length equal to *AB*.

    2 Name an angle equal to ∠*BAC*.

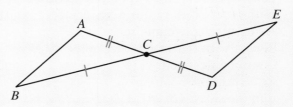

3. Sketch these quadrilaterals and mark in any axes of symmetry and any centres of rotational symmetry. State the orders of rotational symmetry.

1   **2**   **3**   **4**

4. **1** What is the sum of the angles of a pentagon ?

    2 One of the angles of a pentagon is 80°, and the other 4 angles are equal. What size are they ?

    3 What is the size of each angle in a regular pentagon ?

    4 *PQRST* is a regular pentagon. *RS* and *PT* are extended to meet at *U*. Find the size of ∠*SUT*.

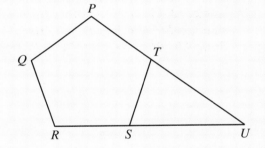

5. A regular polygon has interior angles of 135°.

    1 What is the size of an exterior angle ?
    2 How many sides has it ?

6. Sketch this regular hexagon and join points as necessary.

    What sort of quadrilaterals are
    1 *ABCD*,
    2 *ABDE* ?

    What sort of triangles are
    3 △ *ABC*,
    4 △ *ABD*,
    5 △ *ACE* ?

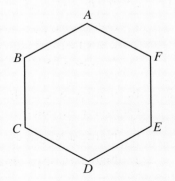

20 Functions

> **The topics in this chapter include:**
>
> - expressing simple functions in words and representing them in graphical or tabular form,
>
> - making and interpreting tables and using graphical representation of mappings expressed algebraically,
>
> - recognising, describing and using properties of linear and square functions.

Functions

If a set of values, x, is connected to another set of values, y, and for each value of x there is only one value of y, then y is said to be a function of x.

A function can be represented by ordered pairs of numbers.
e.g. (1, 1), (2, 4), (3, 9), (4, 16).
The 1st number of each pair is the value of x, the 2nd number is the value of y.

A **function** can be represented by a mapping diagram.
e.g.

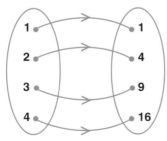

A function can be represented by a table.

e.g.

x	1	2	3	4
y	1	4	9	16

A function can be represented by an equation.
The equation for this function is $y = x^2$.
The notation $x \mapsto x^2$ can also be used. This is read as 'the function such that x is mapped onto x^2'.

Function machines

Starting with the first number, x, the instructions in the box or boxes are followed to give the second number, y.
The first number can be called the **input** and the final number the **output**.

e.g. The function $y = 5x - 4$.

When $x = 1$, $1 \times 5 = 5$, $5 - 4 = 1$, so $y = 1$,
when $x = 2$, $2 \times 5 = 10$, $10 - 4 = 6$, so $y = 6$,
when $x = 3$, $3 \times 5 = 15$, $15 - 4 = 11$, so $y = 11$,
and so on.

Use the function machine when $x = 4, 5, 6$, and copy and complete this table.

x	1	2	3	4	5	6
y	1	6	11			

Exercise 20.1

1.   Here is a function machine.

Find y when $x = 1, 2, 3, 4, 5$, and show the results
in a mapping diagram.

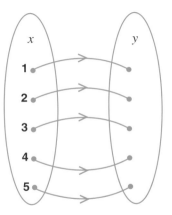

2. Here is a function machine.

| Begin with x | → | square x | → | add 1 | → | end with y |

Find y when $x = 0, 1, 2, 3, 4$, and show the results in a table.

x	0	1	2	3	4
y					

3. For each of these functions and for $x = 1, 2, 3, 4, 5$, represent the function by a mapping diagram.

1 $y = 3x$
2 $y = 10 - x$
3 $y = 2x + 3$

4. Make a table of values for $x = 0, 1, 2, 3, 4$, for these functions.

1 $y = 4x$
2 $y = 5x + 1$
3 $y = 12 - 2x$

5. Here is a function machine.

| INPUT x | → | multiply by a | → | add b | → | OUTPUT y |

Here is a mapping diagram showing some results
What are the values of a and b which produce this table ?

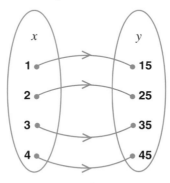

6. Find the equations, in the form $y = $ 'expression in x', for these functions given as pairs of numbers.

1   (0, 4), (1, 8), (2, 12), (3, 16).
2   (0, 7), (1, 6), (2, 5), (3, 4).
3   (1, 5), (2, 6), (3, 7), (4, 8).
4   (1, 4), (2, 6), (3, 8), (4, 10).
5   (1, 1), (2, 4), (3, 9), (4, 16).

Graphs of functions

If the values of x are continuous, the function
can be represented by its graph.

This is the graph of $y = x^2$.

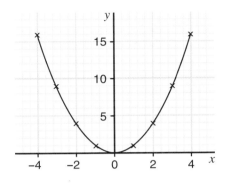

Examples

1   For this question, use graph paper with x from -1 to 3 and y from -3 to 9 using scales
of 1 cm to 1 unit on both axes.

(1)   This is a table connecting values of x and y, for the function $y = x$ or $x \mapsto x$.

x	-1	0	1	2	3
y	-1	0	1	2	3

To represent this table on graph paper, plot the points $(-1, -1)$, $(0, 0)$, $(1, 1)$, $(2, 2)$,
$(3, 3)$.
These points lie on a straight line. Draw it, using a ruler.
$y = x$ is the equation of the line.

(2)   Here is another table, for the function $y = 2x$ or $x \mapsto 2x$.

x	-1	0	1	2	3
y	-2	0	2	4	6

To represent this, plot the points $(-1, -2)$, $(0, 0)$, $(1, 2)$, $(2, 4)$, $(3, 6)$ on the same
graph as before, and draw the straight line through these points.
The equation of this line is $y = 2x$.
It is a steeper line than the first one.

(3)   Make a similar table for $y = 3x$, and plot this line on your graph.

2   For this question use graph paper with x from -1 to 3 and y from -4 to 5, using equal scales on both axes.
Plot the points given in this table, and draw the line.

x	-1	0	1	2	3
y	1	2	3	4	5

The equation of this line is $y = x + 2$.
Draw the line $y = x$ on the same graph.
These lines are parallel. $y = x + 2$ cuts the y-axis at $(0, 2)$, but $y = x$ passes through the origin $(0, 0)$.
Make a table of values for the line $y = x - 3$, and draw this line on the same graph.

3   Draw the graph of $y = 5 - 2x$.

Find the values of y when $x = -1$, 0 and 3.
When $x = 0$, $y = 5 - (2 \times 0) = 5$.
When $x = 3$, $y = 5 - (2 \times 3) = 5 - 6 = -1$.
When $x = -1$, $y = 5 - (2 \times (-1)) = 5 + 2 = 7$.

Here are these results in a table.

x	-1	0	3
y	7	5	-1

Draw axes with x from -1 to 3 and y from -1 to 7.
Plot the points $(-1, 7)$, $(0, 5)$, $(3, -1)$ and draw the line.
It slopes downwards.

(It is unnecessary to plot many points when you know the graph is a straight line. Two points are sufficient but a third point is also useful as a check on accuracy.)

Exercise 20.2

1.   Make tables of values for these functions, for values of $x = -2, -1, 0, 1, 2, 3$.

1 $y = x + 3$ **3** $y = 7 - x$
2 $y = 2x - 1$ **4** $y = 4 - 2x$

Draw axes for x from -2 to 3 and for y from -5 to 9, using a scale of 2 cm to 1 unit on the x-axis and 1 cm to 1 unit on the y-axis.
Plot the points given in the tables and draw the lines, labelling each one.

2. Make tables of values for these functions, for $x = 0, 1, 2, 3, 4$.

    1 $y = 2x - 4$ **3** $y = 9 - 3x$
    2 $y = 5 - x$

    Draw axes for x from 0 to 4 and for y from -4 to 9, using a scale of 2 cm to 1 unit on the x-axis and 1 cm to 1 unit on the y-axis.
    Plot the points given in the tables and draw the lines, labelling each one.

3. Draw the x-axis from -3 to 5 using 2 cm to 1 unit, and draw the y-axis from -4 to 12 using 1 cm to 1 unit.
    Plot the points and draw the lines represented by these tables.

    1

x	-3	-1	1	3	5
y	-4	0	4	8	12

    2

x	-3	-1	1	3	5
y	12	10	8	6	4

    3 Make a similar table for the equation $y = x - 1$ and draw this line on the graph.

    4 Make a similar table for the equation $y = 12 - 3x$ for $x = 0, 1, 2, 3, 4, 5$ and draw this line on the graph.

    5 Find the coordinates of the point where the line $y = 12 - 3x$ intersects the line drawn in part **1**.

    6 Draw the line $x = -2$ on the graph. Find the coordinates of the point where this line intersects the line drawn in part **1**.

4. Make a table of values for $x = -5, -1, 3, 7$ for the function $y = 3 (x + 1)$.
    Draw the x-axis from -5 to 7 using 1 cm to 1 unit and the y-axis from -12 to 24 using 1 cm to 4 units.
    Plot the points from the table and draw the graph.

Graphs of curves

Equations involving x^2

Exercise 20.3

1. **To draw the graph of $y = x^2$**

    This is not a straight line and several points must be plotted.

    1 Copy and complete this table showing the connection between x and y.

    Note that when $x = -4$, $x^2 = (-4)^2 = (-4) \times (-4) = 16$, (not -16).

x	-4	-3	-2	-1	0	1	2	3	4
y	16	9				1			

    2 Draw the x-axis from -4 to 4 and the y-axis from 0 to 16, taking a scale of 2 cm to 1 unit on the x axis and 1 cm to 1 unit on the y-axis.

    3 Plot these 9 points and join them with a smooth curve, drawn freehand. This shape is called a parabola.

2. To draw the graph of $y = x^2 + 3$.

    1 Copy and complete the table of values, working out x^2 and then adding 3.

x	-4	-3	-2	-1	0	1	2	3	4
x^2	16	9				1			
$+3$	3	3				3			
y	19	12				4			

    2 Draw the x-axis from -4 to 4 and the y-axis from 0 to 19 taking a scale of 2 cm to 1 unit on the x-axis and 1 cm to 1 unit on the y-axis.

    3 Plot these 9 points, $(-4, 19)$, $(-3, 12)$, etc. and join them with a smooth curve. Compare the graph with that of question 1.

    4 What is the least value of y on this curve ?

    5 Draw the line $y = 10$ on your graph and find the x-coordinates of the two points where it meets the curve, giving the answers correct to 1 decimal place.

3. 1 Copy and complete this table for the function $y = x^2 - 2$.

x	-4	-3	-2	-1	0	1	2	3	4
x^2	16	9			0				
-2	-2	-2			-2				
y	14	7			-2				

2 Draw the x-axis from -4 to 4 and the y-axis from -2 to 14, taking a scale of 2 cm to 1 unit on the x-axis and 1 cm to 1 unit on the y-axis.

3 Plot the points from the table and draw the graph of the function, joining the points with a smooth curve.

4 Find the x-coordinates of the two points where the curve meets the x-axis, correct to 1 decimal place.

Exercise 20.4   Applications

1. Here is a table of values for a function.

x	0	1	2	3	4	5
y	10	8	6	4	2	0

Copy and complete the instructions for the function machine of this function.

Input x → multiply by _ _ _ → subtract from _ _ _ → Output y

2. Draw the x-axis from 0 to 7 and the y-axis from 0 to 10 using equal scales on both axes.

1 Plot the points A (3, 6) and B (5, 10).
Draw the line OAB, where O is the origin. What is the equation of this line ?

2 Plot the point C (7, 9) and join BC.
Find the point D such that $ABCD$ is a rectangle.
Join AD and DC.
What are the coordinates of D ?

3 What is the equation of the line BD ?

3. Make a table of values for these functions, for $x = -4, -2, 0, 2, 4, 6$.

1 $y = 10 - 2x$ 2 $y = 3x - 2$

3 Draw the x-axis from -4 to 6 and the y-axis from -14 to 18, taking a scale of 1 cm to 1 unit on the x-axis and 1 cm to 2 units on the y-axis.
Plot the points given in the table and draw the lines, labelling each one.

4 What is the x-coordinate of the point where the lines intersect ?

4. **1** Continue the pattern of numbers:

(0, 0), (1, 1), (2, 4), (3, 9), (4, 16), (   ), (   ), (   ).

2 If the first number in the bracket is x, and the second number is y, what is the connection between x and y in any bracket ?

3 On graph paper, use a scale of 2 cm to 1 unit on the x-axis, with x from 0 to 7, and a scale of 2 cm to 10 units on the y-axis, with y from 0 to 50.

4 Plot the 8 points given above and also the 2 points $(5\frac{1}{2}, 30\frac{1}{4})$, $(6\frac{1}{2}, 42\frac{1}{4})$. Join all these points to form a smooth curve.

5 On the curve, what is the value of y when $x = 4\frac{1}{2}$?

5. A builder has a plot of land on which he can build 40 houses.
If he builds x luxury houses and y standard houses, write down an equation connecting x and y, and, if necessary, re-write this in the form which begins $y = \dots$
Use the equation to find the values of y when $x = 0, \ 20, \ 40$.
Draw x and y axes from 0 to 50 using a scale of 2 cm to 10 units on both axes.
Draw the graph of the equation found above, for values of x from 0 to 40.

The luxury houses each need $300 \, \text{m}^2$ of land and the standard houses need $150 \, \text{m}^2$.
Altogether the builder has $7500 \, \text{m}^2$ of land to be used.
Write down a second equation connecting x and y.
Simplify this equation by dividing each term by 150, and write it in the form $y = \dots$
Use this equation to find the values of y when $x = 0, \ 10, \ 25$.
Draw the graph of this equation on the same axes as before, for values of x from 0 to 25.

Write down the x and y coordinates of the point where the two lines intersect.

How many houses of each type did the builder build ?

Using a computer or graphics calculator

If you have the use of a computer then you probably have a graph-plotting program which you can use to plot graphs of various functions. You could also use a graphics calculator, although the graphs are shown much smaller than on a computer screen.

One use of plotting the graphs on the computer screen or calculator is so that you can see the general shape of the graph. If you need to find solutions of equations from the points of intersection of 2 graphs, you can see where these values are, approximately.

By zooming into an area around a value, or by re-scaling the axes to draw that area to a larger scale, you can get a more accurate value. The trace facility will help you to find approximate values of x and y at a point of intersection. This is equivalent to using trial and improvement methods algebraically. It is also useful to use a computer or calculator to check graphs you have drawn, and the solutions of equations you have found.

Practice test 20

1. Here is a function machine.

    | INPUT x | → | add 1 | → | multiply by 3 | → | subtract 7 | → | OUTPUT y |

    Find y when $x = 1, 3, 5, 7, 9$, and show the results in a mapping diagram.

2. Make tables of values for these functions, for $x = -2, -1, 0, 1, 2, 3, 4, 5$.

    1 $y = 4x - 1$ **2** $y = 10 - 3x$

    3 Draw the x-axis from -2 to 5 and the y-axis from -9 to 19, taking a scale of 2 cm to 1 unit on the x-axis and 1 cm to 2 units on the y-axis.

    4 Plot the points given in the table and draw the lines, labelling each one.

    5 Find the x-coordinate of the point where the lines intersect, correct to 1 decimal place.

3. To draw the graph of $y = x^2 - 5$.

    1 Make a table of values, for $x = -3, -2, -1, 0, 1, 2, 3$.

    2 Draw the x-axis from -3 to 3 and the y-axis from -5 to 4, taking a scale of 2 cm to 1 unit on both axes.

    3 Plot the 7 points and join them with a smooth curve.

    4 What is the least value of y on this curve ?

    5 Find the x-coordinates of the two points where the curve meets the x-axis, correct to 1 decimal place.

PUZZLES

32. Barry was given a box containing 125 small bars of chocolate. On the wrapper of each bar there was a token, and Barry could exchange 5 tokens at the local shop for a similar bar of chocolate. How many extra bars of chocolate did he get ?

33. By crossing out just SIX LETTERS in the following, leave the name of a topic in this book.

     P S R I O X B L A E B T I T L E I R T S Y

34. A group of people on a coach outing went into a cafe for a snack. The party leader ordered a cup of tea and a sandwich for everyone, and the total bill came to £18.49. How many people were on the coach ?

21 Solid figures

The topics in this chapter include:

- visualising, describing and representing shapes including 2-D representations of 3-D shapes,

- knowing, using the properties of, and classifying, cube, cuboid, cylinder, square based right pyramid, triangular prism, cone and sphere,

- understanding and using the terms face, edge, vertex, net and plane,

- understanding and using the symmetry properties of solid shapes,

- interpreting and drawing nets, and constructing 3-D shapes.

Solid figures

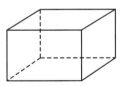

Cuboid, or rectangular block

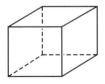

Cube

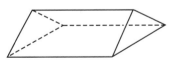

Triangular prism

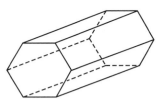

Hexagonal prism

Triangular pyramid, or tetrahedron

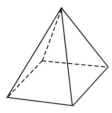

Pyramid with square base

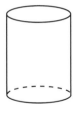

Cylinder

Cone

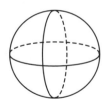

Sphere

Exercise 21.1

Practise drawing solid figures by using these methods.

1. **Drawing a cube**

    Draw a square.   Draw 4 parallel lines of equal length.   Draw a square joining the 4 ends.

      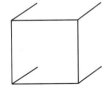 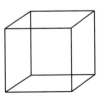

    Make some lines into dotted lines.   or   Leave out the dotted lines.

    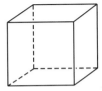 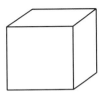

2. **Drawing a cuboid**

    Use a similar method to that of question 1.

    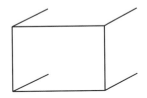 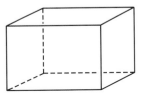

3. **Drawing a cube or a cuboid using isometric paper**

    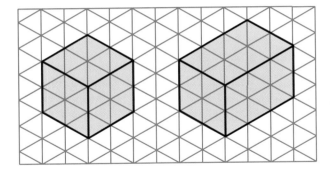

4. **Drawing a triangular prism**

    Draw a triangle and translate it to form a second triangle.

    Join the corresponding points of the triangles, making the rectangular faces.

    Make some lines into dotted lines.

    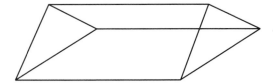

5. **Drawing a triangular pyramid**

    Draw a triangle and put a dot somewhere inside it.

    Draw dotted lines from the dot to the vertices of the triangle.

    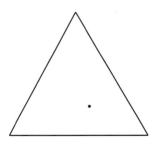 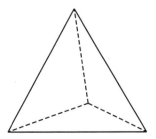

6. **Drawing a pyramid with a square base**

    Draw a parallelogram *ABCD* as shown. Find where the diagonals cross and put a dot vertically above this point.

    Join the dot to *A*, *B* and *C*, using solid lines, and to *D* with a dotted line. Make *AD* and *DC* into dotted lines.

    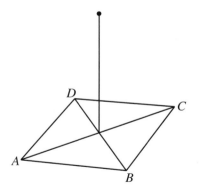 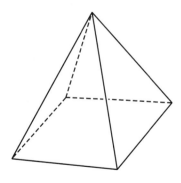

7.   **Drawing a cylinder**

Begin with a rectangle.
Make curved lines at the top and the bottom.
Rub out the straight lines there, and make part of the bottom curve dotted.

8.   **Drawing a cone**

Begin with an isosceles triangle.
Make curved lines at the bottom.
Rub out the bottom straight line and make some of the curve dotted.

Nets of solid figures

These are patterns which when cut out and folded will make the solid figures.

Net of a cube

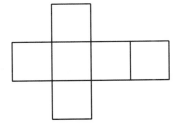

Here are nets for some other figures you can make. Decide which lengths on the nets should be equal.

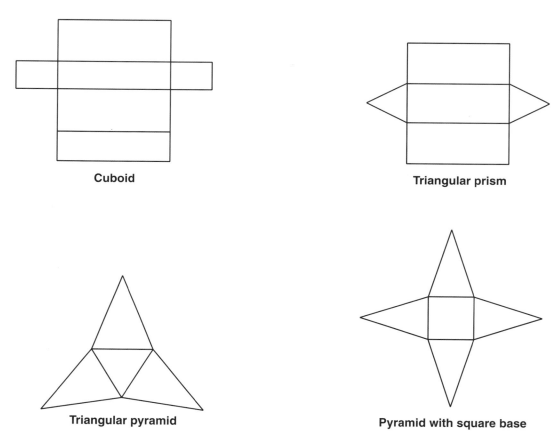

Cuboid   **Triangular prism**

Triangular pyramid   **Pyramid with square base**

There are other arrangements possible, to make the same solid figures.

Exercise 21.2

1. Name the solid figures with these shapes.

    1   **2**   **3**   **4**

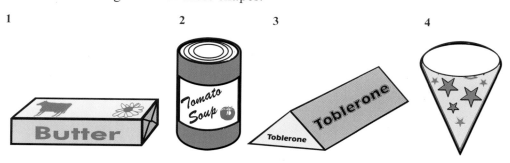

2. Give an example of a common object, not shown in question 1, which has the shape of

    1 a cuboid,   **3** a sphere,
    2 a cube,   **4** a cylinder.

3. Of the solid figures shown on page 276, which have

    1 one or more faces which are square,
    2 one or more faces which are rectangular,
    3 one or more faces which are circular,
    4 one or more faces which are curved,
    5 faces which are all plane (i.e. not curved) ?

4. The net of a cube can be arranged in several different ways. Which of these drawings of arrangements of six equal squares, if cut out and folded, would make a cube ?

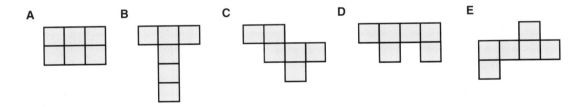

5. Name the solid figures which can be made from these nets.

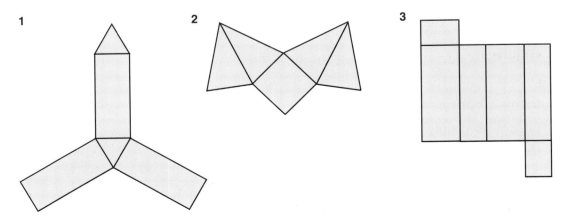

6. This net can be folded to make a triangular prism.
    Which letter(s) will point A join ?

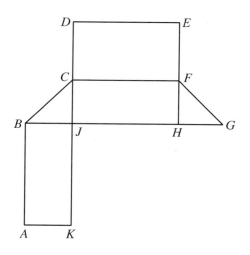

Exercise 21.3   Applications

1. Look at drawings of solid figures which have no
    curved faces, or look at actual objects if you
    have them available.
    Count the number of faces, vertices (corners)
    and edges on each.
    For example, this prism with pentagonal ends
    has 7 faces, 10 vertices and 15 edges.

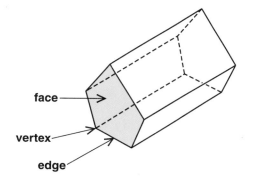

    Copy and complete this table and add other
    solid figures to the list.
    F = number of faces, V = number of vertices,
    E = number of edges.

Solid figure	F	V	E
cuboid			
triangular prism			
prism with pentagonal ends	7	10	15
tetrahedron			
pyramid on square base			

Can you discover the relationship between $F + V$ and E ?

2.   If a small triangular pyramid is sliced off one
      corner of a cube, how many faces, vertices and
      edges has the remaining solid figure ?

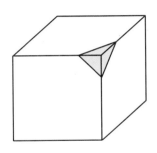

3.   ## Making models from thin cardboard, using their nets

   1   Draw the pattern of the net of the solid figure, on paper. Then place it over thin
       cardboard, with something underneath to protect the desk or table, and prick
       through the main points using the point of your compasses. Remove the pattern and
       join up the marks on the cardboard. (Keep the pattern for future use.)

   2   Draw a tab on every alternate edge, i.e. starting
       at any edge, put tabs on edges $1, 3, 5, 7, \ldots$ in order.
       Tabs can be drawn freehand. They should be large
       enough to stick easily.

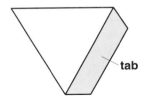

   3   Score every line.
       This means making a nick in the line so that it folds neatly. Put your ruler along the
       line and drag your compass point along it. (When you fold the cardboard, always
       fold **away** from the side you scored on. Do not bend the cardboard backwards **and**
       forwards.)

   4   Cut out the net and fold it along the scored lines.

   5   Glue it together, doing one tab at a time and waiting until it has stuck before doing
       the next one, except at the last face where more than one tab may have to be glued at
       the same time. You may need to poke your compass point through a corner hole to
       help to make the last tab stick down properly.

   To make a cube

   Making the sides of the squares 4 cm long, copy the net of the cube shown on page 279
   onto paper. (Graph paper or squared paper is useful.)
   Carry out the instructions above for making the model.

To make a cuboid

Decide on the measurements your finished
cuboid will have, and design and draw the net.
Here is the net for a cuboid which will be
8 cm by 3 cm by 2 cm.
Carry out the instructions for making the model.

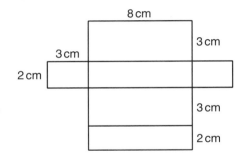

To make a triangular prism

Decide on the measurements your finished prism
will have. Here is the net for a prism with ends
which are right-angled triangles.
You can draw the net on graph paper or
squared paper.
Carry out the instructions for making the model.

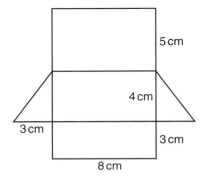

4.   This is a triangular pyramid with all edges 4 cm long.
Since all the faces are equilateral triangles it can also
be called a **regular tetrahedron**.

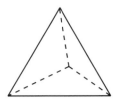

Which of these arrangements of 4 triangles can be used as nets of the pyramid ?

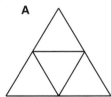

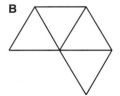

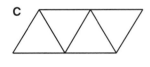

Draw a net of the pyramid accurately. (Isometric paper is useful.)
Make the model.

5. **To make a pyramid with a square base**

Begin by drawing a semicircle, centre O, of radius 10 cm, and from it make 4 triangles, as shown.

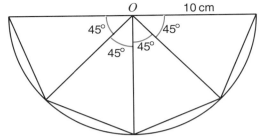

Add tabs. Score all lines and cut out the figure. Make an open pyramid by glueing along the long tab.

Make a square base of side 7.7 cm and glue it to the other tabs.

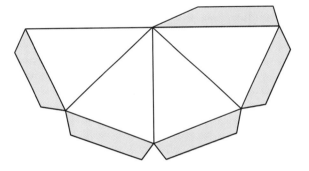

6. The curved surface of a cone is made from a sector of a circle. Draw a circle centre O, radius 8 cm. Cut out the sector AOB, bend it round and join OA to OB. (The shape of the cone will depend on the size of $\angle AOB$.)

What shape is needed to make the curved surface of a cylinder ?

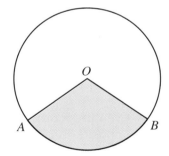

7. **Axes of symmetry**

This cone has an axis of symmetry shown by the vertical dotted line. Sketch 3 other solid figures which have an axis of symmetry.

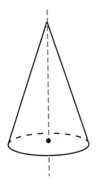

8. **Planes of symmetry**

This cylinder has a plane of symmetry.
The plane divides the cylinder into two equal halves.
One half is a reflection of the other half.

The cylinder has other planes of symmetry.
These cut the end circles into two halves.

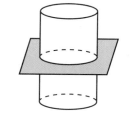

These solid figures have planes of symmetry. How many do they have ?

1

Cuboid
with rectangular
(not square) faces

2

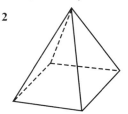

Pyramid
with square base

3

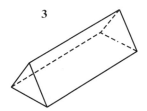

Prism
with equilateral
triangular ends

Practice test 21

1. Name the solid figures with the shape of

   1 a cricket ball,
   2 a box of drawing pins,
   3 a simple tent,
   4 a tube of sweets,
   5 a lump of sugar.

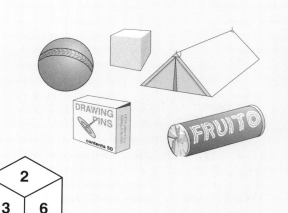

2. On a proper die, the numbers on
   opposite faces add up to 7.

A cardboard cube was to be made into a die by labelling the squares on the net with
the numbers 1, 2, 3, 4, 5, 6.

On these nets, some of the squares have been labelled. Sketch these diagrams and label
the other squares correctly.

1 | 1 | 2 |
          | 3 |

2
| 4 | 1 |
| 2 |

3
| 1 |
| 5 | 3 |

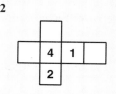
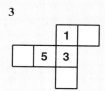

3. The diagram shows a net of a solid figure.
What sort of solid figure is it ?
When the solid is constructed, which letter(s)
will point *A* join ?

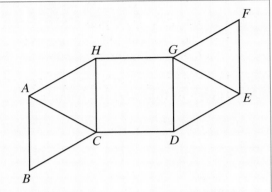

4. A solid figure consists of a pyramid fitted
exactly on top of a cube.
State how many faces, vertices and edges
the solid figure has.

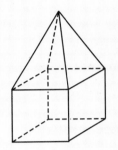

5. Draw full-size and complete the net of this prism.
The triangular ends are isosceles triangles and
the prism is 9 cm long.

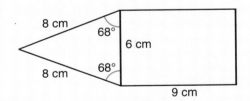

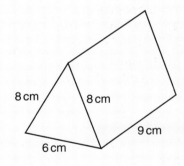

PUZZLES

35. Arrange (a) three 1's, (b) three 2's, (c) three 4's, without using any mathematical signs,
so that you represent the highest possible number in each case.

36. Practical maths.
Fold a piece of paper in half, then in half again, and again, . . . , 9 times altogether.

22 Probability (2)

The topics in this chapter include:

- using a probability line and ordering the likelihood of events,

- recognising situations where probabilities can be based on equally likely outcomes,

- identifying all the outcomes of a combination of two experiments,

- knowing that if the probability of an event is p then the probability of the event not happening is $1 - p$,

- knowing and using the fact that the total probability of all mutually exclusive outcomes of an event is 1,

- comparing the estimated probability from experimental results with the theoretical probability.

Probability

Probability or chance is the likelihood of an event happening.
It is measured on a numerical scale from 0 to 1 and it can be given as a fraction, a decimal or a percentage.

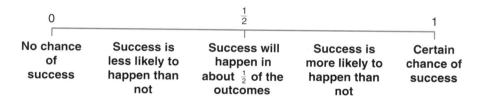

0	$\frac{1}{2}$	1
No chance of success	**Success is less likely to happen than not**	**Success will happen in about $\frac{1}{2}$ of the outcomes**	**Success is more likely to happen than not**	**Certain chance of success**

We can calculate the value of the probability of a certain result in an experiment or trial if there are two or more outcomes which are equally likely.

Equally likely outcomes

If a trial has n equally likely outcomes, then the probability of each outcome occurring is $\frac{1}{n}$.

If a trial has n equally likely outcomes, and of these s outcomes are successful ones, then:

$$\text{Probability (or chance) of a successful outcome} = \frac{\text{number of successful outcomes}}{\text{total possible outcomes}} = \frac{s}{n}$$

Examples

1 Find the probability of a tossed coin showing heads.

   There are 2 outcomes, heads or tails, and these are equally likely.

   Probability of heads $= \frac{1}{n} = \frac{1}{2}$.

2 Find the probability of a fair die showing a five when thrown.

   There are 6 outcomes, the numbers 1, 2, 3, 4, 5, 6, and these
   are equally likely.

   Probability of a five $= \frac{1}{n} = \frac{1}{6}$.

3 Find the probability of a number picked at random from the numbers 1 to 10 being
   exactly divisible by 4.

   There are ten equally likely outcomes of which two (4 and 8) are successful.

   Probability of picking a number exactly divisible by 4 $= \frac{s}{n} = \frac{2}{10} = \frac{1}{5}$.

4 If a letter is chosen at random from the 11 letters of the word PROBABILITY, what is
   the probability that it is A, B, either A or B ?

   There are 11 equally likely outcomes, including one A and two B's.

   Probability of letter A $= \frac{1}{n} = \frac{1}{11}$,

   probability of letter B $= \frac{s}{n} = \frac{2}{11}$,

   probability of either A or B $= \frac{s}{n} = \frac{3}{11}$.

Exercise 22.1

1. A fair die is thrown once. What is the probability of getting
    1   a three,
    2   a square number ?

2. 20 discs, numbered from 1 to 20, are placed in a bag and one is drawn out at random.
    What is the probability of getting a disc with
    1   a number greater than 15,
    2   a number which includes the digit 1,
    3   a number which is divisible by 3 ?

3. In a fairground game a pointer is spun and you win
    the amount shown in the sector where it comes
    to rest. Assuming that the pointer is equally likely to
    come to rest in any sector, what is the probability that
    1   you win some money,
    2   you win 20p ?

    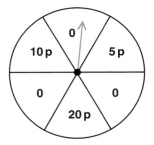

4. In a tombola game, $\frac{7}{8}$ of the counters are blank. The rest have a number on them and
    they win a prize. If you take a counter out of the drum at random what is the probability
    that you win a prize ?

5. If you choose a card at random from a pack of 52
    playing-cards, what is the probability that it is
    1   an ace,
    2   a diamond,
    3   a red card with an even number ?

6. A letter is chosen at random from the 11 letters of the word MATHEMATICS.
    What is the probability that it is
    1   the letter M,
    2   a vowel,
    3   a letter from the second half of the alphabet ?

7. In a pack of playing-cards, the 2 of diamonds and the 2 of hearts have been removed. If
    you choose a card at random from the remaining cards, what is the probability that it is
    1   a diamond,
    2   a two,
    3   the 2 of diamonds ?

8. A box contains 2 red, 3 yellow and 5 green sweets. One is taken out at random, and
    eaten. A second sweet is then taken out.
    1   If the 1st sweet was green, what is the probability that the 2nd sweet is also green ?
    2   If the 1st sweet was not red, what is the probability that the 2nd sweet is red ?

9.   Two cards are drawn from a pack of 52 cards. What is the probability that the second card is from the same suit as the first
     1   if the 1st card is replaced before the 2nd card is drawn,
     2   if the 1st card is not replaced before the 2nd card is drawn ?

Two events combined

Example

Five discs numbered 1 to 5 are placed in a bag and one is drawn out at random and not replaced. A second disc is then drawn out at random.

(1)   What is the probability that the second disc has a number higher by at least 2 than the first disc ?
(2)   What is the probability that the total of the two numbers is 6 ?

Set down the possible equally likely results in a diagram called a sample space.

		1st disc				
		1	2	3	4	5
2nd disc	1		.	.	.	.
	2	.		.	.	.
	3	.	*a*	.		.
	4	.	.		.	.
	5	.	.	.	.	

A dot represents one of the equally likely outcomes, e.g. dot (*a*) represents the outcome that the first disc is 2 and the second disc is 4. There are 20 dots so there are 20 equally likely outcomes. (It might be more useful to write the actual outcomes e.g. (2, 4), or the total score, instead of just dots.)

We will mark in some way all the outcomes where the second disc has a number higher by at least 2 than the first disc, and in a different way where the total of the two numbers is 6. (Normally these would go on the original diagram but here to make it clearer we have two new diagrams.)

(1)

		1st disc				
		1	2	3	4	5
2nd disc	1		.	.	.	.
	2	.		.	.	.
	3	⊡	.		.	.
	4	⊡	⊡	.		.
	5	⊡	⊡	⊡	.	

(2)

		1st disc				
		1	2	3	4	5
2nd disc	1		.	.	.	⊙
	2	.		.	⊙	.
	3	.	.		.	.
	4	.	⊙	.		.
	5	⊙	.	.	.	

⊡ represents a successful outcome. There are 6 successful outcomes.

⊙ represents a successful outcome. There are 4 successful outcomes.

(1)   The probability that the 2nd disc has a number higher by at least 2 than the first disc $= \dfrac{s}{n} = \dfrac{6}{20} = 0.3$

(2)   The probability that the total of the two numbers is 6 $= \dfrac{s}{n} = \dfrac{4}{20} = 0.2$

Exercise 22.2

1. In a bag there are 5 cards numbered 1, 3, 5, 7, 9.
    In a second bag there are 4 cards numbered 2, 4, 6, 8.
    One card is drawn at random from each bag.
    Copy and complete the sample space diagram
    showing the sum of the numbers on the two cards.

		1st card				
		1	3	5	7	9
	2	3	5			
2nd	4	5				
card	6					
	8					

What is the probability that
    1 the sum is an odd number,
    2 the sum is an even number,
    3 the sum is 13,
    4 the sum is less than 10,
    5 the sum is exactly divisible by 5 ?

2. A regular triangular pyramid (tetrahedron) has its four faces numbered 1, 2, 3, 4 and it is used as a die by counting as the score the number on the bottom face.

    Copy and complete a sample space diagram showing the outcomes when this die is thrown twice.

		1st throw			
		1	2	3	4
	1	1, 1	2, 1	·	·
2nd	2	1, 2	2, 2	·	·
throw	3	1, 3	·	·	·
	4	·	·	·	·

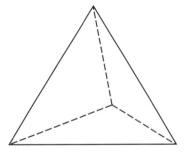

Find the probability that
    1 in both of the two throws the score is 4,
    2 in the two throws the sum of the scores is 4,
    3 in the two throws the product of the scores is 4.

3. These five tiles are placed in a bag.
    One tile is drawn out and replaced and
    then a second tile is drawn out.
    Make a sample space diagram of the
    equally likely results.

    Find the probability of getting
    1 A first and then B,
    2 A and B in either order.

    3 Repeat the questions if the second
    tile is drawn out without the first
    tile being replaced.

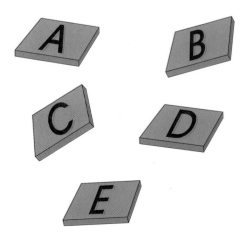

4. Two dice are thrown together. Copy and complete the sample space showing the total scores.

		1st die					
		1	2	3	4	5	6
	1	2	3	4	.	.	.
	2	3	.	.	.	.	.
2nd die	3	.	.	.	.	.	.
	4	.	.	.	.	.	.
	5	.	.	.	.	.	.
	6	.	.	.	.	.	.

List in a table the probability of scoring each total from 2 to 12.

Score	2	3	4	5	6	7	8	9	10	11	12
Probability	$\frac{1}{36}$										

What is the probability
1 that the sum of the two numbers is greater than 10,
2 that the sum of the two numbers is 7,
3 of a double (the two dice showing the same number),
4 of both dice showing numbers less than 3 ?

5. There are six cards numbered 1 to 6. One card is selected at random and not replaced, and then a second card is selected. Make a sample space diagram of the equally likely results.
What is the probability
1 that the sum of the two numbers is greater than 10,
2 that the sum of the two numbers is 7,
3 that the product of the two numbers is odd ?

Mutually exclusive events

When there are two or more outcomes of an event and at each time only one of the outcomes can happen (because if one outcome happens, this prevents any of the other outcomes happening), then the outcomes are called **mutually exclusive events**.

The sum of the probabilities of all possible mutually exclusive events is 1, because it is certain that one of them will occur.

If the probability of an event happening is p, then the probability of the event not happening is $1 - p$.

Examples

1   In the last year in a certain school, pupils must study one of the subjects music, or art, or Latin.
The probability that a pupil studies music is $\frac{1}{4}$, and the probability that a pupil studies art is $\frac{5}{8}$.
If a pupil from that year is chosen at random, what is the probability that the pupil studies Latin?

P(music) $= \frac{1}{4}$,
P(art) $= \frac{5}{8}$.

The sum of the probabilities of all events $= 1$.

P(Latin) + P(music) + P(art) $= 1$.
P(Latin) $= 1 - \frac{1}{4} - \frac{5}{8} = 1 - \frac{2}{8} - \frac{5}{8} = 1 - \frac{7}{8} = \frac{1}{8}$.

P(music) is a short way of writing 'the probability of a pupil studying music'.

2   The weather forecaster said that there was a probability of 20% that it would rain tomorrow.
What is the probability that it will not rain?

P(rain) $= 20\% = 0.2$
The probability of it not raining $= 1 - $ P(rain)
$$= 1 - 0.2$$
$$= 0.8, \text{ as a decimal,}$$
$$= 80\%, \text{ as a percentage.}$$

Exercise 22.3

1.   A biscuit jar contains 7 shortbread biscuits, 8 cream biscuits, 10 chocolate biscuits and 15 wafer biscuits. If a biscuit is picked out at random, what is the probability that
1   it is either a cream biscuit or a chocolate biscuit,
2   it is not a wafer biscuit?

2.   6 men, 4 women, 3 girls and 7 boys enter for a contest.
If they each have an equal chance of winning, what is the probability that the winner is
1   a man,
2   a child,
3   a female?

3.   In a raffle, Mrs Andrews buys 10 tickets and
     Mr Andrews buys 5 tickets. There are 200
     tickets sold altogether.
     What is the probability that the 1st prize is
     won by either Mr or Mrs Andrews ?

4.   A bag contains a number of sweets, some red and some green. The probability of taking
     out a red sweet, at random, is 0.6.
     1   What is the probability of taking out a green sweet ?
     2   If 36 of the sweets are green sweets, how many red sweets are there ?

5.   A box contains cartons of orange juice, grapefruit
     juice and pineapple juice.
     If a drink is taken out at random the probability
     that it is orange or pineapple is $\frac{5}{8}$.

     1   What is the probability that it is grapefruit ?

     2   The probability that it is orange is $\frac{3}{8}$. What is
         the probability that it is not orange ?

6.   Jan estimates that the probability of the bus being early is 0.1,
     of it being on time is 0.7, and otherwise it will be late.
     1   What is the probability that the bus will be late ?
     2   If the bus is early, Jan will miss it, and be late
         for school. If the bus is late, Jan will also be
         late for school.
         What is the probability that Jan will be late
         for school ?

7.   1   In an archery game the probability of Helen hitting a target is 0.7.
         What is the probability of her missing the target ?

     2   The probability of Helen hitting one of the 4 outer
         rings is 0.65. What is the probability of her hitting the
         centre circle ?

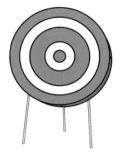

Exercise 22.4 Applications

1.   Write down a list of all possible results if a coin is
      tossed 3 times in succession, e.g. HHH, HTH, HHT, ...

      What is the probability of getting
      1   3 heads,
      2   2 or more tails,
      3   exactly 2 heads and 1 tail ?

2.   100 discs, numbered from 1 to 100, are placed in
      a bag and one is drawn out at random.

      What is the probability of getting a disc with
      1   a number greater than 70,
      2   a number which includes the digit 1,
      3   a two-digit number whose digits add up to 9 ?

3.   Seeds are planted with 5 in each pot. The probabilities of 0, 1, 2, 3, 4 or 5 seeds in a pot
      germinating are as follows:

Number of seeds germinating	0	1	2	3	4	5
Probability	0.002	0.008	0.02	0.14	0.39	0.44

      What is the probability of having a pot in which
      1   at least 1 seed germinates,
      2   less than 5 seeds germinate ?

4.   A number of corks are placed in a bag. The corks are marked with a number 1, 2, 3, 4 or
      5. If a cork is picked out at random the probabilities of the different scores are:
      P(1) = 0.15
      P(2) = 0.1
      P(3) = 0.25
      P(4) = 0.2

      What is the probability of getting
      1   a cork marked 5,
      2   a cork not marked 5 ?
      3   Which number has the least chance of being picked ?
      4   What is the probability of this number not being picked ?

5.   This table shows the numbers of boys and girls in 200 families.

		Number of boys				
		0	1	2	3	4
Number of girls	0	45	6	7	8	3
	1	7	15	25	12	1
	2	5	23	13	1	0
	3	10	9	2	0	0
	4	2	3	0	2	1

For example, there are 45 families with no children, and 6 families with 1 boy but no girls.

Find the probability that in a family chosen from these at random, there are
1   two boys and one girl,
2   an equal number of boys and girls (at least one of each),
3   more than two boys.

6.   A   B   C   D

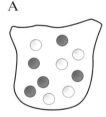   

A collection of green or white table-tennis balls are placed in 4 bags, as shown.
Sheila wants to pick a green table-tennis ball from a bag, without looking.

1   Find the probability of selecting a green ball from each of the 4 bags.
2   Which bag should Sheila choose to pick from, to have least chance of picking a green ball ?
3   Which bag should Sheila choose to pick from, to have most chance of picking a green ball ?
4   Of the other two bags, which one would give Sheila a greater chance than the other one, of picking a green ball ?

The table-tennis balls from two of the bags are put together in a box. A ball is picked out at random from the box.
Which two bags were used if the probability of picking out a green ball is
5   $\frac{1}{2}$,   6 $\frac{8}{17}$?

7   Which two bags should be used together to make the probability of drawing out a green ball from the box as small as possible, and what is this probability ?
8   Which two bags should be used together to make the probability of drawing out a green ball from the box as large as possible, and what is this probability ?

7.   Two dice are thrown together. One of them is numbered from 1 to 6, as is usual. The other one has the six faces marked 1, 2, 2, 3, 3, 3.
Copy and complete the sample space diagram showing the results.

		1st die					
		1	2	3	4	5	6
	1	1, 1	2, 1	3, 1			
	2	1, 2					
2nd	2						
die	3						
	3						
	3						

Find the probability that
1 the sum of the numbers on the two dice is 5,
2 the numbers on the two dice are the same,
3 at least one of the numbers on the two dice is a 3.

8.   In a batch of components the probabilities of the number of faults per component are as follows:
P(0 faults) = 0.8,
P(1 fault) = 0.12,
P(2 faults) = 0.06.
The other components have more than 2 faults.

What is the probability that a component picked at random has
1 more than 2 faults,
2 at least 1 fault ?

9.   Find the theoretical results for the experiments you carried out in Exercise 14.3, questions 1, 2, 3, 6 and 7, and compare them with your experimental results.

Practice test 22

1.   The students in a school club belong to two forms 11X and 11Y.

	11X	11Y
Girls	12	16
Boys	8	14

If from this club one member is chosen at random, what is the probability that it is
1 a boy,
2 a member of 11Y,
3 a girl from 11X ?

4 If a girl has to be chosen at random, what is the probability that she is from 11X ?

2. Some parachute jumpers are landing on the
    target shown.
    There is an equal probability of them landing on
    any of the small squares.
    They never fail to land somewhere within the
    target.
    Points, ranging from 1 to 10, are scored
    for landing on different squares. These points
    are shown in the diagram.

1	2	3	4	3	2	1
2	5	6	7	6	5	2
3	6	8	9	8	6	3
4	7	9	10	9	7	4
3	6	8	9	8	6	3
2	5	6	7	6	5	2
1	2	3	4	3	2	1

    What is the probability of a parachutist scoring
    1   10 points,
    2   8 or 9 points,
    3   5 or more points,
    4   3 or less points ?

3. A bag contains 4 cards numbered 1 to 4. Two cards are selected at random. (The first
    card is not replaced before the second card is selected.) Show the outcomes in a
    sample space diagram.

    Find the probability that
    1   there is a difference of 2 between the numbers on the two cards,
    2   the two cards have a sum of 5 or 6.

4. Raffle tickets are sold from books of three different colours, blue, green and pink. The
    probability that the winning ticket is blue is 0.35 and the probability that the winning
    ticket is pink is 0.4. What is the probability that the winning ticket is green ?

5. At a certain set of traffic lights,
    the probability of the lights showing red = 0.3,
    the probability of the lights showing red and amber = 0.04,
    the probability of the lights showing green = 0.6,
    the probability of the lights showing amber = x.

    1   What is the value of x ?

    2   A motorist passes through the junction every day.
        Unless the lights are showing green he has to stop.
        What is the probability that he has to stop ?

    3   A pedestrian crosses the road at the junction every day.
        He can cross safely when the lights are showing red.
        Unless the lights are showing red, he has to wait.
        What is the probability that he has to wait ?

23 Perimeters, areas and volumes

> **The topics in this chapter include:**
>
> - measuring and calculating the perimeters of plane rectilinear shapes,
> - estimating areas by counting squares,
> - calculating areas of plane rectilinear shapes,
> - finding volumes by counting cubes,
> - calculating the volumes of cubes and cuboids.

Perimeters

The perimeter of a plane figure is the total length of the edges.

> The perimeter of a rectangle $= 2 \times$ (length + breadth)
> $$= 2(l + b)$$

Examples

1. Find the perimeter of a rectangle with sides $10\,\text{cm}$ and $8\,\text{cm}$.

    Perimeter $= 2(l + b)$

    $\qquad = 2 \times (10 + 8)\,\text{cm}$

    $\qquad = 2 \times 18\,\text{cm}$

    $\qquad = 36\,\text{cm}$

2   Measure the sides of this figure, to the nearest mm, and find its perimeter.

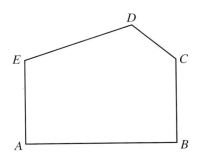

$AB = 4.0$ cm

$BC = 2.3$ cm

$CD = 1.5$ cm

$DE = 3.0$ cm

$EA = 2.3$ cm

$\overline{13.1 \text{ cm}}$

The perimeter $= AB + BC + CD + DE + EA$

$= 13.1$ cm

Exercise 23.1

1.   Find the perimeters of these figures.

1   **2**   **3**

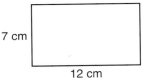   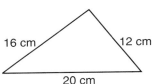   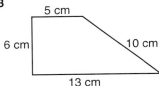

2.   Measure the sides of these figures, to the nearest mm, and find their perimeters.

1   **2**   **3**

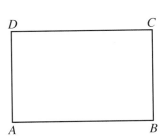   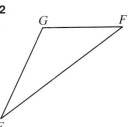   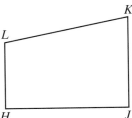

3.   **1**   Find the perimeter of a rectangle with length $4\frac{1}{2}$ cm and width $2\frac{1}{2}$ cm.
     2   Find the perimeter of a square of side $5\frac{1}{4}$ cm.
     3   Find the perimeter of an equilateral triangle with sides 7.2 cm.

4.   The perimeter of a rectangle is 30 cm and its length is 9 cm. Find its width.

5.   The perimeter of a triangle is 19 cm and one side has length 6 cm. The other two sides are equal. Find their lengths.

Areas

When we measure area we compare it with a unit area.
We can use the area of a square of side 1 cm for the unit.
This is called 1 square centimetre and written $1\,\text{cm}^2$.

1 cm

1 cm

If we are measuring larger areas we will compare them with
$1\,\text{m}^2$ or $1\,\text{km}^2$.

Area of a rectangle = length × breadth = lb

Area of a square = (length)^2 = l^2

Area of a triangle = $\frac{1}{2}$ × base × perpendicular height = $\frac{1}{2}bh$

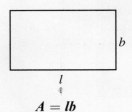

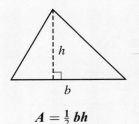

$A = lb$ $A = l^2$ $A = \frac{1}{2}bh$

Examples

1   **Rectangle**

Area = lb

$= 10 \times 8\,\text{cm}^2$

$= 80\,\text{cm}^2$

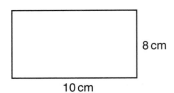
8 cm
10 cm

2   **Square**

Area = l^2

$= 8^2\,\text{cm}^2$

$= 64\,\text{cm}^2$

8 cm

3   **Triangle**

Area = $\frac{1}{2}bh$

$= \frac{1}{2} \times 10 \times 6\,\text{cm}^2$

$= 30\,\text{cm}^2$

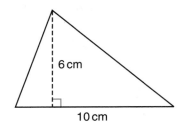
6 cm
10 cm

Exercise 23.2

1. Find the areas of these figures.

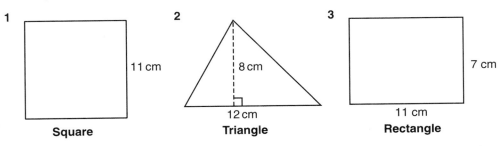

2. Find the areas of these figures. They are drawn full-size. Make any measurements you need, measuring in cm, to the nearest $\frac{1}{2}$ cm.

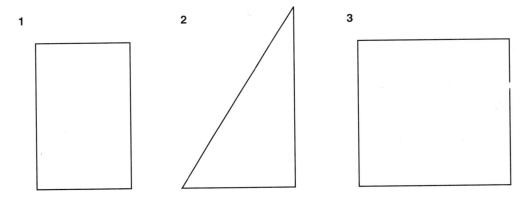

3. Draw these figures full-size:

   (a) a right-angled triangle with sides 5 cm and 2.2 cm next to the right angle,
   (b) a square side 2.4 cm,
   (c) a rectangle length 3.6 cm, breadth 1.4 cm.

   Decide by estimation which of these 3 shapes has
   1 the largest area,
   2 the smallest area.
   3 Calculate the areas to check your estimates.

4. Find the area and perimeter of a rectangular lawn 7 m long and 4 m wide.

5. Find the area and the perimeter of this triangle.

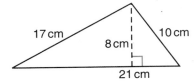

6.   What is the length in metres of a side of a square lawn which has an area of $144\,\text{m}^2$?
      What is the perimeter of the lawn ?

Examples

1   Find the area of this figure, which represents the side of a shed.

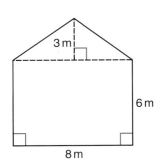

Area of rectangle $= lb$

$$= 8 \times 6\,\text{m}^2$$

$$= 48\,\text{m}^2$$

Area of triangle $= \tfrac{1}{2}bh$

$$= \tfrac{1}{2} \times 8 \times 3\,\text{m}^2$$

$$= 12\,\text{m}^2$$

Total area $\quad = (48 + 12)\,\text{m}^2$

$$= 60\,\text{m}^2$$

2   Find the area of a path $2\,\text{m}$ wide round a rectangular lawn $11\,\text{m}$ by $6\,\text{m}$.

1st method

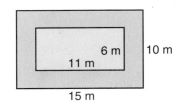

The complete rectangle is $15\,\text{m}$ long and $10\,\text{m}$ wide.

Total area of lawn and path $= lb$

$$= 15 \times 10\,\text{m}^2$$

$$= 150\,\text{m}^2$$

Area of lawn $= 11 \times 6\,\text{m}^2$

$$= 66\,\text{m}^2$$

Area of path $= (150 - 66)\,\text{m}^2$

$$= 84\,\text{m}^2$$

2nd method

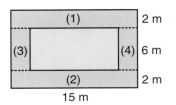

Split the path into 4 rectangles, which are all $2\,\text{m}$ wide.

Area of (1) $= 15 \times 2\,\text{m}^2 = 30\,\text{m}^2$
Area of (2) $= 15 \times 2\,\text{m}^2 = 30\,\text{m}^2$
Area of (3) $= 6 \times 2\,\text{m}^2 = 12\,\text{m}^2$
Area of (4) $= 6 \times 2\,\text{m}^2 = 12\,\text{m}^2$

Total area $\; = (30 + 30 + 12 + 12)\,\text{m}^2$
$$= 84\,\text{m}^2$$

Exercise 23.3

1. Find the area of this trapezium, by considering it as a rectangle and a right-angled triangle.

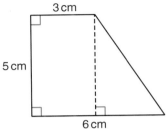

2. Find the total area of the quadrilateral *ABCD*.

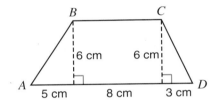

3. There is a path 1 m wide all round a rectangular lawn of size 10 m by 8 m.
    Find the area of the path.

4. Find the areas of these figures. They are drawn full-size.
    Make any measurements you need, measuring in cm, to the nearest $\frac{1}{2}$ cm.

    1

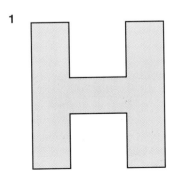

    2

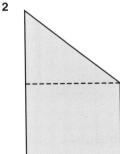

5. If the perimeter of a square is 36 cm, what is its area ?

6. The area of a rectangle is 54.4 cm². It breadth is 6.4 cm.
    Find
    1   the length of the rectangle,
    2   the perimeter.

7. A rectangle $9\frac{1}{2}$ cm by 6 cm is cut out of the corner of a square piece of paper of side
    12 cm. What area is left ? What is the perimeter of the piece that is left ?

8. Find the areas of these figures, assuming that they are drawn on a grid of squares of
    edge 1 cm.

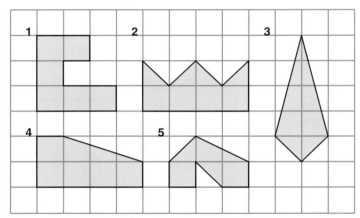

9. ABCD is a square.
    Find the areas of
    1   the square,
    2   △ ABE,
    3   △ CEF,
    4   △ ADF,
    5   △ AEF.

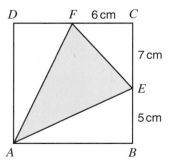

10. A room is 4 m wide, 3 m long and $2\frac{1}{2}$ m high. What is the total area of the
    four walls ?

Areas of irregular shapes

One way to estimate these areas is to draw
them on a squared grid and count the squares.
For those squares on the boundary, where more
than half the square is included in the area,
count it as a whole one, and where less than
half the square is included, do not count it
at all. This method will give an approximate
value for the area.

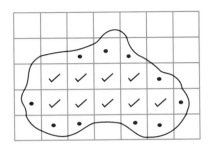

In the diagram,
Whole squares: 9
Boundary squares counted: 10
Other boundary squares not counted.
Total area 19 squares.

If each square has edge 1 cm, area $= 19\,\text{cm}^2$.
If the squares are larger, e.g. edge 5 cm, their areas are $25\,\text{cm}^2$, so
area $= 19 \times 25\,\text{cm}^2 = 475\,\text{cm}^2$.
If the squares are smaller, e.g. edge 2 mm, their areas are $4\,\text{mm}^2$,
so area $= 19 \times 4\,\text{mm}^2 = 76\,\text{mm}^2 = 0.76\,\text{cm}^2$.

Can you think of other ways to estimate such areas ?

Exercise 23.4

1.   Estimate the areas of these shapes by counting squares, assuming that they are drawn on
a grid of squares of edge 1 cm.

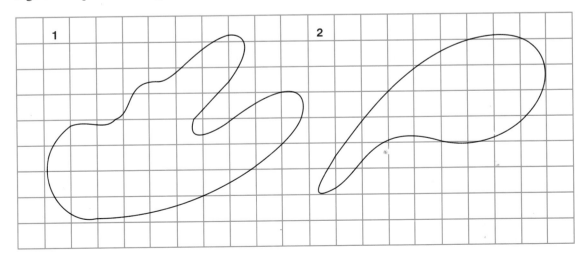

2.   Estimate the areas of these shapes by counting squares.
      They are drawn on a grid of squares of edge 5 mm.
      Give the answers in mm².

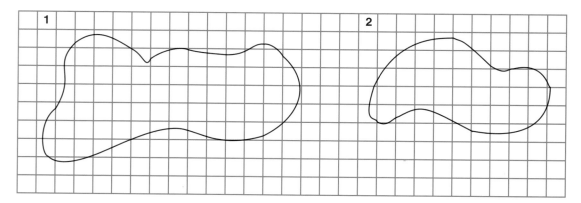

Volumes

When we measure volume we compare it with a unit volume.
We can use the volume of a cube of side 1 cm for the unit.
This is called 1 cubic centimetre and written as 1 cm^3, sometimes
as 1 c c.

1 cm

If we are measuring larger volumes we will compare them with 1 m^3.

Volume of a cuboid = length × breadth × height = lbh

Volume of a cube = $(\text{length})^3 = l^3$

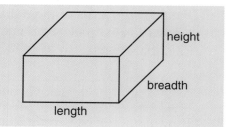

height

breadth

length

Examples

1   **Cuboid**

     Volume = lbh

            = $10 \times 8 \times 5 \text{ cm}^3$

            = 400 cm^3

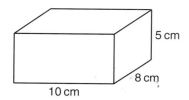

5 cm

8 cm

10 cm

2   Cube

Volume $= l^3$

$= 6 \times 6 \times 6 \, \text{cm}^3$

$= 216 \, \text{cm}^3$

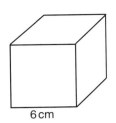

6 cm

Exercise 23.5

1. These figures are built with cubes of edge 1 cm. By finding how many cubes are used, find their volumes.

1

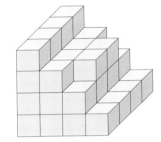

2

2.   Find the volumes of these figures.
   1 A rectangular box 12 cm by 10 cm by 5 cm.
   2 A cube of edge 5 cm.
   3 A rectangular room 5 m by 4 m with height $2\frac{1}{2}$ m.
   4 A matchbox 7.5 cm by 4 cm by 1.5 cm.
   5 A case 50 cm by 30 cm by 18 cm.

3.   This swimming pool is 1.8 m deep.
      Find the volume of water which it will hold.

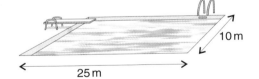

10 m

25 m

4.   How many cubic metres of concrete will be needed to make a path 25 metres long, 1.6 metres wide, if the concrete is to be laid to a depth of 0.1 m ?

5.   A rectangular tank is 4 m long, $2\frac{1}{2}$ m wide and 3 m deep. How many cubic metres of water does it contain when it is half-full ?

6.   A new road 4 km long and 25 m wide is to be constructed.

   1 How many square metres of land will be required ?
   2 If the soil has to be removed to a depth of 0.3 m how many cubic metres of soil will have to be removed ?

7.   If a large rectangular room has length 9 m, breadth 8 m and its volume is 360 m³, what is its height ?

Exercise 23.6   Applications

1.   On a graph, draw the x-axis from -7 to 3 and the y-axis from 0 to 6, using a scale of 1 cm to 1 unit on both axes.
     Plot the points A, B, and C where A is $(-7, 1)$, B is $(3, 1)$ and C $(1, 6)$.
     Join AB, BC, CA.
     Find the area of $\triangle ABC$.

2.   A floor 6 m long and 5 m wide is to be covered by carpet which is sold in rolls 1 m wide. How many metres of carpet will be required ?
     What will be the cost at £12 per metre ?

3.   A firm prints photographs on paper of size 10 cm square. They decide to make larger prints, size 11.2 cm square.

     1   What is the area of the larger prints ?
     2   The firm have advertised their prints as being 25% larger. It this correct ?

4.   A field is 80 m longer than it is wide.
     If it is x metres wide, how long is it, in terms of x ?
     What is the perimeter of the field, in terms of x ?
     If the perimeter of the field is 640 m, write down an
     equation and solve it to find the value of x, and then
     find the area of the field.

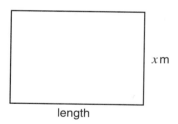

x m

length

5.   A floor 12 m long and 7.5 m wide is to be covered by tiles 30 cm square. How many tiles will be needed ?
     If the tiles are sold in boxes of 24, how many boxes must be bought ?

6.   A child's sandpit is rectangular in shape, 2 m long and $1\frac{1}{2}$ m wide. What weight of sand is needed to fill it to a depth of $\frac{1}{2}$ m ?

     (Assume 1 m³ of sand weighs 1500 kg.)

7.   A box measures 10 cm by 6 cm by 4 cm.

     1   Find its volume.
     2   How many cubes of edge 2 cm will fit in the box ?

8. A room is 5.5 m long and 4 m wide.
    What is the distance around the room
    (the perimeter of the floor) ?
    Use the table to find approximately how many rolls
    of wallpaper will be needed if the walls are to be
    papered to a height of 2.8 m.

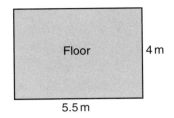

Floor   4 m

5.5 m

How many rolls are needed ?

Figures show you approximate number of rolls required

WALLS	Distance around the room (doors and windows included)										
Height from skirting	9 m	10 m	12 m	13 m	14 m	15 m	16 m	17 m	18 m	19 m	21 m	22 m
2.15–2.30 m	4	5	5	6	6	7	7	8	8	9	9	10
2.30–2.45 m	5	5	6	6	7	7	8	8	9	9	10	10
2.45–2.60 m	5	5	6	7	7	8	9	9	10	10	11	12
2.60–2.75 m	5	5	6	7	7	8	9	9	10	10	11	12
2.75–2.90 m	6	6	7	7	8	9	9	10	10	11	12	12
2.90–3.05 m	6	6	7	8	8	9	10	10	11	12	12	13
3.05–3.20 m	6	7	8	8	9	10	10	11	12	13	13	14

Extra rolls may be required where two patterns are used on the same wall.

9. A square sheet of cardboard has sides length 17 cm.
    Out of each corner a square of side 4 cm is cut, and the flaps
    remaining are turned up to form an open box of depth 4 cm.
    What are the measurements of the box ?
    Find its volume.

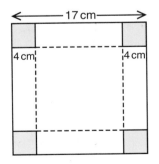

17 cm

4 cm   4 cm

10. Ice 0.1 m thick covered a rectangular paddling pool 20 m long and 15 m wide.
    Find the weight of ice, if 1 m^3 of ice weighs 920 kg.

11.   A bath is in the shape of a cuboid with length 150 cm, breadth 60 cm, and the water in
       the bath is 25 cm deep.
       Find the volume of water in the bath, in cm^3.
       Find how many litres of water there are. $(1000\,cm^3 = 1\,\ell)$

       A shower uses 3 ℓ of water each minute.
       How much water would be saved by having a 10-minute shower instead of a bath ?

Practice test 23

1.   Find the perimeters of these figures. All angles are right angles.
      By dividing the figures into rectangles, find their areas.

1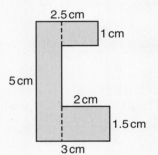

2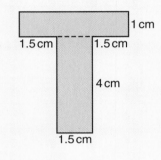

2.   Draw the x-axis from 0 to 6 and the y-axis from 0 to 4 using a scale of 1 cm to 1 unit.

      1   Plot the points A (6, 0), B (6, 4) and C (0, 4). O is the origin.
              Join AB and BC.
              What is the area of the rectangle $OABC$?

      2   Plot the points D (6, 2) and E (2, 4). Join OD and OE. What are the areas of
              $\triangle OAD$ and $\triangle OCE$?

      3   What is the area of the quadrilateral $ODBE$?

3.   Find the approximate area of this
      oval shape.
      (Assume that the lines on the grid
      are 1 cm apart.)

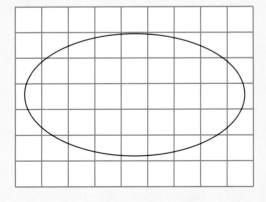

4. Construct a triangle ABC with $AB = 9$ cm, $\angle A = 75°$ and $\angle B = 65°$.
    Measure AC and BC and find the perimeter of the triangle.
    Draw and measure an additional line needed to calculate the area of $\triangle ABC$, and find this area.

5. A greenhouse has a rectangular concrete base 4 m long and 2.5 m wide.

    1 Find the area of the greenhouse floor.
    2 Find the volume of the concrete base, if the concrete is 0.12 m thick.

6. This shape is made from cubes of edge 1 cm.
    Find the total volume of the shape.

    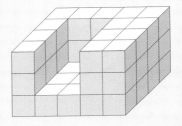

7. A box has length 15 cm and width 12 cm. If its volume is 1080 cm^3, find its height.

PUZZLES

37. Lorraine said 'Two days ago I was 13, next year I shall be 16'. What is the date today and when is her birthday?

38. Write the numbers from 100 to 200 as the sum of consecutive integers.
    e.g. $100 = 18 + 19 + 20 + 21 + 22$
    $101 = 50 + 51$
    $102 = 33 + 34 + 35$
    $104 = 2 + 3 + 4 + \cdots + 13 + 14$

    It is possible to do this for every number except one of them. Which number is this?

39. If 1 m^3 of earth weighs 1600 kg, how much would there be in a hole 50 cm by 50 cm by 50 cm?

40. How many triangles are there in this figure?

    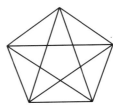

24 *Frequency distributions*

The topics in this chapter include:

- sorting, classifying and tabulating discrete or continuous data,
- extracting information from tables, graphs and lists,
- making frequency tables to group discrete or continuous data,
- constructing appropriate graphs to represent data including bar-line graphs and frequency polygons,
- identifying the modal class for grouped data,
- drawing conclusions based on the shapes of graphs,
- finding the mean, median, mode and range of a discrete, ungrouped, frequency distribution.

Frequency distributions

Discrete data

(i.e. the variables are numbers, not measurements.)

Example

The numbers of children in 50 families (with at least 1 child) are as follows:

4 5 2 2 3 4 4 3 5 4 7 3 3 4 2 2 2 2 2 6 3 2 3 3 1
2 3 2 2 6 5 5 3 2 4 4 2 4 1 2 2 2 1 3 3 2 2 4 5 3

Tally chart

Number of children	Number of families	f
1	|||	3
2	||||| ||||| ||||| |||	18
3	||||| ||||| ||	12
4	||||| ||||	9
5	|||||	5
6	||	2
7	|	1
		50

(Remember the 5th tally mark goes through the other 4.)

f is short for **frequency**, the number of times each item occurs.

Frequency distribution table

Number of children	Number of families f
1	3
2	18
3	12
4	9
5	5
6	2
7	1
	50

The most suitable diagram to represent the data is a bar-line graph, but a histogram is sometimes used.

Bar-line graph

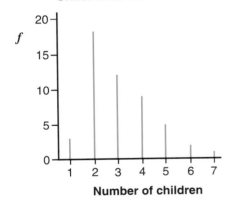

Histogram

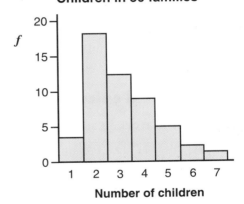

Averages and range

Mode. There are most families with 2 children (18), so the mode is 2 children per family.

Median. If the numbers were arranged in order of size

1 1 1 2 2 2 . . . 5 6 6 7

the middle value would be halfway between the 25th and 26th numbers, and these are both 3, so the median is 3 children per family.

Formula for the mean

$$\bar{x} = \frac{\Sigma fx}{\Sigma f}$$

where Σf is the total of the frequencies,
        Σfx is the total of the fx values.

Mean. Write down a frequency table. x is the number of children, f is the frequency. Add a
column for fx. Find the sums of the columns f and fx.

x	f	fx
1	3	3
2	18	36
3	12	36
4	9	36
5	5	25
6	2	12
7	1	7
	50	155

(1×3)
(2×18)

$$\bar{x} = \frac{\Sigma fx}{\Sigma f} = \frac{155}{50} = 3.1$$

The mean is 3.1 children per family.

The range = highest value − lowest value = $7 - 1 = 6$ children.

Check that your answers seem to be reasonable.
Do not give too many decimal places. If the data is in whole numbers then it is reasonable to
give the averages correct to 1 decimal place.

Using a statistical calculator to find the mean

Set the calculator to work in statistical mode then press

1 $\boxed{\times}$ 3 $\boxed{\text{DATA}}$ 2 $\boxed{\times}$ 18 $\boxed{\text{DATA}}$ and so on.

When you have entered all the data,
$\boxed{n}$ will tell you the number of items, Σf, and gives 50,
$\boxed{\Sigma x}$ will tell you the sum of the items, Σfx, and gives 155,
$\boxed{\bar{x}}$ will tell you the mean, and gives 3.1.

Exercise 24.1

Questions 1 to 6.

For each frequency distribution, find:
1   the mean,
2   the median,
3   the mode,
4   the range, of the distribution.
5   Draw a bar-line graph or a histogram of the distribution.

1.   Number of people per household in a sample of 50 households.

Size of household, x	1	2	3	4	5	6
Number of households, f	10	18	9	7	4	2

2.   Number of goals scored by 30 teams in a league.

Goals	0	1	2	3	4	5
f (number of teams)	8	9	5	4	2	2

3.   Apexa plays a computer game in which she can score
      from 0 to 10 in each game.
      The scores she achieved in several games are shown here.

Score	0	1	2	3	4	5
Frequency	2	3	0	4	3	8

Score	6	7	8	9	10
Frequency	5	9	3	1	2

4.   Number of heads when 8 coins were tossed together 60 times.

Number of heads	0	1	2	3	4	5	6	7	8
Frequency	1	2	7	15	17	11	5	2	0

5.   A manufacturer notes the number of faults in 100 machines.

Number of faults	0	1	2	3	4	5	6 or more
Number of machines	14	31	25	16	9	5	0

6.   The weekly wages of 30 women are shown in the table.

Wage (to nearest £20)	60	80	100	120
Number of women	3	7	15	5

7.   The goals scored by 20 football teams were as follows:
      8 teams scored no goals, 4 teams scored 1 goal, 3 teams scored 2 goals, 1 team scored
      3 goals, 3 teams scored 4 goals, 1 team scored 5 goals.

      1   What was the total number of goals scored by the 20 teams ?
      2   What was the mean number of goals scored by the 20 teams ?

8.   In a year-group of 60 pupils, the number of subjects each pupil passed in an examination
     was as follows:

     | 5 | 8 | 8 | 7 | 8 | 7 | 6 | 4 | 8 | 7 | 8 | 7 | 7 | 8 | 5 |
     | 6 | 6 | 3 | 6 | 6 | 8 | 7 | 9 | 5 | 7 | 8 | 7 | 7 | 8 | 6 |
     | 7 | 9 | 4 | 7 | 8 | 9 | 6 | 5 | 9 | 8 | 3 | 8 | 7 | 4 | 5 |
     | 8 | 4 | 5 | 6 | 9 | 9 | 9 | 9 | 7 | 8 | 8 | 5 | 6 | 7 | 6 |

     1   Tally the results to form a frequency distribution.
     2   Draw a bar-line graph or histogram of the distribution.
     3   Find the mean, median and mode of the number of subjects passed.

Grouped data

If the range of data is wide we can put it into convenient groups, called classes.

Example

The distribution of examination marks of 120 students.

Mark	0–9	10–19	20–29	30–39	40–49	50–59	60–69
f (number of students)	5	14	22	29	27	19	4

The data can be represented by a frequency polygon.

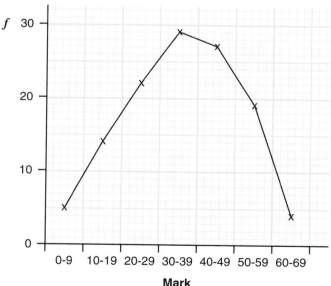

Frequency polygon to show the distribution of marks

The points on the frequency polygon are plotted at the centres of the classes, and they
are joined by straight lines.
The **modal class** is the class with the greatest frequency.
Here the modal class is the class 30–39 marks (with 29 students).

A histogram is sometimes used instead of a frequency polygon.

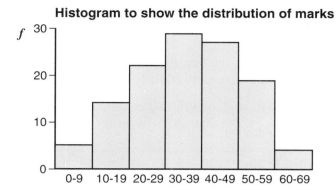

Histogram to show the distribution of marks

We often draw a frequency polygon or a histogram because we can deduce things from its general shape.

Many distributions have graphs like this one, with a peak near the centre of the values and lower frequencies towards both ends.

This is because most data are near an average value, with fewer data further away from it. In this example, the mean mark is 35.5 and the modal class is 30–39 marks. 65% of students have marks between 20 and 49, with fewer students having marks which are lower or higher than these, and very few students having very low or very high marks compared to the average for the group.

Exercise 24.2

1. The marks of 30 children in an examination were as follows:

62	73	52	59	66	82	73	51	37	42
86	63	32	77	49	57	85	65	79	93
46	68	60	83	79	56	84	74	98	61

   1 Tally these marks in classes 30–39, 40–49, etc. and record the frequencies.
   2 Draw a frequency polygon of the distribution.
   3 What is the modal class of the distribution ?
   4 Comment briefly on the distribution.

2. The number of goals scored by 22 teams in a football league during a season were as follows:

81	81	56	77	83	65	67	68	57	52	65
52	41	71	46	53	51	56	54	45	64	57

   1 Tally these data in classes 40–44, 45–49, 50–54, etc, and record the frequencies.
   2 Draw a frequency polygon of the distribution.
   3 What is the modal class of the distribution ?

3.   The marks of 40 children in a test were as follows:

Mark	0–2	3–5	6–8	9–11	12–14	15–17	18–20
Number of children	4	3	5	7	10	6	5

1   Draw a frequency polygon of the distribution.
2   What is the modal class of the distribution ?

4.   The distributions of examination marks in two examinations are shown in this table. Draw frequency polygons for these distributions on the same graph and comment on them.

Mark	0–9	10–19	20–29	30–39	40–49	50–59	60–69	70–79	80–89	90–99
1st exam	3	8	7	11	14	18	21	10	6	2
2nd exam			1	3	6	8	15	38	22	7

Continuous data

(i.e. the variables are measurements, such as lengths, weights, times, which go up continuously, not in jumps.)

Example

The lengths of leaves from a bush, using a sample of 60 leaves.

Length in cm	5.0–5.4	5.5–5.9	6.0–6.4	6.5–6.9	7.0–7.4	7.5–7.9
f	2	12	20	15	8	3

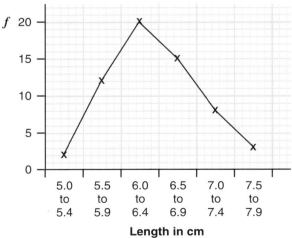

Frequency polygon of lengths of leaves

The modal class is the class 6.0–6.4 cm (with 20 leaves).

A histogram is sometimes used instead of a frequency polygon.

Exercise 24.3

1. The times taken by 25 children to travel to school are as follows:
    (Times in minutes to the nearest minute.)

6	10	14	16	16	21	7	12	9
18	19	13	23	5	17	20	12	14
11	24	20	10	12	4	15		

    1 Tally these data in classes 1–5, 6–10, 11–15, etc. and record the frequencies.
    2 What is the modal class of the frequency distribution ?

2. The heights of 20 students are as follows:
    (Heights in cm to the nearest cm.)

166	177	164	171	175	170	173
182	173	176	160	163	174	180
167	172	177	168	165	175	

    1 Tally these data in classes 160–164, 165–169, 170–174, etc. and record the frequencies.
    2 What is the modal class of the frequency distribution ?

3. The weights of a group of children are shown in this frequency polygon. (Weights are found to the nearest kilogram.)

    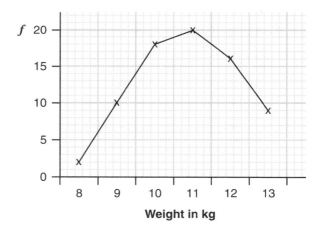

    1 Show the frequencies of each class of weights, in a table.
    2 How many children were there altogether ?
    3 What is the modal class of the distribution ?
    4 Comment briefly on the distribution of weights.

4. The table shows the ages of 100 cars in a survey.

Age in years	0–2	2–4	4–6	6–8	8–10	10–12	12–14
Number of cars	16	23	24	17	12	7	1

    (The 1st class includes cars up to just under 2 years old, the 2nd class includes cars from 2 years to just under 4 years old, and so on.)

    1 Draw a frequency polygon of the distribution.
    2 State the modal class of the distribution.
    3 Comment briefly on the distribution.

5. 30 students were asked in a survey to say how many hours they spent watching television in the previous week. Their answers, in hours to the nearest hour, were as follows:

    12 20 13 15 22 3 6 24 20 15   9 12   5   6   8
    30   7 12 14 25 2 6 12 20 20 18   3 18   8   9

    1 Tally these data in classes 1–5, 6–10, 11–15, etc.
    2 Draw a frequency polygon of the distribution.
    3 Comment briefly on the distribution of times.

6. The lengths of 50 rods were measured to the nearest cm.
    Here are the results, in cm:

87	80	69	90	80	84	73	78	79	71
74	85	62	79	72	81	65	76	82	70
74	75	82	66	71	78	72	73	86	76
81	73	70	67	78	84	75	70	77	82
83	76	77	88	75	75	83	78	79	68

    1 Tally the data using classes 60–64, 65–69, etc. and show the frequencies.
    2 Draw a frequency polygon of the distribution.
    3 Comment briefly on the distribution of lengths.

Exercise 24.4 Applications

1. The number of goals scored in the 1st 4 divisions of the football league were written down in order as they were heard on the radio.
    Results:

0	2	0	2	2	2	0	3	1	4	1	0	1	0
2	1	4	1	5	1	5	0	3	2	2	1	1	4
2	0	3	0	1	1	2	1	0	1	1	2	2	1
2	0	1	1	1	2	0	0	2	2	1	2	0	3
2	0	1	0	0	0	1	0	1	2	1	0	2	2
3	0	2	0	3	1	1	2	1	2	2	2	1	3

    1 Make a frequency table to show these results.
    2 Draw a bar-line graph of the distribution.
    3 Find the mean, median, mode and range of the number of goals scored.

2. The number of matches in 50 boxes of matches was as follows:

34	36	40	37	37	38	37	42	36	41	37	38	38	39	39	37	36
41	36	39	37	32	36	38	37	38	40	41	37	38	38	33	34	35
37	41	40	37	42	39	35	35	37	32	37	35	37	41	41	41	

    1 Make a tally chart and an ungrouped frequency distribution table of the data.
    2 Draw a bar-line graph of the distribution.
    3 Find the median, mode and range of the number of matches per box.

3. Use 5 cards with numbers 1, 2, 3, 4, 5 printed, one number on each.
    Draw 3 cards at random and add the numbers together to get the 'score'.
    Mix the cards again and repeat this several times, putting the scores in a tally chart.

    Make a frequency distribution of the results and show this in a bar-line graph.
    Find the mode score.

    Make a list of all the possible different outcomes of the experiment, with their 'scores',
    e.g. 1, 3, 4; score 8. (Disregard the order so that 3, 1, 4 is not counted as a different
    outcome.)
    Since these are equally likely outcomes you can find the theoretical probability of each
    score.
    Multiply each probability by the number of times you did your experiment to get a
    theoretical frequency distribution.
    Compare this with your experimental results.

4. Throw two dice and note the total score shown. Repeat this 180 times altogether.
    (If you have already recorded the results of throwing 1 die, as on page 194, question 3,
    use the results in pairs, as if you had thrown two dice together.

    e.g. if the results were 1 6   5 5   4 6   6 2   ...

           the scores are   7   10   10   8   )

    Before you begin it is interesting to estimate the most likely score (the mode) and the
    average score (the mean).
    Make a frequency table of the results.

    Draw a bar-line graph of the distribution, and find the mode score and the mean score.

    (You can compare your results with the theoretical frequencies. As on page 293, question
    4, find the theoretical probabilities of scoring each total from 2 to 12. Multiply each of
    these by 180, the total number of throws in this experiment, to get a list of theoretical
    frequencies. Your experimental results should not match completely.)

5. The scores of the first 5 batsmen in each team for the 8 Sunday League matches on a
    particular Sunday were

5	48	20	3	8	6	0	48	21	22
17	15	48	13	0	4	19	1	12	39
25	5	64	51	20	31	49	0	4	17
117	34	24	61	61	11	6	86	0	5
55	3	0	17	96	3	69	0	63	0
14	18	36	103	4	42	0	33	29	28
85	26	8	2	10	16	63	41	39	8
101	1	33	25	13	4	40	19	70	3

    1   Tally these data in classes 0–19, 20–39, 40–59, etc, and record the frequencies.
    2   Draw a frequency polygon of the distribution.
    3   What is the modal class of the distribution ?
    4   Comment briefly on the scores.

6. The number of words per sentence in the first 50 sentences of two books are recorded below.
    Draw frequency polygons on the same graph to represent the data.
    Compare the two sets of data and comment on them.

    (1)   'The Children of the New Forest'
    (2)   'The Adventures of Tom Sawyer'

Number of words	Number of sentences	
	(1)	(2)
1–10	2	27
11–20	9	11
21–30	14	9
31–40	7	0
41–50	4	3
51–60	8	0
61–70	3	0
71–80	2	0
81–90	1	0

7. The frequency polygon shows the times taken by a group of boys to run a race.
    (The times were recorded to the nearest minute.)

    1 Show the frequencies of each class of times, in a table.
    2 How many boys were there altogether ?
    3 What is the modal class of the distribution ?
    4 Comment briefly on the distribution of times.

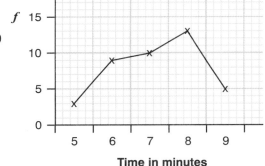

8. The table shows the age distribution of the population of the UK in 1901 and 1981.
    Draw frequency polygons on the same graph to represent the data, and comment on them.
    (Figures in 100 000's.)

Age (years)	Population	
	1901	1981
0–9	85	70
10–19	78	90
20–29	70	78
30–39	53	76
40–49	40	62
50–59	28	64
60–69	18	56
70–79	8	40
80–89	2	15

(A few people in the last group are over 89 years old.)

9.   In Chapter 9, Exercise 9.3 and in Chapter 12, Exercise 12.2, several suggestions were
      given for data which could be collected for statistical investigations.
      If you have carried out any investigation where the data can be listed in a frequency
      distribution, you can illustrate the distribution with a suitable diagram.

Practice test 24

1.   The number of seeds germinating in 40 pots when 6 seeds were
      planted in each pot were as follows:

Number of seeds	0	1	2	3	4	5	6
Number of pots	0	1	3	12	10	11	3

      1 Draw a bar-line graph of the distribution.
      2 Find the mean, median and mode of the distribution.
      3 If you pick a pot at random from this batch what is the
            probability that it will have 4 or more germinating seeds ?

2.   The number of pupils per class in 30 classes in a school was as follows:

Number in class	29	30	31	32	33
f	6	10	5	5	4

      Find the mean, median, mode and range of the distribution.

3.   The marks of 25 children in an examination were as follows:

      68   78   64   67   73   94   69   86   62   67   82   79   61
      87   71   81   79   82   77   73   81   84   74   76   66

      1 Tally these data in classes 60–64, 65–69, 70–74, etc. and record the frequencies.
      2 Draw a frequency polygon of the distribution.

4.   The heights of 30 women are as follows:
      (Heights were measured in cm, to the nearest cm.)

      164   164   167   172   167   161
      163   153   156   156   155   150
      171   158   151   159   161   165
      158   165   163   155   174   172
      157   163   162   169   160   168

      1 Tally these data in classes 150–154, 155–159, 160–164, etc. and record the
            frequencies.
      2 What is the modal class of the frequency distribution ?

Miscellaneous Section D

Exercise D1   Aural Practice

If possible find someone to read these questions to you.
You should do the questions within 20 minutes.
Do not use your calculator.
Write down the answers only.

1.   What is 0.75 as a fraction in its lowest terms ?

2.   If the time is 'quarter to three in the afternoon', write this in the 24-hour clock system.

3.   How many faces has a pyramid with a square base ?

4.   In the function $y = 10 - 2x$, what is the value of y when $x = 3$?

5.   Each side of a hexagon is 8 cm long. What is the perimeter of the hexagon ?

6.   The probability of Sally winning her next game of table tennis is 0.9. What is the probability of her not winning ?

7.   What is 4% of £500 ?

8.   Two angles of a triangle are each 55°. What is the size of the other angle of the triangle ?

9.   A rectangle 4 cm by 3 cm is cut out of a square piece of paper of side 5 cm. What area is left ?

10.   In a bag there are 5 discs. 3 are red and 2 are blue. What is the probability of drawing out a blue disc ?

11.   What is the order of rotational symmetry of a rectangle ?

12.   The base of a triangle is 8 cm and the height is 5 cm. What is its area ?

13.   Which is the larger number, 0.18 or 0.081 ?

14.   What is the size of an interior angle of a regular pentagon ?

15.   A cube has edges of length 3 cm. What is its volume ?

Additional aural questions using data from pages 444 to 447.

16.   Use table **4**.
      I am in Kereva, wanting to go to Veefield, and I miss the train which leaves just after half-past one in the afternoon. At what time is the next train ?

17.   Use diagram **10**.
      AB is 6 cm long. Estimate the length of *AC*.

18.   Use the function machine **15**.
      Find *y* when *x* = 2.5.

19.   Use the graph **16**.
      Approximately how many items of product *D* were sold last year ?

20.   Use diagram **19**.
      Which of these drawings have an axis of symmetry ?

Exercise D2   Revision

1.   **1**   In a school of 800 pupils, 440 are girls. What fraction of the school is girls ?

     2   What fraction is £4.80 of £6.40 ?

     3   What fraction of $1\frac{1}{2}$ km is 50 metres ?

2.   From the letters N, U, M, B, E, R, S, write down

     1   the letters which have a vertical axis of symmetry,
     2   the letters which have a horizontal axis of symmetry,
     3   the letters which have rotational symmetry.

3.   **1**   Here is a function machine.

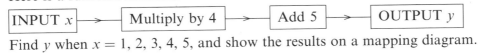

INPUT *x* ⟶ Multiply by 4 ⟶ Add 5 ⟶ OUTPUT *y*

Find *y* when *x* = 1, 2, 3, 4, 5, and show the results on a mapping diagram.

     2   Here is a function machine.

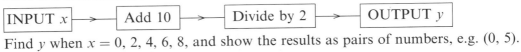

INPUT *x* ⟶ Add 10 ⟶ Divide by 2 ⟶ OUTPUT *y*

Find *y* when *x* = 0, 2, 4, 6, 8, and show the results as pairs of numbers, e.g. (0, 5).

4.   There are a lot of coloured beads in a bag, and some of them are green ones.
     When picking a bead at random the probability that it is green is 0.64.
     What is the probability of picking a bead that is not green ?

5.   Calculate the sizes of the angles a, b, c, d, e.

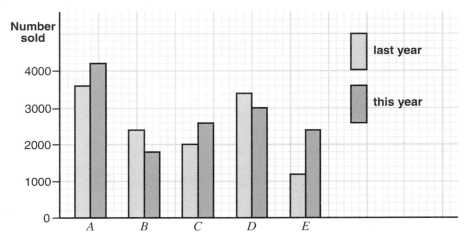

1   83°   60°   128° a

2   34° b c 72°

3 d 86° e 37°

6.   The bar chart shows sales of 5 products A, B, C, D and E, by a manufacturing company in two years, this year and last year.

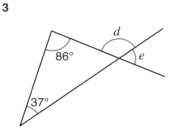

1   How many items of product A were sold last year ?
2   Of which products were fewer sold this year than last year ?
3   Of which product were approximately 2000 sold last year ?
4   Find the total sales of all 5 products this year, to the nearest 1000.

7.   If $A = 5.14$, $B = 3.709$ and $C = 13.3$, find, without using your calculator,

1    $A + B + C$ 2 $A \div 100$ 3 $10(C - A)$

8.   In the rectangle $ABCD$, $\triangle BEC$ is an isosceles triangle and $\angle BEC = 42°$. $\angle CED = \angle AEB = 90°$.

Find the size of $\angle CDE$.

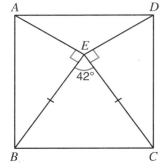

9. On graph paper, draw the x-axis from −3 to 4 and the y-axis from −2 to 5, taking equal scales on both axes.
    Plot the points A (−3, −2), B (2, −1), C (4, 5), D (−1, 4).
    Join AB, BC, CD, DA.
    What sort of figure is ABCD ?
    Draw the diagonals AC and BD. If these diagonals cross at E, write down the coordinates of E.

10. In a road survey, the cars passing a certain point in 1-minute intervals were counted, for 30 minutes. Here are the results.

9	11	3	15	11	1	13	12	1	10
15	0	9	11	0	10	5	5	4	5
11	7	13	7	9	12	5	9	10	6

    1 Show the results in a tally chart in classes 0–3, 4–7, 8–11, 12–15.
    2 Draw a frequency polygon of the distribution.
    3 What is the modal class ?

Exercise D3 Revision

1. Do not use your calculator in this question. Show your working.

    What is the least number of coaches needed to take 600 people on an outing, if each coach can carry 48 passengers ?

2. Find the perimeter and area of △ABC.

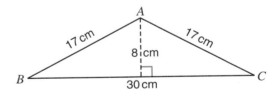

3. The following numbers were written on pieces of paper, put into a hat, and drawn out at random.

    10,   13,   16,   17,   21,   25,   30,   36,   39,   49,   110,   121.

    What is the probability of drawing out
    1 a number greater than 100,
    2 a number less than 20,
    3 a prime number,
    4 a square number ?

    5 If an odd number is drawn out and not replaced, what is the probability of drawing out a second odd number ?

4.   These diagrams represent the nets of solid figures. Give the names of the solid figures.

1

2

3

5.   A man buys a painting as an investment. He pays
£2000 for it and estimates that its value should
increase by 10% each year. He plans to sell it in
3 years time.

   1   If it increases as he hopes, how much will it
be worth at the end of the first year ?
   2   How much will its value increase during
the second year ?
   3   How much will it be worth at the end of
the second year ?
   4   How much will its value increase during
the third year ?
   5   How much will it be worth at the end of
the third year ?
   6   How much profit does he hope to gain on
this investment ?

6.   Solve these equations.

   1 $7x + 1 = x + 31$
   2 $4(x - 5) + 5(x + 1) = 3$
   3 $44 - 8x = 9 - 3x$

7. $ABCDEFGH$ is a regular octagon, whose point
of symmetry is O.
   1   What is the size of $\angle AOB$?
   2   What is the size of $\angle ABC$?
   3   If AC, CE, EG and GA are joined, what sort
of quadrilateral is formed ?

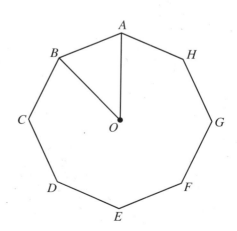

8. The air service between London and Kereva, together with connecting train services to Veefield, are given in a time-table as follows:

London dep.	23.00	10.20	11.20	15.25	16.55
Kereva airport arr.	00.30	11.40	12.50	16.45	18.10
Kereva station dep.	04.30	13.31	15.17	17.55	20.01
Veefield arr.	06.13	14.43	16.25	19.03	21.09

1   What is the time of departure from London of the fastest service to Kereva ?

2   What is the time taken for the slowest journey from London to Veefield ?

3   The single fare from London to Kereva is £90, and the distance is 750 km. How much is the cost per km ?

4   From Kereva to Veefield is 84 km. What is the average speed of the 13.31 train ?

9. 1   What is 5% as a fraction ?

2   In a pie chart, what angle will represent 5% ?

3   A soil sample is found to have the following composition.

Air	25%
Water	25%
Mineral material	45%
Organic material	5%

Draw a pie chart showing this information.

10. Construct a quadrilateral $ABCD$ as follows:
Draw a line AC, 10 cm long.
Draw the perpendicular bisector of AC, cutting AC at M.
(The perpendicular bisector is the line at right angles to AC, through the mid-point M of AC.)
Find points B and D on the bisector, such that $BM = MD = 3$ cm.
Join AB, BC, CD, DA.

Measure AB, to the nearest mm.
Measure $\angle ABC$,
What sort of quadrilateral is $ABCD$?

Exercise D4   Revision

1. 1   Find 36% of $2\frac{1}{2}$ hours.

2   What percentage is 40 cm of 5 m ?

2. The diagram shows a thermometer marked in °C.

    1   What temperature does it show ?

    2   If the temperature rises 10 degrees, what will it be then ?

    3   If the temperature one morning is −2°, and it rises by
        8 degrees during the day and then falls by 11 degrees at
        night, what is that night's temperature ?

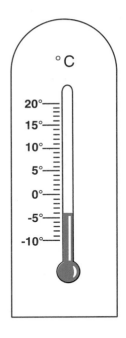

3. Find the square root of 1369 by trial (and without using the square root key on your
    calculator).

    You can copy and continue this table.

Number	Square
10	100
20	400
30	. . .
. . .	

4. A group of people were asked how they prefer to spend their leisure time, choosing from
    reading (R), playing sports (S), watching television (T), other activities (U). The results
    were as follows:

R	T	T	S	T	R	T	R	T	S	R	T	R	S	T
U	T	R	U	R	T	S	U	U	S	S	T	U	T	T
T	T	T	T	R	R	T	R	S	U	S	T	R	U	S
T	R	T	U	R	T	R	R	U	T	R	T	U	S	U

    Tally these results.

    What is the modal category ?
    Comment briefly on the results of the survey.

5. One number in each of these sequences is incorrect. Copy them, replacing the wrong number with the correct number.

   1   1, 3, 6, 9, 15, 21, 28.
       What is this sequence of numbers called ?
       Write down the next 3 numbers in the sequence.

   2   1, 1, 2, 3, 5, 8, 13, 22, 34.
       (Each number is connected to the previous two numbers.)
       Write down the next 3 numbers in the sequence.

   3   1, 6, 27, 64, 125, 216.
       Is 1000 a member of this sequence ?

   4   100, 93, 86, 79, 72, 66, 58, 51.
       Write down the next 3 numbers in the sequence.

6. In the diagram, AB is a straight line.
   Use angle properties to write down an equation
   involving x and solve it to find the value of x.

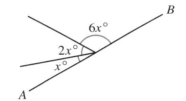

7. In an experiment, several coloured balls were placed in a bag and drawn out one at a time. Each ball was replaced and the bag shook up before the next ball was drawn.

   Here are the results of 100 drawings.

Colour	Red	Yellow	Green	Blue
Number of times	40	15	24	21

   Using these results, find the probability of drawing
   1   a red ball,
   2   a ball that is not red,
   3   a ball that is yellow or red.

8. This table shows the number of children in 100 families.

Children in family	0	1	2	3	4	5	6
Number of families	11	24	30	21	8	5	1

   Draw a bar-line graph to illustrate the data.
   Find the mean, median and mode number of children per family.

9. Name the solid figures with the shape of

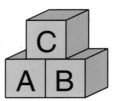

    1 a tennis ball,
    2 a tin of beans,
    3 a clown's hat,
    4 a match box,
    5 a child's building block.

10. Make tables of values for $x = -2, -1, 0, 1, 2, 3$, for these functions.
    1 $y = 3 - x$
    2 $y = x + 6$

    Draw axes for x from -2 to 3 and for y from 0 to 9, using a scale of 2 cm to 1 unit on both axes.
    Plot the points given in the tables and draw the lines, labelling each one.
    Write down the coordinates of the point where the two lines intersect.

Exercise D5   Activities

1. **The Fibonacci sequence**

    1 Write down the 1st 15 terms of the Fibonacci sequence 1, 1, 2, 3, 5, 8, 13, ...

    2 Find what happens to the results in this pattern, where you divide a Fibonacci number by the number before it, and then by the number after it, and find the difference.

    $$\frac{1}{1} - \frac{1}{2} = 0.5$$

    $$\frac{2}{1} - \frac{2}{3} = 1.333\ldots$$

    $$\frac{3}{2} - \frac{3}{5} =$$

    $$\frac{5}{3} - \frac{5}{8} =$$

    $\ldots$

    3 Continue this pattern for the sums of squares of the numbers in the sequence

    $$1^2 + 1^2 + 2^2 \qquad\qquad = \quad 6 = 2 \times 3$$

    $$1^2 + 1^2 + 2^2 + 3^2 \qquad\quad = 15 = \ldots$$

    $$1^2 + 1^2 + 2^2 + 3^2 + 5^2 \quad =$$

    $$1^2 + 1^2 + 2^2 + 3^2 + 5^2 + 8^2 =$$

    $\ldots$

2. **Cube numbers**

Work out the cubes of numbers from 1 to 10.
$1^3 = 1 \times 1 \times 1 = 1$, $2^3 = 2 \times 2 \times 2 = 8$, and so on.

Copy and complete this pattern.

Sums of numbers	Total	Sums of cubes of numbers	Total
1	1	1^3	1
$1 + 2$	3	$1^3 + 2^3$	9
$1 + 2 + 3$	6	$1^3 + 2^3 + 3^3$	36
...		...	
$1 + 2 + \cdots + 10$	55	$1^3 + 2^3 + \cdots + 10^3$	

What do you notice about the connection between 2nd and 4th columns ?
Double the numbers in column (2) and divide each by the largest number of the
same row in column (1). What do you notice ?
Can you use this pattern to find

1   $1 + 2 + 3 + \cdots + 20$,
2   $1^3 + 2^3 + 3^3 + \cdots + 20^3$?

3. **A budget for a year**

Imagine that you plan to move away from home into your own flat, in a few year's time.
This is a big step to take and it deserves proper consideration.
You will have your wages from your work or your grant as a student. Plan how you are
going to manage financially.

Firstly, there is necessary spending on the flat, e.g. rent, bills for water, electricity, gas
and other fuel, insurance, TV licence, phone bills, etc. If you are over 18 and working
you may have to pay a local tax.
Secondly, there is the necessary spending on yourself, e.g. food, travelling expenses
(including car expenses if you have a car), clothes, etc.
Then there are all the extras such as things for the flat, holidays, presents, entertainment,
sports or hobbies, etc.
If you have borrowed money or bought things on credit you will have regular
repayments to make.

Make a complete list of expenditure (what you need to spend) with estimated costs for
each item. Find the total amount.
Estimate the total income you will have. If you are working, deductions will be made
from your wages for National Insurance contributions and Income Tax.
If the expenditure total exceeds the income total you will have to decide what you can do
about it.

(If you prefer, instead of this you can work out a similar budget for a family.)

4. A study-bedroom

Design a study-bedroom suitable for a teenager.

Make a scale model of the room, showing the door, windows and heating source. Make scale models of the furniture and include those. Show where the lighting is and where the power points are. Paint your model to show the colour scheme.

A more ambitious project would be to make a model of a house, a famous building or a village.

5. Models of the main solid figures

Make a set of models of the cube, cuboid, prism, etc., and display them.
As well as making models you could make a collection of tins and boxes of different shapes, arrange them in a display and take a photograph of them.

6. Shapes in everyday life

Make a display about these, with drawings, pictures, postcards, photographs and models.

Ideas:
symmetry in nature, and in man-made objects,

triangles: pylons, etc.,

circles: wheels, drainpipes,

tins and boxes of different solid shapes,

shapes in nature: spirals in snails, jellyfish, pattern on a sunflower centre, cone of a volcano,

shapes in building: unusual modern designs, bridges, the Pyramids, radio telescopes (paraboloid), cooling towers (hyperboloid), spheres of an early warning system.

7. **Income Tax**

This is tax taken as a proportion of any money you earn. Most employees pay tax as PAYE which means 'Pay as you earn', so the tax is deducted from the pay by the employer, and the amount depends on how much is earned.

You are allowed a Personal Allowance, and maybe other Allowances. These give an amount you can earn without paying tax on it, then any income above that is taxed at a Basic Rate. There is also a Higher Rate tax so that people with high incomes pay more.

Example

Mr Taylor earns £12 000 a year. How much income tax will he pay ?

(We will imagine that the Personal Allowance is £3000 and the Basic rate of tax is 25%. The questions in this book use imaginary rates, since every year, on Budget Day, the tax rates can be altered and we cannot foresee what they will be when you are reading this book.)

Income	£12000
Personal Allowance	£3000
Taxable Income	£9000

Tax. 25% of £9000 = £2250   (This is $\frac{1}{4}$ of £9000 or £0.25 × 9000.)

Mr Taylor pays £2250 income tax in that year. That leaves him with £9750.

(The tax will be deducted in equal amounts each week, if he is paid weekly, or each month if he is paid monthly. In addition to having tax deducted from his earnings he will also have National Insurance contributions deducted.)

If you know the up-to-date tax rates, work out this example using them.

Work out these questions.

1 Mr Yates had a taxable income of £8800. How much income tax did he pay if the tax rate was 25% ?

2 In one year Mr Burke's taxable income was £9100. He paid income tax at the rate of 24%. How much tax did he pay ?
The money was deducted from his wages weekly. How much tax was taken out per week ? (In one year there are 52 weeks.)

3 Assuming that the income tax rates were:
Personal Allowance £3300, Basic rate of tax 24%,
find how much tax Miriam Kirby paid in the year if her salary was £18 000.
If this tax was paid in equal monthly instalments, how much did she pay per month ?
(Taxable income = salary − personal allowance.
Tax paid in the year = 24% of taxable income.)

8.   **The arrangement of red cards in a pack of cards**

If a pack of cards has been shuffled properly, then when you turn up the top card it is equally likely to be a red card (heart or diamond) or a black one (club or spade). In this experiment you should investigate how many cards are turned over before a red card appears.

Shuffle the pack of cards and turn over the cards one-by-one, counting until a red card appears. If it is the first card it counts as 1. If it is only the second card it counts as 2, and so on. Record the result. Then continue turning the cards over, beginning the count again at 1, and carrying on until another red card appears. Repeat until you have 10 results.

Before you go any further, make two guesses:
1   What is the mode number of the results ?
2   What is the mean of the results ?

To continue the experiment, shuffle all the cards again properly and begin again using the full pack.
Carry on in this way. After every 10 results shuffle the cards and begin again with a full pack.
Repeat until you have got 100, or more, results.

Make a frequency table of the results and show them in a bar-line graph. Comment on the shape of the graph.
Find the mode. Does it agree with your guess ?
Find the mean. Does it agree with your guess ?

9.   **Using a computer**

If you have the use of a computer and a selection of computer programs then there are many investigations or activities which you can do.
The choice of activities will depend on the programs available, but here are a few general suggestions. If you have not got suitable software, it is often possible to do some investigations using simple programs which you can write yourself.

1   Statistical investigations, using spreadsheets to produce graphs and diagrams, and to calculate averages and measures of dispersion. Inserting and interrogating data in a database and drawing conclusions from it.
2   Probability investigations, using computer-generated random numbers to simulate throws of dice, tosses of coins, selections of discs, etc.
3   Investigating prime numbers and prime factors of numbers.
4   Investigating sequences, number chains, etc.
5   Drawing graphs of functions, and other graphs.
6   Solving problems by trial and improvement methods.
7   Calculating using mathematical formulae, e.g. finding areas and volumes.
8   Using LOGO or similar methods to generate and transform 2-D shapes, and devising instructions for the computer to produce certain shapes and paths.

The computer is a very powerful tool. Do make use of it.

To the student : 5

Learning formulae

There are certain formulae which you will need to know by heart. The best way to learn a formula is to know where it comes from.

There is a formula checklist on page 448. Copy the list, completing each formula, then check your answers from the relevant chapters of the book. Learn those you do not know.

Learning formulae in isolation is not very useful. You need to link this with learning methods, so that you can use the formulae correctly.

Practice exams

You may have a practice exam at school. This will give you some idea of your present standard. It will show you that you can do well if you have learnt the work. It will give you practice in working to time and working under pressure.

After the exam, you will be told your marks or grade and given back your paper. Perhaps your teacher will go through all the questions with the class or you may have to correct them yourself. Ask about anything you do not understand.

If you get a low mark, do not be too discouraged if you know that you can do better next time. But decide what you are going to do to improve your standard.

In an exam it is the marks which count. Could you have got more marks if you had spent less time on some questions and more on others ? Should you have revised some topics more thoroughly ?

Did you throw away any marks by:
not reading a question carefully enough,
not showing the necessary working with the answer,
writing so badly that the marker could not read it,
writing so badly that **you** could not read it and copied it wrongly on the next line,
not checking an answer that was obviously wrong,
not giving an answer to the accuracy asked for, e.g. to the nearest cm ?

Since this was a practice exam, having made some of these mistakes, you can see that by avoiding them in future you can gain more marks.

Make a list of topics you still need to revise, and plan how you will use the remaining time before the proper examination.

Your teacher may give you further practice papers to do at home. If not, you may like to give yourself some. You can use the practice test questions or the revision exercises in this book. Try to do them as in a proper exam, spending the correct time on them and working in a quiet room without referring to books or notes.

25 Ratios

The topics in this chapter include:

- understanding and using ratios, and the equivalence between decimals, fractions, percentages and ratios,

- calculating using ratios in a variety of situations,

- working out proportional changes,

- solving problems involving compound measures, including speed,

- solving problems involving foreign currency.

Ratio

A ratio is a way of comparing the sizes of two quantities.
e.g. A quantity divided in the ratio $2:3$ (read as 2 to 3)
means that the 1st share is $\frac{2}{3}$ of the 2nd share,
and the 2nd share is $\frac{3}{2}$ times the 1st share.
Ratios have no units, they are just numbers.

Here are some examples using ratios.

Examples

1   Express $25\,\text{cm} : 1\frac{1}{2}\,\text{m}$ as a ratio in its simplest form.

$$\frac{25\,\text{cm}}{1\frac{1}{2}\,\text{m}} = \frac{25\,\text{cm}}{150\,\text{cm}} = \frac{25}{150} = \frac{1}{6}. \text{ Ratio is } 1:6.$$ Both quantities must be in the same units before simplifying.

2   Divide £24 in the ratio $3:5$.

$3:5$ gives 8 parts.

1 part is $\dfrac{£24}{8} = £3$.

Shares are $3 \times £3$ and $5 \times £3$, i.e. £9 and £15.

3   The angles of a triangle are in the ratio $4:5:6$. Find their sizes.

     $4:5:6$ gives 15 parts. The sum of the angles is $180°$.

     1 part is $\dfrac{180°}{15} = 12°$.

     The angles are $4 \times 12°$, $5 \times 12°$, $6 \times 12°$, i.e. $48°$, $60°$ and $72°$.

4   Increase $12\,kg$ in the ratio $5:3$.

     New weight is $\frac{5}{3}$ of $12\,kg = \dfrac{5}{3} \times 12\,kg = 20\,kg$.

5   Decrease £120 in the ratio $9:10$.

     New amount is $\frac{9}{10}$ of £120 $= £\dfrac{9}{10} \times 120 = £108$.

Exercise 25.1

1.   Express the following as ratios in their simplest forms.

     1    $24:64$ 6 $13.2\,cm:16.5\,cm$
     2    $1.5 \ : \ 3.5$ 7 $75p:£1.80$
     3    $18\,cm:12\,cm$ 8   3 hours 20 minutes : 5 hours 20 minutes
     4   £9 : £27   9 $750\,g:3.6\,kg$
     5    $16\,kg:8\,kg$ 10 $600\,ml:2$ litres

2.   1   Divide £2.25 in the ratio $2:3$.
     2   Divide £1.54 in the ratio $4:7$.
     3   Divide 60p in the ratio $7:3$.
     4   Divide £1.75 in the ratio $6:1$.
     5   Divide £4 in the ratio $7:3$.

3.   1   Increase £270 in the ratio $5:3$.
     2   Increase £37.50 in the ratio $9:5$.
     3   Decrease £280 in the ratio $4:7$.
     4   Decrease £12 in the ratio $5:8$.
     5   Increase £25 in the ratio $11:10$.

4.   A line AB of length $9\,cm$ is divided at P so that $AP:PB = 3:7$. Find the length of AP.

5.   Children aged 12 years, 9 years and 4 years share £5 in proportion to their ages. How much does the youngest child get ?

6.   The angles of a triangle are in the ratio $2:3:5$. Find their sizes.

7. A concrete mixture is made by mixing cement, sand and gravel by volume in the ratio $1:2:4$. How much sand and gravel must be added to 0.5 m³ of cement ?

8. The angles of a quadrilateral are in the ratio $2:3:5:8$. Find their sizes.

9. A shade of paint is made up of 3 parts blue and 4 parts purple. How many litres of blue are needed to make up 10.5 litres of this paint ?

10. To make gunmetal, copper, tin and zinc are used in the ratio $43:5:2$. What quantities of tin and zinc are used with 21.5 kg of copper ?

11. Two boys share some apples in the ratio $4:3$. The boy with the larger share took 56 apples. How many did the other boy take ?

Ratios, fractions, decimals and percentages

The ratio $4:5$ is equivalent to the fraction $\frac{4}{5}$, the decimal 0.8 and the percentage 80%.

If a quantity is divided into two parts A and B in the ratio $4:5$, then A is $\frac{4}{5}$ (or 0.8 or 80%) of B.

Also the ratio $B:A = 5:4$,
so B is $\frac{5}{4}$ or $1\frac{1}{4}$ (or 1.25 or 125%) of A.

Also, A is $\frac{4}{9}$ of the whole amount and B is $\frac{5}{9}$ of the whole amount.

Exercise 25.2

1. Copy this table and complete it, also including the fractions $\frac{1}{5}$, $\frac{2}{5}$, $\frac{3}{5}$, $\frac{4}{5}$, $\frac{1}{10}$, $\frac{1}{20}$, $\frac{1}{25}$, $\frac{1}{50}$, $\frac{1}{100}$.

Equivalent fractions, ratios, decimals and percentages

Fraction	Ratio	Decimal	Percentage
$\frac{1}{2}$	$1:2$	0.5	50%
$\frac{1}{4}$			
$\frac{3}{4}$			
$\frac{1}{3}$	$1:3$	0.333...	$33\frac{1}{3}\%$
$\frac{2}{3}$			

2.   A load of 52 kg is divided into two parts A and B in the ratio 3 : 10.

    1   What are the weights of A and B?
    2   What fraction of B is A?
    3   What percentage of B is A?
    4   What fraction of the whole load is A?
    5   What fraction of the whole load is B?

3.   84 ℓ of liquid is poured into two containers C and D in the ratio 7 : 5.

    1   What are the quantities of liquid in C and D?
    2   What fraction of C is D?
    3   What percentage of D is C?
    4   What fraction of the whole amount is C?

4.   £25 is divided between two people E and F so that E gets 40% of the total amount.

    1   What percentage does F get?
    2   What amounts do E and F get?
    3   In what ratio is the money divided?
    4   What fraction of the amount that F gets does E get?

Unitary method and proportion

Quantities which increase in the same ratio are in **direct proportion**.

Example

1   If 21 notebooks cost £7.56, what do 28 similar notebooks cost?

1st method, unitary method

21 notebooks cost £7.56
 1 notebook costs £0.36   (dividing by 21)
28 notebooks cost £10.08 (multiplying by 28)

2nd method, proportion

The prices are in direct proportion to the quantities.
Ratio of quantities, new : old = 28 : 21 = 4 : 3
Ratio of prices = 4 : 3

New price = $\frac{4}{3}$ of £7.56 = £$\frac{4}{3} \times 7.56$ = £10.08.

Quantities which vary so that one increases in the same ratio as the other decreases are in **inverse proportion**.

Example

2 If there is enough food in an emergency pack to last 12 men for 10 days, how long would the food last if there were 15 men ?

1st method, unitary method

The food lasts 12 men for 10 days.
The food lasts 1 man for 120 days.   (multiplying by 12 because it would last twelve
                                      times as long)
The food lasts 15 men for 8 days.   (dividing by 15)

2nd method, proportion

As the number of men increases, the time the food will last decreases.
Ratio of number of men, new : old = 15 : 12 = 5 : 4
Ratio of times, new : old = 4 : 5

New time the food lasts for = $\frac{4}{5}$ of 10 days = 8 days.

Rate

The word **rate** is used in many real-life situations.

Examples

A woman is paid for doing a job at the rate of £6.75 per hour.
Grass seed is sown to make a lawn at the rate of 2 oz per square yard.
Income tax is paid at the standard rate of 25p in the £ (or whatever the current rate is).
A car uses petrol at the rate of 40 miles to the gallon.

Best buys

Example

3 In one shop, $1\frac{1}{2}$ lb of frozen peas cost 57p, in another shop 2 lb of the same brand of frozen peas cost 79p.
Which packet is the better value for money ?

One way to do this is to find the cost of 1 lb of peas in each packet.

1st shop

$1\frac{1}{2}$ lb cost 57p.
$\frac{1}{2}$ lb would cost 19p.
1 lb would cost 38p.

2nd shop

2 lb cost 79p.
1 lb would cost 39.5p.

Since 38p is less than 39.5p, the $1\frac{1}{2}$ lb packet from the 1st shop is the better value for money.

Exercise 25.3

1. 28 bars of chocolate cost £6.16. What would be the cost of 35 similar bars ?

2. If 20 boxes weigh 36 lb, what is the weight of 45 similar boxes ?

3. If a car travels for 100 miles on fuel costing £6.80, what would the fuel cost be, at the same rate, for a journey of 250 miles ?

4. If a store of emergency food would last 20 men for 36 days, how long would the same food last if there were 45 men ?

5. 10 men can build a wall in 9 days. How long would 6 men take, working at the same rate ?

6. A carpet to cover a floor of area 20 square yards costs £250. How much would it cost for a similar carpet to cover a floor of area 24 square yards ?

7. In an hour 10 people can pick 40 kg of fruit. How much can be picked in an hour if there are 25 people ?

8. A farmer has enough food for his 30 cows for 12 days. If he buys 6 more cows, how long will the food last then ?

9. A plumber charges £143 for a job taking 22 hours. What rate does he charge per hour ?

10. A car used 12 litres of petrol on a journey of 150 km. What is the petrol consumption in km per litre ?

11. Two bottles of detergent are shown.

    1 What is the cost per litre of the two brands ?
    2 Which one is the better value for money if the two brands are equally effective in use ?

12.   Water flows from a tap at the rate of 20 litres per minute. How long will it take to fill a
       tank holding 240 litres ?

13.   The insurance for the contents of a house is charged at £6.50 per £1000 of value. How
       much will the insurance cost for contents valued at £37 500 ?

14.   This 2.5 litre tin of paint will cover an area of $45 \, m^2$.
       What is the rate in square metres per litre ?

15.   A firm offers a discount of 5p in the £. What will you actually pay for goods which are
       priced at £7.00 ?

Speed

The rate at which distance is travelled is called **speed** and it is found from the formula

$$Speed = \frac{distance}{time}$$

It is measured in units such as miles per hour, kilometres per hour, metres per second. The
abbreviation for metres per second is m/s or ms^{-1}.

The formula can be rearranged to give:

$$Time = \frac{distance}{speed}$$

$$Distance = speed \times time$$

The units have to correspond, e.g. metres, seconds, metres per second or km, hours, km per
hour.
If the speed is variable, these formulae will give or use the **average speed**.

Examples

1   A train travels 75 km in $1\frac{1}{4}$ hours. What is its average speed ?

$$Speed = \frac{distance}{time} = \frac{75}{1.25} \, km/h = 60 \, km/h$$

2   A boat travels 21 km at a speed of 36 km/h. How long does it take ?

$$\text{Time} = \frac{\text{distance}}{\text{speed}} = \frac{21}{36} \text{ hour} = \frac{7}{12} \text{ hour} = \frac{7}{12} \times 60 \text{ min}$$

$$= 35 \text{ min}$$

Exercise 25.4

1.   Find the time taken to travel 72 km at an average speed of 48 km/hour.

2.   Find the distance travelled by a train going for 3 hours at an average speed of 66 miles/hour.

3.   Mrs Owen travels 21 miles to work and the journey normally takes 30 minutes. What is her average speed ?

4.   1   A car travels 210 km in 3 hours. What is its average speed ?
     2   A train is travelling at 60 km/h. How far will it travel in $1\frac{1}{2}$ hours ?
     3   A plane is travelling at 900 km/h. How long will it take to travel 300 km ?

5.   A helicopter passes a point A at 3.58 pm and reaches a point B 25 km distant at 4.03 pm. What was its average speed ?

6.   A main road through a village has a speed limit of 40 miles per hour. A motorist covers the $1\frac{1}{2}$ mile section in 2 minutes. Did he break the speed limit ?

Foreign currency

In USA the currency is in dollars and cents, with 100 cents = 1 dollar. The symbol for dollars is $.

In France, Switzerland and Belgium, the currency is in francs and centimes, with 100 centimes = 1 franc.

Many other countries have a similar system, where the main unit of currency is divided into 100 smaller units.

Calculations in such currencies are carried out in a similar way to calculations in £'s and pence.

Rate of exchange

At Banks and a few other places you can change money into different currencies. The Banks make a small charge (commission) for changing the money. The rate of exchange varies slightly from day to day and may change considerably at times, depending on the financial situations in the countries concerned. In order to attract customers, some banks may offer slightly better rates than others.

Here are some of the rates quoted on one particular day. These amounts are equivalent to £1.

Australia	1.94 dollars
Austria	15.20 schillings
Belgium	44.60 francs
Canada	2.04 dollars
Denmark	8.45 kroner
France	7.43 francs
Germany	2.19 marks
Greece	365 drachmae
Holland	2.46 guilders
Ireland	0.96 punts
Israel	4.58 shekels
Italy	2325 lire
Malta	0.54 lire
New Zealand	2.23 dollars
Norway	9.56 kroner
Portugal	227 escudos
Spain	183 pesetas
Switzerland	1.78 francs
United States	1.50 dollars

For example,
£10 will be worth 10×7.43 French francs
$= 74.3$ francs

£15 will be worth 15×2.04 Canadian dollars
$= 30.6$ dollars

1500 Spanish pesetas will be worth $£\dfrac{1500}{183}$
$= £8.20$

10 Irish punts will be worth $£\dfrac{10}{0.96}$
$= £10.42$

Exercise 25.5

1. Find the total cost in dollars of articles bought in New York costing $1.25, $2.80 and $5.15.

2. If 3 dollars is shared among 3 children in the ratio 3 : 4 : 5, how much do they each get ?

3. Find the total cost of 5 books at $4.95 each.

4. In Switzerland a packet of sweets cost 0.45 francs. What was the total cost in francs of 12 packets ?

5. Find the total cost of food bought in Switzerland costing 9.50 f, 12.30 f, 4 f, 7.90 f. How much change is there from 50 francs ?

6.   In a market, 5 pairs of socks are sold for 13.90 francs. How much is this per pair ?

Using the rates of exchange given in the list, say how much you get if you change these amounts.

7.   £100 into Greek money.
8.   £150 into Swiss francs.
9.   £12 into U.S. dollars.
10.   £3000 into Danish money.
11.   £200 into Italian money.

Using the rates of exchange given in the list, change this money into British currency, to the nearest penny.

12.   5000 Australian dollars.
13.   2000 Belgian francs.
14.   4000 German marks.
15.   1000 Portuguese escudos.
16.   200 Norwegian kroner.

If you know the up-to-date exchange rates, repeat questions 7 to 16 using them.

17.   Whilst on holiday, Mr Wood bought a carton containing 10 packets of cigarettes for 1080 pesetas. On returning home he sold these packets to his friends for £1 each. How much profit (in £'s) did he make ?
The rate of exchange at the time was 180 pesetas = £1.

18.   Two tourists, Alan and Bill, returned to England, each with 300 francs to change back into British money. When Alan changed his the rate was 8.0 francs to the £, and a week later when Bill changed his the rate was 7.5 francs to the £. Who got more British money, and how much more ?

19.   If the rates of exchange are £1 = 1.50 dollars and £1 = 7.5 francs, how much is 24 dollars worth

    1   in British currency,
    2   in francs ?

Exercise 25.6   Applications

1.   The costs of manufacture of an article are divided among labour, materials and overheads in the ratio 8 : 4 : 1. If the materials for 1000 articles cost £640, what are the costs for labour, and for overheads ? What is the total cost of these articles ?

2.   The measurements of two rectangles are (a) length 12 cm and width 9 cm, (b) length 24 cm and width 7 cm.

Find
1   the ratio of their perimeters,
2   the ratio of their areas.

3   If all the sides are increased by 3 cm, find the new ratio of their areas.

3.   The edges of two cubes are 4 cm and 6 cm. Find the ratio of their volumes.

4.   A firm buys petrol and diesel oil in the ratio 5 : 7, spending £2700 altogether per week. How much is spent on each ?
If the price of petrol is increased by 5% and the diesel oil by 3%, find the increase in the total cost.

5.   A man gave £500 to his four children in the ratio 2 : 4 : 5 : 9. What was the difference between the largest and the smallest shares ?

6.   The weekly wages paid by a firm to 8 workers total £760. What will be the weekly wages if they employ 2 extra women and pay them all at the same rate ?

7.   If grass seed is to be sown at the rate of 2 oz per square yard, how many lbs will be needed to make a rectangular lawn, 10 yards long by 8 yards wide ?
(16 oz = 1 lb)

8.   A pond can be emptied in 12 hours using 4 pumps. If the owner wants it emptied in 8 hours, how many extra pumps, which work at the same rate, will be needed ?

9.   A recipe for 12 small cakes uses 75 g butter, 75 g castor sugar, 100 g flour and 2 eggs.
1   How much flour is needed to make 30 of these cakes ?
2   How many eggs are needed to make 30 of these cakes ?

10. Mrs Modi wants to buy some toothpaste. Which size, 50 ml, 125 ml or 175 ml, is the best value for money ?

11. The internal dimensions of the base of a rectangular tank are 3 m by 2 m and it can contain water to a depth of 1.5 m. How long will it take to fill the tank by means of an inlet pipe delivering water at the rate of 50 litres per minute ?
($1 \text{ m}^3 = 1000 \ell$)

12. When Ron visits his mother, the journey takes $2\frac{1}{2}$ hours if he goes at an average speed of 30 miles per hour. If he reduces his average speed to 25 miles per hour in wet weather, how much longer will his journey take ?

13. Two motorists, Mr Bowen and Mrs Crane, set off at 9 am to travel to a town 120 km away. Mr Bowen arrives there at 11.30 am and Mrs Crane arrives there at noon.

   1 What is the ratio of their times taken ?
   2 What is the ratio of their average speeds ?

14. On a holiday journey the car mileage indicator readings and times were as follows:

Time	9.05 am	11.35 am	12.15 pm	2.15 pm
Mileage indicator reading	16335	16455	16455	16525

(I had stopped to visit a place of interest from 11.35 am to 12.15 pm.)

   1 What was the average speed for the part of the journey up to 11.35 am ?

   2 What was the average speed for the part of the journey from 12.15 pm ?

   3 I estimate that my car used 5 gallons of petrol on the journey. What is the approximate fuel consumption in miles per gallon ?

15. Maureen went on holiday to Belgium taking £200 which she changed into francs at the rate of 45 francs to the £. She spent on average 500 francs each day for 12 days on holiday expenses, and also she bought for presents a watch costing 599 francs, a doll for 30 francs, perfume for 49 francs and a necklace for 207 francs.
How many francs had she left ?

On her return home she changed this money back into British currency at the same rate as before. How much did she get ?

16. Brian is spending 10 days holiday in Austria. On the first day he changed his spending money of £300 into schillings at the rate of 15 schillings to the £.
He spent 340 schillings, 195 schillings, 265 schillings and 295 schillings in the first four days. Then he saw a camera which he would like to buy, costing 1485 schillings.

If he buys the camera, how much will he have left to spend each day, on average, for the next 6 days ?

What is the value of the camera in British currency ?

Practice test 25

1. Express as ratios in their simplest forms

    1 12 cm : 15 cm   4 50 g : 240 g
    2 25p : 60p   5 60 ml : 20 ml
    3 20 minutes : 32 minutes

2. £900 is raised and is divided among 3 charities, *A*, *B* and *C* in the proportion 4 : 5 : 6. Find the amount each charity receives.

3. Three men invest £2000, £3500 and £4500 respectively into a business and agree to share the profits in the ratio of their investments.

    1 What was the ratio of their investments in its simplest form ?
    2 The profits in the first year were £8000. How much did they each receive ?

4. Write
    1 the ratio 1 : 4 as a percentage,
    2 the ratio 2 : 3 as a fraction,
    3 the ratio 3 : 5 as a decimal,
    4 the fraction $\frac{3}{4}$ as a ratio,
    5 the decimal 0.9 as a ratio.

5.   A party of 4 volunteers can pack a batch of emergency parcels in 7 hours. How long would it take if there were 10 more volunteers helping, and they all worked at the same rate ?

6.   Tanya saves £12 in 8 weeks. How long would it take her to save £45, if she saved at the same rate ?

7.   If a car travels 48 miles in 45 minutes, what is its average speed in miles per hour ?

8.   What are 30 Dutch guilders worth in British currency, when the rate of exchange is 2.4 guilders to £1 ?

PUZZLES

41.   There are three married couples having dinner together.
George is older than Michelle's husband.
Frank's wife is older than Nadia.
Lynnette's husband is older than George.
Michelle is not Edward's wife.
The oldest man is married to the youngest woman.
The oldest woman paid the bill. Who was this ?

42.   You are given 27 coins and told that 26 of them are of equal weight but 1 is slightly lighter.
You are also given balance-type weighing scales so that you can weigh some coins on one side against some on the other side.
However, you are only allowed to make 3 weighings.
How can you find the lighter coin ?

43.   There are two discs; one is red on both sides, the other is red on one side and green on the other, but they are otherwise identical. Without looking, one is picked at random and placed flat on the table. If the top of this disc is red, what is the probability that the hidden side is also red ? Is it $\frac{1}{4}, \frac{1}{3}, \frac{1}{2}, \frac{2}{3}$ or $\frac{3}{4}$?

26 Circles

The topics in this chapter include:

- understanding and using the terms circle, diameter, radius, circumference, arc, chord, tangent,
- constructing circles,
- calculating the circumference of a circle,
- calculating the area of a circle.

Circles

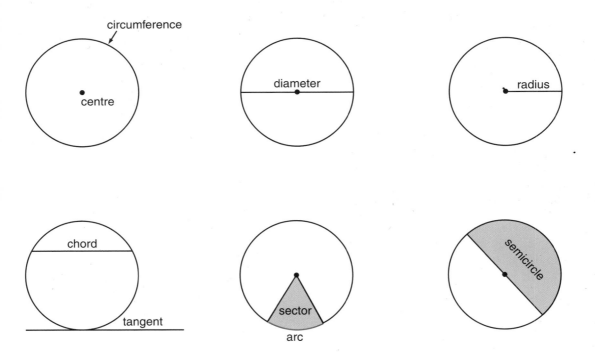

Note that:

An arc is part of the circumference.
A tangent is a line which just touches a circle.
The plural of radius is radii.

Exercise 26.1

1. Using the same centre O, draw circles with radii 2 cm, 3.6 cm, 4.5 cm and 6 cm. (Circles with the same centre are called **concentric** circles.)

2. Draw a line AB of length 9 cm.
   Using centres A and B in turn, draw circles with radii 6 cm.
   Let the points where these circles cross each other be C and D.
   Draw the line CD.
   What do you notice about this line ?

3. In the diagram, O is the centre of the circle.

   Give the names of parts of the circle shown by
   1   OB,
   2   AC,
   3   CD,
   4   the straight line AB,
   5   the curved line AB.

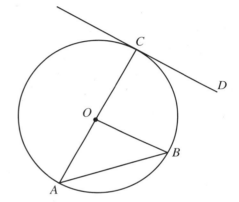

Circumference of a circle

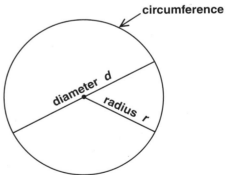

The perimeter of a circle is called the **circumference**.

> Circumference $= \pi \times$ diameter $= 2 \times \pi \times$ radius
>
> $$C = \pi d$$
>
> $$C = 2\pi r$$

π (pi) is the Greek letter which represents the special number 3.14159... used in circle formulae.
This number cannot be written as an exact decimal.
For practical purposes we use 3, 3.1, 3.14 or 3.142, depending on how accurate we need to be.
If you use 3.14 or 3.142 for π, your answer should normally be given corrected to 3 figures.

There may be a special key labelled π on your calculator, and if so, it is quicker to use that.
e.g. For 9π press $9 \; \boxed{\times} \; \boxed{\pi} \; \boxed{=}$ getting 28.274... To 3 figures this is 28.3.

Examples

1   Find the circumference of a circle with radius 25 cm.

$$C = 2\pi r$$

$$= 2 \times \pi \times 25\,\text{cm}$$

$$= 157.07\ldots\text{cm, if using the } \pi \text{ key,}$$

   or 157.1 cm, if using $\pi = 3.142$,

$$= 157\,\text{cm, correct to 3 figures.}$$

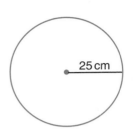

2   Find the circumference of a circle with diameter 8.4 cm.

$$C = \pi d$$

$$= \pi \times 8.4\,\text{cm}$$

$$= 26.38\ldots\text{cm, if using the } \pi \text{ key,}$$

   or 26.3928 cm, if using $\pi = 3.142$,

$$= 26.4\,\text{cm, correct to 3 figures.}$$

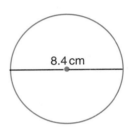

Exercise 26.2

In this exercise, take π as 3.142 or use the π key on your calculator.
In questions 1 and 2, give the answers correct to 3 figures.

1.   Find the circumferences of these circles.

   1   Diameter 11 cm.   **4**   Diameter 3.5 cm.
   2   Diameter 4 m.   **5**   Diameter 6.2 m.
   3   Diameter 15 cm.

2.   Find the circumferences of these circles.

   1   Radius 14 cm.   **4**   Radius 1.6 m.
   2   Radius 6 cm.   **5**   Radius 10.8 cm.
   3   Radius 4.5 m.

3.   A wheel has a radius of 0.8 m. What is the distance
      all round the edge of the wheel, to the nearest cm ?

4.   Measure the diameters of these circles in centimetres, to the nearest centimetre.
     Calculate the lengths of their circumferences. Give the answers to the nearest cm, and
     write them in order of size, smallest first.

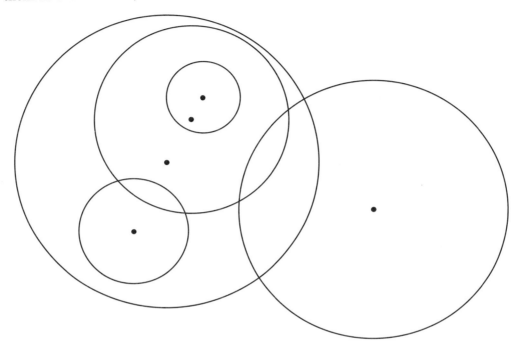

5.   There is a circular running-track with diameter 35 m.
     How far has Peter run, to the nearest metre, when he has made 10 complete circuits ?

6.   A cotton reel has diameter 3.4 cm. The cotton is wound round
     500 times. What is the length of cotton, to the nearest metre ?

7.   A car wheel has a diameter of 50 cm. What is its circumference ?
     When the wheel has rotated 1000 times, what distance has the car travelled, to the
     nearest 100 metres ?

Area of a circle

Area of a circle $= \pi \times (\text{radius})^2$

$$A = \pi r^2$$

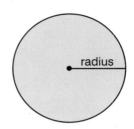

Example

Find the area of a circle with diameter 8 cm.

(If the diameter is 8 cm, the radius is 4 cm.)

$A = \pi r^2$

$\quad = \pi \times 4^2 \text{ cm}^2$

$\quad = \pi \times 4 \times 4 \text{ cm}^2$

$\quad = 50.26\ldots \text{ cm}^2$, if using the π key,

$\quad$ or 50.272 cm^2, if using $\pi = 3.142$,

$\quad = 50.3 \text{ cm}^2$, correct to 3 figures.

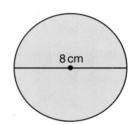

Exercise 26.3

In this exercise take π as 3.142 or use the π key on your calculator.

1. Find the areas of these circles, giving them correct to 3 figures.

    1 Radius 5 cm.   **4** Diameter 16 cm.
    2 Radius 9 cm.   **5** Diameter 4.2 cm.
    3 Radius 7.5 cm.

2. The circle is touching a square of side 12 cm.

    Find
    1 the area of the square,
    2 the area of the circle,
    3 the total shaded area.

    Give answers to parts **2** and **3** to the nearest 0.1 cm^2.

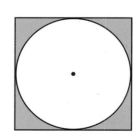

3. A flower bed is marked out at the corner of a
    garden by drawing a quarter circle with radius 2.5 m,
    as shown in the diagram.

    1   Find the area of a circle of radius 2.5 m.
    2   Find the area of the flower bed.

    Give answers to the nearest 0.1 m^2.

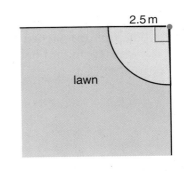

2.5 m

lawn

Exercise 26.4 Applications

Where necessary, take π as 3.142 or use the π key on your calculator.

1.   Here are some patterns made with circles. Copy these patterns and design others.

     1 Keep the same radius.   2   Extend to outer circles.

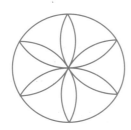

     3   4

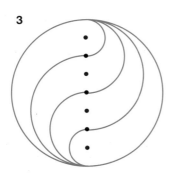

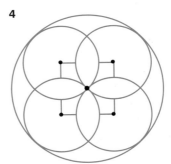

2. Some cylindrical tins have radius 3.5 cm and height 10 cm.
    The tins are packed in a rectangular box of length 28 cm,
    width 21 cm and height 10 cm. How many tins will fit
    in a box ?

3. This rug is in the shape of a semicircle with
    radius 80 cm. A strip of tape is sewn all round
    the edge of the rug. How much tape is
    needed, to the nearest cm ?

4. It is planned to plant a bush with a circle of flowering plants round it.
    The plants have to be 1.5 m from the centre of the bush so the radius of the circle for the
    plants is 1.5 m.
    What is the circumference of this circle, to the nearest cm ?

    A box of 25 plants is bought.
    Approximately how far apart should they be planted around the circle, if they are spaced
    out evenly ?

5. A circular pond of radius 2.6 m is surrounded
    by a circular path of width 0.4 m.

    1   Find the area of the pond.

    2   Find the total area of the pond and the path.

    3   Find the area of the path.

    Give the answers to the nearest 0.1 m^2.

6. **1**   By counting squares find the approximate area of the circle.

    2   Measure the radius of the circle to the nearest mm and use this answer to calculate a more exact value for the area of the circle, to the nearest $0.1\,\text{cm}^2$.

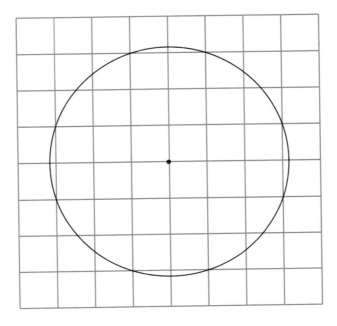

7.   The diagram shows a hemisphere. It has a plane surface, which is a circle, and a curved surface.

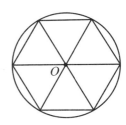

  1   Find the area of the circle.

  2   The area of the curved surface is twice the area of the circle. Find the total surface area of the hemisphere, to the nearest cm^2.

8.   6 equilateral triangles of side $3.6\,\text{cm}$ are arranged to form a hexagon inside a circle.

  1   What is the perimeter of the hexagon ?

  2   What is the radius of the circle ?

  3   Find the circumference of the circle, to the nearest mm.

  4   How much larger is the circumference of the circle than the perimeter of the hexagon ?

  5   Find the area of the circle, to the nearest $0.1\,\text{cm}^2$.

  6   The area of each triangle is $5.6\,\text{cm}^2$. How much larger is the area of the circle than the area of the hexagon ?

9.   **Using formulae in reverse**

The formula $C = \pi d$ can be rearranged as $d = \dfrac{C}{\pi}$.

The formula $C = 2\pi r$ can be rearranged as $r = \dfrac{C}{2\pi}$.

The formula $A = \pi r^2$ can be rearranged as $r = \sqrt{\dfrac{A}{\pi}}$.

Use these rearranged formulae in these questions. Give the answers correct to 3 figures.

1   Find the diameter of a circle if its circumference is 100 cm.

On your calculator for $\dfrac{C}{\pi}$, press C $\boxed{\div}$ π $\boxed{=}$.

2   Find the radius of a circle if its circumference is 64 cm.

On your calculator for $\dfrac{C}{2\pi}$, press C $\boxed{\div}$ 2 $\boxed{\div}$ π $\boxed{=}$.

3   Find the radius of a circle if its area is 8 cm².

On your calculator for $\sqrt{\dfrac{A}{\pi}}$, press A $\boxed{\div}$ π $\boxed{=}$ $\boxed{\sqrt{}}$.

Practice test 26

Where necessary, take π as 3.142 or use the π key on your calculator.

1.   The minute hand of a church clock is 1.3 m long.
How far does the tip of the hand travel in an
hour, to the nearest 0.1 m ?

2.   Draw a line *AB* of length 14 cm, and find its mid-point *O*.
      Through *O* draw a line crossing *AB* at right angles.
      With centre *O*, radius 7 cm, draw a circle. Let the points where it cuts the second line
      be *C* and *D*.
      Join *AC, BC, AD, BD*. Measure *AC* to the nearest mm.
      What sort of figure is *ACBD* ?

3.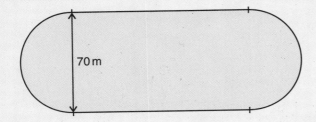

      An athletics track has two straight lengths and two semicircles.
      If the diameter of the semicircular parts is 70 m, find the total length of the two
      semicircles, to the nearest metre.
      If the total distance round the track is 400 m, find the length of each straight part.

4.   The diameter of a £1 coin is 2.25 cm. What is the area of a circular surface, to the
      nearest 0.1 cm^2 ?

5.   A door is shaped as a rectangle 3 m high and 1.6 m wide,
      with a semicircle above it.

      1   What is the total height of the door ?

      2   Find the area of one side of the door, to the
          nearest 0.1 m^2.

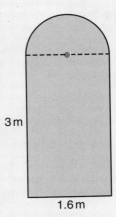

27 *Travel graphs and other graphs*

The topics in this chapter include:

- constructing and interpreting graphs that describe real-life situations, including travel graphs and conversion graphs.

Travel graphs

Distance-time graphs

On a distance-time graph, the horizontal axis is the time axis and the vertical axis is the distance axis.

The graph is a straight line when the speed is steady. If the speed is not steady, the graph will not be a straight line.

When the speed is steady, its value is given by the gradient (slope) of the line. The greater the speed, the greater the gradient of the line.

To find the speed, divide the distance travelled by the time taken.

$$\text{Speed} = \frac{\text{distance}}{\text{time}}$$

Example

This graph represents a boy's journey from a town P.
He leaves at 12 noon and walks for 30 minutes at a steady speed. This is represented by the line AB.

How far does he walk ?
At what speed does he walk ?

The line BC represents the next stage, where he cycles.
For how long does he cycle ?
What distance does he cycle ?
At what speed does he cycle ?

The line CD represents a rest of 30 minutes.
How far is he away from P ?

The line *DE* represents his journey home by bus.
What time does the bus journey begin ?
How long is the bus journey ?
What is the speed of the bus ?

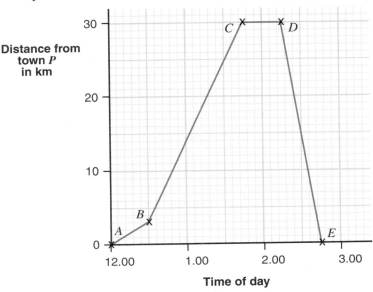

He walks for 3 km in $\frac{1}{2}$ hour.
His speed is $3 \div \frac{1}{2}$ km/h $= 6$ km/h.

He cycles for $1\frac{1}{4}$ hours, and cycles 27 km.
His speed is $27 \div 1\frac{1}{4}$ km/h $= 21.6$ km/h.

At *CD* he is 30 km from *P*.

The bus journey begins at 2.15 pm and ends at 2.45 pm, taking $\frac{1}{2}$ hour.
The speed of the bus is $30 \div \frac{1}{2}$ km/h $= 60$ km/h.

Exercise 27.1

1.   The graph represents the journey of a
     cyclist.
     What is the cyclist's speed ?

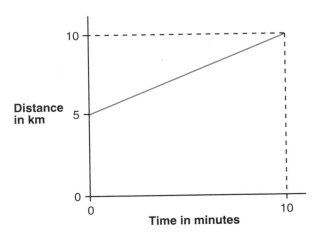

2. The diagram represents the journeys of four trains.
    Three of them are travelling from town *A* to town *B*, 100 km away, and one is going in
    the opposite direction.

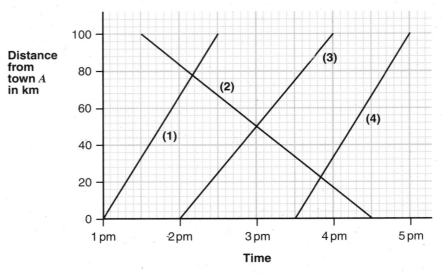

1   Which two trains travel at the same speed ?
    What speed is it ?

2   Which train has the slowest speed ?
    What speed is it ?

3   Train (2) should have been travelling at a speed of 40 km/h.
    How many minutes late was it on reaching town *A* ?

3. John cycled from home to a friend's house. He stayed for a while and then cycled home,
    stopping on the way to buy some sweets at a shop.
    The graph shows his journeys.

1   How long did it take John
    to cycle to his friend's house ?
2   How long did he stay at his
    friend's house ?
3   How far from his friend's
    house was the shop ?
4   How long did he spend in
    the shop ?
5   After leaving the shop,
    what was John's speed on
    the homeward journey ?

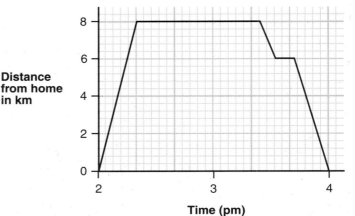

4.   The graph represents the journeys of two motorists, one in a car and one in a van.

    1   At what time did the car reach B ?
    2   What was the speed of the van ?
    3   At what time, and how far from A, did the car pass the van ?
    4   How far apart were the car and the van at 2 pm ?
    5   What was the average speed of the car over the whole journey from A to B ?

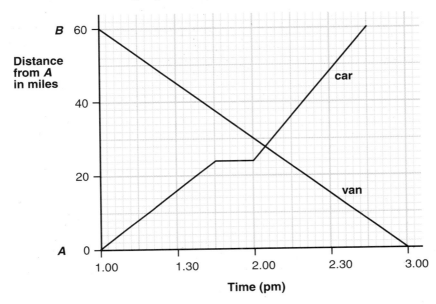

5.   Paula leaves home to go to school. She walks at a steady speed of 5 km/h to her friend's home, which is $2\frac{1}{2}$ km away.
There she waits for 20 minutes until her friend is ready to leave.
The two girls are then taken by car to the school, which is 5 km away. The car travels at a steady speed of 30 km/h.

Draw a graph to represent Paula's journey. Draw the time axis from 0 to 60 minutes and the distance axis from 0 to 8 km.

6.   A rocket is fired vertically into the air from ground level, and its height h metres after t seconds is given in the table.

t	0	5	10	15	20	25	30
h	0	625	1000	1125	1000	625	0

Draw a distance-time graph, joining the points with a smooth curve.

    1   What is the greatest height achieved by the rocket ?
    2   At what times is the rocket at half of its greatest height ?
    3   For how many seconds is the rocket 900 m or more above the ground ?

Speed-time graphs

Example

Draw a graph to represent the journey of a car which starts from rest and increases its speed at a constant rate for 10 seconds, reaching a speed of 30 m/s. It maintains this speed for 30 seconds and then decreases its speed constantly for 15 seconds until it comes to rest.

Put time on the horizontal axis, from 0 to 55 s.
Put speed on the vertical axis, from 0 to 30 m/s.
For the first part of the journey, join the point (0, 0) to the point (10, 30) with a straight line.
Then draw a straight line with the speed 30 for the next 30 seconds.
Finally, the slowing down period takes 15 seconds. Draw the line to represent this.

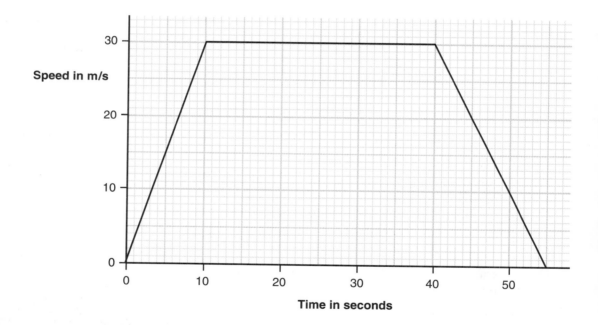

Use your graph to find the speed of the car at time 6 seconds, and at time 42 seconds.

At time 6 seconds the speed is 18 m/s,
at time 42 seconds the speed is 26 m/s.

Exercise 27.2

1. A train starts from rest at a station *A* and increases speed at a steady rate for 2 minutes until it reaches a speed of 100 km/h. It maintains this steady speed for 12 minutes, and then slows down at a steady rate for 5 minutes until it comes to a stop at station *B*.

   Represent this information graphically on a speed-time graph.
   Draw the time axis from 0 to 20 minutes and the speed axis from 0 to 100 km/h.

   1 How far does the train travel at its highest speed ?

   2 What is its speed after 1 minute, and at what time is it next travelling at this speed ?

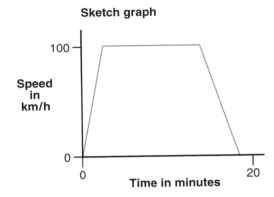

Sketch graph

2. The table shows the speed of a train at various times as it travels between two stations.

Time from start, in seconds	0	15	30	45	60	75	90	105	120
Speed, in m/s	0	9	14	18	21	21	18	11	0

   1 Draw a speed-time graph, joining the points with a smooth curve.
   Draw the time axis from 0 to 120 seconds and the speed axis from 0 to 25 m/s.

   Find from the graph
   2 the greatest speed,
   3 the two times when the train was travelling at half its greatest speed.

Conversion graphs

Example

Draw a graph to convert kilometres into miles, given that 1 km = 0.62 miles.

Draw the 'kilometres' axis horizontally, label from 0 to 100.
Draw the 'miles' axis vertically, label from 0 to 70.

You know that 0 km = 0 miles, so plot a point at (0, 0).
Also 100 km = 100 × 0.62 miles = 62 miles, so plot a point at (100, 62).
A third point would be useful as a check.
50 km = 50 × 0.62 miles = 31 miles, so you can plot a
point at (50, 31).
Join the points with a straight line.

You can use this graph to convert km into miles or miles
into km.

1   Convert 23 km into miles.
2   Convert 50 miles into km.

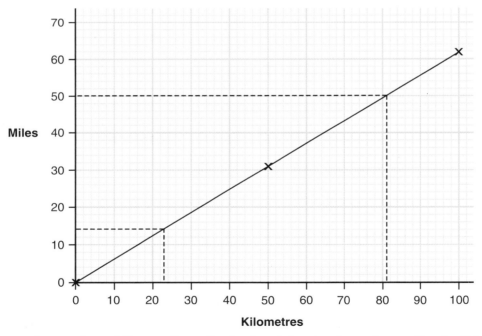

For 1, draw a dotted line up from the horizontal axis where the reading is 23 km, to the graph. Then draw a dotted line sideways from this point on the graph to the vertical axis, where its value can be read. (It is 14 miles.)

For 2, start with a dotted line sideways from the vertical axis where the reading is 50 miles, to the graph. Then draw a dotted line downwards from this point on the graph to the horizontal axis, where its value can be read. (It is 81 km.)

Exercise 27.3

1. Draw a graph to convert U.S. dollars into £'s at a time when the rate of exchange was 1 dollar = £0.69. Draw the 'dollars' axis horizontally, label from 0 to 100. Draw the £'s axis vertically, label from 0 to 70. Plot the point representing 100 dollars on the graph and join it to the origin (0, 0) with a straight line.

    Use your graph to convert
    1   75 dollars into £'s,
    2   £22 into dollars.

    (If you know the up-to-date rate of exchange you may prefer to use that.)

2. Draw a graph to convert gallons into litres.
    Draw the 'gallons' axis horizontally, label from 0 to 10.
    Draw the 'litres' axis vertically, label from 0 to 50.
    10 gallons is equivalent to 45.5 litres.
    Plot this point on the graph and join it to the origin (0, 0) with a straight line.

    Use your graph to convert 6.5 gallons into litres, and to convert 10 litres into gallons.

3. Draw a graph to convert between British and Spanish currency at a time when the rate of exchange was £1 = 190 pesetas.
    On the horizontal axis, for £'s, label from 0 to 10 with 1 unit to 1 cm. On the vertical axis, for pesetas, label from 0 to 2000 with 200 units to 1 cm.
    Plot the point representing £10 in pesetas and join this to the origin with a straight line.

    From your graph find
    1   the amount you would get if you changed £3 into pesetas,
    2   the value in British money of a present which cost you 1500 pesetas.

    (If you know the up-to-date rate of exchange you may prefer to use that.)

4. Draw a graph to convert temperature from °F to °C.
    Draw the °F axis horizontally, labelling it from 0 to 220, and draw the °C axis vertically, labelling it from 0 to 100.
    When the temperature is 32°F, it is 0°C. (Freezing point.)
    When the temperature is 212°F, it is 100°C. (Boiling point.)
    Plot these two points on the graph, and join them with a straight line.

    Use your graph to convert 70°F into °C, and to convert 80°C into °F.
    A person's 'normal' temperature is 98.4°F. What is the approximate value in °C ?

Other graphs

Example

A Gas Company makes a standing charge of £10 a quarter plus a cost of 1.5p for every kilowatt hour (kWh) of gas used.
What would be the total bill if 8000 kWh were used ?
What would be the total bill if 4000 kWh were used ?
If no gas was used, there would still be the £10 standing charge to pay.

Draw an accurate graph, with the number of kWh on the horizontal axis, from 0 to 8000, using a scale of 2 cm to represent 1000 kWh, and with cost in £'s on the vertical axis, from 0 to 130, using a scale of 2 cm to £20.
Plot the 3 points corresponding to 0 kWh, 4000 kWh and 8000 kWh used, and join them with a straight line.

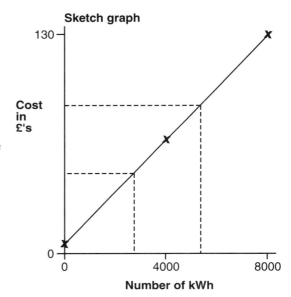

Sketch graph

Use your graph to find the amount of the bill when 2800 kWh were used. Also find the number of kWh used if a gas bill was for £88.

(This sketch graph shows how your accurate graph will look, and how it can be used.)

8000 kWh cost £130,
4000 kWh cost £70.

2800 kWh cost £52,
£88 is the cost of 5200 kWh.

Exercise 27.4

1. When a local firm is called out to service machinery, it charges £40 for coming to the job plus an amount for time spent on the job, at the rate of £30 per hour.

    Draw a graph of the costs for jobs taking up to 5 hours.

    Use the graph to find
    1   the cost for a job taking $2\frac{1}{4}$ hours,
    2   the time spent, if the bill was for £175.

2. A tank contains water, and when it is drained by means of a tap the water level falls by 2.5 cm each second. At the start, the depth of the water in the tank is 50 cm.

Draw a graph to show the depth of water at different times after opening the tap.

Use the graph to find
1 the depth of water in the tank after 12 seconds,
2 the time taken for the tank to empty.

3. The cost, £C, of making n articles in a certain factory is given by the formula $C = 160 + 20n$.

1 Copy and complete this table showing the costs.

Number of articles n	0	5	10	15	20	25	30
Cost £C	160	260					

2 Draw a graph showing the cost for making up to 30 articles.
3 From the graph find how many articles can be made for £500.

4. These times are taken from a table of 'lighting-up times for vehicles', on the Sunday of each week.

Week number	1	2	3	4	5	6	7	8
Time of day	16.32	16.40	16.50	17.02	17.14	17.26	17.39	17.52

Plot these values on a graph.
Draw the 'week number' axis horizontally with 2 cm to each unit.
Draw the 'time of day' axis vertically, from 16.00 hours to 18.00 hours taking 1 cm to 10 minutes.
Join the plotted points with a smooth curve.

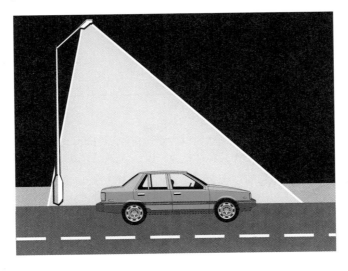

5.   The graph shows the temperature recorded
      in the room of a house between 6 am
      and 6 pm.
      Describe the changes in temperature and
      suggest likely reasons for them.

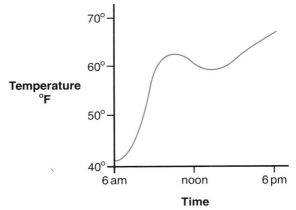

Exercise 27.5   Applications

1.   The graph shows the journeys of 2 girls, Pam and Ruth.
      Pam cycles from town A to village B, stopping for a rest on the way.
      Ruth cycles from village B to town A.

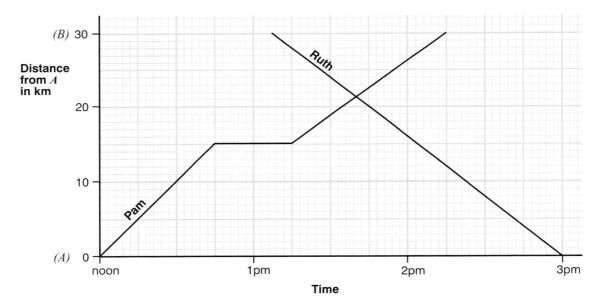

   1   For how long did Pam rest ?
   2   What was Pam's average speed on the part of her journey after her rest ?
   3   When did the two girls pass each other and how far from B were they at this time ?
   4   How far apart were the girls at 2.00 pm ?
   5   How far did Ruth travel between 2.00 pm and 3.00 pm ?
   6   What was Ruth's average speed ?

2.   Two cars start at 9 am, one from place *A* and the other from place *B*, which is 60 miles from *A*. They move towards each other, the first car travelling at 30 mph and the other one at 40 mph.
Show these journeys on a graph.
At what time do the cars meet, and how far are they from *A* when they meet ?

Sketch graph

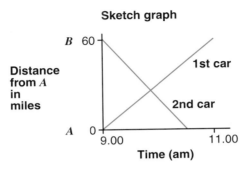

3.   Three workmen charge for doing a job as follows:
Mr A charges £240 for the 1st 40 hours and £10 an hour for any hours over 40.
Mr B charges a flat-rate of £12 per hour.
Mr C charges £300 for the job regardless of how long it will take.

Copy and fill in this table showing the charges by the three men for jobs up to 50 hours.

Number of hours	1	10	20	30	40	50
Mr A	£240					
Mr B	£12					
Mr C	£300					

Draw a graph with time on the horizontal axis, from 0 to 50 hours, and cost on the vertical axis from £0 to £600.
Plot the points in the table for Mr B, and join them with a straight line.
Draw the straight line representing the costs for Mr C.
For Mr A the graph consists of two straight lines, one to the point (40, 240) and one past that point. Draw this graph.
Label the graphs for Mr A, Mr B and Mr C.

From your graphs find
1   which man charges least for a job taking 15 hours,

2   which man charges least for a job taking 25 hours,

3   which man charges least for a job taking 48 hours.

4. The following values of the speed of an object at different times are obtained by experiment. Plot the values on a graph with time on the horizontal axis and speed on the vertical axis, and show that the plotted points lie approximately on a straight line. Draw this line and use it to estimate the speed at time 3.5 seconds.

Time in seconds	1	2	3	4	5	6
Speed in m/s	2.0	2.7	3.6	4.4	5.3	5.9

Practice test 27

1. Karen walks from school to a bus stop and then catches a bus which takes her to the village. She then walks the remaining distance home. The journey is shown by the graph.

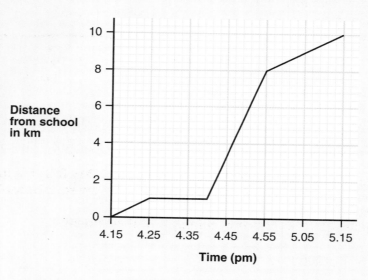

1   How long does Karen wait at the bus stop ?
2   At what speed does the bus travel ?
3   How far does Karen walk after getting off the bus ?

2. Draw a graph to convert metres/second into km/h for speeds up to 50 m/s. Label the horizontal axis from 0 to 50 (m/s) and the vertical axis from 0 to 180 (km/h). Use the information that 0 m/s = 0 km/h and 50 m/s = 180 km/h to draw the straight-line graph.

    What speed is equivalent to
    1   13 m/s,
    2   100 km/h ?

3. The temperature of water in a jug is shown in this table.

Time in minutes	0	2	4	6	8	10	12
Temperature in °C	100	60	40	30	25	23	21

Plot the points on a graph with time on the horizontal axis, from 0 to 12 minutes, and temperature on the vertical axis, from 0° to 100°.
Join the points with a smooth curve.

Use the graph to estimate the temperature of the water after 7 minutes.

4. The graph shows how the depth of water in a harbour varies throughout the day.

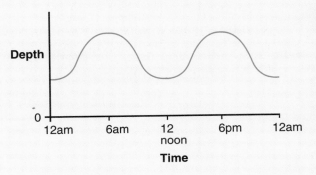

1   At what times were high tide ?
2   At what times were low tide ?
3   Estimate the time of the next high tide.

PUZZLES

44. The ages of my father, my son and myself total 85 years. My father is just twice my age, and the units figure in his age is equal to the age of my son. How old am I ?

45. How many squares can be formed by joining 4 of these points ?

46. Down the corridor next to the school hall there are five classrooms, numbered from 1 to 5, and these are occupied by the five forms, 7A, 7B, 7C, 7D and 7E.
7A is not in room 1, 7B is not in room 5, 7C is not in room 1 or room 5.
7D is in a room with a lower number than 7B. 7C's room is not next to 7B's room.
7E's room is not next to 7C's room.
Which class is in room 1 ?

28 Transformations

The topics in this chapter include:

- recognising and using transformations:
    translation,
    reflection in axes or mirror line,
    rotation through $\frac{1}{4}$, $\frac{1}{2}$ or $\frac{3}{4}$ turns,
    enlargement of a shape with a positive whole number scale factor,

- understanding and using the properties of transformations to create patterns and to understand the properties of shapes,

- understanding the congruence of simple shapes.

Transformations

The three main transformations which change the position of a figure without altering its size or shape are translation, reflection and rotation.

Translation

The dotted lines show the translation of the triangles when every point has been moved an equal distance in the same direction.

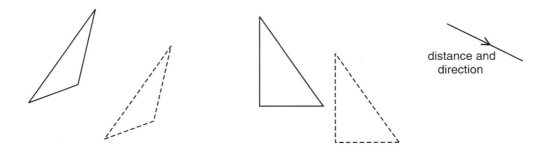

distance and direction

Example

The translation 4 units in the *x*-direction,
1 unit in the *y*-direction.

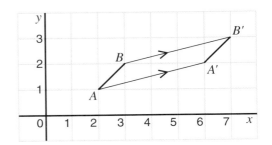

A (2, 1) is transformed into A' (6, 2).
B (3, 2) is transformed into B' (7, 3).

The line AB is translated into the line $A'B'$.

Reflection

The dotted lines shows the reflections of the triangles in the line AB, which is an axis of symmetry of the completed figure.

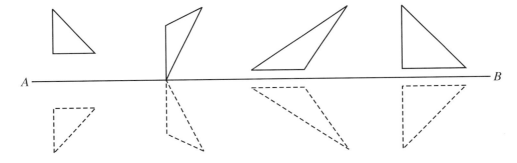

Rotation

The dotted lines show the new positions of the triangles when they have been rotated about the point marked • through a half-turn.

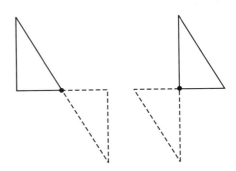

These triangles have been rotated about the point marked • through a quarter-turn anticlockwise.

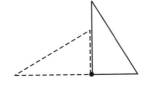
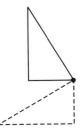

Exercise 28.1

1. Draw x and y axes from -8 to 8. Draw the triangle ABC where A is $(1, 1)$, B is $(4, 2)$ and C is $(3, 7)$.

    A is translated to A_1 $(-5, -6)$. Describe this translation.
    Using the same translation, translate B and C and draw the new triangle $A_1B_1C_1$.
    Write down the coordinates of B_1 and C_1.

2. Sketch these flags and reflect them in the dotted lines.

    1    **2**    **3**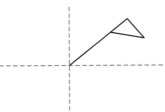

3. The diagram shows a shape and a mirror line.
    Copy the diagram on squared paper and draw
    the reflection of the shape.

    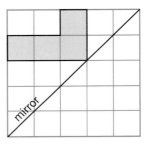

4. Sketch these flags and rotate them about the points marked •

    1 through 90°   **2** through 180°,   **3** through 90°
           anticlockwise,   clockwise.

5. The diagram shows a shape.
    Copy the diagram on squared paper and draw the
    shape after it has been rotated a
    half-turn about the point •

    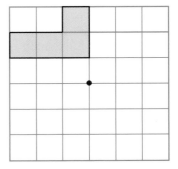

6. Describe the transformations (reflection, rotation or translation) which map the triangles

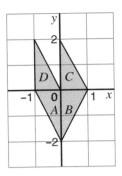

    1   *A* into *B*,

    2   *A* into *C*,

    3   *B* into *C*,

    4   *C* into *D*.

7. Draw the *x*-axis from −5 to 5 and the *y*-axis from −4 to 4.
    Draw the triangle *OAB* where *O* is (0, 0), *A* is (0, 3) and *B* is (−2, 3).

    1   Draw the line $x = 1$, and then draw the reflection of $\triangle OAB$ in the line $x = 1$, labelling the new triangle (1).

    2   Rotate $\triangle OAB$ through 90° clockwise about the point *B*, labelling the new triangle (2).

    3   Translate $\triangle OAB$ by moving all points 1 unit left and 3 units downwards, labelling the new triangle (3).

Congruent figures

Congruent figures are the same shape and the same size.

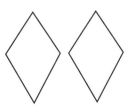
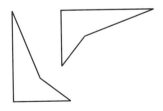
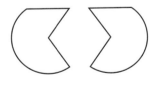

Congruent triangles

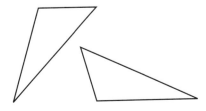

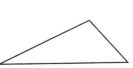

If one triangle can be reflected into the position of a second triangle, then the triangles are congruent.

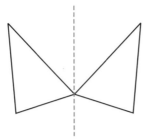 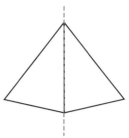

If one triangle can be rotated into the position of a second triangle, then the triangles are congruent.

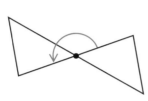 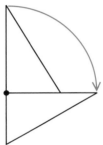

Exercise 28.2

1. Name the pairs of congruent figures in the diagram.

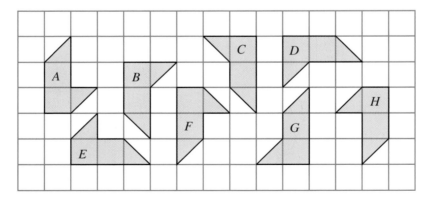

2. *ABCD* is a rectangle and *M* and *N* are points on *AB* and *DC* such that *AM = DN*.

    Which triangle is congruent to △ *AMC* ?

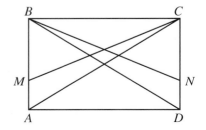

3.   Name the pairs of congruent triangles in the diagram.

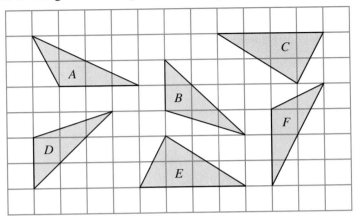

Enlargement

This transformation alters the size of the figure, but not its shape.

The **scale factor** of the enlargement is the number of times the original has been enlarged.
e.g. If the scale factor is 2, all lines on the enlargement are twice as long as corresponding lines on the original.
If the scale factor is 3, all lines on the enlargement are three times as long as corresponding lines on the original.

Examples

1   Enlargement with scale factor 2.

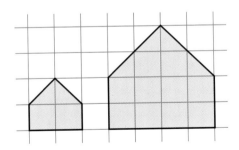

2   Enlargement with scale factor 3.

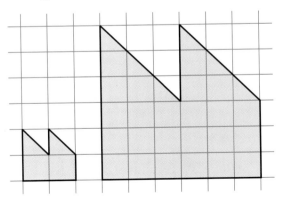

Length of line on enlargement = scale factor × length of line on original

Scale factor = $\dfrac{\text{length of line on the enlargement}}{\text{length of line on the original}}$

Example

3   Trapezium $PQRS$ is an enlargement of trapezium $ABCD$.
Find the scale factor of the enlargement, and the lengths of QR, RS and SP.

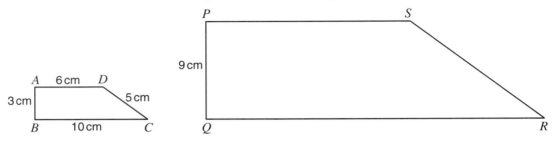

$$\text{Scale factor} = \frac{\text{length of } PQ}{\text{length of } AB} = \frac{9\,\text{cm}}{3\,\text{cm}} = 3$$

$$
\begin{aligned}
\text{Length of } QR &= \text{scale factor} \times \text{length of } BC\\
&= 3 \times 10\,\text{cm}\\
&= 30\,\text{cm}
\end{aligned}
$$

$$
\begin{aligned}
\text{Length of } RS &= 3 \times 5\,\text{cm}\\
&= 15\,\text{cm}
\end{aligned}
$$

$$
\begin{aligned}
\text{Length of } SP &= 3 \times 6\,\text{cm}\\
&= 18\,\text{cm}
\end{aligned}
$$

Centre of enlargement

Examples

$\triangle ABC$ is enlarged with centre of enlargement O, to form $\triangle A_1 B_1 C_1$ and $\triangle A_2 B_2 C_2$.

When the scale factor is 2.   When the scale factor is 3.

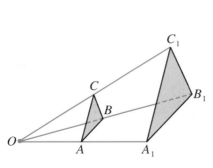 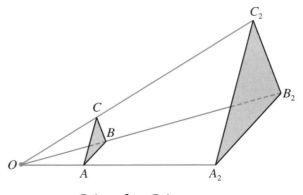

$OA_1 = 2 \times OA$ $OA_2 = 3 \times OA$

$OB_1 = 2 \times OB$ $OB_2 = 3 \times OB$

$OC_1 = 2 \times OC$ $OC_2 = 3 \times OC$

Exercise 28.3

1.   Copy these figures and for each one draw an enlargement with scale factor 2.

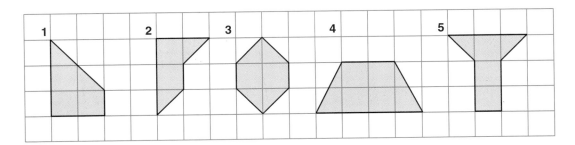

2.   What is the scale factor
     of the enlargement
     which transforms figure
     A into figure *B* ?

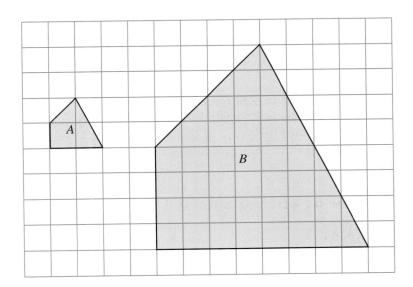

3.   This rectangle is to be enlarged with a scale factor 5.
     What are the measurements of the enlarged rectangle ?

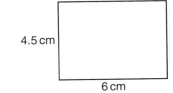

4.   Copy this drawing of a box, on
     squared paper, and then draw
     an enlarged box using a scale
     factor of 2.

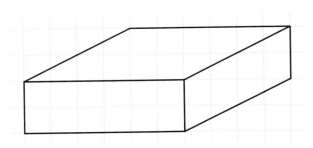

5. Copy these diagrams onto squared paper.
    Using O as the centre of enlargement and a scale factor 2, transform the line AB into a
    line $A'B'$. Do this by making OA' twice as long as OA and OB' twice as long as OB.

1
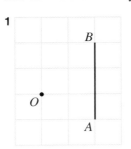

2
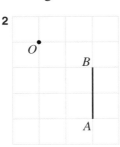

3
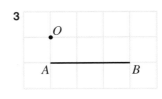

4
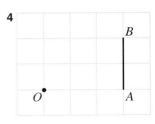

6. Copy this diagram onto squared
    paper. Triangle ABC has been
    enlarged into triangle $A'B'C'$.
    What is the scale factor of the
    enlargement ?

    By joining $A'A$, $B'B$, $C'C$ and
    continuing these lines, find on
    your diagram the position of the
    centre O of the enlargement.

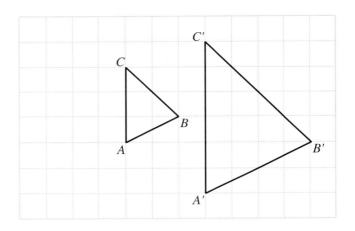

7. Each figure consists of a semicircle
    above a rectangle.
    B is an enlargement of A.

    1 By what scale factor must the lengths
        of A be multiplied to give the
        corresponding lengths of B ?

    2 If the perimeter of A is 35 cm,
        what is the perimeter of B ?

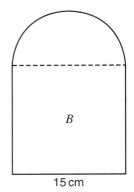
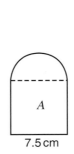

8. A triangle is transformed by enlargement with scale factor 3 into a similar triangle.

    1 One side of the new triangle has length 4.5 cm. What is the length of the
        corresponding side of the original triangle ?

    2 One angle of the new triangle has size 66°. What is the size of the corresponding
        angle of the original triangle ?

Exercise 28.4 Applications

1. **1** Draw x and y axes from -4 to 8 using equal scales on both axes. Draw the triangle ABC where A is $(1, 1)$, B is $(4, 2)$ and C is $(3, 7)$.

    2 Translate triangle ABC to triangle $A_1B_1C_1$ by moving each point 3 units in the x-direction and then -2 units in the y-direction.
    What are the coordinates of the image points A_1, B_1, C_1 ?

    3 Translate triangle $A_1B_1C_1$ to triangle $A_2B_2C_2$ by moving each point -8 units in the x-direction and then 3 units in the y-direction.
    What are the coordinates of the image points A_2, B_2, C_2 ?

    4 What single transformation would map triangle ABC onto triangle $A_2B_2C_2$?

2. If $\triangle ABC$ is reflected in the line BC, with A reflected into a point D, what sort of quadrilateral is $ABDC$?

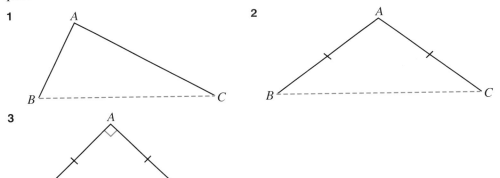

3. If $\triangle ABC$ is rotated about M, the mid-point of BC, through $180°$, so that B is rotated into C, C into B, and A into a point E, what sort of quadrilateral is $ABEC$?

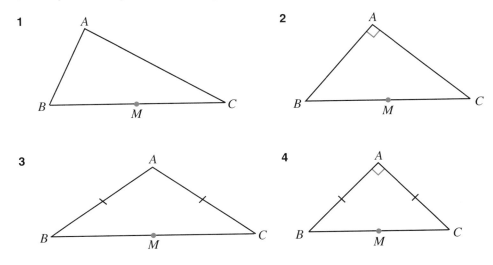

4. ## Geometric patterns

We see many examples of patterns in our daily lives.
Notice the patterns on wallpaper and fabric and see how they involve reflections, rotations and translations.
Look for symmetry in buildings and in natural objects such as flowers.

1   Patterns made with triangles. Copy and continue these patterns and design others.

Reflection and translation.

Rotation and translation.

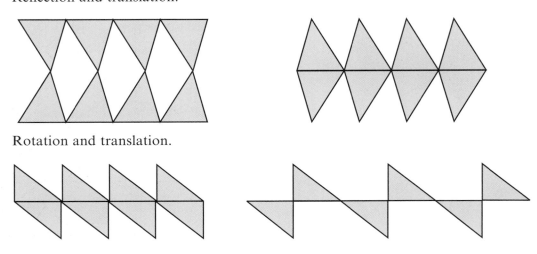

2   Copy and continue these three patterns, or design similar patterns for yourself.

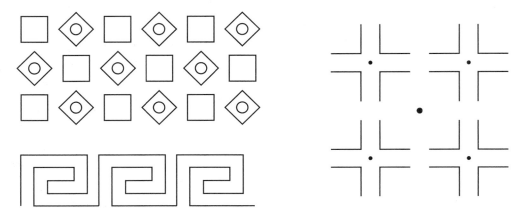

3 Start with an equilateral triangle of side 8 cm.
Mark points every 2 cm along each side.
By joining points, design a pattern.
Here is one idea.

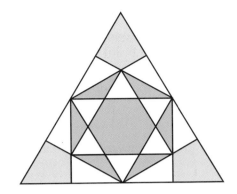

4 Start with a square with sides divided into
4 equal parts. By joining points make a
symmetrical pattern.
Here is one idea.

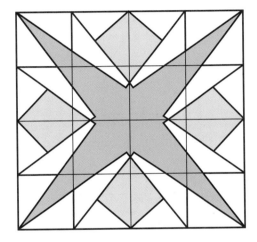

5 Start with a circle and mark 12 points
equally spaced round the circumference.
(Make the radius of the circle just larger
than the radius of your protractor, then
mark points every 30° round the circle.)
By joining some of these points make a
symmetrical pattern.
Here is one idea.

5. **Tessellations**

These are congruent shapes arranged in a pattern to cover an area.
At every point where shapes join, for them to fit exactly, the sum of the angles is 360°.

Examples

triangles covering a surface

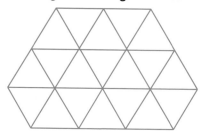

hexagons

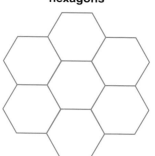

rhombuses

Tessellations can also be made using some combinations of regular polygons.
The sum of the angles at each point must be 360°, for the pieces to fit together.

Examples

equilateral triangles and regular hexagons

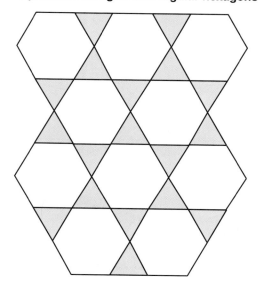

squares, hexagons and dodecagons

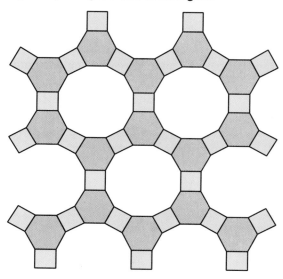

(Dodecagons are 12-sided polygons.)

1   Draw a regular hexagon with side 4 cm on thick card. Cut it out. By drawing round the outside, make several more hexagons. Also make some equilateral triangles and some squares of side 4 cm.

Draw sketches of these tessellated areas:

(1)   Use equilateral triangles and regular hexagons, so that every point is the join of 1 hexagon and 4 triangles.

(2)   Use equilateral triangles, regular hexagons and squares. How many of each meet at every point ?

(3)   Use equilateral triangles and squares.

2   Draw a regular octagon. Cut it out, and make several more of the same size.
Make several squares with sides the same length as those of the octagon.
Arrange the octagons and squares to make a tessellated area and show your design on a sketch.

3   Draw on squared paper and cut out several pieces of each of these shapes. Draw outlines on squared paper to show how each shape can be used to tessellate an area.

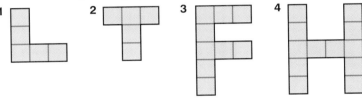

The possibilities are endless. Notice any tessellations you see, for example, on tiled floors. Make up your own designs.

Practice test 28

1.   Name the pairs of congruent figures in the diagram.

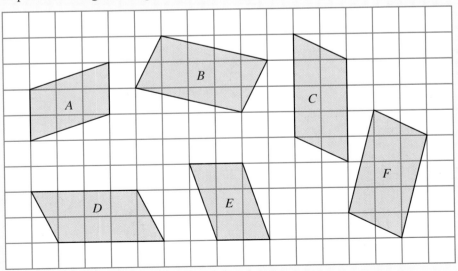

[Turn over]

2. On graph paper, draw the x-axis from -4 to 7 and the y-axis from -6 to 8.
    Plot these points and join them in order, to make a letter Z, $(-4, 6)$, $(-1, 6)$, $(-4, 2)$, $(-1, 2)$.

    1   Reflect this letter in the x-axis and label the reflection (1).

    2   Translate the original letter 8 units in the x-direction and 7 units downwards in the y-direction, and label the translation (2).

    3   Enlarge the original letter, starting with the top left-hand point at $(1, 8)$, and using a scale factor of 2. Label the enlargement (3).

3. On separate diagrams, copy the letter F and rotate it

    1   about the point A through $180°$,
    2   about the point B through $90°$ clockwise,
    3   about the point C through $90°$ anticlockwise.

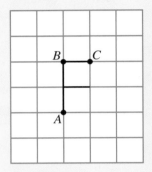

4. $\triangle DEF$ is an enlargement of $\triangle ABC$.

    1   What is the scale factor of the enlargement ?

    2   What is the length of DF ?

    3   What is the length of BC ?

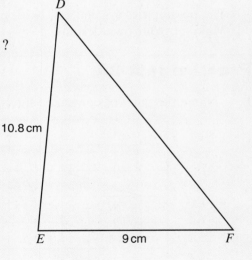

5. A photograph with length 15 cm is enlarged and the corresponding length on the enlargement is 75 cm.

    1   What is the scale factor of the enlargement ?

    2   The breadth of the original photograph is 10 cm.
        What is the breadth of the enlargement ?

PUZZLES

47.   Seasonal greetings. On graph paper, label the x axis from 0 to 12 and the y-axis from 0 to 8, using the same scale on both axes. Mark these points. Join each point to the next one with a straight line, except where there is a cross after the point.

(5, 6)	(4, 6)	(4, 8)	(5, 8)×	(8, 6)	(8, 8)	(8.8, 8)	(9, 7.8)
(9, 7.2)	(8.8, 7)	(8, 7)	(9, 6)×	(1, 2)	(3, 4)×	(1, 6)	(1, 8)
(2, 7)	(3, 8)	(3, 6)×	(11, 7)	(12, 8)×	(6, 6)	(6, 8)	(6.8, 8)
(7, 7.8)	(7, 7.2)	(6.8, 7)	(6, 7)	(7, 6)×	(10, 8)	(11, 7)	(11, 6)×
(4, 7)	(4.8, 7)×	(3, 2)	(1, 4)×				

Complete the diagram.

48.   Jill has lost her timetable. She remembers that tomorrow's lessons end with Games, but she cannot remember the order of the first 5 lessons. She asks her friends, who decide to tease her.

Alison says, 'Science is 3rd, History is 1st'.
Brenda says, 'English is 2nd, Maths is 4th'.
Claire says, 'History is 5th, Science is 4th'.
Denise says 'French is 5th, English is 2nd'.
Emma says 'French is 3rd, Maths is 4th'.

Naturally, Jill is very confused by all this. Then her friends admit that they have each made one true statement and one untrue one.
When is Maths ?

49.   **Tangrams**. Use thin cardboard to make this.
Start with two equal squares and cut into 7 pieces as shown.
Rearrange these 7 pieces to make one large square.
This is an ancient puzzle. The pieces make many more shapes, using all 7 pieces each time. The pieces can be turned over.
Make a parallelogram, an isoceles trapezium, a rectangle, an isosceles right-angled triangle and a trapezium with 2 adjacent right angles. Here are some other designs to make, and you can invent others.

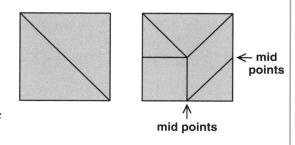

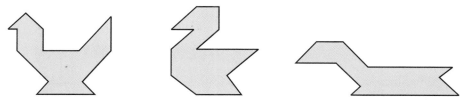

29 Scatter diagrams

The topics in this chapter include:

- constructing scatter diagrams,
- drawing conclusions from scatter diagrams (understanding the basic ideas of correlation).

Scatter diagrams

Scatter diagrams can be drawn to look at the relationship between 2 sets of data.

Simple scatter diagrams

This type of graph is drawn when the data has few values.

Example

The number of goals scored by the home team and the number of goals scored by the away team in football matches.
Here are the results for one particular Saturday.

4–0	1–0	1–0	1–1	1–3	0–1	2–0	1–2	1–1	2–2
0–2	3–2	1–2	2–1	3–1	0–0	0–0	1–1	2–4	0–1
2–1	3–1	1–1	2–2	3–3	3–0	2–3	1–1	1–1	0–2
2–2	1–0	1–0	1–1	2–1	1–1	0–2	4–2	3–1	3–2
3–0	2–4								

Show these results on a simple scatter diagram.

Draw and label the axes like this.

If the first score is 4–0, put a cross in the space which represents 4 goals by the home team and 0 by the away team.

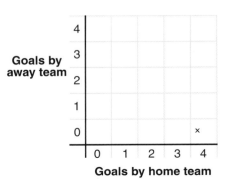

Here is the graph showing the results.

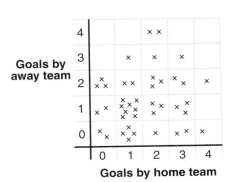

Exercise 29.1

1. The marks out of 10 for some students in two
   tests are given below.
   Draw axes like these and put crosses in the
   squares to represent the marks.
   Comment about the relationship shown by
   the graph.

   The marks are given for each student in turn.
   6, 7 means 6 in the first test and 7 in the
   second test.

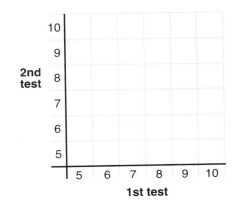

6, 7	5, 6	10, 10	7, 8
9, 10	8, 9	5, 7	6, 9
9, 10	9, 9	7, 7	8, 7
6, 8	9, 9	8, 7	9, 9
8, 6	8, 8	6, 8	7, 9
10, 9	8, 9	9, 9	7, 8
8, 9	9, 8	9, 8	9, 9
9, 9	7, 6	5, 7	8, 8
8, 8	7, 9	8, 8	7, 8
6, 7	8, 7	6, 5	9, 8
6, 6	10, 10	9, 9	10, 10
9, 10			

2. The football results on a particular Saturday are given below.
   Draw axes with blocks labelled from 0 to 5 and put crosses in the squares to represent
   the goals scored by the home team and by the away team.

1–0	1–1	1–0	0–2	1–5	4–2	2–0	1–1	0–1	0–1	1–1
2–0	4–1	0–0	0–0	0–1	2–0	0–1	1–1	2–1	2–0	1–2
3–1	2–3	1–0	0–2	1–0	1–3	1–1	2–0	4–0	0–0	4–1
0–0	1–0	3–0	0–4	3–2	5–1	1–3	3–3	1–0		

Comment on the results.

Scatter diagrams

The previous questions used a few whole numbers only, on each axis, and these were represented in blocks.
When the numbers have a bigger range, or if the data involves measurements, we label the axes in a different way.

Example

The lengths and widths of 10 leaves from a bush.

Length (in cm)	6.4	7.5	6.7	7.3	6.8	5.6	5.1	4.7	5.5	6.2
Width (in cm)	2.6	3.9	2.8	3.4	3.7	2.1	2.3	1.5	2.2	2.6

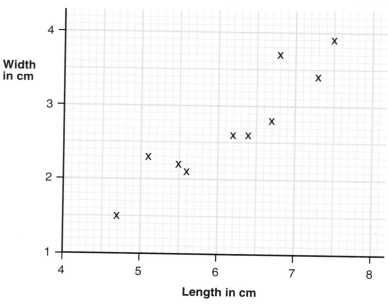

Scatter diagram of the lengths and widths of 10 leaves

This diagram shows that there is some relationship between the length and width of a leaf from the bush. Longer leaves tend to be wider, although the relationship is not exact. This relationship is called **correlation**.

Note that the labelling on the axes need not start at 0.

The 1st set of data is usually plotted on the horizontal axis.
You do not need to use the same scale on both axes.

Exercise 29.2

For the graphs in this exercise, the axes should be labelled as in the example on page 396, labelling lines, not blocks.

Keep the graphs you draw to use again in Exercise 29.3.

Questions 1 to 5.

Sets of two related variables x and y are given in the tables.
Plot the values on scatter diagrams, with x on the horizontal axis, from 10 to 70, and y on the vertical axis, from 0 to 50.

1.

x	10	20	30	40	50	60	70
y	2	3	12	25	33	36	47

2.

x	10	15	20	25	30	40	50	55	60	70
y	44	40	39	32	31	25	17	15	9	7

3.

x	15	20	25	30	40	50	60	70
y	8	17	20	19	24	39	41	46

4.

x	15	20	25	30	35	40	50	55	60	70
y	45	31	35	25	22	12	15	8	5	6

5.

x	10	15	20	25	30	40	50	55	60	65	70
y	6	7	18	17	25	26	42	39	43	49	48

6.   8 plots were treated with different amounts of fertilizer and the crop yield recorded.

Amount of fertilizer (units/m^2)	1	2	3	4	5	6	7	8
Yield (in kg)	36	41	58	60	70	76	75	92

Plot a scatter diagram of these results.

7.   The marks of 10 students in a Maths exam were as follows:

Paper 1	32	38	42	45	48	51	57	62	70	72
Paper 2	45	44	49	51	50	55	60	60	68	70

Plot the marks on a scatter diagram.

Correlation

This is the relationship between the two sets of data.
Here are some pictures of scatter diagrams, with axes not labelled.

This shows that there is good (positive) correlation between the variables.

Here there is an exact relationship. This can be described as perfect correlation.

There is some correlation but it is not very close.

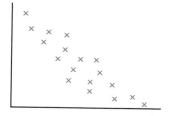

This is a relationship where as one variable increases, the other decreases.
This is said to be inverse or negative correlation.

Perfect inverse correlation.

There does not seem to be any relationship. There is no correlation, or there is zero correlation.

With a suitable computer program, a scatter diagram can be plotted on a computer screen. This is very useful if you have a large amount of data, because it is much quicker than drawing your own graph and plotting the points on it. You can see if there seems to be evidence of correlation.

Statisticians use a formula to work out a numerical value for correlation. They would not make any assumptions about whether two variables have correlation unless they had at least 30 pairs of data. However, we have used fewer items here, so that the questions do not take too long.

When there is evidence of correlation between two sets of data, you have to decide if they are really connected, or whether they are both linked to a third item.

For example, someone found a strong positive correlation between size of feet and maths ability, but the real reason for the connection was that the boys with the bigger feet were older boys, and they had learnt more maths. Both these items, size of feet, and maths knowledge, would show some correlation with the age of the boys, but there is no other connection.

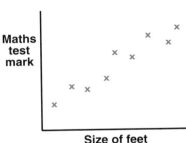

Exercise 29.3

Questions 1 to 5.

Look at the scatter diagrams you have drawn for questions 1 to 5 of Exercise 29.2 on page 397. In each case, say whether the correlation is positive or negative, or if there is no correlation. Use each graph to estimate a y-value which would correspond with an x-value of 45.

6.   Look at the scatter diagram for question 6 of Exercise 29.2.
        Comment on the relationship between the amount of fertilizer and the yield.

7.   Look at the scatter diagram for question 7 of Exercise 29.2.
        Comment on the relationship between the marks in the two papers.

Exercise 29.4   Applications

1.   30 children were asked about the numbers of boys and girls in their families.
     Here is the information, with the number of girls given first, so 3, 2 means 3 girls and
     2 boys.

1, 2	0, 2	1, 0	2, 1	1, 1	2, 0	2, 1	2, 0	2, 1
3, 1	2, 2	2, 1	2, 3	1, 1	0, 2	4, 2	0, 1	2, 1
2, 0	1, 1	2, 1	1, 1	2, 1	1, 3	1, 1	1, 3	1, 1
2, 1	1, 5	0, 1						

     Show the information on a simple scatter diagram.
     Label the blocks on the horizontal axis for the number of girls, and those on the vertical
     axis for the number of boys.
     Comment on the graph.

2.   In each of the following cases say whether you think that the correlation would be
     positive, negative or if there is no correlation.
     Give reasons and sketch the kind of scatter diagram you would expect.

     1   The daily rainfall, and the number of
         umbrellas sold.

     2   The number of empty chairs, and the
         number of occupied chairs in a
         classroom in each lesson during the week.

     3   The heights of children, and their
         house numbers.

     4   The distances that children live from
         school, and the cost of their fares to school.

     5   The daily air temperature, and the
         amount of fuel used for heating by households
         in a certain town.

3.   A manufacturing company gives these figures for each quarter in a two-year period.

Quarter	1	2	3	4	1	2	3	4
Output units	10	20	40	25	30	40	50	45
Total cost (in £1000's)	41	48	67	53	61	70	79	73

     Draw a scatter diagram for the data, with output units on the horizontal axis and total
     cost on the vertical axis.
     Comment on the relationship between the output units and the total cost.
     Find an estimate for the total cost likely to be incurred at an output level of 35 units.

4. The marks gained by 10 students in each of two papers of a Maths examination were as follows:

Student	A	B	C	D	E	F	G	H	J	K
Marks for Paper 1	30	39	44	60	28	64	70	56	32	46
Marks for Paper 2	48	55	56	75	35	78	86	70	46	56

Draw a scatter diagram for the data, putting the marks for Paper 1 on the horizontal axis.
Another student got 52 marks on Paper 1 but was absent for Paper 2. Use the graph to estimate a mark for this student for paper 2.

5. The heights of 10 boys and their fathers are given in this table.

Height of father (in cm)	167	168	169	171	172	172	174	175	176	182
Height of son (in cm)	164	166	166	168	169	170	170	171	173	177

Plot the points on a scatter diagram.
Use your diagram to estimate the height of a boy of this age if his father is 1.7 m tall.

6. A test was carried out on seven fields by treating them with different amounts of nitrogen fertilizer and measuring the percentage of protein in the grass.
Here are the results.

Units of fertilizer applied	0	1	2	3	4	5	6
Percentage of protein	14.0	15.2	17.0	19.4	21.4	22.6	23.2

Plot a scatter diagram of these results.
Comment on the relationship between the amount of fertilizer and the percentage of protein.

7. Eight paintings were entered for a competition and were examined by two judges, who marked them out of 100.
The marks are shown in the table.

Painting	1	2	3	4	5	6	7	8
1st Judge	45	55	65	40	25	45	35	65
2nd Judge	50	65	80	50	35	60	40	75

Plot a scatter diagram of the data.
Another painting arrived unavoidably late, and was given a mark of 50 by the 1st judge, but it was not possible for the 2nd judge to examine it.
Use the graph to estimate the mark it might have gained from the 2nd judge.

8.   Carry out an investigation using data with which you expect to find some kind of paired relationship.
Collect the data and represent it on a scatter diagram.
Comment on the relationship, but do not be too disappointed if your scatter diagrams do not show good correlation. Statistical data rarely matches perfectly as the figures are often affected by other factors as well as those you are measuring.

Here are some suggestions for possible investigations.

Heights and weights of children of the same age.
Heights of mothers and their 16 year old daughters.
Ages of young children and their bedtimes.
Heights and arm-spans.
Exam marks in similar subjects such as Maths and Science, French and German, or in different subjects such as Art and Science.
Times spent learning a piece of work, and marks gained in a test on it.
Times taken to do a piece of work using (1) normal hand and (2) other hand.
Shoe sizes and collar (or hat) sizes.
Amounts of pocket money and amounts saved.

Practice test 29

1.   In a handicraft competition 10 entries were examined by two judges A and B, who awarded marks out of 10, shown below.

Entry number	1	2	3	4	5	6	7	8	9	10
Judge A	5	5	3	6	8	4	8	4	7	6
Judge B	5	4	3	5	7	3	6	3	6	5

Show these results on a simple scatter diagram.
Label the blocks on the horizontal axis, for Judge A, from 3 to 8.
Label the blocks on the vertical axis, for Judge B, from 3 to 7.

Comment on the marks.
Which competitor do you think should win the competition ?

2.   Draw 5 sketch diagrams, with 10 crosses shown on each, to show examples of pairs of variables which have
1   positive correlation,
2   perfect negative correlation,
3   no correlation.
(Do not label axes or show scales.)

3. x and y are two related variables. Plot the values on a scatter diagram.

x	53	57	66	70	72	85	90	97
y	42	37	35	37	30	28	25	24

Comment on the relationship between the variables.
Use the graph to find an estimated value for y when $x = 80$.

4.   The heights and weights of 8 young men are given in this table.

Height (in cm)	168	170	173	178	181	182	183	185
Weight (in kg)	68	70	70	74	75	76	78	79

Plot the points on a scatter diagram.
Comment on the relationship between the heights and the weights.
Use the graph to estimate the likely weight of a young man if he is 1.75 m tall.

PUZZLES

50.   Mark, the racing driver, did his first practice lap at 40 miles per hour. What speed
       would he have to average on his second lap if he wanted to produce an average for the
       two laps of 80 miles per hour ?

51.   An explorer wants to estimate the width of a river, flowing East-West. He stands due
       South of a tree growing on the opposite bank, and then walks due West, counting his
       paces, until the tree is in the North-East direction. If by that time he has taken 120
       paces, and his usual pace-length is 90 cm, what estimate can he make of the width of
       the river.

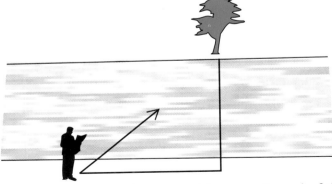

52.   How far would someone have to travel to get to 'the opposite end of the Earth'
       assuming that the Earth is a sphere of diameter 12 750 km ?
       If instead of travelling over the surface, the person went by plane which travelled at a
       height of 10 km over the earth, how much further would the journey be ?

30 Scale drawings and bearings

> **The topics in this chapter include:**
>
> - developing an understanding of scale drawings including using and interpreting maps or drawings,
> - understanding and using bearings.

Scale drawing

Scales can be given in various ways, such as
  1 cm represents $\frac{1}{2}$ m,
or, 2 cm represents 1 m,
or, Scale 1 : 50 (1 to 50),
or, $\frac{1}{50}$ scale.

The symbol ≡ can be used for 'represents', e.g. 2 cm ≡ 1 m.

In any scale drawing, the scale should be stated.

The scale of a map

Some possible scales are 1 : 1250, 1 : 2500, 1 : 10 000, 1 : 25 000, etc.
A scale of $\frac{1}{100\,000}$ or 1 : 100 000 means that 1 unit represents 100 000 units, so 1 cm represents 100 000 cm, which is 1 km.

Example

On a plan, 30 cm represents 150 m. What is the scale of the plan ?

30 cm represents 150 m,
1 cm represents 5 m.
Since 5 m = 500 cm, the scale can also be written as $\frac{1}{500}$ or 1 : 500.

Exercise 30.1

1.   The scale of a map is 5 cm to 1 km. What is the distance between two places which are 35 cm apart on the map ?

2. The scale of a map is '1 cm represents 250 m'. What is the actual distance in kilometres between two places which are 8 cm apart on the map ?

3. A hall is 20 m long and 15 m wide. What measurements should be used on a plan drawn to a scale of 1 cm to represent 2 m ?

4. On a map the distance between two villages is 9 cm. The villages are actually 45 km apart. What is the scale of the map ?

5. On a scale drawing, a rectangular enclosure which is 240 m long and 60 m wide is drawn with a length of 12 cm.
What is the scale of the drawing ?
What is the width of the enclosure on the drawing ?

6. A map has a scale of 2 cm to represent 1 km. If two villages are 8.4 cm apart on the map, what is the actual distance between them ?

7. 1 On this plan of the park, the scale is '1 cm represents 50 m'.
How far is it from the main gate to the swings ?
(Measure to the crosses.)

2 How far is it from the swings to the aviary ?

3 A jogger goes all round the park, running on a path at the edge of the park. How far does she run ?

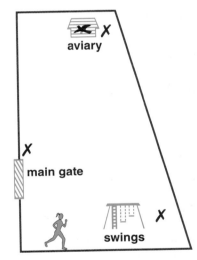

8. The diagram shows two trees in a field, drawn to scale. If the smaller tree is 9 m tall, estimate the height of the other one.

Example

This diagram shows a sketch of one end of a building.
Draw an accurate scale drawing, using a scale of 1 : 100.
By measurement, find how high the highest point is from
ground level.

1 : 100 means that 1 cm will represent 1 m.
Begin by drawing the line AB, 10 cm long. Make accurate
right angles at A and B, and draw the lines AE and BC, both 4 cm long.
To find point D, use compasses. With centre E, radius 5.5 cm, draw an arc, and with
centre C, same radius, draw an arc which will cut the first arc at D. Join CD and ED.

To find the height of D above AB, construct a perpendicular line from D to AB. (By
symmetry, this will be the line from D to the mid-point of AB.) This distance is 6.3 cm on
the scale drawing.
So the highest point is 6.3 m above ground level.

Exercise 30.2

1. Draw an accurate scale drawing of a rectangular field, 75 m long and 45 m wide, using a
    scale of 1 cm to represent 10 m.
    By measurement on your drawing, find the actual distance from a corner of the field to
    the opposite corner.

2. Draw an accurate scale drawing of this garden which is
    25 m long and 15 m wide, using a scale of 1 cm to
    represent 2 m.

    The lawn is 17 m long and 11 m wide and the path
    round three sides of it is 1 m wide.

    In the centre of the lawn, draw in a circular pond
    of diameter 5 m.

    Find the area of the vegetable plot.

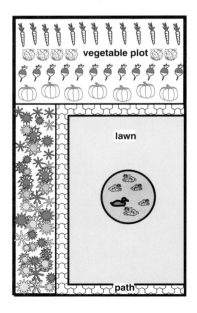

3.   The diagram shows a tower seen from a point A
     80 m away on level ground. The angle at A is 38°.
     By scale drawing, find the height of the tower.

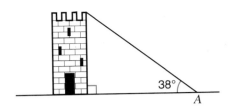

4.   Here is a sketch of a shed.

   1   Make a scale drawing suitable for making a
       model of the shed, of the two rectangular
       sides and the two sides of the roof all
       joined together.

   2   Make a separate drawing for the side
       marked A.

     Use a scale of 1 cm to represent 1 m.

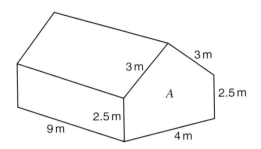

3-figure bearings

Bearings (directions) are measured from North, in a clockwise direction.
They are given in degrees, as 3-figure numbers.

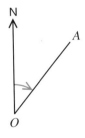

Example

1   Show the directions given by the bearings 040°, 310°.

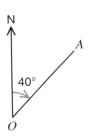

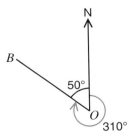

Direction OA has a bearing of 040°.   Direction OB has a bearing of 310°.

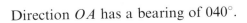

Opposite directions

To face the opposite direction, you turn through 180°. So to find the bearing of a reverse direction, add 180°. If this comes to 360° or more, subtract 180° instead.

Example

2   Find the bearings of the directions AO and BO from example 1.

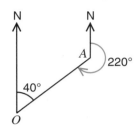   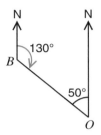

The bearing of A from O is 040°
The bearing of O from A is 040° + 180°
$\qquad\qquad\qquad = 220°$

The bearing of B from O is 310°
The bearing of O from B is 310° − 180°
$\qquad\qquad\qquad = 130°$

Exercise 30.3

1.   Find the bearings given by the directions OA, OB, OC, OD and OF.

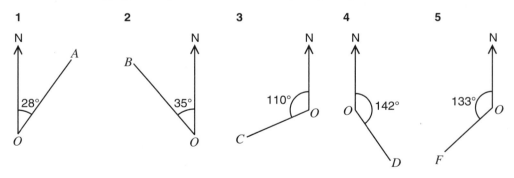

2.   Draw sketches to show the directions given by the bearings

   1   200°,   2   020°,   3   290°,   4   135°,   5   002°.

3.   Find the bearings of the directions AO, BO, CO, DO and FO in question 1.

4.   Find the bearings of these places from a point O.

   1   A is south-west of O.   4 D is north-east of O.
   2   B is east of O.   5 F is west of O.
   3   C is north-west of O.

5. **1** The bearing of *P* from *Q* is 080°. What is the bearing of *Q* from *P* ?

2 The bearing of *P* from *Q* is 125°. What is the bearing of *Q* from *P* ?

3 The bearing of *P* from *Q* is 260°. What is the bearing of *Q* from *P* ?

4 The bearing of *P* from *Q* is 015°. What is the bearing of *Q* from *P* ?

5 The bearing of *P* from *Q* is 301°. What is the bearing of *Q* from *P* ?

6. By measuring with your protractor, find the bearings given by the directions *OA*, *OB*, *OC*, *OD*, *OF* in these drawings.

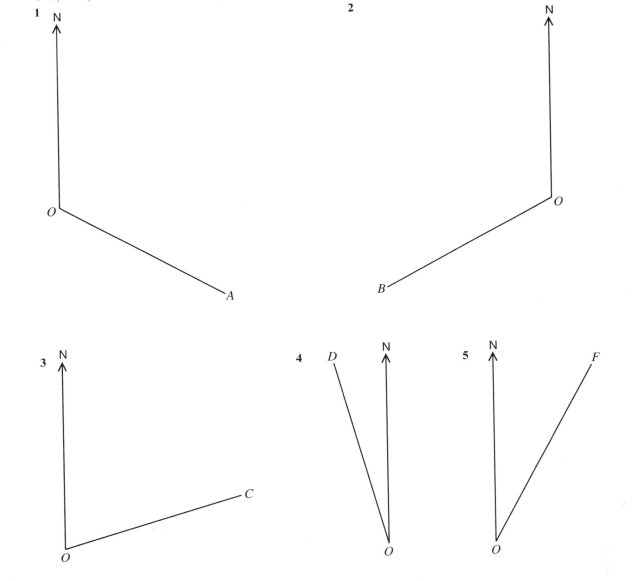

7. **1** Find the bearings of *B* and *C* from *A*.

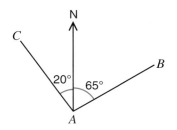

2 Find the bearings of *B* and *C* from *A*.

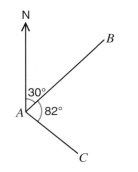

3 The bearing of *B* from *A* is 068° and the bearing of *C* from *B* is 130°.
Find the size of ∠*ABC*.

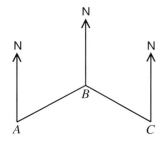

4 The bearing of *B* from *A* is 070° and ∠*ABC* is 109°.
Find the bearing of *B* from *C*.

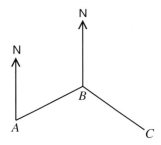

5 Find the bearing of *C* from *A*, and of *C* from *B*.

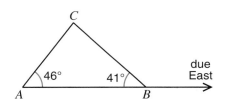

Using scale drawings to solve problems

Example

An explorer walks 1000 m on a bearing of 070° and he then walks 2000 m on a bearing of 160°.
Draw an accurate scale drawing of his route.
By measurement, find how far he has to go to return directly to his starting point.

First draw a sketch map of the route.
Begin with a direction for North. Usually this is towards the top of the page although this is not essential.

Sketch map

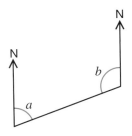

Use the sketch map to see how the drawing is going to fit on the page.
Choose a suitable scale.
1 cm to represent 200 m will mean that the first line is 5 cm long and the second line is 10 cm long.
If this will fit on your paper, this is a suitable scale.

Draw a line at A in the direction of North.
Measure an angle of 70° clockwise from the North direction and draw the line AB making it 5 cm long. Then at B draw another line pointing North. (Draw a line parallel to the first North line.)
At B, draw a line at an angle of 160° with the North line and mark point C on this line 10 cm from B.
The line CA is the line showing the return journey.
Join CA and measure the line.

The line CA is 11.2 cm long, so the actual distance is 11.2×200 m $= 2240$ m.

Note. The method for drawing parallel lines with a set-square is explained on page 22.

If you use a protractor instead, the two angles in the position of a and b in this diagram add up to 180°.
If $a = 70°$, $b = (180 - 70)° = 110°$.

Exercise 30.4

1.

A speedboat travels 8 km North and then 3 km East.
Draw an accurate scale drawing and find on what bearing the boat must be steered to go directly back to the starting point.

2.   There are four towns A, B, C, D.
B is 100 km North of A, C is 90 km on a bearing of 140°
from A, D is 120 km on a bearing 260° from A.

1   Draw an accurate scale drawing.

Find the distances between the towns
2   B and C,
3   C and D,
4   B and D.

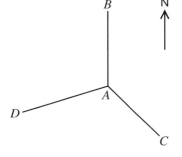

3.   There are 2 coastguard stations, A and B, 50 km apart,
with B being due East of A.
A ship is shown on radar on a bearing of 068° from A,
and on a bearing of 316° from B.
Draw an accurate scale drawing showing A, B and
the ship.
(Use a scale of 1 cm to represent 5 km.)

How far is the ship from A, and from B?

4.   A man walks 10 km North-East and then 7 km South-East.

1   Show his route on a scale drawing.

2   How far is he from his starting-point?

3   On what bearing must he walk to go directly back to his starting-point?

5.   (On tracing paper mark the positions shown for *A*, *B*, *C* and also mark the North
      direction.)

   1   A boat is just off the cape at *A* and it wants to reach the harbour at *B*. On what
        bearing must the boat sail ?

   2   The distance *AB* is actually 6.8 km. What is the scale of the map ?

   3   After reaching *B*, the boat then sails to a bay at *C*. What is the actual distance from
        B to *C* ?

   4   From *C*, on what bearing must the boat sail to return round the cape at *A* ?

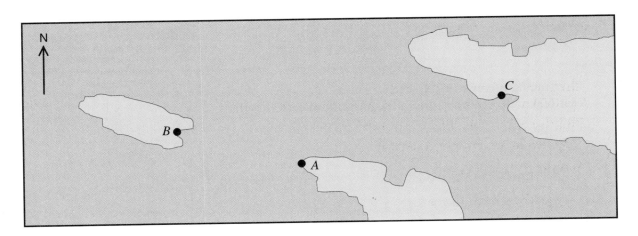

Exercise 30.5 Applications

1.   The diagram represents a field *ABCD*.

   1   Make a scale drawing using a scale of 1 cm
        to represent 10 m.
   2   Find the length of *DC*, in metres.
   3   What is the perimeter of the field ?
   4   There are straight paths in the field from *A* to *C*
        and from *B* to *D*. Draw these paths and measure
        their lengths.
   5   The paths cross at point *T*. A boy runs from
        A to *T* and then to *D*. How much further does
        he run than if he had gone directly from *A* to *D* ?

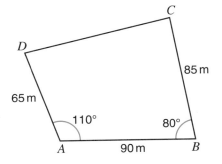

2.

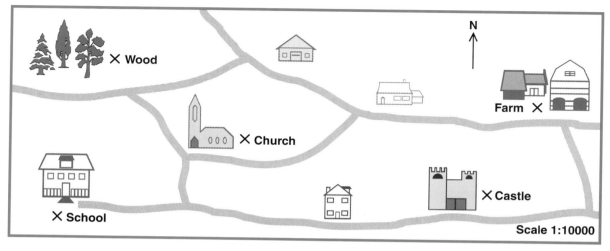

Use tracing paper to mark the positions shown by the crosses for the school, church, castle, wood and farm, and also mark the North direction.

Find the distances and bearings of

1	the church from the school,	
2	the farm from the wood,	
3	the wood from the castle,	

4   the farm from the church,

5   the castle from the farm.

3.   **Alternative notation for bearings**

You may still find instances where the old method of stating bearings is used, so here are some examples of how the method works.

Bearings are measured from North or South, whichever is the nearer direction, and they are measured towards the East or towards the West.
N 20° E means measure 20° from the North, turning towards the East.

Examples

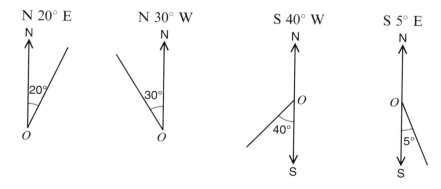

Using this notation, find the bearings given by OA, OB, OC, OD, OF.

1

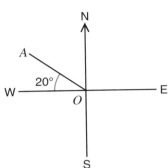

2

3

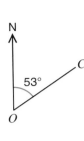

4

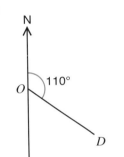

5

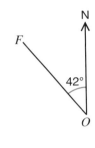

Draw sketches to show the directions given by the bearings

6 N 40° E, **7** S 15° W, **8** N 80° W, **9** N 4° E, **10** S 10° E.

4. In a sailing race the boats go round a triangular course ABC, with $AB = 7$ km, $BC = 5$ km and $CA = 6$ km. The direction of AB is due North.

1 Show this information on a scale drawing, with C to the East of the line AB.
(Draw the line representing AB first, then find the position of C using compasses.)

2 On what bearing do the boats head from B to C ?

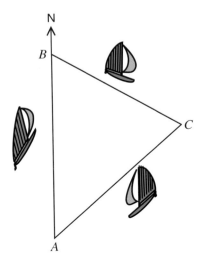

5. A fishing boat is 20 km due North of its harbour.
    It sails on a bearing of 110° at an average speed
    of 12 km/h.

    After 2 hours there is a gale warning on the radio.
    Show on a scale drawing the position of the boat
    at that time.

    In what direction should the boat be headed to
    get straight back to the harbour, and how far
    has it to go ?
    If it increases its speed to 16 km/h, how long will it take ?

Sketch map

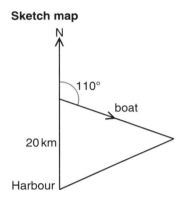

6. Assuming that the bus stop sign is placed
    on the lamppost 2.2 m from the ground, estimate
    the height of the lamppost

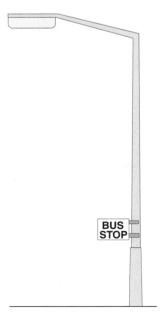

7.   A surveyor who wishes to find the width
     of a river stands on one bank at a point X
     directly opposite a tree T. He then walks
     80 m along the river bank to a point C.
     The angle XCT is found to be 52°.
     By scale drawing find the width of the
     river.

Practice test 30

1.   A model of a hall of rectangular shape is made using a scale of 2 cm to 1 m.
     The height of the model is 16 cm and its floor measurements are 25 cm by 32 cm.
     Find the height and floor measurements of the hall.

2.   This plan of the ground floor of a house is drawn to a scale of 1 cm represents 1 m.

     What are the measurements of
     1   the lounge,   **2**   the dining-room,   **3**   the kitchen ?

     4   What is the area of the lounge ?
             A carpet for this room costs £28 per m^2. What is the cost of the carpet ?

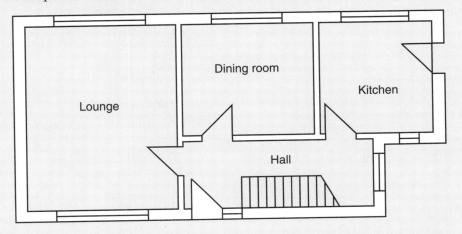

[Turn over]

3. The diagram shows a church steeple seen from
    a point A 120 m away, on level ground.
    The angle at A is 32°.
    Draw a scale drawing to find the height of
    the steeple.
    State the scale you have used.

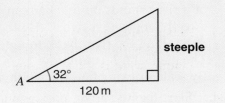

4. The bearing of OA is 240°.
    The angle OAB is 80°.
    $OA = AB$.

    1   What is the size of $\angle AOB$?

    2   Find the bearing of OB.

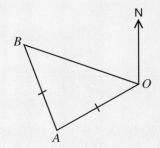

5. A ship sailing in the direction 258° alters course to
    sail in the opposite direction.
    What is its new course ?

6. P and Q are places 900 m apart on a coastline running East-West.
    A ship S is at sea on a bearing of 341° from P, and on a bearing of 071° from Q.

    1   Draw an accurate scale drawing.
        State the scale you have used.

    Find
    2   the distance SP,
    3   the distance SQ,
    4   the distance of S from the nearest point
        on the coast.

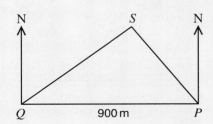

PUZZLES

53. A bag contains several discs, some red and some yellow. I have to take some out of the bag without looking. If I want to be sure that I pick at least 4 discs of the same colour, what is the least number of discs that I should take out of the bag ?

54. Start from ∗, going horizontally or vertically (not diagonally), and spell out the names of 7 plane figures.

T	A	N	T	R	I	X	A
N	G	O	R	T	A	E	G
E	G	O	A	E	N	H	O
P	R	L	P	L	G	M	N
M	A	E	E	Z	I	U	Q
A	L	L	A	R	E	A	U
R	A	*P	L	S	T	D	R
E	R	A	U	Q	A	L	I

55. Make 5 equal squares out of cardboard. Leave one square whole, and divide the other four into two pieces as shown. Rearrange the 9 pieces to make one large square.

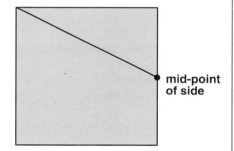

mid-point of side

56. The most famous problem connected with a network is 'The Bridges of Königsberg'.

There were 7 bridges over the various parts of the river. The townspeople suspected that the 7 bridges could not be crossed in one continuous walk without recrossing the route somewhere.

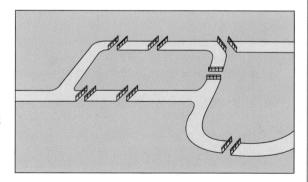

In 1735, Euler, one of the world's great mathematicians, was asked to give a proof of this, which he did. Now, if there was an 8th bridge, just out of view on the left side of the picture, would it be possible to cross the 8 bridges in one continuous walk ?

Miscellaneous Section E

Exercise E1   Aural Practice

If possible find someone to read these questions to you.
You should do the questions within 20 minutes.
Do not use your calculator.
Write down the answers only.

1.   What is the ratio, in its simplest form, of the two amounts £20 and £24 ?

2.   If 5 similar books weigh 3.5 kg, what will 2 of them weigh ?

3.   How many axes of symmetry does a square have ?

4.   A water tank is 6 m long, 5 m wide and 2 m deep. How many cubic metres of water can it hold ?

5.   When throwing a fair die, what is the probability of getting an even number ?

6.   A model statue is enlarged by a scale factor of 4. How tall is the original if the enlarged statue is 32 cm tall ?

7.   If prices are increased by 10%, what is the new price of a chair which used to cost £30 ?

8.   What is the name of a quadrilateral which has all four sides equal, but no angles are right angles ?

9.   If £1 is equal to 7.5 francs, how many francs will I get for £100 ?

10.   If 6 men can build a wall in 10 days, how long would 3 men take ?

11.   The sides of a triangle have lengths 4 cm, 8 cm and 10 cm. What is its perimeter ?

12.   If the scale on a drawing is 1 to 100, what length does 3 cm on the drawing represent ?

13.   How many edges has a triangular prism ?

14.   How long will it take to travel 10 km when driving at an average speed of 60 km per hour ?

15.   A rectangular piece of paper measuring 40 cm by 30 cm is cut into squares with side 5 cm. How many squares can be made ?

Additional aural questions using data from pages 444 to 447.

16.   Use table **6**.
       I have 20 Australian dollars. How many £'s are these worth, approximately ?

17.   Use the graph **13**.
       How many kilometres are approximately equal to 20 miles ?

18.   Use diagram **18**.
       If the two trees are drawn to scale and the smaller one is 4 m tall, estimate the height of
       the larger one.

19.   Use diagram **19**.
       Which of these drawings have rotational symmetry ?

20.   Use diagram **19**.
       Which of these drawings are nets of a cube ?

Exercise E2   Revision

1.   Draw diagrams to represent
      1   a cuboid,
      2   a triangular prism,
      3   a pyramid with a square base.

      Say how many faces, vertices and edges each figure has.

2.   **1**   A bag of sugar contained 1 kg and after using some to bake a cake it contained
               0.85 kg. How many grams of sugar had been used ?

      2   A medicine spoon holds 5 ml. How many spoonfuls are there in a bottle containing
               $\frac{1}{4}$ litre of medicine ?

3.   Find the size of angle *a*.

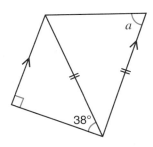

4. In a certain school, students must learn either French or Spanish, or both languages. The numbers studying each subject are shown in this list.

French only	630
Spanish only	126
French and Spanish	84
Number of students	840

1   If a student of the school is chosen at random, what is the probability that this student studies both French and Spanish ?

2   If a student is chosen at random from those who study Spanish, what is the probability that this student also studies French ?

5. The angles of a quadrilateral, in order, are $(x + 5)°$, $(x - 25)°$, $(2x - 95)°$ and $(175 - x)°$.
1   Write down an equation and solve it to find the value of x.
2   What are the numerical values of the sizes of the angles ?
3   What sort of quadrilateral is it ?

6. The design shows 8 isosceles right-angled triangles arranged in a square.

State which triangle results if
1   triangle (1) is reflected in the line DF,
2   triangle (2) is rotated through 90° anticlockwise about E,
3   triangle (3) is rotated through 180° about E.

State the transformation (reflection or rotation), which would map
4   triangle (4) into triangle (7),
5   triangle (5) into triangle (1),
6   triangle (6) into triangle (3).

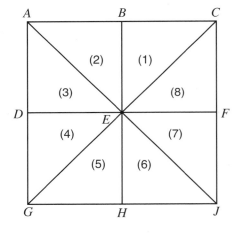

7. Make tables of values for these functions, for $x = 0, 1, 2, 3, 4, 5$.
1   $y = 3x - 5$
2   $y = 12 - 2x$

Draw axes for x from 0 to 5 and for y from -5 to 12 using a scale of 2 cm to 1 unit on the x-axis and 1 cm to 1 unit on the y-axis.
Plot the points given in the tables and draw the lines, labelling each one.
Write down the coordinates of the point where the two lines intersect, correct to 1 decimal place.

8. A spherical wire cage for holding a plant pot is formed by
    fastening together 3 circular hoops of diameter 30 cm and one
    smaller hoop of diameter 20 cm. Find the total length of wire
    needed, giving the answer to the nearest 0.1 m.
    (Take π as 3.142 or use the π key on your calculator.)

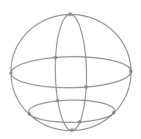

9. The number of different ways of choosing two items from a total of n items is given by
    multiplying n by the number which is one less than n, and then dividing by 2.

    1 Write down a formula for T, the number of different ways.
    2 Use the formula to find the number of different ways of choosing 2 items from
       10 items.

10. A group of 6 children held a money-raising event and raised £90, which they decided to
    split between 2 charities, X and Y.
    They each wrote down the amounts they wanted to send to each, (in £'s).

Child	Adam	Ben	Claire	Donna	Edward	Farida
To charity X	70	85	20			
To charity Y	20	5		55		

    Edward wanted to send equal amounts to each charity. Farida wanted to send twice as
    much to charity X as to charity Y.
    Copy and complete the table.

    Plot the data on a scatter diagram with charity X on the horizontal axis and charity Y on
    the vertical axis. Label the x-axis from 20 to 90 and the y-axis from 0 to 70.
    Describe the correlation shown by the diagram.

    The children found the mean of the amounts they wished to send to X, and this was the
    money they sent, with the rest going to Y. How much did each charity receive ?

Exercise E3 Revision

1. Find the values of the following:

    1 $(-4) + (+6)$
    2 $(-4) - (+1)$
    3 $5 - (-3)$
    4 $1 - (+2)$
    5 $0 + (-4)$

    6 $(-7) - (-9)$
    7 $8 - (+7)$
    8 $2 + (-5)$
    9 $(-1) + (+3)$
    10 $(-6) - (+2)$

2.   **1**   Express $50\,g : 2\,kg$ as a ratio in its simplest form.

     2   A shortbread recipe uses flour, butter, sugar and nuts in the ratio, by weight, of $9 : 6 : 3 : 2$. How much butter is used in making $1\,kg$ of the mixture ?

3.   Find the size of angle a.

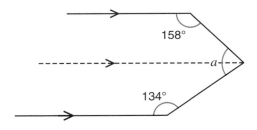

4.   **1**   What is the probability of getting a six when a fair die is thrown ? In 120 throws, what is the approximate number of sixes you would expect to get ?

     2   What is the probability of getting an ace if a card is dealt to you from a full pack of 52 cards ? If a card was dealt in this way 120 times, what is the approximate number of times you would expect to get an ace ?

     3   If the probability that the bus to take you to school is late on any one morning is reckoned to be $\frac{1}{10}$, how many times approximately would you expect to be late out of 120 mornings ?

5.   A vegetable plot is rectangular in shape, $20\,m$ long and $18\,m$ wide.

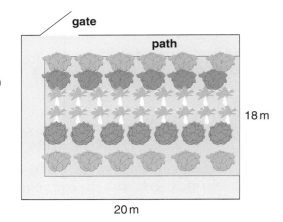

     1   A hedge is to be planted round the boundary, except at the gateway which is $2\,m$ wide. The hedging plants cost £1.20 per metre. Find the cost of the hedge.

     2   Inside the plot, there is a path $1\,m$ wide round 3 sides, as shown. The remaining area is to be fertilized at the rate of $75\,g$ per m^2. How much fertilizer is needed ?

6.   In the diagram, $\triangle ABC$ is an enlargement of $\triangle APQ$.

     1   What is the scale factor of the enlargement ?

     2   If $PQ = 2.5\,cm$, what is the length of BC ?

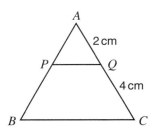

7. The graph represents the journey of a boy who cycles from a town *A* to a town *B*, and
    after a rest there, cycles back to *A*.

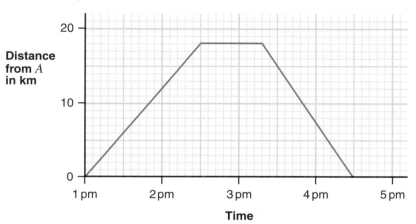

Distance from *A* in km

Time

1   For how long did the boy stay in town *B* ?
2   What was his speed on the outward journey ?
3   What was his speed on the return journey ?

8. The rule for a number chain for 2-figure numbers is:
    Square the tens digit and add the units digit.
    Stop the chain when you get a single figure.
    e.g. $36 \rightarrow 3^2 + 6 = 9 + 6 = 15 \rightarrow 1^2 + 5 = 1 + 5 = 6$

    Carry out this rule starting with the numbers 52, 84 and 92.

9. An explorer setting out from his base camp *C* walks
    due West for 8 km and then due North for 5 km.
    1   Use scale drawing to find on what bearing he
        must now travel to go directly back to camp.
    2   How far is he away from his base camp ?

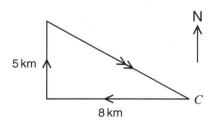

10. The distributions of examination marks in two examinations are shown in this table.
    Draw frequency polygons for these distributions on the same graph and comment on
    them.

Mark	20–29	30–39	40–49	50–59	60–69	70–79	80–89	90–99
1st exam	4	14	38	30	11	3		
2nd exam		5	18	25	31	15	4	2

Exercise E4   Revision

1.   Simplify, without using your calculator.

   1 5.32×100 **5** 8.34×5
   2 $6.8 \div 10$ **6** $25.2 \div 7$
   3 $18.1 + 5.05 + 9.37$ **7** 12.1×20
   4 $18.1 - 5.05$ **8** $24.6 \div 30$

2.   In this quadrilateral, the angles a and b are equal.
     Find the size of angle a.

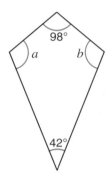

3.   The opening hours of a shop are shown on this poster.
     For how many hours per week is the shop open ?

Mon	9.30–5.30
Tues	9.30–5.30
Wed	9.30–5.30
Thurs	9.30–8.00
Fri	9.30–8.00
Sat	9.00–5.30
Sun	—

4.   A hair shampoo is sold in two sizes costing 92p and £1.34.
     The cheaper bottle is marked as holding 100 ml and the other one holds 150 ml.
     Which bottle is the better value for money ?

5.   Draw the net of a cube making all edges 3 cm long. (You may use squared paper or
     graph paper.)

     Label one square A, and label square B such that A and B will be opposite faces when
     the cube is constructed.
     Label another square C and label square D such that C and D will be opposite faces
     when the cube is constructed.
     Label the remaining squares E and F. Will these be opposite faces ?

6. Mary and Ann are hoping to be chosen for the position of shooter in the netball team. The probability that Mary will be chosen is 0.5 and the probability that Ann will be chosen is 0.3.

1   What is the probability that someone else will be chosen ?
2   What is the probability that Mary or Ann will be chosen ?

7. The time spent on homework by 30 students in a certain week was as follows:
(Times in hours, to the nearest hour.)

8	3	3	6	9	5	20	7	12	14	25	2	6	12	20
20	18	18	12	9	20	15	24	5	3	22	15	13	16	20

Make a frequency distribution table of the data using class intervals 1–5, 6–10, 11–15, 16–20, 21–25.

Draw a frequency polygon of the distribution.
What is the modal class of the distribution ?

8. A right-angled triangle ABC has sides of length 3.5 cm, 12 cm, 12.5 cm.

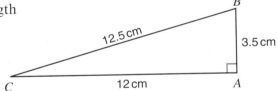

1   Find its perimeter.
2   Find its area.

9. A certain estate of 720 hectares consists of ploughed land, pasture land and woodland. This is represented in the pie chart shown.

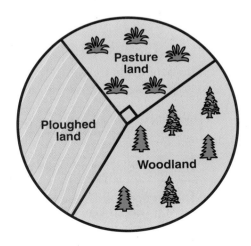

1   The angle in the pasture land sector is 90°. How many hectares are pasture land ?
2   There are 240 hectares of ploughed land. The angle in this sector has not been drawn accurately. What should it be ?
3   How many hectares are woodland ?

10. *A* and *B* are two harbours 15 km apart on a
straight coastline running West–East. A ship,
C, out at sea is seen from *A* on a bearing of 056°
and from *B* on a bearing of 288°.
Use scale drawing to find the distance of the ship
from *B*, to the nearest 0.1 km.

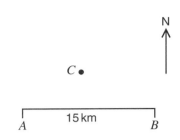

Exercise E5   Revision

1. A new road is being paid for by four towns *A*, *B*, *C* and *D*.
   Town *A* pays $\frac{1}{8}$ of the cost and *B* and *C* each pay $\frac{1}{4}$ of the cost.

   1   What fraction of the cost does *D* pay ?
   2   What does the road cost if *D* pays £60 000 ?

2. The data gives the marks of 10 students in Papers 1 and 2 of an examination. Show the
   data on a scatter diagram.

Student	A	B	C	D	E	F	G	H	I	J
Mark on Paper 1	56	52	45	53	51	67	64	58	69	56
Mark on Paper 2	68	61	53	57	62	74	79	73	81	70

   1   Comment on the correlation between the marks.
   2   Another student gained 60 marks for Paper 1 but she was absent through illness for
   Paper 2. Use the diagram to estimate the mark she might have gained on Paper 2.

3. The temperatures in the 1st 8 days of July in a recent year in London and Rome were as follows (in °C):

| London | 24 | 24 | 28 | 24 | 21 | 19 | 22 | 26 |
| Rome | 29 | 30 | 29 | 29 | 30 | 28 | 29 | 28 |

Find the mean temperature for the 8 days
1   in London,
2   in Rome.

Find the range of temperature for the 8 days
3   in London,
4   in Rome.

Comment briefly on the temperatures.

4. When boxes are stacked in piles of 5 there are 2 left over. When they are stacked in piles of 8 there are still 2 left over. If the number of boxes is between 50 and 100, how many are there ?

5. There are 7 discs in a bag numbered from 1 to 7.
    A disc is drawn (and not replaced) and a second disc is drawn.
    Show the sample space of all possible pairs of results.

Find the probability that
1   the sum of the numbers drawn is odd,
2   the 1st disc drawn has a higher number than the 2nd one.

		1st disc						
		1	2	3	4	5	6	7
2nd disc	1							
	2							
	3							
	4							
	5							
	6							
	7							

6. Copy this drawing of a prism on your own squared paper, then using the squares to help you, draw an enlargement of your prism with scale factor 2.

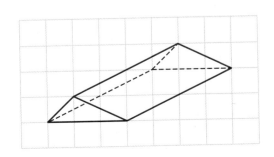

7. A boy is playing near a circular pool of diameter 20 m.
    He sends his toy boat across the centre of the pool
    from A to B at a speed of 2.5 m/s, and at the same
    time as the boat leaves A he starts to run round the
    edge of the pool from A to B at a speed of 4 m/s.

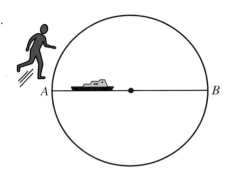

    1   How long does the boat take to go from A to B ?
    2   How far is it from A to B round the edge of the
        pool, to the nearest 0.1 m ?
    3   How long will the boy take to run from A to B,
        to the nearest 0.1 second ?
    4   Which gets to B first, the boy or his boat ?

    (Take π as 3.142 or use the π key on your calculator.)

8. The table shows the takings, in £1000's, in the four departments of a shop during the last
    year.

    | Food | 60 |
    | Wines and spirits | 30 |
    | Fruit and vegetables | 20 |
    | Sweets and tobacco | 15 |

    Represent the data on a pictogram or bar chart.
    Which department is the modal department ?

9. Draw a graph to convert between British and French currency at a time when the rate of
    exchange was £1 = 7.5 francs.
    On the horizontal axis, for £'s, label from 0 to 10 with 1 unit to 1 cm. On the vertical
    axis, for francs, label from 0 to 80 with 10 units to 1 cm.

    From your graph, find
    1   the amount you would get if you changed £3 into francs,
    2   the value in British money of a present which cost you 50 francs.

10. Carol's father was 24 years old when Carol was born. Now he is four times as old as
    Carol. How old is Carol now ?
    (Let Carol be x years old, write down an equation and solve it.)

Exercise E6 Revision

1. Change these fractions to percentages.

    1 $\frac{1}{4}$ **2** $\frac{3}{5}$ **3** $\frac{7}{25}$

    Change these decimals to percentages.

    4 0.3   **5** 0.65   **6** 0.02

    Change these percentages to fractions, in their simplest forms.

    7 35%   **8** 36%   **9** 40%

2. Which pairs of these triangles are congruent to each other ?

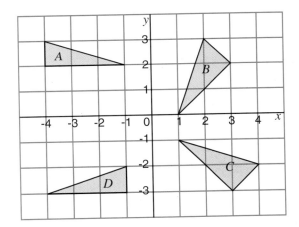

3.

The average prices of semi-detached houses in five districts is given in this table.

District	A	B	C	D	E
Price in £1000's to nearest £1000	43	45	50	58	69

Draw a bar chart to illustrate the data.

4. The following information is given by a travel agent for holidays in Spain.

Prices in £ per person from London	Departure commencing between			Single room supplements per person per night
	1 May–18 Jun	19 Jun–9 Jly	10 Jly–26 Aug	
Hotel Marti 11 days (10 nights)	348	407	479	} £4
12 days (11 nights)	364	425	502	
15 days (14 nights)	414	481	564	
Hotel Parki 15 days (14 nights)	454	526	616	£2
Supplements for flights from:	11 days	12 days	15 days (dep. Mon)	15 days (dep. Sat)
Glasgow	£49	£47	£39	£57
Manchester	£31	£33	£23	£39

1   Mr and Mrs Dee are going on their honeymoon for 12 days, departing Saturday, 4th July, flying from Manchester. They want a double room. Which hotel must they stay at ? Find the total cost.

2   Three friends are going for 15 days holiday, flying from Glasgow, departing on Saturday, 13th June. They each want single rooms and will stay at the Hotel Parki. Find the cost for each person, and the total cost.

3   Mr and Mrs Ede and their 7-year old daughter Mary want an 11-day holiday, flying from London and departing on Saturday, 8th August. (Mary will occupy a bed in her parents' room and there is a $\frac{1}{5}$ reduction in cost for her.) Find the total cost.

5. Draw axes as shown and show the journey of a boy on his bicycle and his father in the car.

The boy starts from A at 1 pm and cycles at a steady speed of 10 km/h for 2 hours. He then rests for $\frac{1}{2}$ hour and then continues cycling at a steady speed to B, which is 40 km from A, and he arrives at 6 pm.

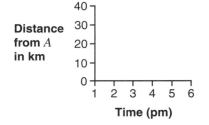

His father starts from A at 4 pm and arrives at B at 5.20 pm, travelling at a steady speed.

1   What was the boy's speed on the second part of his journey ?

2   What was his father's speed ?

3   When and where did the father overtake his son ?

6. A boat sails from a port A for 10 km on a bearing
   of 135° to an island B and then 14 km on a bearing
   of 070° to a port C.

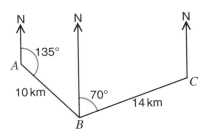

   Choose a suitable scale and draw an accurate scale
   drawing of the course sailed.

   If the boat then sails directly back to A, how far is
   the return journey and in what direction ?

7. A rectangular shallow tray is 120 cm long, 80 cm wide and 5 cm high.
   How many litres of water will it hold ? $(1000\, cm^3 = 1$ litre).

8. Identify whether the quadrilateral $ABCD$ is necessarily
   a parallelogram, trapezium, rectangle, square or
   rhombus, if it has the following properties.

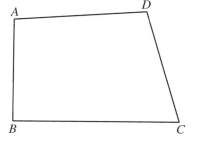

   1   AD is parallel to BC.
   2   $AB = DC$ and $AD = BC$.
   3   $\angle A = \angle C$ and $\angle B = \angle D$.
   4   Angles A, B, C, D are right angles.
   5   $AB = BC = CD = DA$.

9. Copy and complete the following table of values for the function $y = x^2 - 8$.

x	-4	-3	-2	-1	0	1	2	3	4
x^2	16	9			0				
-8	-8	-8			-8				
y	8	1			-8				

   Draw the x-axis from -4 to 4 and the y-axis from -8 to 8, taking a scale of 2 cm to
   1 unit on the x-axis and 1 cm to 1 unit on the y-axis.
   Plot the points from the table and draw the graph of the function, joining the points with
   a smooth curve.
   Find the x-coordinates of the 2 points where the curve meets the x-axis, correct to
   1 decimal place.

10. Imagine that you are running a pre-school playgroup.
    Design a questionnaire which you could ask the parents of the children to fill in, to give
    you their views on how well the playgroup meets their needs and those of their children.
    (Include about 4 to 8 questions.)

Exercise E7   Revision

1.   A man earns £25 000 and he gets a pay rise of 6%. What is his new salary ?
      The following year he gets a pay rise of 4%. What does he earn then ?

2.   State how many axes of symmetry these figures have.

      1   Isosceles triangle   4   Rhombus
      2   Equilateral triangle   5   Regular hexagon
      3   Parallelogram

      State the order of rotational symmetry of these figures.

      6   Square   9   Regular pentagon
      7   Rectangle   10   Outline of a 50 pence coin
      8   Equilateral triangle

3.   If oranges are packed 150 to a box, 12 boxes are needed.
      How many boxes are needed if they are packed 200 to a box ?

4.   The diagram shows a woman walking under a motorway bridge.
      Estimate the height AB of the bridge above the ground. (You can assume the woman is
      1.6 m tall.)

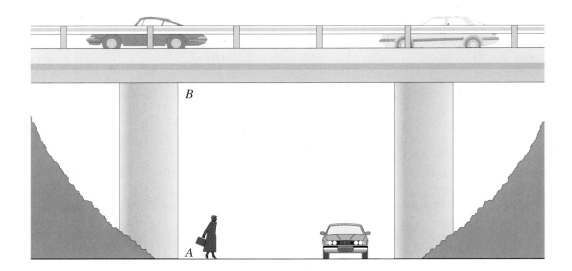

5.   Construct a triangle ABC with $BC = 7$ cm, $\angle B = 95°$ and $\angle C = 40°$. Bisect $\angle A$, letting the
      bisector cut BC at D. Measure the length of BD, to the nearest mm.

6. The diagram represents an octagon formed by cutting equal isosceles triangles with short sides 3 cm from the corners of a square of side 12 cm.
Find the total area of the four corners.
Hence find the area of the octagon.

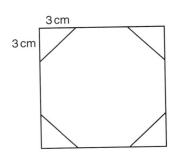

7. The quantities, w grams, of a salt which can be dissolved in a given volume of water at different temperatures, t °C, are given in the table.

t (°C)	10	20	25	30	40	50	55	60
w (g)	41	44	45.5	47	50	53	54.5	56

Draw a scatter diagram to show this information.
Comment on the relationship between the temperatures and the quantities of the salt which can be dissolved.

8. Three years ago the cost of an article was £24, made up of charges for labour, materials and other expenses in the ratio 9 : 4 : 3.

1 Find the separate costs for each item.

2 Since then labour costs have increased by one-third, the price of materials has increased by one-fifth and the cost of other expenses has increased by one-tenth. What is the cost of the article now ?

9. These circles with the same centre have radii 11 cm and 9 cm.

Find the area of each circle and use your answers to find the shaded area.
(Take π as 3.142 or use the π key on your calculator.)

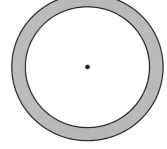

10. Copy and complete this table showing the size of an interior angle of a regular polygon.

Number of sides	3	4	5	6	8	9	10
Size of each interior angle (in degrees)	60					140	144

On graph paper, label the horizontal axis for 'number of sides' from 3 to 10, and label the vertical axis for 'size of angle in degrees' from 0 to 180.
Plot the values in the table on the graph.
Join the points with a smooth curve. (Note that intermediate points on the curve have no meaning, except where the number of sides is 7.)
Use the graph to estimate the size of an interior angle of a regular polygon with 7 sides.

Exercise E8   Activities

1.   **My house**

Imagine that it is a few years into the future and you are about to buy a house.
Design the house and draw a plan of each floor.
Then draw the plan of each room, showing where the doorways and windows are, and
where each item of furniture will go.
Find the approximate cost of each item of furniture (by looking in shops, catalogues or
advertisements).
For each room make a list of the furniture and fittings you will need and find the total
cost. Find the total cost for all the rooms in the house.
If you intend to have a garden you could include a plan for this, and add on the costs of
garden tools and garden furniture.
Find the up-to-date price of a similar house by looking at advertisements, and find the
total cost of everything.

Cut pictures from magazines and catalogues to illustrate your booklet, and make an
attractive cover for it.

This is your dream house so you need not be too practical about being able to afford it,
if you wish to design a really luxurious one, on the other hand you may prefer to be
practical and plan for an inexpensive one. You may prefer to choose a flat, or a
bungalow, instead of a house.

2. **The probability that two numbers have a common factor**

If you choose 2 numbers at random they can have a common factor, e.g. 35 and 40 have a common factor 5, but 35 and 44 do not have a common factor although they both have factors.

Get 200 pairs of numbers from 1 to 50, from random number tables, a computer, the phone directory or elsewhere.

Write them down in a list.

Find how many pairs have a common factor.
Look first for pairs with numbers which are both even.
They have a common factor 2. Mark them with F for factor.

Then look from those left for pairs with numbers which both end in 5 or 0, they have a common factor 5. Mark them with F.

Then look from those left for pairs with numbers which both divide by 3, and mark them with F. (What is a quick test for deciding which numbers are divisible by 3 ?)

Then write down all the multiples of 7 up to 49, and look for pairs with a common factor 7.

35	F	40
35	×	44
1	×	17
12	F	32
10	×	9
5	F	50
41	×	29
43	×	9
48	F	3
8	F	46
...		

Then look for pairs with numbers which both divide by 11 (multiples 11, 22, 33, 44), 13 (multiples 13, 26, 39), 17 (multiples 17, 34), 19 (multiples 19, 38) and 23 (multiples 23, 46), or other pairs where both numbers are the same.

The remaining pairs of numbers have no common factors. Mark them with a cross.

Find the experimental probability that two numbers have a common factor using the formula

$$\text{experimental probability} = \frac{\text{number with a common factor}}{\text{total number of pairs}}.$$

Compare your result with the theoretical probability which is 0.38, and comment on this.

$\left(\text{If you do this experiment with whole numbers of any size, the theoretical probability}\right.$

$\text{is } 1 - \dfrac{6}{\pi^2}\ .\Big)$

3. **Pascal's triangle**

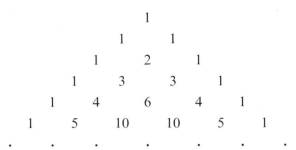

Pascal was a French Mathematician who lived in the 17th century.
See if you can find out more about him from library books.
This triangle of numbers is named after him, although it was known long ago in Ancient China.
Decide how each number is formed from the numbers in the row above, and copy the triangle and continue it for a few more rows.
(As a check, a later row is 1 8 28 56 70 56 28 8 1)

What do you notice about the sum of each row ?
What do we call the numbers in the diagonal which begins 1, 3, 6, 10 ?

Further investigations

1   If you toss three coins in turn, there are 8 possible results, HHH, HTH, etc. which can be summarised like this.

	0 heads	1 head	2 heads	3 heads
Number of ways	1	3	3	1

Investigate the results when 4, or more, coins are tossed.

2   Suppose there are 7 people and 3 of them have to be selected for some purpose. How many ways are there of making the selection ?
To find this number you could first select 3 from 3, (1 way), then 3 from 4, (4 ways), and so on.
See how this connects with Pascal's triangle.

3   The diagram shows the railway station and the roads to the beach. From the station, how many ways are there of getting to each access point A, B, C, D, E or F ?
How does this link with Pascal's triangle ?
Why is the beach more crowded in the centre ?

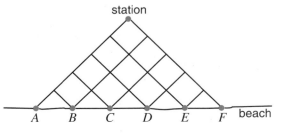

4 Start with Pascal's Triangle, move the numbers along so that the first number starts one column further along each time, and add the column totals.

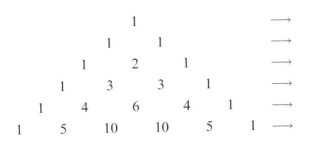

What do you notice about the totals ?

5 Using the upright △ triangles on a sheet of isometric paper, write down several rows of Pascal's Triangle.
Colour in one colour all the triangles with odd numbers and colour in a different colour all the triangles with even numbers.
Continue if possible to the row beginning 1, 15, ... (There is no need to work out the actual numbers on the later rows, since you only need to know whether they are odd or even.)

Comment on the patterns.

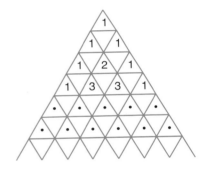

4. **A packaging problem**

A square piece of cardboard has sides of length 30 cm. Out of each corner a square of side x cm, where x is less than 15, is cut. The flaps remaining are turned up to form an open box.
Show that the volume of the box is $x(30 - 2x)^2$ cm^2.
Find the volume when $x = 1, 2, 3, \ldots$, and then find the value of x which gives the greatest volume.
State this volume.

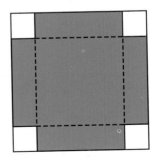

5.   ## Solid figures with pentagonal holes

These are easier to make than closed solid figures as you can get your fingers inside the solids to press the glued faces together.

1   Rhombicosidodecahedron

The basic figure is a square (of side 3 cm) with equilateral triangles on two opposite sides. You need 30 pieces like this.

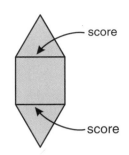

One way is to draw several squares in a line, on cardboard, then with compasses, radius 3 cm, find the points above and below for the third points of the equilateral triangles. When you have the pattern for some pieces, copy them by putting another piece of cardboard underneath, then prick through the main points using your compasses. (Put something underneath to protect the desk.) Then join these points.

You must score the two lines by putting a ruler along them and then drag your compass point along so that it makes a nick in the lines. Always fold away from the side you scored on. Fold these lines slightly.

Now take 5 pieces and glue them together with triangles exactly on top of each other, to make a ring like this.

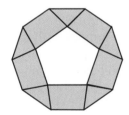

Then glue a third triangle on the top of each other two to start off 5 more rings like this.

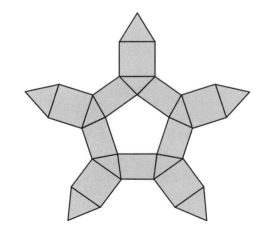

Complete these rings with 2 more pieces each. (Every ring has an edge of 5 squares because it is a pentagonal hole, i.e. a hole with 5 edges.)
Continue in this way so that there are 3 triangles stuck together every time.

2   Snub dodecahedron

This is made in a similar way to the previous
model.
The basic figure is 4 equilateral triangles.
Make the edges 3 cm long.
You need 30 pieces. As before, you can make
a block of several pieces together and then
copy them.
Score the 3 inside lines and bend slightly.
Glue together as for the last model, only using
the triangles at the ends of the strips for glueing together.

3   Spherical truncated icosahedron

The basic figure is a regular hexagon in a circle.
(See page 263 question 9.)
You need 20 pieces like this.
Cut off three alternate segments.
Score the other 3 lines and bend away from
the scored line.

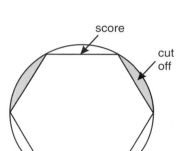

Glue 2 pieces together by the small curved segment. Add pieces until 5 hexagons are
joined together in a circle, with the curved segments on the outside.
Add other pieces to the unused segments and continue making pentagonal holes.

6.   **The number of beads drawn to get a blue one**

This experiment involves 8 beads in a bag. 6 are red and 2 are blue. You draw out the
beads one at a time until a blue one appears.

Before you begin, estimate
1   what is the most likely number (mode number) of beads drawn out,
2   what is the average number (mean number) of beads drawn out.

Put the beads in a bag and shake them up and then draw out the beads one at a time
until a blue one appears. If it is the third one out, count that result as 3.
Replace the beads and repeat the experiment about 100 times.

Put the results in a tally chart, then find the mode number and mean number of draws.
How close were your estimates ?
(If you have not got any beads, anything suitable will do, as long as the items feel the
same and two of them are marked differently from the rest.)

7.   **Magic squares**

Here is a 4 by 4 magic square, used by the German artist Albrecht
Durer in an engraving 'Melancholia' to show the date, 1514.

16	3	2	13
5	10	11	8
9	6	7	12
4	15	14	1

What are the totals of each row, each column and the two main
diagonals ?

Make a 3 by 3 magic square using the numbers 1 to 9.

If a 5 by 5 magic square uses numbers 1 to 25, what is the number to which all rows and
columns should add up ?

One way of constructing a magic square with an odd number of rows or columns is:
(1)   Put 1 in the middle of the top row.
(2)   Put each following number above and to the right of the preceding number. If this
       is above the top row go to the bottom row and if it is to the right of the right-hand
       column go to the left-hand column.

The 1st 5 numbers are shown.

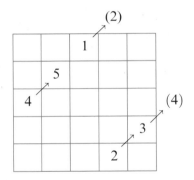

(3)   If a number cannot be placed because its square has already been filled (as 6 cannot
       be placed because 1 is there), put the number below the last number written. (Thus
       put 6 below 5 and continue as before.)

Copy and complete this magic square according
to this method.
Check that the rows, columns and main diagonals
all add up to the same number.

Make a 7 by 7 magic square using the same method.

Here is an 8 by 8 magic square.
Check that the rows, columns and main diagonals
all add up to the same number.

Look for other patterns in the square.
For example, copy the square just writing in
the odd numbers and leaving the other squares
blank, or just writing in the numbers 1 to 32
and leaving the other squares blank.

7	53	41	27	2	52	48	30
12	58	38	24	13	63	35	17
51	1	29	47	54	8	28	42
64	14	18	36	57	11	23	37
25	43	55	5	32	46	50	4
22	40	60	10	19	33	61	15
45	31	3	49	44	26	6	56
34	20	16	62	39	21	9	59

8. ## A plaited cube and tetrahedron

It is interesting to make a plaited cube. It has a different pattern to an ordinary net since faces have to overlap.
Copy the pattern. (It is useful to use the 2 cm squares on graph paper.)
Cut it out and crease all the lines, bending the paper away from the numbers so that the numbers stay on the outside. Now cover up number 1, by putting the square above number 5 sideways on top of it. Next cover up number 2, then 3 and so on. 5 is covered by 6, 7 is covered by 8. Finally there is one square left. Cut the corners off this one and tuck it in.

If you make several such cubes you can use them to investigate volumes and surface areas of different rectangular shapes. You can also use them as dice, but they may not give fair results. (You could investigate to see if the results were fair.)

Here also is a pattern for a plaited tetrahedron. The triangles are equilateral. Perhaps you can find out how to make other solid figures by plaiting.

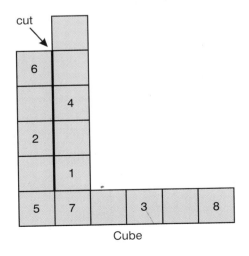

Cube

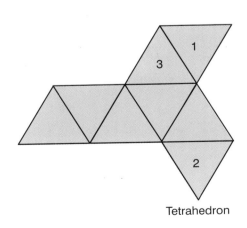

Tetrahedron

Data for additional aural questions

1 Distance chart
(Distances in km)

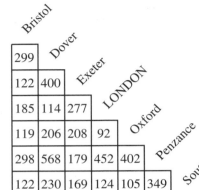

Bristol
Dover
Exeter
LONDON
Oxford
Penzance
Southampton

299					
122	400				
185	114	277			
119	206	208	92		
298	568	179	452	402	
122	230	169	124	105	349

2

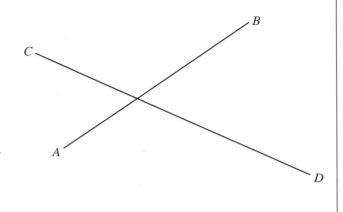

3 Travel insurance
(Prices per person.)

	United Kingdom only	Europe	Worldwide
up to 8 days	£5.65	£13.10	£30.60
up to 12 days	£6.00	£13.90	£31.95
up to 17 days	£6.95	£15.25	£33.55
up to 24 days	£7.75	£16.40	£39.10

Winter sports in Europe insured at $1\frac{1}{2}$ times the Europe premium.
Double premium for persons aged over 65, Worldwide.

4 Air service and connecting rail timetable

London dep.	23.00	10.20	11.20	15.25	16.55
Kereva airport arr.	00.30	11.40	12.50	16.45	18.10
Kereva station dep.	04.30	13.31	15.17	17.55	20.01
Veefield arr.	06.13	14.43	16.25	19.03	21.09

5 Value of £100 worth of Savings Certificates

Years after purchase	Value at end of year
1	£103.75
2	£108.06
3	£113.46
4	£120.44
5	£129.77

6   Exchange rates

Australia	1.94 dollars
Austria	15.20 schillings
Belgium	44.60 francs
Canada	2.04 dollars
Denmark	8.45 kroner
France	7.43 francs
Germany	2.19 marks
Greece	365 drachmae
Holland	2.46 guilders
Ireland	0.96 punts
Israel	4.58 shekels
Italy	2325 lire
Malta	0.54 lire
New Zealand	2.23 dollars
Norway	9.56 kroner
Portugal	227 escudos
Spain	183 pesetas
Switzerland	1.78 francs
United States	1.50 dollars

7   TV Programmes

6.25	Weather
6.30	News
6.50	Entertainment 88
7.20	Sports Today
9.30	The Golden Age (play)
11.05	Local lives
11.45	Closedown

8

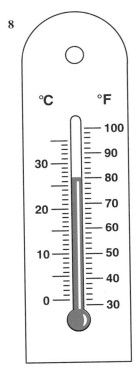

9   Curtains

Very good value ! Price per pair			
54 × 46	£29.99	54 × 66	£49.99
72 × 46	£42.99	72 × 66	£59.99
90 × 46	£49.99	90 × 66	£74.99
108 × 46	£59.99	108 × 66	£89.99
54 × 90	£68.99	90 × 90	£99.99
72 × 90	£86.99	108 × 90	£124.99

(Measurements in inches)

10

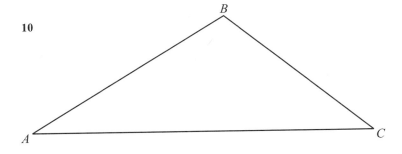

11   Bus passengers in one week

Number of
Passengers
(in 100's)

[Line graph with y-axis "Number of Passengers (in 100's)" marked 0, 10, 20, 30, 40, 50, 60 and x-axis days Sun, M, Tu, W, Th, F, Sat. Points plotted at approximately Sun=10, M=40, Tu=30, W=40, Th=45, F=51, Sat=24, and a final point at 20]

12

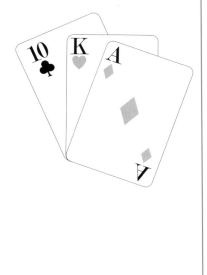

13   Conversion graph

Miles

[Line graph with y-axis "Miles" marked 0, 10, 20, 30 and x-axis "Kilometres" marked 0, 10, 20, 30, 40, 50. A straight line from origin through a point marked × at about (50, 31)]

Kilometres

14   The Fares Table on the local bus

(Fares in pence)

Town centre				
25	Pollard Street			
35	30	Victoria Road		
40	37	25	Addison Road	
55	50	40	35	Long Lane

15   Function machine

| INPUT x | → | Multiply by 10 | → | Subtract 7 | → | OUTPUT y |

16 **Sales of 5 products A, B, C, D, E**

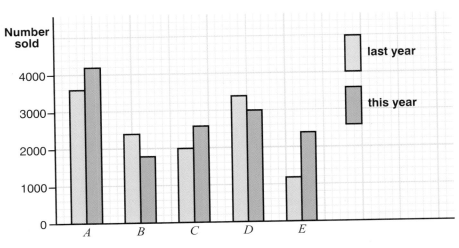

17 **Advertisement for a loan**

	Secured Loans		
	Weekly Equivalent Payments		
LOAN	10 yrs	$7\frac{1}{2}$ yrs	5 yrs
£2250	£10.52	£11.69	£14.34
£3200	£14.96	£16.63	£20.40
£5500	£25.71	£28.58	£34.89

18

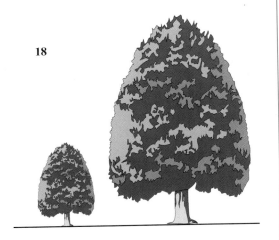

19

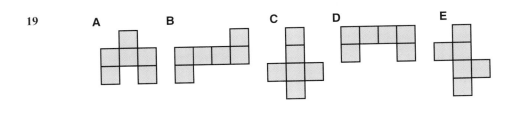

Checklist for formulae and facts

I   This is a list of the more important formulae. Copy it, complete and check the formulae, and learn the ones you do not know.

Angles
1.   Sum of angles of a triangle =
2.   Exterior angle of a triangle =
3.   Sum of angles of a quadrilateral =
4.   Sum of exterior angles of a polygon =
5.   Sum of angles of a pentagon =
6.   Sum of angles of a hexagon =
7.   Sum of angles of an octagon =
8.   Each angle in a regular pentagon =
9.   Each angle in a regular hexagon =
10. Each angle in a regular octagon =

Statistics
11. Mean of a set of numbers =
12. Range of a set of numbers =
13. Mean of a frequency distribution =

Probability
14. Relative frequency =
15. Probability of a successful outcome =
16. Sum of probabilities of mutually exclusive events =
17. Probability of an event happening (in terms of it not happening) =

Perimeters, areas and volumes
18. Perimeter of a rectangle =
19. Area of a rectangle =
20. Area of a square =
21. Area of a triangle =
22. Volume of a cuboid =
23. Volume of a cube =
24. Circumference of a circle =
25. Area of a circle =

Time, distance, speed
26. Speed =
27. Time =
28. Distance =

Enlargement
29.   Length of line on enlargement =
30.   Scale factor of enlargement =

II   Here are some questions to remind you of the more important mathematical facts. You could answer these questions orally, or in some cases draw sketches. Find out the answers to those you do not know.

31.   What different kinds of numbers do you know ?
32.   What is an even number ?
33.   What is an odd number ?
34.   What is a prime number ?
35.   What is a factor of a number ?
36.   What is a multiple of a number ?
37.   What is a square number ?
38.   What is a cube number ?
39.   What is the square root of a number ?

40.   What are the main metric measures of length ? How are they connected with each other ?
41.   What are the main metric measures of weight ? How are they connected with each other ?
42.   What are the main metric measures of capacity ? How are they connected with each other ?
43.   Name some British measures of length, and give their approximate comparisons with the metric measures.
44.   Name some British measures of weight, and give their approximate comparisons with the metric measures.
45.   Name some British measures of capacity, and give their approximate comparisons with the metric measures.
46.   In which units do we measure time ? How are these units connected with each other ?

47.   What is an angle ? How do we measure angles ?
48.   What kinds of angles are there ?
49.   What are parallel lines ?
50.   What are perpendicular lines ?

51.   What is a triangle ?
52.   What kinds of triangles are there ?
53.   What do you know about the angles of a triangle ?
54.   What is an isosceles triangle ?
55.   What do you know about the angles of an isosceles triangle ?
56.   What is an equilateral triangle ?
57.   What do you know about the angles of an equilateral triangle ?

58.   What is a quadrilateral ?
59.   What do you know about the angles of a quadrilateral ?

60. What special kinds of quadrilaterals do you know ? What is special about each one ?
61. What is a diagonal of a quadrilateral ?
62. What is a polygon ?
63. What is special about a regular polygon ?
64. Name the polygons with 5, 6 and 8 sides.
65. What names of parts of a circle do you know ? Describe each one.

66. What kinds of solid figures do you know ? Describe each one.
67. What is the net of a solid figure ?
68. How many faces, edges and vertices has a cuboid ?
69. How many faces, edges and vertices has a triangular prism ?
70. How many faces, edges and vertices has a pyramid with a square base ?

71. What are congruent figures ?
72. What is a horizontal line ?
73. What is a vertical line ?
74. What are the 8 main compass directions ?
75. How are bearings measured ?
76. What is an axis of symmetry ?
77. What is rotational symmetry ?

78. What is the perimeter of a figure ?
79. What is the area of a figure ?
80. What is the volume of a solid figure ?
81. What is the circumference of a circle ?
82. What is π ?

83. Name some kinds of statistical diagrams and describe them.
84. Name 3 kinds of averages and say how you would find each of them.

85. What is meant by correlation ?
86. What is the difference between positive correlation and negative correlation ?

87. What do we mean by the probability of an event happening ?
88. When we give the probability as a number, what range of numbers do we use ?
89. How do we calculate the probability of an event happening ?
90. What does it mean if the probability of an event happening is $\frac{1}{2}$?

PUZZLES

57. Here is the final table in the local league. Every team has played every other team once. What was the score in the match between the Allsorts and the Dribblers ?

	played	won	drawn	lost	goals for	goals against	points
Allsorts	3	3	0	0	4	0	6
Buskers	3	1	1	1	4	4	3
Cobblers	3	0	2	1	3	4	2
Dribblers	3	0	1	2	0	3	1

58. When Katie and Roger were married, they hadn't much money, and on their first wedding anniversary Roger was unable to buy his wife a decent present. So he gave her 1p, and said that it was all he could afford, but he would try to double the amount each year from then on. Sure enough, the next year he gave her 2p, and the following year 4p. Katie was quite pleased to get £5.12 this year, and says she is looking forward to their Silver Wedding anniversary when they will have been happily married for 25 years. Roger, however, doesn't seem quite so enthusiastic about this. Why ?

59. Decode this bill. Each capital letter stands for a figure and each figure stands for the corresponding letter.

R	6480	at	LI pence each	U I
I	6489520	at	BI pence each	U I
L	372430	at	BN pence each	R P
L	3711430	at	C pence each	B N
				£L. S E

60. What is the area of a square of side 21 cm ?

   Draw a square of side 21 cm on cardboard and divide it into 4 pieces as shown.
   Cut the pieces out and rearrange them to form a rectangle.
   What are the measurements of the rectangle ?
   What is the area of the rectangle ?
   Where has the extra 1 cm^2 come from ?

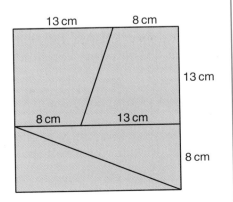

To the student: 6

The day before the examination

Get all your equipment ready:
Pen,
Pencil and sharpener,
Rubber,
Ruler,
Compasses, protractor, set square.
Calculator,
Watch.

For your calculator, buy new batteries and make sure they work. Spend a few minutes playing with your calculator to recall what functions you can get with the various keys. How do you find $\sqrt{40}$, 40^2, $\frac{1}{40}$, $(2 \times 40) - 3$, $\frac{20+40}{3}$? Remove the instruction booklet which you must not take into the examination room.

Although there should be a clock in the examination room, you may not be able to see it from where you are sitting so it is advisable to wear your watch. Does it also need new batteries ? If you have not got a watch then borrow one or buy a cheap one.

You want to be comfortable in the exam room so plan to wear a jacket or pullover to keep you warm if it is cold, but which you can take off if you get too hot. (If it gets very stuffy during the exam, ask the invigilator if a window can be opened. If you are in a chilly draught, ask him if it can be closed.)

Check your exam timetable. If you think the exam is in the **afternoon**, check very carefully, because you will be too late if you turn up in the afternoon for an exam that actually took place that morning. Check with someone else in your class to make sure.

Have a last-minute glance at last year's paper or a practice paper. See what instructions were given on that. Plan ahead as to how you will allocate your time. Have a final look at your revision checklist and maybe do just a little more revision, but not too much, as this should be a time for relaxation. Get out into the fresh air and have some exercise. Then go to bed at a reasonable time.

The day of the examination

Get to the exam room in good time, with all your equipment, and have nothing on your desk or in your pockets which you are not supposed to have with you.

When the exam begins, make a note of the time shown on your own watch, and note the time it is due to end.

Check the instructions at the beginning of the paper so that you know whether you must answer all the questions or whether you have to make a choice from one section. Note any other important points.

Do not rush into the first question too quickly. Read it carefully. Decide how to answer it, then do so. If you have to show your working, set it down neatly. You have plenty of time. It is so easy to make a mistake at this stage as you have not settled down, so do not be in too much of a rush.

When you have finished this question, and this applies to all the other questions as well, read the printed question again. Have you done what you were asked to do ? Have you answered all of it ? Is the answer reasonable ? Is the answer given to the accuracy required, e.g. to the nearest whole number, and have you given the units, e.g. cm^2 ?

Continue answering questions carefully until you have done a few. Then check the time. If you are going very slowly it might be sensible to leave out any long questions so as to do a few quick ones at this stage. Remember it is the marks which count so spend the time on what will gain you the most marks.

If you cannot do a question, read it again carefully. What is it about ? Are you using all the information given ? Is there a diagram ? Is there any other information you could deduce from the diagram ? If there is not a diagram, would a sketch diagram help ? If so, draw one. What facts or formulae do you know about this topic ? Do they help ? If the question is in several parts, often an answer to an earlier part may be needed in working out a later part. Even if you cannot finish the question, put something down on paper because your attempt might be worth some marks and it cannot be marked if it is not written down. If you cannot do part (1) of a question but can do part (2), then do part (2) so that you will get the marks for that. You can always go back to thinking about part (1) later if you want to, and have the time. If you cannot get any further on any part of the question then abandon it and try a different one.

If the numbers in a question turn out to be complicated it is possible that you have made a simple mistake. Check that you have copied the numbers or expression correctly, and check your calculations again.

Keep your writing clear. Show all necessary working with your answer as you cannot gain marks for it if it is in a jumbled mess at the bottom of the page. You can do rough work at the side of the page near the answer, and then cross it out if you wish, but cross it out neatly so that it can still be read, in case it is worth some marks.

Do not use white paint correction fluid to blot out your mistakes. Some Examination Boards do not allow you to use this, but even if allowed, it wastes time, and if you write over it the new writing might get soaked up and be illegible by the time your script has reached the examiner.

Once the examination is over, forget it, until the results come out. You have done your best and that is all that matters. We hope you will be satisfied with your final grade.
GOOD LUCK!

Index

Answers

Some answers have been given corrected to reasonable degrees of accuracy, depending on the questions. There may be variations in answers where questions involve drawings or graphs. Sometimes it will not be possible to give answers to the same degree of accuracy, depending on the scale used.
There may be wide variations in answers involving estimates.

Page 4   **Exercise 1.1**

1. 56   120   15   72   20
    24   15   6   0   106
    20   121   240   8   0
    60   8   12   13   144

2. 8   3   11   6   3
    6   12   8   5   7
    8   10   12   7   9
    7   12   5   12   9

3. **1** 3   **4** 0
    2 4   **5** 4
    3 2

4. **1** 4   **4** 3
    2 8   **5** 19
    3 5

5. **1** 15   **5** 2500   **8** 12
    2 0   **6** 188   **9** 90
    3 60   **7** 36   **10** 110
    4 96

6. **1** 2   **4** 2
    2 4   **5** 2
    3 3

7. **1** 4, 9   **4** 9, 8
    2 5, 6   **5** 8, 3
    3 4, 12

8. **1** 4   **4** 106
    2 1024   **5** 105
    3 8

9. **1** 8
    2 4
    3 10

10. **1** 19   **4** 15
    2 7   **5** 16
    3 9

11. **1** 21
    2 6
    3 7

Page 8   **Exercise 1.2**

1. 23, 29

2. **1** 37
    2 89

3. **1** 16   **5** 8   **8** 88
    2 343   **6** 72   **9** 2700
    3 100 000 **7** 140   **10** 450
    4 11

4. **1** 132, 156, 400
    2 135, 225, 400
    3 132, 135, 156, 225

5. **1** 11   **5** 4   **8** 8
    2 9   **6** 8   **9** 2
    3 5   **7** 3   **10** 7
    4 3

6. **1** 15   **5** 20   **8** 6
    2 24   **6** 22   **9** 10
    3 20   **7** 18   **10** 21
    4 24

7. **1** 121, 36, 4, 100, 1
   2 8, 12, 7, 3, 5
   3 5, 6
   4 9, 10
   5 3, 4, 5

8. **1** $2 \times 3 \times 5$
   2 $2 + 5 + 23$ or $2 + 11 + 17$

9. **1** 19   **4** 12
   2 16   **5** 16, 20
   3 20   **6** 8, 19

10. **1** 19, 23   **4** 27
    2 25   **5** 19, 25
    3 18, 27

11. **1** 61, 63, 65, 67, 69
    2 64
    3 63, 70
    4 60, 65, 70
    5 60
    6 66
    7 61, 67
    8 64

12. 41

13. 66

Page 11   Exercise 1.3

1. **1** 33   **5** 3   **8** 33
   2 48   **6** 65   **9** 9
   3 39   **7** 121   **10** 33
   4 55

2. **1** 50   **5** 7   **8** 4
   2 64   **6** 100   **9** 28
   3 20   **7** 28   **10** 4
   4 28

Page 11   Exercise 1.4

1. **1** 80, 81, 82, 83, 84, 85, 86, 87, 88, 89, 90
   2 80, 82, 84, 86, 88, 90
   3 81, 84, 87, 90
   4 80, 85, 90
   5 84
   6 83, 89

2. **1** 81   **5** 8
   2 8   **6** 360
   3 37, 73   **7** 81
   4 91   **8** 50

3. **1** even   **4** even
   2 even   **5** odd
   3 odd

4. **1** 23
   2 48

5. **1** 45
   2 99

7. 28

8. **1** 31
   2 30

Page 13   Practice test 1

1. **1** 3   **4** 12
   2 3   **5** 100
   3 8

2. 49, 25, 144, 1, 36

3. 11, 10, 4, 9, 2

4. 64, 1000, 125

5. **1** 36
   2 50
   3 86

6. **1** 20, 22, 24, 26, 28, 30
   2 21, 28
   3 25
   4 27
   5 24
   6 30
   7 22
   8 23, 29
   9 23

7. 4

Page 17   Exercise 2.1

1. **1** acute   **3** obtuse
   2 reflex   **4** reflex

4. **1** $27°$ **2** $118°$ **3** $70°$

5. $a = 40°, b = 71°, c = 90°, d = 148°$

Page 20   Exercise 2.2

1. **1** $a = 136°, b = 78°, c = 50°, d = 96°$
   2 $e = 154°, f = 26°$
   3 $g = j = 110°, h = k = 70°$
   4 $k = n = 47°, m = 133°, p = 49°, q = 84°$

2. **1** $a = 26°, b = 334°$
   2 $a = 132°, b = 228°$

3. **1** $a = 160°$
   2 $b = 40°$
   3 $c = 35°, d = e = 145°$

4. 1 $a = 80°$
    2 $b = 67°$
    3 $c = 125°, d = 55°, e = 40°$

5. 1 $a = 72°$
    2 $75°$

Page 23　　　　Exercise 2.3

1. 1 $a = b = 127°$
    2 $c = d = 29°$
    3 $e = 64°, f = 116°$

2. 1 $f = 67°$
    2 $g = 54°$
    3 $h = 70°$

3. 1 $a = 56°, b = 124°$
    2 $c = 102°, d = 78°$
    3 $e = f = 41°$

4. 1 $a = b = 74°, c = 106°$
    2 $d = 117°, e = 63°$

5. 1 $j = 60°, k = 50°, m = 70°$
    2 $n = 125°, p = 145°, q = 35°$

Page 25　　　　Exercise 2.4

1. 1 AB, BC, GH, HD, FE
    2 AG, BH, CD
    3 FG, FH, ED

2. 1 clockwise
    2 decreasing

3. 1 135°   3 NE
    2 90°   4 SE
                   5 W

Page 26　　　　Exercise 2.5

1. 1 30°
    2 75°
    3 105°

2. 1 Turn through 180° (clockwise or
       anticlockwise).
       Forward 5 squares.
       Turn clockwise through 90° (or
       anticlockwise through 270°).
       Forward 1 square.
       Turn clockwise through 90°.
       Forward 2 squares.
       Turn clockwise through 90°.
       Forward 6 squares.
       Turn anticlockwise through 90°.
       Foward 3 squares.

2 Turn clockwise through 90°.
   Forward 5 squares.

4. $BC = 6\,cm, DC = 10\,cm, \angle C = 57°$

5. 1 General Store
    2 NE
    3 Post Office
    4 Inn
    5 90° clockwise

6. 1 d, alternate angles
    2 e, alternate angles
    3 180°, adjacent angles
    4 $a + b + c = 180°$

Page 28　　　　Practice test 2

2. $\angle ACD = 48°$

3. 1 $a = 42°, b = 138°$
    2 $c = d = 69°$

4. 1 $a = 72°$
    2 $b = 78°$
    3 $c = 102°$

5. 1 AB, AG, DC, DF, CE, EF
    2 AD, BC, GF

6. 1 SE
    2 NW
    3 N

Page 31　　　　Exercise 3.1

1. 1 Two hundred and thirty-six
    2 One thousand and seventy-nine
    3 Four hundred and forty-one thousand,
       three hundred and fifty-eight
    4 Ten thousand, two hundred and one
    5 Eight million, three hundred thousand

2. 1 265 384   4 30 000
    2 12 040   5 4 440 404
    3 1500

3. 1 200, 9901, 220, 4010, 1000
    2 298, 4998, 919, 7098, 9080

4. 1 1700, 66 275, 2013, 10 197, 4913
    2 1386, 9219, 181 274, 10 967, 370 000

5. 1 One hundred thousands, five hundreds,
       six tens (or sixty)
    2 Two millions, eight thousands

6. 1   50, 7690, 30, 1530, 100
    2   700, 9700, 300, 3800, 2000
    3   7000, 3000, 86 000, 12 000, 254 000

Page 34   Exercise 3.2

1. 1   21 008   4   4805
    2   2891   5   2477
    3   2920

2. 1   223   4   311
    2   445   5   1329
    3   4042

3. 1   84   4   105
    2   92   5   80
    3   82

4. 1   82   4   23
    2   59   5   39
    3   16

5. 36

6. 1   23   4   138
    2   82   5   786
    3   477

7. 1   20 137
    2   4840

8. 1   334 km
    2   66 km

Page 37   Exercise 3.3

1. 1   5000   5   12 300   8   1960
    2   92 000   6   10 600   9   1000
    3   6500   7   1700   10 20 000
    4   500

2. 1   600   5   800 000   8   140 000
    2   4000   6   240 000   9   300 000
    3   15 000   7   180 000   10 28 000
    4   4800

3. 1   138   5   3703   8   5635
    2   4010   6   6669   9   1090
    3   424   7   720   10 2220
    4   990

4. 1   36 180   5   21 438   8   10 545
    2   8683   6   14 256   9   72 197
    3   61 916   7   32 550   10 12 180
    4   9792

5. 1   17 600
    2   5224 m, 5200 m
    3   752

Page 42   Exercise 3.4

1. 1   700   5   57   8   179
    2   300   6   160   9   100
    3   6   7   10   10 18
    4   40

2. 1   3   5   300   8   400
    2   30   6   20   9   2
    3   100   7   30   10 250
    4   90

3. 1   19   5   75   8   118
    2   161   6   49   9   134
    3   61   7   83   10 78
    4   27

4. 1   100 r 5   5   26 r 2   8   125 r 3
    2   36 r 5   6   29 r 1   9   50 r 2
    3   13 r 7   7   60 r 4   10 91 r 4
    4   32 r 2

5. 1   38   5   9   8   13
    2   6   6   29   9   22
    3   31   7   17   10 34
    4   7

6. 1   52 r 4   4   15 r 10
    2   12 r 8   5   22 r 6
    3   12 r 33

7. £48

8. 45 days

9. 116 cartons, 8 left over

Page 43   Exercise 3.5

1. 1   Ten thousand, four hundred and seventy
    2   7635
    3   22 218
    4   22 000

2. 1089 (or sometimes 198)

3. 1   14 miles
    2   9 miles
    3   612 miles

4. £424

5. £2016, 224 tickets

6. £1577, £25

7. 368

Page 45   Practice test 3

1. 13 090

2. 598

3.   **1**   3490
    2   3500
    3   3000

4.   6 (kg)

5.   **1**   62 782
    2   10 948

6.   **1**   10 000   **4**   10
    2   35 000   **5**   162
    3   152

7.   40 min

8.   11 111

9.   15

10.   35 books, £10 over

Page 47   Exercise 4.1

1.   **1**   600 pence, $5a$ pence
    2   180 min, $120b$ min
    3   20 francs, $(c - d)$ francs
    4   110 pence, $(3e + 2f)$ pence
    5   15 pence, $(50 - gh)$ pence

2.   **1** $12k$ pence
    2 $\dfrac{m}{3}$ pence or $\frac{1}{3}m$ pence
    3 $180n$ seconds
    4 $\dfrac{x}{q}$ pence
    5 st seconds

3.   **1** $V = E - F + 2$
    2 $B = \dfrac{r}{w}$
    3 $T = 40c + 6n$
    4 $M = \dfrac{T - D}{12}$ or $M = \frac{1}{12}(T - D)$
    5 $t = \sqrt{\dfrac{d}{5}}$

Page 49   Exercise 4.2

1.   **1** $8a$ **5** c **8** $3g - 4h$
    2 $4b$ **6** 0 **9** $6j + 4k$
    3 $7c$ **7** $8c$ **10** m
    4 $5d$

2.   **1** $2a^2$ **5** $20e$ **8** $\dfrac{3j}{k}$
    2 b^3 **6** $3f^2$ **9** 5
    3 1 **7** $6gh$ **10** $5pq$
    4 $4d$

3.   **1** $2a + 6b$ **5** $18g - 15h$ **8** $5c + 7d$
    2 $15c - 5d$ **6** $3a + 3$ **9** $e + 24$
    3 $20e - 30$ **7** $7b + 2$ **10** $2f^2$
    4 $6f + 10$

Page 51   Exercise 4.3

1.   **1**   18   **5**   2   **8**   4
    2   10   **6**   36   **9**   16
    3   12   **7**   12   **10**   2
    4   12

2.   **1**   32   **5**   2   **8**   0
    2   25   **6**   18   **9**   2.5
    3   5   **7**   27   **10**   4
    4   24

3.   **1** $x = 23$ **4** $x = 0$
    2 $x = 34$ **5** $x = 5$
    3 $x = 50$

4.   **1**   210   **4**   150
    2   2.5   **5**   7
    3   880

5.   **1** $a = 900$ **4** $C = 10$
    2 $s = 6$ **5** $s = 300$
    3 $b = 10$

6.   35

Page 52   Exercise 4.4

1. $\dfrac{100p}{q}$ pence

2.   £85, £110, £135;
    $A = 60 + 25n$;
    Total amount £360

3.   **1** $2a$ **4**   1
    2   0   **5** a
    3 a^2

4.   **1** $3a$ **5** $9e$ **8** h
    2 $3b$ **6** $2f$ **9** $4j$
    3 $5c$ **7**   0   **10** k
    4 d

5.   **1** $16xy$ **5**   1   **8** x
    2 $4x^2$ **6** $6xy$ **9** $9x^2$
    3   2   **7** $24x^2$ **10**   0
    4 $27x$

6.   **1** $7x - 1$ **4** $20 - 4x$
    2 $3x + 2y$ **5** $15x + 2$
    3 $3x + 17$

7. **1** 6   **5** 52   **8**   24
    2 22   **6** 2   **9**   0.5
    3 1   **7** 6   **10** 22
    4 48

8. **1** $A = 770$ **4** $y = 30$
    2 $t = 360$ **5** $P = 5$
    3 $speed = 30$

9. 78

10. **1** £190
    2 £290

Page 53   Practice test 4

1. **1** $20(x - y)$ pence or $(20x - 20y)$ pence
    2 £8x
    3 1000x grams
    4 $x - 5$

2. 60 min, 100 min, 140 min;
    $T = 40c + 20$

3. **1** 12a **4** 5f
    2 b **5** $9g + 1$
    3 $2c - d$

4. **1** 12a **4** 4
    2 12bc **5** $5f^2$
    3 d

5. **1** $6a - 10$ **4** $e^2 + 2e$
    2 $18b + 15c$ **5** $3f - 12$
    3 $4d^2 + 4d$

6. **1** 19   **4** 1
    2 37   **5** 100
    3 30

7. £44

8. **1** $c = 14$ **4** $s = 56$
    2 $E = 300$ **5** $area = 84$
    3 $v = 50$

Page 58   Exercise 5.1

1. **1** 7.61   **4** 10.02
    2 7   **5** 7.86
    3 0.63

2. **1** 20.96   **4** 9.09
    2 6.95   **5** 4.88
    3 0.37

3. **1** 15.48   **4** 9.42
    2 0.6   **5** 9.6
    3 5.6

4. **1** 0.97   **4** 2.2
    2 0.007   **5** 5.9
    3 0.16

5. **1** 13.2   **4** 2.7
    2 250   **5** 310
    3 1030

6. **1** 0.379   **4** 0.0031
    2 0.0015   **5** 0.034
    3 0.0213

7. **1** 182   **4** 3.1
    2 180   **5** 1.4
    3 0.41

8. 1

9. 148 cm (1.48 m)

10. 8.8 g

Page 60   Exercise 5.2

1. 0.7, 0.75, 0.778, 0.8, 0.81

2. 60.9, 62.49, 62.5, 63.7, 63.72

3. **1** 57   **4** 207
    2 83   **5** 1000
    3 253

4. **1** 29.71   **4** 4.68
    2 1.63   **5** 0.04
    3 202.92

5. **1** 2.9   **5** 6.6   **8** 2.8
    2 1.9   **6** 5.3   **9** 3.4
    3 1.6   **7** 0.2   **10** 13.0
    4 36.1

Page 63   Exercise 5.3

1. **1** £10.20
    2 £9.80

2. **1** £4227
    2 £773

3. £50

4. 4p

5. 91p

6. £2.65

7. £735

8. £35.71

Page 63   **Exercise 5.4**

1.   264.9 g, 666.9 g

2.   **1** 16.2 m
     2 16 m

3.   **1** 0.365
     2 0.4

4.   **1** 62.9 mm
     2 63.1 mm
     3 11.1 mm more
     4 37.8 hours, 13.9 hours less

5.   1.5 m

6.   0.06 mm

7.   6.25 g, 125 g

8.   **1** 74p
     3 84p
     4 51p

9.   **1** £2.72
     2 £2.22

Page 66   **Practice test 5**

1.   **1** 13.8   **5** 2030   **8** 8, 7
     2 13.6   **6** 910   **9** 30
     3 316.2   **7** 0.31   **10** 0.9
     4 32.7

2.   **1** 0.059, 0.06, 0.59, 0.6, 0.66
     2 24.59, 24.95, 25.0, 25.19, 25.9

3.   **1** 379   **4** 105.93
     2 20   **5** 18.60
     3 27.4

4.   2.8

5.   **1** 100   **4** £30
     2 16p   **5** £3.96
     3 10p

6.   £3.34

7.   24p

Page 70   **Exercise 6.1**

1.   **1** 13   **5** 410   **8** 600
     2 0.2   **6** 1200   **9** 6
     3 35   **7** 0.5   **10** 200
     4 10

2.   **1** 13.3   **5** 420.36   **8** 640
     2 0.189   **6** 1016.4   **9** 6.6
     3 40   **7** 0.55   **10** 210
     4 10.46

3.   **1** 3.248   **4** 35.38
     2 88.8   **5** 416.7
     3 2.3

5.   **1** 11.0
     2 16.7
     3 0.7

6.   **1** 30 r 11   **4** 285 r 5
     2 35 r 22   **5** 6 r 40
     3 78 r 10

7.   **1** 15   **5** 75   **8** 44
     2 42   **6** 14   **9** 65
     3 33   **7** 21   **10** 101
     4 16

8.   10 each, 9 over

9.   383

10. 4.95 kg

11. 65 cm^3

Page 72

1.   4.35   4.   222

2.   43.75   5.   56.04

3.   26.5

Page 74   **Exercise 6.2**

1.   **1** 35
     2 42
     3 73

2.   **1** 7.5   **5** 6   **8** 8
     2 12   **6** 51   **9** 18
     3 27   **7** 7   **10** 2
     4 54

3.   **1** 2   **4** 4
     2 300   **5** 10
     3 4

4.   **1** 1.89   **4** 4.75
     2 324.89   **5** 9.5
     3 3.84

5.   **1** 169, 841, 973.44
     2 512, 9261, 970 299

6.   **1** 143 000 000
     2 2 601 000 000
     3 12 801 000 000

Page 76   Exercise 6.3

1. £7.77

2. £12

3. £17.79

4. £51.80

5. £224

6. 60

7. 40

8. 78

9. 38 stamps, 12p change

10. £5.62, 16p over

11. £134.17

Page 79   Exercise 6.4

1. 27, 34

2. 32, 38

3. 18

4. 23, 25, 27

5. 12, 16

6. 26

Page 80   Exercise 6.5

1.
1	80.6	5	21	8	9
2	1.7	6	770	9	3.6
3	18	7	0.8	10	10
4	3.6				

2.
1	7.61	4	32.718
2	9.082	5	38 562.5
3	37.2		

3.
1	200 000
2	150 000 000

4.
1	£5.65
2	£41.70
3	£78.20

5.
1	£150
2	£149.97

6.
1	£5.64	3	£90
2	£67.68	4	£118.80

7. 1185 units, cost £78.21, total £94.72

Page 83   Practice test 6

1.
1	36.736	4	6.3
2	2.9	5	501.76
3	39.69		

2.
1	8	4	39
2	0.6	5	35
3	9.08		

3. 33

4. £55.80

5. 8p

6. 42 pens, 30p change

7.
1	186 000
2	510 000 000

8. 34, 39

Page 84   Exercise A1

1. 4 053 00

2. 42, 49

3. $(100 - x)$ pence

4. 30

5. 7500

6. £2.50

7. 2, 12

8. £4.95

9. 110°

10. $12x^2$

11. 29

12. 1200

13. 0.2

14. 12 packets, 4p

15. 77

16. Penzance, 452 km

17. 60° (or near)

18. £15.25

19. £240.88

20. £25.71

Page 85   Exercise A2

1.
1	1506
2	Three thousand and ninety-one miles

2.
1	891, 1161
2	800, 900
3	800

3.
1	135°
2	West
3	South–East

4.
1	563	4	10
2	323	5	7
3	3728		

5.
1	5, 8, 9, 10, 2
2	4, 3, 1, 5, 2

6. **1** 12 **4** 9
    2 59 **5** 5
    3 0

7. Missing numbers in order in columns:
    31, 24, 127, 22, 27, 27, 106, 103, 529
    1 Thursday
    2 £114.30

8. 10.09, 10.9, 10.91, 10.99, 11.19

9. **1** £187.20
    2 50 hours

10. $\angle DAB = 53°$

Page 87   Exercise A3

1. **1** 690 **4** 64 000
    2 530 **5** 26 000
    3 270 **6** 10 000

2. **1** 28 **4** 70
    2 27 **5** 24
    3 50

3. **1** $11a$ **4** $4d$
    2 b **5** 5
    3 $12c^2$

4. **1** $c = 94°, d = 35°, e = 145°$
    2 $a = d = 45°, e = 135°$

5. £648.85

6. **1** fp pence **4** $(x - 2)$ years
    2 $\frac{y}{x}$ pence **5** £$(12x + 52y)$
    3 $12 - x$

7. **1** 32 **4** 14
    2 150 **5** 5
    3 2

8. 43

9. **1** AB, BC, AC, DE, EF, DF
    2 AD, BE, CF

10. **1** 853 **5** 315 **8** 891
    2 26 **6** 334 **9** 20
    3 3147 **7** 22 **10** 52
    4 69 984

Page 97   Exercise 7.1

1. **1** 34, 40, 46. Add 6 each time.
    2 18, 21, 24. Add 3.
    3 160, 320, 640. Double each time.
    4 729, 2187, 6561. Multiply by 3.
    5 17, 14, 11. Subtract 3.
    6 18, 24, 31. Add 1 more each time.
    7 $\frac{1}{81}, \frac{1}{243}, \frac{1}{729}$. Divide by 3.
    8 127, 255, 511. Adding 4, 8, 16, ... (doubling)
    9 158, 318, 638. Adding 5, 10, 20, ... (doubling)
    10 720, 5040, 40 320. Multiplying by 2, 3, 4, ...

2. **1** 12, 16, 20, 24, 28
    2 12, 10, 8, 6, 4
    3 12, 60, 300, 1500, 7500
    4 12, 6, 3, 1.5, 0.75
    5 12, 13, 15, 18, 22

3. **1** 9, 14, 23 **4** 5, 9, 14
    2 18, 28, 46 **5** 11, 18, 29
    3 2, 3, 5

4. Lines 1, 3, 6, 10, 15, 21, 28, 36, 45

6. The sum is a square number.

Page 99   Exercise 7.2

2. $85^2 = 7225$

5. $1 + 3 + 5 = 9$;
    20th row total is 400.

Page 101   Exercise 7.3

1. **1** 19 **4** $5\frac{1}{2}$
    2 56 **5** 42
    3 55

2. **1** 44 **4** 58
    2 1 **5** 7
    3 102

3. **1** 19, 23; $4n - 1$
    2 12, 11; $17 - n$
    3 22, 25; $3n + 7$
    4 66, 61; $91 - 5n$
    5 38, 44; $6n + 8$

4. **1** 2, 5, 8, 11 **4** 14, 13, 12, 11
    2 90, 80, 70, 60 **5** $3\frac{1}{2}, 4, 4\frac{1}{2}, 5$
    3 13, 21, 29, 37

Page 102   **Exercise 7.4**

1. **1** 16, 25, 36; n^2
    2 12, 15, 18; $3n$
    3 13, 16, 19; $3n + 1$
    4 28, 34, 40; $6n + 4$

3. **1** 10, 6, 12, 8, 16, 12, 24, 20
    2 First time multiply by 3, next time subtract 5
    3 43, 129
    4 2

6. **1** 41, 55, 71   **4** 44, 58, 74
    2 37, 47, 58   **5** 80, 110, 145
    3 43, 60, 80

Page 105   **Practice test 7**

1. **1** 26, 37   **6** $\frac{1}{15}$, $\frac{1}{18}$
    2 18, 9   **7** 9, 0
    3 16, 20   **8** 14, 17
    4 1, $\frac{1}{3}$ **9** 10 000, 100 000
    5 19, 23   **10** 64, 55

4. **1** 43, 51, 59; $8n + 3$
    2 20, 24, 28; $4n$
    3 9, 5, 1; $29 - 4n$
    4 24, 30, 36; $6n - 6$
    5 26, 21, 16; $51 - 5n$

Page 108   **Exercise 8.1**

1. **1** 2.38 kg   **5** 260 cm   **8** 5.12 m
    2 0.2 m   **6** 3100 g   **9** 32 ℓ
    3 5000 ml   **7** 2.8 cm   **10** 250 g
    4 120 mm

2. **1** 17
    2 24 (cm)

3. 2.5 kg

4. 7

5. **1** 6 g
    2 0.14 mm

6. 920 mm

7. £15

8. 250 g for £1.25

9. 50

10. £13.50

Page 111   **Exercise 8.2**

1. **1** metres   **6** tonnes
    2 grams   **7** litres
    3 litres   **8** grams
    4 metres   **9** km
    5 metres and cm   **10** cm and mm

2. **1** to the nearest cm
    2 to the nearest kg

3. **1** 8.7 m   **5** 156.9 cm   **8** 5.44 kg
    2 280 g   **6** 4.1 ℓ **9** 2500 ℓ
    3 4200 ℓ **7** 5.0 ℓ **10** 47.0 s
    4 6 m

4. **1** 10.64 kg
    2 1.25 kg
    3 4 ml

5. **2** $AB = 4.9$ cm
       $CD = 9.7$ cm
       $EF = 4.0$ cm
       $GH = 12.0$ cm

Page 115   **Exercise 8.3**

1. 04.05, 14.00, 15.15, 18.05, 23.55;
    1.10 am, 5.18 am, 10.30 am, 5.05 pm, 9.50 pm

2. **1** 4 h 10 min
    2 6 h 40 min
    3 1 h 15 min

3. 4.05 pm

4. **1** 3.40 pm
    2 15.40

5. 40 min

6. £37.80

7. to the nearest 5 min

8. 5 h 10 min, 01.20 (1.20 am)

Page 118   **Exercise 8.4**

1. 10 inches

2. 864

3. **1** 15 cm   **4** 2 tonnes
    2 1.8 kg, 2 kg   **5** 16 km
    3 45 ℓ

4. **1** 10 feet   **4** $7\frac{1}{2}$ inches
    2 10 lb, 11 lb   **5** 6 tons
    3 7 pints, 1 gallon

5.   **1**   7 cm
     2 $1\frac{1}{2}$ inches

6.   40 000 km

7.   5 balls

Page 119   Exercise 8.5

1.   **1**   50   **5**   4000   **8**   52
     2   3000   **6**   2000   **9**   30
     3   50   **7**   150   **10**   1000
     4   365

2.   **1**   3 kg
     2   1.1 kg

3.   4

4.   **1**   1.8
     2 $3\frac{1}{2}$ kg, 35 kg
     3   £30

5.   **1**   45p   **3**   5p
     2   15p   **4**   £4.15

6.   **1**   46°F, 8°C
     2   95°F
     3   20°C

7.   6 (gall)

8.   **1**   Dover and Exeter
     2   124 km
     3   77 miles

9.   **1**   1 h 35 min
     2   4 h 55 min

10. **1**   16.16 (4.16 pm), 25 min
     2   16.08 (4.08 pm), 36 min

Page 122   Practice test 8

1.   **1**   750 g   **6**   1.52 kg
     2   12.6 cm   **7**   70 cl
     3   260 cm   **8**   78 mm
     4   0.4 ℓ   **9**   120 cm
     5   1.6 m   **10**   3.04 tonnes

2.   **1**   1 kg
     2   4 min
     3   30 m

3.   11.4 cm

4.   **1**   8.7 kg
     2   650 ml
     3   3.1 cm

5.   **1**   5 lb (5.5 lb)
     2   3 m
     3   9 ℓ
     4   15 miles

6.   4 h 43 min

Page 125   Example 2

40, 37

Page 126   Exercise 9.1

1.   Totals 44 to 50 are:
     1, 6, 8, 10, 12, 20, 3

2.   Columns in order:
     30, 12, 18, 60; 35, 19, 14, 68; 65, 31, 32, 128;
     fraction $\frac{1}{4}$

Page 130   Exercise 9.3

4.   Totals by home teams in order:
     7, 16, 12, 4, 1, 2;
     totals by away teams in order:
     14, 10, 13, 3, 2;
     total number of goals by home teams, 66;
     total number of goals by away teams, 53.

Page 133   Practice test 9

1.   **1**   Totals in order 1 to 6:
             5, 18, 13, 4, 1, 2; total 43

4.   Totals (daily):
     187, 305, 463, 600, 842;
     Adults 908, children 1489, total 2397.
     1   1489
     2   Sunday
     3   13
     4   2397

Page 136   Exercise 10.1

1.   **1** $\frac{2}{5}$ **4** $\frac{1}{4}$
     2 $\frac{1}{6}$ **5** $\frac{1}{3}$
     3 $\frac{2}{3}$

2.   **1**   44, 9, 4, 7, 30, 12, 21, 26, 45, 48
     2   6, 33, 20, 8, 15, 9, 1, 7, 13, 25
     3   2, 7, 20, 25, 13, 11, 1, 6, 40, 9
     4   12, 4, 9, 2, 20, 3, 7, 15, 11, 40
     5   4, 10, 16, 6, 20, 40, 22, 60, 50, 12

3. **1** $\frac{2}{3}$ **5** $\frac{3}{10}$ **8** $\frac{3}{8}$
    2 $\frac{5}{6}$ **6** $\frac{2}{5}$ **9** $\frac{4}{9}$
    3 $\frac{1}{6}$ **7** $\frac{5}{8}$ **10** $\frac{3}{4}$
    4 $\frac{3}{10}$

4. **1** $\frac{14}{18}$ **4** $\frac{21}{24}$
    2 $\frac{12}{20}$ **5** $\frac{6}{20}$
    3 $\frac{15}{18}$

5. **1** $\frac{7}{4}$ **5** $\frac{23}{8}$ **8** $\frac{15}{2}$
    2 $\frac{7}{3}$ **6** $\frac{22}{5}$ **9** $\frac{10}{3}$
    3 $\frac{37}{10}$ **7** $\frac{9}{8}$ **10** $\frac{23}{10}$
    4 $\frac{11}{6}$

6. **1** $4\frac{3}{5}$ **5** $2\frac{3}{4}$ **8** $4\frac{1}{4}$
    2 $2\frac{5}{6}$ **6** $6\frac{2}{3}$ **9** $8\frac{1}{3}$
    3 $3\frac{1}{10}$ **7** $2\frac{3}{5}$ **10** $3\frac{1}{4}$
    4 $2\frac{5}{8}$

Page 140   Exercise 10.2

1. **1** $\frac{1}{3}$ **5** $\frac{3}{5}$ **8** $\frac{1}{9}$
    2 $\frac{2}{9}$ **6** $\frac{2}{3}$ **9** $\frac{2}{5}$
    3 $\frac{1}{10}$ **7** $\frac{1}{4}$ **10** $\frac{1}{3}$
    4 $\frac{3}{4}$

2. **1** £2.70   **5** 15 cm   **8** 40 g
    2 8 inches   **6** 15°   **9** 50 cm
    3 60p   **7** 6 ℓ   **10** 700 g
    4 1 hour

3. **1** 0.75   **4** 0.37
    2 0.4   **5** 0.875
    3 0.7

4. **1** $\frac{3}{5}$ **4** $\frac{1}{8}$
    2 $\frac{1}{4}$ **5** $\frac{2}{25}$
    3 $\frac{3}{20}$

5. $\frac{1}{6}$

6. 150

Page 141   Exercise 10.3

1. **1** $\frac{5}{8}$ **4** $5\frac{1}{4}$
    2 $\frac{11}{16}$ **5** $6\frac{3}{16}$
    3 $6\frac{3}{4}$

2. **1** $\frac{3}{8}$ **4** $2\frac{1}{8}$
    2 $\frac{7}{16}$ **5** $2\frac{3}{8}$
    3 $1\frac{5}{8}$

3. $\frac{5}{8}$

4. **1** $\frac{7}{8}$ **2** $\frac{1}{8}$

5. $8\frac{3}{4}$ feet

Page 142   Exercise 10.4

1. Mr B, $\frac{5}{12}$; Mr A won; 400 votes extra

2. 32

3. $\frac{1}{20}$ second

4. 27

5. $\frac{2}{5}$

6. 180 (litres)

7. £180.60, 45 hours

8. $5\frac{1}{2}$ inches

9. $9\frac{3}{8}$ inches

10. $13\frac{5}{8}$ inches by $9\frac{1}{2}$ inches

11. **1** 15 miles
    2 $\frac{5}{24}$

Page 145   Practice test 10

1. **1** $\frac{5}{8}$ **3** $\frac{19}{5}$
    2 $\frac{18}{24}$ **4** $5\frac{1}{5}$

2. **1** 0.8   **4** 0.06
    2 0.75   **5** 0.15
    3 0.7

3. **1** $\frac{3}{5}$ **4** $\frac{1}{4}$
    2 $\frac{3}{100}$ **5** $\frac{4}{25}$
    3 $\frac{1}{1000}$

4. **1** $\frac{3}{8}$
    2 £1.50

5. 48

6. 60 cows, $\frac{1}{4}$

7. £147

Page 148   Exercise 11.1

1. **1** $\angle A = 81°$, $\angle B = 55°$, $\angle C = 44°$
    2 $\angle A = 116°$, $\angle B = 37°$, $\angle C = 27°$

2.   **1** $\angle A = 24°$, $\angle B = \angle C = 78°$
    2 $\angle A = \angle C = 18°$, $\angle B = 144°$

3.   **1** $72°$ **4** $30°$
    2 $48°$ **5** $118°$
    3 $24°$

4.   **1** $14°$, obtuse-angled
    2 $72°$, acute-angled, isosceles
    3 $90°$, right-angled
    4 $60°$, acute-angled, equilateral
    5 $120°$, obtuse-angled

5.   **1** $a = 141°$ **3** $c = 28°$
    2 $b = 50°$ **4** $d = 36°$

6.   **1** $a = 30°$ **3** $c = 60°$
    2 $b = 38°$ **4** $d = 35°$

7. $\angle ACB = 48°$, $\angle DCB = 70°$

8. $a = 68°$, $b = 90°$,
    right-angled triangle

Page 153   Exercise 11.2

1. $BC = 7.6\,\text{cm}$, $\angle B = 34°$, $\angle C = 88°$

2. $AB = 4.8\,\text{cm}$, $AC = 6.4\,\text{cm}$, $\angle A = 76°$

3. $\angle A = 48°$, $\angle B = 39°$, $\angle C = 93°$

4. $AC = 11.3\,\text{cm}$, $\angle A = 34°$, $\angle C = 18°$

5. $AC = 5.1\,\text{cm}$, $BC = 9.0\,\text{cm}$, $\angle C = 56°$

Page 153   Exercise 11.3

1. B; angles add up to $180°$

2. $a = b = 60°$, $c = 30°$

3. $a = b = 45°$

4. $f = g = 38°$

5. $\angle ABC = \angle BCA = 68°$, $\angle ACD = 46°$,
    $\angle CDB = 90°$, $\angle BCD = 22°$

6.   **1** $a = b = 50°$, $c = d = 40°$
    2 $e = f = g = 20°$
    3 $h = j = 75°$, $k = 30°$
    4 $m = p = 40°$, $n = 100°$, $q = r = 70°$

7.   **1** $\angle ABC = 70°$
    2 $\angle IBC = 35°$
    3 $\angle BIC = 110°$

8. $AC = 10.4\,\text{cm}$, $BC = 7.0\,\text{cm}$, $\angle C = 23°$;
    $BE = CE = 3.5\,\text{cm}$

9. $EF = 6.2\,\text{cm}$, $\angle E = 42°$, $\angle F = 90°$

Page 156   Practice test 11

1. $a = 34°$, $b = 53°$, $c = 37°$

2. $j = k = 60°$, equilateral triangle

3. $p = 47°$, $q = 56°$, $r = 77°$

4.   **1** $\angle ACD = 32°$ **3** $\angle DBC = 64°$
    2 $\angle CDB = 64°$ **4** $\angle BCD = 52°$

5. $PR = 9.3\,\text{cm}$, $\angle P = 45°$, $\angle R = 70°$,
    $ST = 3.6\,\text{cm}$

Page 161   Exercise 12.1

1.   **1** 9   **4** 40.7
    2 44   **5** 1.9
    3 8

2.   **1** 8   **4** 35
    2 39   **5** 1.95
    3 7

3.   **1** 9
    2 28
    3 4.5

4.   **1** 12
    2 27
    3 5

5.   **1** 64.4   **4** 2.5 cm
    2 £917.40   **5** 2.9 kg
    3 121 min

6.   **1** mean 57 kg, median 55 kg
    2 12 y 1 m
    3 164 g

7. $22°C$

8.   **1** 13   **4** 76
    2 73   **5** 0.7
    3 12

9.   **1** 57.4   **4** 2.5 cm
    2 £122   **5** 2.1 kg
    3 117 min

Page 162   Exercise 12.2

1.   **1** 8
    2 5

2.   **1** 73.7 kg
    2 76.3 kg

3.   **1** mean 8.3 miles, median 4 miles
    3 mean 5.8 miles, median 4 miles
    5 29 miles
    6 16 miles

4. **1** mean 4.3 h, median 4.5 h
    2 6.2 h

5. **1** mean 110 g, median 108 g
    2 29 g
    3 mean 121 g, median 119.5 g
    4 28 g

Page 163   Practice test 12

1. **1** mean 11, median 10, mode 9, range 8
    2 mean £20, median £20.50, mode £21, range £8

2. **1** 72 min
    2 75 min
    3 20 min

3. **1** 411
    2 340
    3 449

4. **1** 54 miles
    2 38 miles
    3 156 miles

5. **1** mean 4.9, median 5, mode 5
    2 mean 5.6, median 6, mode 6
    3 group A 6, group B 4
    4 group B
    5 group A

Page 166   Exercise B1

1. 17 min
2. $\frac{1}{3}$
3. 22 km
4. 6
5. 10 or 11
6. 9
7. £16
8. $5x$
9. 8 kg
10. West
11. $1000\,k$ (g)
12. 6.12 pm
13. $27\,\ell$
14. 35p
15. 6 kg
16. 8 cm (or near)
17. 2 h 10 min
18. 27°C
19. 110° (or near)
20. £1.20

Page 167   Exercise B2

1. **1** 100   **5** 1000
    2 1000   **6** 100
    3 60   **7** 1000
    4 1000   **8** 60

2. **1** $\frac{29}{6}$ **4** $3\frac{7}{10}$
    2 $\frac{77}{10}$ **5** $3\frac{1}{8}$
    3 $\frac{100}{11}$ **6** $6\frac{1}{9}$

3. **1** 20 (ℓ)
    2 £9.44
    3 £2.40

4. $m = p = 40°, n = 100°, q = r = 70°$

5. **1** 47   **4** 34, 51
    2 15, 51   **5** 27, 15
    3 47, 57

6. 9 amps

7. 171 m

8. mean 52 g, range 11 g

10. **1** 1 h 25 min
    2 10 min
    3 4 h 35 min

Page 169   Exercise B3

1. **1** $\frac{3}{11}$ **4** $\frac{2}{3}$
    2 $\frac{5}{7}$ **5** $\frac{3}{8}$
    3 $\frac{1}{4}$ **6** $\frac{1}{10}$

2. 39°

3. 90 kg

4. mean 8, median 7, mode 2

5. £5.90, £14.10 change

6. **1** 41, 48   **4** 29, 40
    2 41, 45   **5** 2, 1
    3 12 500, 62 500

7. **1** A 6.2 kg, B 3.8 kg
    2 2.4 kg
    3 10 kg

8. $a = 60°, b = 40°, d = 80°$

9. **1** £9
    2 8

Page 180   Exercise 13.1

1. **1** $\frac{3}{10}$ **4** $\frac{2}{5}$
    2 $\frac{7}{20}$ **5** $\frac{3}{5}$
    3 $\frac{3}{20}$

2. **1** 0.47   **4** 0.06
    2 0.95   **5** 0.99
    3 0.22

3. **1** 75%   **4** 70%
    2 80%   **5** 87%
    3 15%

4. 1 £3.60   4 £2.40
   2 60p   5 13p
   3 63p

5. 1 96   4 5 cm
   2 120 g   5 31 ℓ
   3 2 min

6. 1 72%   4 $37\frac{1}{2}$ %
   2 8%   5 $66\frac{2}{3}$ %
   3 60%

7. 1 10%
   2 75 learn French, 60 learn German, 15 learn Spanish
   3 7 classes

Page 182   Exercise 13.2

1. 1 £6.24   4 £60
   2 £2.99   5 £336
   3 £108

2. 1 £5.40   4 £528
   2 £3   5 £2
   3 £896

3. 1 20%   4 20%
   2 $16\frac{2}{3}$ %   5 12%
   3 $22\frac{1}{2}$ %

4. 1 £1680   4 £9720
   2 £3.24   5 £16.50
   3 330 ml

Page 185   Exercise 13.3

1. 1 £63, £423   4 £13.65, £91.65
   2 £5.60, £37.60   5 £155.75, £1045.75
   3 £21.70, £145.70

2. £28.20

3. 1 A
   2 C

4. 1 £180
   2 £60
   3 £16.80

5. 1 £60
   2 £264
   3 £168

Page 185   Exercise 13.4

1. £270 deducted, £180 paid

2. 12%

3. £90, £98.10, £188.10

4. 1 £1120   3 £448
   2 £4480   4 £4032

5. £49 896 (£49 900)

6. 1 22.4% variable
   2 10 years
   3 £7779.20
   4 £5.44 extra, £5304

7. £72.40, £12.67, £85.07

Page 187   Practice test 13

1. 1 50%, 25%, 20%, 10%, 5%, 1%
   2 $\frac{3}{10}$, $\frac{1}{3}$, $\frac{2}{5}$, $\frac{2}{3}$, $\frac{3}{4}$

2. 36%

3. 1 40%
   2 C
   3 16 000

4. 1 £400
   2 £7600

5. 60%

6. £16

Page 197   Practice test 14

1. 1 D   4 C
   2 B   5 A
   3 E

2. 1 $\frac{6}{25}$ (0.24)
   2 $\frac{121}{400}$ (0.30)
   3 $\frac{29}{50}$ (0.58)

Page 200   Exercise 15.1

1. 1 $\angle A = 110°$, $\angle B = 97°$, $\angle C = 63°$, $\angle D = 90°$
   2 $\angle E = \angle G = 88°$, $\angle F = 69°$, $\angle H = 115°$
   3 $\angle J = \angle L = 106°$, $\angle K = \angle M = 74°$
   4 $\angle P = \angle Q = 108°$, $\angle R = \angle S = 72°$

2. 112°

3. 85°

4. 1 $a = 57°$, $b = 108°$, $c = 133°$
   2 $d = 95°$, $e = 85°$, $f = 105°$

5. 74°, 87°

6. $a = c = 115°$, $b = 65°$

7. $a = 60°$, $b = 30°$

8. 110°

9. $a = b = 52°$, $c = 104°$, $d = 49°$, $e = 79°$

10. **1** parallelogram, rectangle
    2 kite
    3 rhombus, square

Page 202   Exercise 15.2

5. $AC = 6.9$ cm, $\angle ADC = 51°$, kite

Page 205   Exercise 15.3

1. Columns in order:
    1 yes, yes, yes, yes
    2 no, no, yes, yes
    3 no, yes, no, yes

2. **1** right-angled triangle
    2 right-angled isosceles triangle
    3 isosceles triangle

3. angle $= 50°$

4. $AC = BD = 7.1$ cm, angles at $X = 90°$

5. $a = 38°$, $b = 76°$

6. $d = e = 45°$, $f = 90°$

Page 206   Exercise 15.4

2. AD and DE both equal DC,
    $a = 90°$, $b = 56°$, $c = e = 17°$, $d = 107°$

3. **1** $AB = CD = 4.2$ cm, $AD = BC = 7.5$ cm,
    parallelogram
    2 $AB = CD = 4.7$ cm, $AD = BC = 8.8$ cm,
    rectangle
    3 $AB = CD = AD = BC = 6.0$ cm,
    rhombus

Page 206   Practice test 15

1. $a = 76°$

2. $a = 79°$, $d = e = 72°$, $c = 36°$

3. **1** parallelogram   **4** trapezium
    2 kite   **5** rectangle
    3 square

4. **1** $\angle XCB = \angle XAD = \angle XDA$
    2 $\triangle AXD$ is isosceles (equal base angles)

5. $AE = EC = 7.8$ cm, $\angle AEB = 90°$

Page 209   Exercise 16.1

1. | | | | | | |
    |---|---|---|---|---|---|
    | **1** | $+1°$ | **5** | $-2°$ | **8** | $-3°$ |
    | **2** | $-7°$ | **6** | $-5°$ | **9** | $-1°$ |
    | **3** | $+9°$ | **7** | $-7°$ | **10** | $+6°$ |
    | **4** | $0°$ | | | | |

2. | | | | | | |
    |---|---|---|---|---|---|
    | **1** | risen 3° | **5** | fallen 6° | **8** | risen 3° |
    | **2** | fallen 9° | **6** | fallen 27° | **9** | fallen 4° |
    | **3** | risen 6° | **7** | risen 10° | **10** | fallen 3° |
    | **4** | risen 2° | | | | |

3. **1** 7 min past 1
    2 12 min to 2
    3 6 min to 3

4. **1** 17 min
    2 20 min
    3 15 min

5. **1** $-2, -1, 4$ **4** $-3, 1\frac{1}{2}, 1\frac{3}{4}$
    2 $-4, 0, 3$ **5** $-4\frac{1}{2}, -3\frac{1}{2}, 4$
    3 $-5, -1, 4$

Page 211   Exercise 16.2

1. | | | | | | |
    |---|---|---|---|---|---|
    | **1** | 7 | **8** | 10 | **15** | -4 |
    | **2** | 3 | **9** | -9 | **16** | -8 |
    | **3** | -1 | **10** | 3 | **17** | -3 |
    | **4** | -6 | **11** | 0 | **18** | -4 |
    | **5** | 0 | **12** | 1 | **19** | 0 |
    | **6** | -8 | **13** | 11 | **20** | 1 |
    | **7** | -3 | **14** | 2 | | |

2. | | | | | | |
    |---|---|---|---|---|---|
    | **1** | -1 | **5** | 2 | **9** | -3 |
    | **2** | -7 | **6** | -3 | **10** | 1 |
    | **3** | -6 | **7** | -5 | **11** | 0 |
    | **4** | 0 | **8** | 7 | **12** | -9 |

Page 212   Example 1

$ABCD$ is a rectangle

Page 213   Example 2

$ABCD$ is a parallelogram

Page 213   Exercise 16.3

1. parallelogram

2. 1 parallelogram
    2 (7, 2)
    3 $y = x + 2$
    4 (2, 4)

3. 1 trapezium
    2 (−5, 7)
    3 rhombus

Page 214   Exercise 16.4

1. 1 +6   5 +3   8 −3
    2 +3   6 −3   9 2
    3 −2   7 2   10 0
    4 −4

2. 1 £150   3 £70
    2 £260   4 £30

3. 1 0   4 −1
    2 4   5 3
    3 −12

4. A and E, B and F, C and D

5. D (−2, 0), parallelogram

6. (1) 1 −16   5 3   9 −9
         2 24   6 0   10 64
         3 −35   7 0   11 −2
         4 −10   8 2   12 −1

    (2) 1 −2   5 −1   9 8
         2 −3   6 −6   10 6
         3 −3   7 −7   11 −2
         4 9   8 −1   12 0

    (3) 1 −5   5 −1   8 −1
         2 25   6 0   9 $-\frac{1}{2}$
         3 0   7 −6   10 9
         4 1

7. (1) 1 −2   4 2
         2 0   5 −10
         3 0

    (2) 1 $v = 90$
         2 $K = 64$
         3 $F = -40$

Page 217   Practice test 16

1. 1 −7°   4 −8°
    2 13 deg 5 −5°
    3 15 deg

2. 1 −2   5 0   8 −8
    2 −8   6 −20   9 −1
    3 2   7 −5   10 −2
    4 2

3. 1 3   4 5
    2 −6   5 0
    3 5

4. D (2, 3)

5. square

Page 220   Exercise 17.1

3. In reserve, 5p

4. Food, $\frac{3}{10}$

5. 1 £20

Page 222   Example

    1 week 9
    2 weeks 1 and 2

Page 222   Exercise 17.2

2. 1 Sunday 1st week, 1000
    2 Friday 2nd week, 5300
    3 Tuesday

Page 225   Exercise 17.3

1. 1 2
    2 15°
    3 angles in order: 135°, 120°, 75°, 30°

2. 1 7
    2 angles in order: 60°, 100°, 40°, 20°, 140°

3. 1 £5
    2 $\frac{1}{6}$
    3 angles in order: 144°, 48°, 84°, 24°, 60°

4. 1 £150
    2 Wages £22 500, food £18 000, fuel £6000, extras £7500

Page 229   Exercise 17.5

1. Food £15, transport £10, camp fee £7, extras £4

2. 1 P £30 000, Q £30 000

3. 1 A 17, B 6, C 25, D 12
    2 angles in order: 102°, 36°, 150°, 72°

Page 230   Practice test 17

1. Modal type: owner occupied

2. **1** $4°$
    2 angles in order: $224°, 44°, 36°, 56°$

3. **1** Monday 1st week
    2 3 deg C
    3 Thursday 1st week
    4 6 days

Page 233   Exercise 18.1

1. $x = 4$	9. $x = 9$	17. $x = 18$	
2. $x = 15$	10. $x = 15$	18. $x = 10$	
3. $x = 21$	11. $x = 0$	19. $x = 9$	
4. $x = 11$	12. $x = 15$	20. $x = 6$	
5. $x = 6$	13. $x = 0$	21. $l = 8$	
6. $x = 36$	14. $x = 9$	22. $x = 11$	
7. $x = 11$	15. $x = 19$	23. $d = 5$	
8. $x = 12$	16. $x = 12$	24. 27	

Page 234   Exercise 18.2

1. | | | |
    |---|---|---|
    | **1** $x = 4$ | **8** $x = 1$ | **15** $x = 0$ |
    | **2** $x = 2$ | **9** $x = 5$ | **16** $x = 3$ |
    | **3** $x = 2$ | **10** $x = 4$ | **17** $x = 5$ |
    | **4** $x = 24$ | **11** $x = 5$ | **18** $x = 4$ |
    | **5** $x = 7$ | **12** $x = 1$ | **19** $x = 2$ |
    | **6** $x = 3$ | **13** $x = 3$ | **20** $x = 3$ |
    | **7** $x = 3$ | **14** $x = 12$ | |

2. $3x + 8 = 7x - 8; x = 4$

3. **1** $3x - 40 = x + 30; x = 35$
    2 $3x + 10 = 5x - 30; x = 20$

Page 235   Exercise 18.3

1. **1** $x = 10$ **4** $x = 16$
    2 $x = 7$ **5** $x = 6$
    3 $x = 0$

2. **1** $x = 5$ **4** $x = 3$
    2 $x = 8$ **5** $x = 2$
    3 $x = 1$

3. $3(x + 7) = 36; x = 5$

4. Ruth has $£(x + 20)$;
    $x + (x + 20) = 44; x = 12$.
    Jane has £12, Ruth has £32.

Page 235   Exercise 18.4

1. $5x + 28 = 8x - 5; x = 11$.
    The number was 11.

2. Woman $3x$ years.
    In 9 years, daugher $(x + 9)$ years,
    woman $(3x + 9)$ years or $2(x + 9)$ years.
    $3x + 9 = 2(x + 9); x = 9$.
    Daughter is 9 years old, woman is 27 years old now.

3. $n + 2, n + 4, n + 6$;
    $n + (n + 2) + (n + 4) + (n + 6) = 48; n = 9$.
    Numbers are 9, 11, 13 and 15.

4. Barbara $(a + 40)$ pence,
    Chris $(a + 100)$ pence;
    $a + (a + 40) + (a + 100) = 500; a = 120$.
    Ann £1.20, Barbara £1.60, Chris £2.20.

5. **1** $(x + 25) + (x + 35) + 2x = 180; x = 30$.
        Largest angle $65°$.
    2 $(x + 10) + (2x - 40) = 4x - 80; x = 50$.
        Angles are $60°, 60°$ and $60°$, the triangle is equilateral.
    3 $7x + 3x + 90 = 180; x = 9$.

6. **1** $8x + 7x = 180; x = 12$.
    2 $6y + 5y + 96 = 360; y = 24$.
    3 $3z + 2z + 120 = 180; z = 12$.

7. | | | |
    |---|---|---|
    | **1** $x = \frac{1}{2}$ | **5** $x = 2\frac{1}{2}$ | **8** $x = -3$ |
    | **2** $x = \frac{1}{4}$ | **6** $x = -7$ | **9** $x = -8$ |
    | **3** $x = \frac{1}{2}$ | **7** $x = -3$ | **10** $x = -1$ |
    | **4** $x = \frac{2}{5}$ | | |

Page 237   Practice test 18

1. **1** $a = 21$ **4** $d = 140$
    2 $b = 19$ **5** $e = 7$
    3 $c = 8$

2. **1** $x = 6$ **4** $x = 7$
    2 $x = 8$ **5** $x = 1\frac{1}{2}$
    3 $x = 4$

3. **1** The number is 6.
    2 The number is 8.

4. Other numbers are $n + 1, n + 2$;
    $n + (n + 1) + (n + 2) = 63; n = 20$.
    The numbers are 20, 21, 22.

5. $2x + 3 = 3x - 1; x = 4$;
    $24 - 3y = 12 + y; y = 3$;
    $AB = DC = 11$ cm;
    $BC = AD = 15$ cm.

Page 238   Exercise C1

1. $\frac{2}{3}$

2. £6000

3. 5

4. 91 cm

5. 60°

6. 5

7. 5.20 pm

8. 6.5 kg

9. 120°

10. 10

11. £12

12. 5

13. 0.7

14. 9

15. 36

16. £25

17. 30° (or near)

18. 5 cm (or near)

19. 1100

20. rhombus

Page 239   Exercise C2

1. 3200

2. 2

3. 99°

4. **1** 65p   **4** 30 min
    2 51 kg   **5** 350 ml
    3 48 cm

5. **1** Jan 10.7 cm
    2 Feb 2.7 cm
    3 April

6. 36, 35.6

7. **1** unlikely   **4** very unlikely
    2 very likely   **5** likely
    3 an even chance

8. **1** equilateral
    2 obtuse-angled isosceles
    3 right-angled

9. 1 h 30 min

10. men: 70, 200, 90, 12; total men 372;
    women: 105, 50, 45, 68; total women 268;
    totals: 175, 250, 135, 80;
    altogether 640 workers.

Page 241   Exercise C3

1. **1** 0.75
    2 0.15
    3 0.375

2. mean 54.2 m, median 55 m, range 4 m

3. **E**

4. **1** $a = 7$ **4** $d = 5$
    2 $b = 6$ **5** $e = 3$
    3 $c = 22\frac{1}{2}$

5. **1** 4 (feet)
    2 12 feet

6. 79p

7. **1** 116   **4** 720
    2 240   **5** 9
    3 7

8. $a = 56°, d = 68°$

9. 25%, 12.5%

10. 3rd month

Page 243   Exercise C4

1. **1** 5.63   **4** 0.10
    2 3.23   **5** 0.06
    3 37.28

2. **1** 6   **3** 8.5
    2 7.5   **4** 12

3. 12%

4. 850 kg

5. 61°

6. **1** £35.10
    2 £2.97

7. **1** 41, 51; $10n - 9$
    2 44, 40; $64 - 4n$
    3 31, 29; $41 - 2n$
    4 32, 35; $3n + 17$
    5 107, 116; $9n + 62$

8. 7

9. **1** £25
    2 59%
    3 angles 212°, 47°, 36°, 22°, 18°, 25°

10. 5.4 cm, trapezium

Page 251   Exercise 19.1

4. **1** 4   **3** 2
    2 1   **4** 3

Page 252   Exercise 19.2

5. **1** 3
    2 6
    3 7

Page 255   Exercise 19.3

1.   **3**   3

2.   **1** $\angle ADC$
     2 DX

3.   **1** AC, BD
     2 $32°$
     3 CE
     4 $\angle BEC, \angle CED, \angle DEA$
     5 $90°$

4.   **1** X
     2 $\angle BCD$
     3 $AX = XC, BX = XD$

5.   **1**   2   **3**   2
     2   2   **4**   4

Page 259   Exercise 19.4

1. $540°, 85°$

2. $720°, 147°$

3. $1080°, 135°$

4. $50°$

5. $\angle BCD = 108°, \angle BCP = 135°, a = 117°$

6.   both columns in order: 3, 4, 5, 6, 8

7.   **1** $120°$
     2 $a = b = c = 60°$
     3   equilateral
     4   rhombus

8.   **1** $45°$
     2 $135°$
     3 $a = 22\frac{1}{2}°$

Page 261   Exercise 19.5

1.   **1**   A, M, T, U, Y
     2   B, C
     3   H, I, X
     4   N, S, Z
     5   H, I, X

2. $T (6, 4), U (3, 5)$

3.   **1** $a = 30°$
     2 $b = 36°$
     3 $c = 28°, d = e = 62°$

5.   **1** $120°$
     2 $135°$

6.   **1** $120°$, hexagons
     2 $90°, 135°, 135°$, square and two octagons

7.   **1** $108°$
     2   isosceles obtuse-angled triangle
     3 $36°$
     4 $72°$
     5   isosceles trapezium
     6   rhombus

8.   (1) $AD = 9.7\,\text{cm}$
     (2) $AB = 5.9\,\text{cm}$

Page 264   Practice test 19

1.   **1**   E
     2   H
     3   S

2.   **1** DE
     2 $\angle CDE$

3.   axes of symmetry: **2**   1,   **3**   1,   **4**   4
     rotational symmetry: **1**   2,   **4**   4

4.   **1** $540°$ **3** $108°$
     2 $115°$ **4** $36°$

5.   **1** $45°$
     2   8

6.   **1**   isosceles trapezium
     2   rectangle
     3   isosceles obtuse-angled
     4   right-angled
     5   equilateral

Page 267   Exercise 20.1

1. y-values: 1, 4, 7, 10, 13

2. y-values: 1, 2, 5, 10, 17

3. y-values:
     1   3, 6, 9, 12, 15
     2   9, 8, 7, 6, 5
     3   5, 7, 9, 11, 13

4. y-values:
     1   0, 4, 8, 12, 16
     2   1, 6, 11, 16, 21
     3   12, 10, 8, 6, 4

5. $a = 10, b = 5$

6.   **1** $y = 4x + 4$ **4** $y = 2x + 2$
     2 $y = 7 - x$ **5** $y = x^2$
     3 $y = x + 4$

Page 270   **Exercise 20.2**

1.   *y*-values:
     1 1, 2, 3, 4, 5, 6
     2 −5, −3, −1, 1, 3, 5
     3 9, 8, 7, 6, 5, 4
     4 8, 6, 4, 2, 0, −2

2.   *y*-values:
     1 −4, −2, 0, 2, 4
     2 5, 4, 3, 2, 1
     3 9, 6, 3, 0, −3

3.   *y*-values:
     3 −4, −2, 0, 2, 4
     4 12, 9, 6, 3, 0, −3
     5 (2, 6)
     6 (−2, −2)

4.   *y*-values: −12, 0, 12, 24

Page 272   **Exercise 20.3**

1.   **1** *y*-values: 16, 9, 4, 1, 0, 1, 4, 9, 16

2.   **1** *y*-values: 19, 12, 7, 4, 3, 4, 7, 12, 19
     4 3
     5 −2.6 or 2.6

3.   **1** *y*-values: 14, 7, 2, −1, −2, −1, 2, 7, 14
     4 −1.4 or 1.4

Page 273   **Exercise 20.4**

1.   multiply by 2, subtract from 10

2.   **1** $y = 2x$
     2 D (5, 5)
     3 $x = 5$

3.   *y*-values:
     1 18, 14, 10, 6, 2, −2
     2 −14, −8, −2, 4, 10, 16
     4 $x = 2.4$

4.   **1** (5, 25), (6, 36), (7, 49)
     2 $y = x^2$
     5 20 (20.25)

5. $y = 40 - x$;
     $300x + 150y = 7500$;
     $y = 50 - 2x$; $x = 10$, $y = 30$.
     10 luxury houses, 30 standard houses.

Page 275   **Practice test 20**

1.   *y*-values: −1, 5, 11, 17, 23

2.   *y*-values:
     1 −9, −5, −1, 3, 7, 11, 15, 19
     2 16, 13, 10, 7, 4, 1, −2, −5
     5 $x = 1.6$

3.   **1** *y*-values: 4, −1, −4, −5, −4, −1, 4
     4 −5
     5 −2.2 or 2.2

Page 280   **Exercise 21.2**

1.   **1** cuboid
     2 cylinder
     3 triangular prism
     4 cone

3.   **1** cube, pyramid with square base
     2 cuboid, triangular prism, hexagonal
         prism
     3 cylinder, cone
     4 cylinder, cone, sphere
     5 cuboid, cube, triangular prism, hexagonal
         prism, triangular pyramid, pyramid with
         square base

4.   **B, C, E**

5.   **1** triangular prism
     2 pyramid with square base
     3 cuboid

6.   *E, G*

Page 282   **Exercise 21.3**

2.   7 faces, 10 vertices, 15 edges

4.   **A, C**

6.   For a cylinder, rectangle.

8.   **1** 3
     2 4
     3 4

Page 286   **Practice test 21**

1.   **1** sphere
     2 cuboid
     3 triangular prism
     4 cylinder
     5 cube

3.   pyramid with square base; *A* to *E*

4.   9 faces, 9 vertices, 16 edges

Page 290   **Exercise 22.1**

1. **1** $\frac{1}{6}$
    2 $\frac{1}{3}$

2. **1** $\frac{1}{4}$
    2 $\frac{11}{20}$
    3 $\frac{3}{10}$

3. **1** $\frac{1}{2}$
    2 $\frac{1}{6}$

4. $\frac{1}{8}$

5. **1** $\frac{1}{13}$
    2 $\frac{1}{4}$
    3 $\frac{5}{26}$

6. **1** $\frac{2}{11}$
    2 $\frac{4}{11}$
    3 $\frac{3}{11}$

7. **1** $\frac{6}{25}$
    2 $\frac{1}{25}$
    3 0

8. **1** $\frac{4}{9}$
    2 $\frac{2}{9}$

9. **1** $\frac{1}{4}$
    2 $\frac{4}{17}$

Page 292   **Exercise 22.2**

1. **1** 1   **4** $\frac{1}{2}$
    2 0   **5** $\frac{1}{5}$
    3 $\frac{3}{20}$

2. **1** $\frac{1}{16}$
    2 $\frac{3}{16}$
    3 $\frac{3}{16}$

3. **1** $\frac{1}{25}$
    2 $\frac{2}{25}$
    3 $\frac{1}{20}$, $\frac{1}{10}$

4. **1** $\frac{1}{12}$ **3** $\frac{1}{6}$
    2 $\frac{1}{6}$ **4** $\frac{1}{9}$

5. **1** $\frac{1}{15}$
    2 $\frac{1}{5}$
    3 $\frac{1}{5}$

Page 294   **Exercise 22.3**

1. **1** $\frac{9}{20}$
    2 $\frac{5}{8}$

2. **1** $\frac{3}{10}$
    2 $\frac{1}{2}$
    3 $\frac{7}{20}$

3. $\frac{3}{40}$

4. **1** 0.4
    2 54

5. **1** $\frac{3}{8}$
    2 $\frac{5}{8}$

6. **1** 0.2
    2 0.3

7. **1** 0.3
    2 0.05

Page 296   **Exercise 22.4**

1. **1** $\frac{1}{8}$
    2 $\frac{1}{2}$
    3 $\frac{3}{8}$

2. **1** $\frac{3}{10}$
    2 $\frac{1}{5}$
    3 $\frac{9}{100}$

3. **1** 0.998
    2 0.56

4. **1** 0.3   **3** 2
    2 0.7   **4** 0.9

5. **1** $\frac{1}{8}$
    2 $\frac{29}{200}$
    3 $\frac{7}{50}$

6. **1** **A** $\frac{1}{2}$, **B** $\frac{3}{8}$, **C** $\frac{3}{5}$, **D** $\frac{3}{7}$
    2 **B**
    3 **C**
    4 **A**
    5 **C and D**
    6 **A and D**
    7 **B and D**, $\frac{2}{5}$
    8 **A and C**, $\frac{8}{15}$

7. **1** $\frac{1}{6}$
    2 $\frac{1}{6}$
    3 $\frac{7}{12}$

3. theoretical probabilities of scores 6 to 12:
0.1, 0.1, 0.2, 0.2, 0.2, 0.1, 0.1

4. theoretical frequencies of scores 2 to 12:
5, 10, 15, 20, 25, 30, 25, 20, 15, 10, 5

5. **1** frequencies in order: 41, 17, 9, 7, 3, 3
3 0–19

7. **1** frequencies in order: 3, 9, 10, 13, 5
2 40
3 8 min (7.5–8.5 min)

Page 325   Practice test 24

1. **2** mean 3.9, median 4, mode 3
3 0.6

2. mean 30.7, median 30, mode 30, range 4

3. **1** frequencies in order: 3, 5, 4, 5, 5, 2, 1

4. **1** frequencies in order: 3, 8, 9, 6, 4
2 160–164 cm

Page 326   Exercise D1

1. $\frac{3}{4}$
2. 14.45
3. 5
4. 4
5. 48 cm
6. 0.1
7. £20
8. 70°
9. 13 cm^2
10. $\frac{2}{5}$ (0.4)
11. 2
12. 20 cm^2
13. 0.18
14. 108°
15. 27 cm^3
16. 15.17 (3.17 pm)
17. 9 cm (or near)
18. 18
19. 3400
20. **A, C, D**

Page 327   Exercise D2

1. **1** $\frac{11}{20}$
   2 $\frac{3}{4}$
   3 $\frac{1}{30}$

2. **1** U, M
   2 B, E
   3 N, S

3. **1** y-values: 9, 13, 17, 21, 25
   2 y-values: 5, 6, 7, 8, 9

4. 0.36

5. **1** $a = 89°$
   2 $b = 73°$, $c = 36°$
   3 $d = 123°$, $e = 57°$

6. **1** 3600   **3** C
   2 B and D **4** 14 000

7. **1** 22.149
   2 0.0514
   3 81.6

8. 69°

9. parallelogram, (0.5, 1.5)

10. **1** frequencies in order: 5, 8, 11, 6
   3 8–11 cars

Page 329   Exercise D3

1. 13

2. perimeter 64 cm, area 120 cm^2

3. **1** $\frac{1}{6}$ **4** $\frac{5}{12}$
   2 $\frac{1}{3}$ **5** $\frac{6}{11}$
   3 $\frac{1}{6}$

4. **1** triangular prism
   2 cuboid
   3 pyramid with square base

5. **1** £2200   **4** £242
   2 £220   **5** £2662
   3 £2420   **6** £662

6. **1** $x = 5$
   2 $x = 2$
   3 $x = 7$

7. **1** 45°
   2 135°
   3 square

8. **1** 16.55   **3** 12p
   2 7 h 13 min   **4** 70 km/h

9. **1** $\frac{1}{20}$
   2 18°
   3 angles 90°, 90°, 162°, 18°

10. $AB = 5.8$ cm, $\angle ABC = 118°$, rhombus

Page 331   Exercise D4

1. **1** 54 min
   2 8%

2. **1** −4°C
   2 6°C
   3 −5°C

3. 37

4. frequencies:
    R 16, S 10, T 23, U 11, total 60;
    modal category: watching television

5. **1** 9 should be 10;
        triangular numbers, 36, 45, 55
    2 22 should be 21;
        55, 89, 144
    3 6 should be 8, yes;
    4 66 should be 65;
        44, 37, 30

6. $6x + 2x + x = 180$; $x = 20$

7. **1** $\frac{2}{5}$ (0.4)
    2 $\frac{3}{5}$ (0.6)
    3 $\frac{11}{20}$ (0.55)

8. mean 2.06 (2.1), median 2, mode 2

9. **1** sphere   **4** cuboid
    2 cylinder   **5** cube
    3 cone

10. y-values:
    1 5, 4, 3, 2, 1, 0
    2 4, 5, 6, 7, 8, 9
    Intersect at $(-1.5, 4.5)$

Page 341   Exercise 25.1

1. **1** $3:8$ **5** $2:1$ **8** $5:8$
    2 $3:7$ **6** $4:5$ **9** $5:24$
    3 $3:2$ **7** $5:12$ **10** $3:10$
    4 $1:3$

2. **1** 90p, £1.35   **4** £1.50, 25p
    2 56p, 98p   **5** £2.80, £1.20
    3 42p, 18p

3. **1** £450   **4** £7.50
    2 £67.50   **5** £27.50
    3 £160

4. 2.7 cm

5. 80p

6. $36°, 54°, 90°$

7. $1\,m^3$ sand, $2\,m^3$ gravel

8. $40°, 60°, 100°, 160°$

9. 4.5 (ℓ)

10. 2.5 kg tin, 1 kg copper

11. 42

Page 342   Exercise 25.2

2. **1** A 12 kg, B 40 kg
    2 $\frac{3}{10}$
    3 30%
    4 $\frac{3}{13}$
    5 $\frac{10}{13}$

3. **1** C 49 ℓ, D 35 ℓ
    2 $\frac{5}{7}$
    3 140%
    4 $\frac{7}{12}$

4. **1** 60%
    2 E £10, F £15
    3 $E:F = 2:3$
    4 $\frac{2}{3}$

Page 345   Exercise 25.3

1. £7.70   6. £300
2. 81 lb   7. 100 kg
3. £17   8. 10 days
4. 16 days   9. £6.50
5. 15 days   10. 12.5 km/ℓ
11. **1** 88p, 84p
    2 Brand Y better value
12. 12 min
13. £243.75
14. $18\,m^2/\ell$
15. £6.65

Page 347   Exercise 25.4

1. $1\frac{1}{2}$ hours
2. 198 miles
3. 42 mph
4. **1** 70 km/h
    2 90 km
    3 20 min
5. 300 km/h
6. Yes, average speed 45 mph

ANSWERS

Page 348   **Exercise 25.5**

1. $9.20

2. 75 cents, $1, $1.25

3. $24.75

4. 5.40 fr

5. 33.70 fr, 16.30 fr

6. 2.78 francs

7. 36 500 drachmae

8. 267 francs

9. 18 dollars

10. 25 350 kroner

11. 465 000 lire

12. £2577.32

13. £44.84

14. £1826.48

15. £4.41

16. £20.92

17. £4

18. Bill, £2.50 more

19. **1** £16
    2 120 francs

Page 349   **Exercise 25.6**

1. labour £1280, overheads £160; total £2080

2. **1** 21:31
   2 9:14
   3 2:3

3. 8:27

4. £1125, £1575; increase £103.50

5. £175

6. £950

7. 10 lb

8. 2 extra

9. **1** 250 g
   2 5

10. 175 ml for 75p

11. 3 hours

12. $\frac{1}{2}$ hour

13. **1** 5:6   **2** 6:5

14. **1** 48 mph
    2 35 mph
    3 38 miles/gall

15. 2115 francs left; £47

16. 320 schillings; camera £99

Page 352   **Practice test 25**

1. **1** 4:5   **4** 5:24
   2 5:12   **5** 3:1
   3 5:8

2. A £240, B £300, C £360

3. **1** 4:7:9
   2 £1600, £2800, £3600

4. **1** 25%   **4** 3:4
   2 $\frac{2}{3}$ **5** 9:10
   3 0.6

5. 2 hours

6. 30 weeks

7. 64 mph

8. £12.50

Page 355   **Exercise 26.1**

3. **1** radius   **4** chord
   2 diameter   **5** arc
   3 tangent

Page 356   **Exercise 26.2**

1. **1** 34.6 cm   **4** 11.0 cm
   2 12.6 m   **5** 19.5 m
   3 47.1 cm

2. **1** 88.0 cm   **4** 10.1 m
   2 37.7 cm   **5** 67.9 cm
   3 28.3 m

3. 5 m

4. 2 cm, 6 cm;
   3 cm, 9 cm;
   5 cm, 16 cm;
   7 cm, 22 cm;
   8 cm, 25 cm

5. 1100 m

6. 53 m

7. 157 cm, 1600 m

Page 358   **Exercise 26.3**

1. **1** 78.5 cm^2 (78.6 cm^2)
    2 254 cm^2
    3 177 cm^2
    4 201 cm^2
    5 13.9 cm^2

2. **1** 144 cm^2
    2 113.1 cm^2
    3 30.9 cm^2

3. **1** 19.6 m^2
    2 4.9 m^2

Page 359   **Exercise 26.4**

2. 12

3. 411 cm

4. 9.42 m (9.43 m), 38 cm apart

5. **1** 21.2 m^2
    2 28.3 m^2
    3 7.1 m^2 (7.0 m^2)

6. **1** 32 cm^2
    2 32.2 cm^2

7. **1** 201 cm^2
    2 603 cm^2

8. **1** 21.6 cm   **4** 1.0 cm
    2 3.6 cm   **5** 40.7 cm^2
    3 22.6 cm   **6** 7.1 cm^2

9. **1** 31.8 cm
    2 10.2 cm
    3 1.60 cm

Page 362   **Practice test 26**

1. 8.2 m

2. 9.9 cm, square

3. 220 m, 90 m

4. 4.0 cm^2

5. **1** 3.8 m
    2 5.8 m^2

Page 365   **Exercise 27.1**

1. 30 km/h

2. **1** (1) and (4), 67 km/h

    2 (2), 33 km/h
    3 30 min

3. **1** 20 min   **4** 10 min
    2 1 h 4 min **5** 20 km/h
    3 2 km

4. **1** 2.45 pm
    2 30 mph
    3 2.05 pm, 28 miles
    4 6 miles
    5 34 mph

6. **1** 1125 m
    2 4.5 s and 25.5 s
    3 13 s

Page 369   **Exercise 27.2**

1. **1** 20 km
    2 50 km/h, 16.5 min

2. **1** 22 m/s
    2 20 s, 105 s from the start

Page 371   **Exercise 27.3**

1. **1** £52
    2 32 dollars

2. 30 ℓ, 2.2 galls

3. **1** 570 pts
    2 £7.90

4. 70°F, 21°C;
    80°C, 176°F;
    98.4°F, 37°C

Page 372   **Exercise 27.4**

1. **1** £108
    2 $4\frac{1}{2}$ h

2. **1** 20 cm
    2 20 s

3. **1** Costs (£): 160, 260, 360, 460, 560, 660, 760
    3 17

Page 374   **Exercise 27.5**

1. **1** $\frac{1}{2}$ hour
    2 15 km/h
    3 1.40 pm, 9 km
    4 10 km
    5 16 km
    6 16 km/h

2. 9.51 am, 26 miles

3. values:
   A, £240, £240, £240, £240, £340
   B, £12, £120, £240, £360, £480, £600
   C, all £300
   1 Mr B
   2 Mr A
   3 Mr C

4. 4.0 m/s

Page 376   Practice test 27

1. **1** 15 min
   2 28 km/h
   3 2 km

2. **1** 47 km/h
   2 28 km/h

3. 27°C

4. **1** 6 am, 6 pm
   2 12 am, 12 noon, 12 am
   3 6 am

Page 380   Exercise 28.1

1. Translation -6 units in x-direction and
   -7 units in y-direction;
   B_1 $(-2, -5)$, C_1 $(-3, 0)$

6. **1** reflection (in the y-axis)
   2 rotation (about the origin through 180°)
   3 reflection (in the x-axis)
   4 translation (-1 units in the x-direction)

Page 382   Exercise 28.2

1. A and H, B and D, C and G, E and F

2. $\triangle DNB$

3. A and F, B and D, C and E

Page 385   Exercise 28.3

2. 4

3. 30 cm by 22.5 cm

6. 2

7. **1** 2
   2 70 cm

8. **1** 1.5 cm
   2 66°

Page 387   Exercise 28.4

1. **2** A_1 $(4, -1)$, B_1 $(7, 0)$, C_1 $(6, 5)$
   3 A_2 $(-4, 2)$, B_2 $(-1, 3)$, C_2 $(-2, 8)$
   4 translation -5 units in x-direction and
   1 unit in y-direction

2. **1** kite
   2 rhombus
   3 square

3. **1** parallelogram   **3** rhombus
   2 rectangle   **4** square

Page 391   Practice test 28

1. A and E, B and F, C and D

4. **1** 3
   2 13.5 cm
   3 3 cm

5. **1** 5
   2 50 cm

Page 399   Exercise 29.3

1. positive, 27 (or near)

2. negative, 21 (or near)

3. positive, 31 (or near)

4. negative, 17 (or near)

5. positive, 33 (or near)

6. positive correlation

7. positive correlation

Page 400   Exercise 29.4

2. **1** positive correlation
   2 (perfect) negative correlation
   3 no correlation
   4 positive correlation
   5 negative correlation

3. positive correlation, £64 000 (or near)

4. 66 (or near)

5. 1.67 m (or near)

6. positive correlation

7. 60 (or near)

Page 402   Practice test 29

1. positive correlation, entry number 5

3. negative correlation, 30 (or near)

4. positive correlation, 72 kg (or near)

Page 404   Exercise 30.1

1. 7 km

2. 2 km

3. 10 cm long and 7.5 cm wide

4. 1 cm represents 5 km (1 : 500 000)

5. 1 cm represents 20 m (1 : 2000); 3 cm wide

6. 4.2 km

7. **1** 200 m
    2 265 m
    3 1020 m

8. 12 m or near

Page 406   Exercise 30.2

1. 87 m

2. 90 m^2

3. 63 m

Page 408   Exercise 30.3

1. **1** 028°   **4** 142°
    2 325°   **5** 227°
    3 250°

3. **1** *AO* 208°   **4** *DO* 322°
    2 *BO* 145°   **5** *FO* 047°
    3 *CO* 070°

4. **1** 225°   **4** 045°
    2 090°   **5** 270°
    3 315°

5. **1** 260°   **4** 195°
    2 305°   **5** 121°
    3 080°

6. **1** 119°   **4** 345°
    2 241°   **5** 029°
    3 074°

7. **1** *B* 065°, *C* 340°
    2 *B* 030°, *C* 112°
    3 118°
    4 321°
    5 044°, 311°

Page 412   Exercise 30.4

1. 201°

2. **2** 179 km
    3 182 km
    4 169 km

3. From *A*, 39 km; from *B*, 20 km

4. **2** 12.2 km
    3 260°

5. **1** 287° (or near)
    2 1 cm represents 2 km (1 : 200 000)
    3 17.0 to 17.5 km
    4 250° (or near)

Page 413   Exercise 30.5

1. **2** 100 m
    3 340 m
    4 *AC* = 113 m, *BD* = 128 m
    5 35 m

2. **1** 540 m, 066°   **4** 780 m, 083°
    2 1120 m, 096°   **5** 280 m, 209°
    3 1050 m, 290°

3. **1** N 70° W   **4** S 70° E
    2 S 25° W   **5** N 42° W
    3 N 53° E

4. **2** 123°

5. 242°, 25 km, 1 h 35 min

6. 8 m (or near)

7. 102 m

Page 417   Practice test 30

1. height 8 m, floor 12.5 m by 16 m

2. **1** 5 m by 4 m   **3** 3 m by 3 m
    2 3.5 m by 3 m   **4** 20 m^2, £560

3. 75 m

4. **1** 50°
    2 290°

5. 078°

6. **2** 290 m
    3 850 m
    4 280 m

Page 420   Exercise E1

1. 5 : 6
2. 1.4 kg
3. 4
4. 60 (m^3)
5. $\frac{1}{2}$
6. 8 cm
7. £33
8. rhombus
9. 750 (francs)
10. 20 days

11. 22 cm
12. 3 m
13. 9
14. 10 min
15. 48
16. £10
17. 32 km
18. 10 m
19. **B, E**
20. **B, C, E**

Page 421   Exercise E2

1. **1** F 6, V 8, E 12
    2 F 5, V 6, E 9
    3 F 5, V 5, E 8
2. **1** 150 g
    2 50
3. a = 64°
4. **1** $\frac{1}{10}$ (0.1)
    2 $\frac{2}{5}$ (0.4)
5. **1** $(x + 5) + (x - 25) + (2x - 95) + (175 - x) = 360; x = 100$
    2 105°, 75°, 105°, 75°
    3 parallelogram
6. **1** (6)
    2 (4)
    3 (7)
    4 reflection (in BH)
    5 rotation (through 180° about E)
    6 reflection (in CG)
7. y-values:
    1 −5, −2, 1, 4, 7, 10
    2 12, 10, 8, 6, 4, 2
    (3.4, 5.2)
8. 3.5 m
9. **1** $T = \dfrac{n(n - 1)}{2}$
    2 45 ways

10. X-values: 70, 85, 20, 35, 45, 60;
    Y-values: 20, 5, 70, 55, 45, 30;
    perfect negative correlation;
    £52.50 to X, £37.50 to Y

Page 423   Exercise E3

1. **1** 2
    2 −5
    3 8
    4 −1

    5 −4
    6 2
    7 1

    8 −3
    9 2
    10 −8
2. **1** 1 : 40
    2 300 g
3. 68°
4. **1** $\frac{1}{6}$, 20
    2 $\frac{1}{13}$, 9
    3 12
5. £88.80, 22.8 kg
6. **1** 3
    2 7.5 cm
7. **1** 48 min
    2 12 km/h
    3 15 km/h
8. 52 to 2, 84 to 4, 92 to 1
9. **1** 122°
    2 9.4 km

Page 426   Exercise E4

1. **1** 532
    2 0.68
    3 32.52
    4 13.05

    5 41.7
    6 3.6
    7 242
    8 0.82
2. a = 110°
3. 53$\frac{1}{2}$ hours
4. 150 ml for £1.34
5. E and F are opposite faces
6. **1** 0.2
    2 0.8
7. frequencies in order: 6, 6, 7, 8, 3;
    modal class 16–20 hours
8. **1** 28 cm
    2 21 cm^2

9. **1** 180 hectares
    2 120°
    3 300 hectares

10. 10.6 km

Page 428   Exercise E5

1. **1** $\frac{3}{8}$
    2 £160 000

2. **1** positive correlation
    2 71 marks (or near)

3. **1** 23.5°C   **3** 9 deg
    2 29.0°C   **4** 2 deg

4. 82

5. **1** $\frac{4}{7}$
    2 $\frac{1}{2}$

7. **1** 8 s   **3** 7.9 s
    2 31.4 m   **4** boy

8. Modal dept, food

9. **1** 22 fr (22.5 fr)
    2 £6.70

10. 8 years

Page 431   Exercise E6

1. **1** 25%   **4** 30%   **7** $\frac{7}{20}$
    2 60%   **5** 65%   **8** $\frac{9}{25}$
    3 28%   **6** 2%   **9** $\frac{2}{5}$

2. A and D, B and C

4. **1** Hotel Marti, £916
    2 £539 each, £1617
    3 £1341.20

5. **1** 8 km/h
    2 30 km/h
    3 5.05 pm, 33 km from A

6. 20.4 km, 274°

7. 48 litres

8. **1** trapezium   **4** rectangle
    2 parallelogram   **5** rhombus
    3 parallelogram

9. $x = -2.8$ or 2.8

Page 434   Exercise E7

1. £26 500, £27 560

2. **1** 1   **5** 6   **8** 3
    2 3   **6** 4   **9** 5
    3 0   **7** 2   **10** 7
    4 2

3. 9

4. 6 m to 7 m

5. 2.7 cm

6. 4 corners 18 cm^2, octagon 126 cm^2

7. perfect positive correlation

8. **1** £13.50, £6.00, £4.50
    2 £30.15

9. 380 cm^2, 254 cm^2, 126 cm^2

10. angles 60°, 90°, 108°, 120°, 135°;
     7 sides 129°